Recent Advances in Corporate Finance

Recent Advances in Corporate Finance

Edited by
Edward I. Altman
Marti G. Subrahmanyam
Professors of Finance
New York University
Schools of Business

1985

RICHARD D. IRWIN Homewood, Illinois 60430

Library of Congress Catalog Card No. 84-82468

Printed in the United States of America

1 2 3 4 5 6 7 8 9 0 K 2 1 0 9 8 7 6 5

This book is available in a professional edition from Dow Jones-Irwin, and in a classroom edition from Richard D. Irwin, Inc.

In memory of our fathers: Sidney Altman and Marti Mannariah Gurunath

Preface

For several decades, financial academicians and practitioners have been working on parallel paths toward the analysis of problems which confront the financial community. Periodically, a number of concerned analysts have attempted to bring these separate efforts toward a central meeting point to foster a dialogue and even engage in joint work. The general line of attack is to take some of the more important conceptual breakthroughs and attempt to apply them to current practical problems and, in so doing, raise the level of performance of financial markets and the financial institutions, firms, and individual investors who deal in these markets. The attempt to integrate financial theory with practice has been particularly observable and successful in the field of *investments*, broadly defined. The works of Harry Markowitz on portfolio theory from the 1950s, William Sharpe, John Lintner, Jan Mossin, and Jack Treynor on the capital asset pricing model from the 1960s, and Fisher Black-Myron Scholes and Robert Merton on option pricing from the 1970s, among others, have found their way into the halls of investment houses and the trading floors of financial institutions around the world. Numerous capital market institutes of research have been funded, mainly by "Wall Street," to build data bases and sponsor inquiry into the concepts and numbers which have now become common practice, even amongst less sophisticated analysts. It is fair to say that there has been a successful meeting of the minds in the field of investments, as is evidenced by the increasing role of academics as researchers and strategists in some of the major financial institutions.

Unfortunately, the same progress has not taken place in another major area of the financial world, namely the *corporate financial theory and management* area. Despite some efforts by professional associations, as well as research institutes through periodic conferences, there has not, in our opinion, been the same level of interaction and dialogue between academicians and practitioners as is found in the investments area. Of course, some of the more prominent works in corporate finance, such as those by Modigliani and Miller, have on occasion found their way to corporate boardrooms and top corporate financial executives, but for the most part, the related concerns and efforts of academics and practitioners in corporate finance are still on a parallel but not intersecting path. The major areas of corporate financial policy, namely liquidity, capital structure, dividend and valuation analysis have been discussed and debated both within and between these two groups with little or no consensus.

Why has this apparent failure to merge ideas and efforts taken place? One possible reason is the lack of a serious attempt to bring the two groups together—both in terms of dialogue and financial resources. In terms of funding, corporate finance research projects have enjoyed nowhere near the level of support available to research on capital markets. Several questions come readily to mind in this connection. Have we tried hard enough to bring the busy corporate financial executive away from his day-to-day pressures to sit back and view the major issues from a more objective and considered vantage point? Have the practitioners reached out to academics and other theorists both in terms of internships and funding? Have the investment banks played their crucial role effectively in this interface? It is difficult to answer these questions in the affirmative.

The purpose of this volume is to make an attempt at improving the interface between the worlds of academia and practice and also to highlight some of the more significant trends and seminal works in the field of corporate finance. We invited some of the most important researchers in the field to present survey papers in their areas that would be rigorous and yet accessible to nonmathematically oriented readers. And we asked a number of sophisticated and concerned senior corporate financial and investment banking practitioners to assess, critique and comment upon the works and the issues presented. We also invited several researchers to present current works in these same areas to round out the discussion. The format for this interface was a conference sponsored by the Salomon Brothers Center for the Study of Financial Institutions at New York University's Graduate School of Business Administration on November 9 and 10, 1983. The compendium of papers and comments written for the conference and edited in subsequent months is the content of this book.

The four areas that we have selected to launch our idea of corporate financial interface are (1) *contingent claims* or the application of option pricing techniques to corporate finance; (2) *agency theory* or the analysis of interface and conflicts of interest between owners, creditors, and managers; (3) *taxation* and its pervasive impact on firm strategy; and (4) *inflation* and its impact. These surveys were written and presented respectively by Robert Merton and Scott Mason (No. 1), Michael Jensen and Clifford Smith, Jr. (No. 2), Robert Hamada and Myron Scholes (No. 3), and Rich Cohn and Franco Modigliani (No. 4). The practitioners who discussed these surveys were respectively Martin Leibowitz and Andrew Kalotay (No. 1), John Hackett and Robert Kay (No. 2), J. P. Valles (No. 3) and Richard Goeltz and L. M. Ribiero Dias (No. 4). The research papers were by Thomas Ho (No. 1), Avner Kalay and Kose John (No. 2), James Poterba and Lawrence Summers (No. 3), and Michel Levasseur and Itzhak Swary (No. 4). The complete list of participants and their biographical notes are provided at the end of this book.

This book on recent advances in corporate finance and its implications is appropriate for sophisticated practitioners in the world of finance, including corporate financial personnel, financial market practitioners and investment analysts. It is also particularly useful for upper-level courses in corporate finance at the MBA level and for doctoral seminars. Students and instructors who may not be familiar with all of the diverse writings in these areas and wish to have a comprehensive survey and discussion of the issues and practical implications will find the book of value, especially since it is written by the individuals credited with seminal contributions and by those who can appreciate the works and their potential for application.

We sincerely appreciate the participation of those authors and commentators who agreed to speak and write on this important area. We are also appreciative of financial support from the Salomon Brothers Center for the Study of Financial Institutions, under the direction of Dr. Arnold Sametz.

Edward I. Altman
Marti G. Subrahmanyam

Contents

Part I

Valuation of Corporate Securities: Applications of Contingent Claims Analysis: Introduction

One of the most significant developments in financial economics in recent years was that of the theory of option pricing. The origin of this literature can be traced to the pioneering work by Fischer Black and Myron Scholes in a paper in the *Journal of Political Economy* in 1973. The Black-Scholes model, in particular, and option pricing theory, in general, is a notable development in financial economics for two important reasons. First, option pricing theory has had a considerable impact on practitioners as evidenced by the widespread use of the Black-Scholes model, or a variant, in the valuation of traded options on common stocks and related instruments. Second, and perhaps equally important from the academic viewpoint, option pricing theory provides a rich framework for the valuation of corporate assets and liabilities.

The popularity of option pricing theory in the investment community can, in part, be traced to the fortuitous timing of the initial work by Black and Scholes which virtually coincided with the opening of the first organized market in options, the Chicago Board Options Exchange. More importantly, the practical appeal of the model is due to the fact that the model relies on observable variables. Unlike many other models in finance, it eschews reliance on both investor preferences and expectations. In fact, the only nonobservable input to the model is the volatility of the stock price, which is certainly less difficult to estimate than, say, the expectation of the future stock price. The reason for the economy in estimating inputs to the model is that the theory of option pricing is largely based on the principle of arbitrage and is oriented toward development of a relative valuation for the option in terms of the value of the underlying stock—an observable variable.

The principles of option pricing theory are surprisingly general in their applicability to the valuation of both financial and real assets. As originally pointed out by Black and Scholes, corporate securities may be viewed as options, or more generally, contingent claims on the value of the firm. The most obvious example of this insight is that the equity of a levered firm may be thought of as a European call option written on the firm's value, with the exercise price being the promised payment on the debt and the expiration date being the maturity date of the debt. Other corporate securities may also be modeled in this framework as contingent claims and valued using the techniques of contingent claims analysis.

More recently, academic researchers in the area have focused attention on another application of the framework. Most of the early applications of contingent claims analysis dealt with the financing side of the firm's activities through the valuation of corporate liabilities such as the call feature on bonds or the value of a convertible bond. In particular, the traditional notion that the risk of a corporate claim depends on business risk, financial risk, the rate of interest, and the nature of the covenants imposed on the firm can be given specific content. For example, it is possible, using the methods of contingent claims analysis, to place a value on individual features of a security such as the covenants imposed on the firm.

The same recent developments in the area apply to the investment decision of the firm as well through the valuation of corporate assets. Specifically, attention is focused on the "option" aspects of investment projects such as project timing, the scale of the investment, and the right to abandon the project. Further, even after the project is accepted, operating choices do exist in terms of the choice of inputs and outputs in the actual production decision.

Although the past achievements and future promise of contingent claims analysis are impressive, it is only proper to point out some of the difficulties in applying the framework, particularly to the valuation of corporate assets. Many of these issues are receiving attention in the literature of the field and may be addressed by researchers over the next several years.

Much of the option pricing theory and its corporate finance counterpart, contingent claims analysis, relies on the principle of arbitrage which, by its very nature, applies only to traded assets. Of course, there are methods of valuation, either when at least some of the assets involved are traded or there are close substitutes to the nontraded ones in the marketplace. However, the option framework is sufficiently rich to be useful for gaining insights into the problem even when the assets are not traded, or when the cost of replicating an options position is prohibitive. An alternative to the arbitrage method that is independent of preferences but requires that the assets be tradable is the preference-based approach first analyzed by Rubinstein in the *Bell Journal of Economics*, in 1976. It is interesting to note that, under certain circumstances, the two approaches lead to the same valuation result. Hence, the precise choice between the two approaches should be made depending on the nature of the specific problem at hand and how closely it approximates the two alternative sets of assumptions.

The method of analysis in the contingent claims approach to valuation of assets requires an exogenous specification of the stochastic process generating firm value. In many cases of corporate asset valuation, such as capital budgeting, the acceptance of the project may itself affect the stochastic process generating firm values. If the asset is to be viewed as a contingent claim on firm value, there is an obvious problem of simultaneity which has to be carefully modeled.

A related issue is the question of asymmetry of information between the owners of various corporate claims. This issue is discussed at length in Part II of the book, which deals with informational issues and agency costs and their impact on corporate financial decisions. The various claimholders of a firm, for example, debt and equity holders, may have different information regarding the firm's future prospects and, further, each class of investors will pursue its own self-interests. In a situation of conflict of interest between the claimholders, the decisions made by the managers who may represent the equity holders may be quite at variance with those implied by a full-information model. This point has particular relevance to contingent claims analysis, which views corporate assets and liabilities as options on the firm. For example, the exercise policies of these options and the issuance of such securities by the firm may be more fully explained by analyzing the problem of information asymmetry. This may explain why the predictions from contingent claims analysis about optimal financial structure policy of the firm are not borne out in actual practice.

Another issue that may be important for the valuation of securities from the viewpoint of corporate finance is the nature of the risk of the firm's investment projects over time. In particular, the pattern according to which the risk of a project is resolved over time will have an impact on how the claims issued against the project are valued. For example, an investment in a timber plantation may have considerable risk when the saplings are young, but the risk diminishes as the trees mature. By contrast, an investment in a typical industrial project may have growing risk over time. Since the pattern of resolution of uncertainty is different in the two cases, it follows that the values of the claims contingent on the pattern of the cash flows of the firm would be different. While much of the literature in the area, so far, has dealt with models where the resolution of uncertainty is smooth, i.e., where risk increases monotonically with futurity, there is increasing interest in models that incorporate more general patterns of risk resolution. There will be more of such models in the future.

The survey paper by Scott Mason and Robert Merton provides a synthesis of option-theoretic approaches in corporate finance. The authors first outline the principles of valuation of options on common stock and provide the motivation for the Black-Scholes model. They then develop the rationale for valuing corporate securities as options and provide a description of the methods of contingent claims analysis. Finally, they shed light on some of the likely future developments in this area the beginnings of which are already evident; in particular, models for valuing corporate assets. Using examples of the various types of options embedded in most investment projects, they provide convincing arguments for explicitly taking into account these options in capital budgeting decisions.

Mason and Merton emphasize the relevance of contingent claim analysis for the formulation of corporate strategy. Since options are virtually the same as "flexibility" in strategic terms, contingent claims analysis provides an integrated view of the valuation of the firm's assets and liabilities. On the financing side, the trade-offs between the various factors involved such as tax shields, financial distress, and the reduction of flexibility can be taken into account explicitly. In the case of investment decisions dealing with corporate assets, the various options that form an integral part of projects such as timing, scale, and the option to abandon the project can be properly evaluated.

Martin Leibowitz and Andrew Kalotay bring the practitioners' viewpoint into the discussion. Leibowitz argues that contingent claims analysis is a useful framework for viewing corporate assets and liabilities in practice. However, he says that the explicit valuation methods used may not always be appropriate, since the practitioner may be more interested in the flavor of the problem than the actual numerical results.

Kalotay is concerned with his perception of the poor predictive power of the prescriptions of contingent claims analysis, particularly for callable convertible bonds. He emphasizes the impact of taxes, which does not receive much attention in the literature of valuing corporate securities. He argues that practitioners are less concerned with the optimality of their decisions than with efficiency and makes a plea for an "engineering" approach to solving actual valuation problems.

In the research paper of the first section, Thomas Ho analyzes the impact of interest rates on the valuation of bonds with a sinking-fund provision. This paper is somewhat different from many others in the literature on option valuation approaches in corporate finance since it focuses on interest-rate risk rather than the risk of default. He argues that issuers of bonds with a sinking-fund provision have a choice between two alternative methods of fulfilling their sinking-fund obligations: retirement of an appropriate portion of the outstanding bonds at par or purchase of this proportion in the open market. He models this choice, which is termed the delivery option, using the methods of contingent claims analysis.

Viewed in the context of contingent claims analysis, the sinking-fund bond may be seen as a combination of a pure discount bond and an options position. Making assumptions about the stochastic processes underlying the term structure of interest rates, Ho derives the relationship for the yield spread or the interest-rate differential resulting from the sinking-fund provision. He then presents some empirical evidence in support of his theoretical analysis.

1

The Role of Contingent Claims Analysis in Corporate Finance

Scott P. Mason
Associate Professor of Business Administration
Harvard University
Graduate School of Business

Robert C. Merton
J. C. Penney Professor of Management & Finance
Massachusetts Institute of Technology
Sloan School of Management

Contingent claims analysis (CCA) is a technique for determining the price of a security whose payoffs depend upon the prices of one or more other securities. The origins of CCA are found in the theory of option pricing. Although formal approaches to the evaluation of call and put options can be traced back to at least the turn of the century, the major breakthrough came a little over a decade ago in a paper by Fisher Black and Myron Scholes (1973). The Black and Scholes analysis contains a qualitative insight which may prove to be of even greater academic and practical significance than their famous quantitative formula: Corporate liabilities, in general, can be viewed as combinations of simple option contracts. This insight provides a unified framework in which to view the structure of corporate liabilities and implies that option pricing models can be used to price corporate securities. In this paper, we present an overview of CCA and its application to a variety of corporate financial problems, including capital budgeting decisions and the characterization of a project's strategic value as a series of "operating options." We demonstrate that CCA is especially well suited to the task of evaluating what strategists call the "flexibility" of a project.

The Role of Contingent Claims Analysis in Corporate Finance

INTRODUCTION

Contingent claims analysis (CCA) is a technique for determining the price of a security whose payoffs depend upon the prices of one or more other securities. It can, for example, be used to determine the value of a convertible bond in terms of the price of the underlying stock into which the bond can be converted. It can also be used to estimate the value of the flexibility associated with a multipurpose production facility. As suggested by these brief examples, the technique is wide-ranging in that it can be applied fruitfully to a number of tactical and strategic corporate financial decision problems.

The origins of CCA are found in the theory of option pricing. Although formal approaches to the evaluation of call and put options can be traced back to at least the turn of the century, the major breakthrough came a little over a decade ago in a paper by Fisher Black and Myron Scholes (1973). Perhaps no other result in academic finance conceived entirely in theory has had so immediate and significant an impact on financial market practice. The ease of use of the Black-Scholes option pricing model and its subsequent empirical validation explain the practical success of this theoretical result. The speed at which it was adopted was, however, surely affected by the coincidence that 1973 also marked the beginning of organized stock options trading on the Chicago Board Options Exchange. The success of the CBOE and the subsequent expansion in markets to include options on fixed-income securities, currencies, and stock and bond indices have added to the practical importance of their model. While these markets represent an increasingly larger component of the financial markets, options are, nevertheless, relatively specialized financial securities. However, the Black and Scholes (1973) analysis contains a qualitative insight which may prove to be of even greater academic and practical significance than their famous quantitative formula: Corporate liabilities, in general, can be viewed as combinations of simple option contracts. This insight provides a unified framework in which to view the structure of corporate liabilities and implies that option pricing models can be used to price corporate securities. Such generalized option pricing models are the quantitative foundation for contingent claims analysis.

In this paper, we present an overview of CCA and its application to a variety of corporate financial problems. The focus is on providing a functional understanding of the technique. The emphasis is, therefore, on formulating the various problems in a CCA framework and not on the methods for solving the derived equations. The balance of this introduction, together with the following section, develops the basic concepts and presents in greater detail the historical development of CCA. The balance of the paper is devoted to applications of CCA broken down roughly along temporal lines: First, a section on the Black and Scholes option pricing model represents the "past" in the sense of applications which are firmly established in financial practice. The next section is the "present" in terms of those applications which are state-of-the-art in financial practice. The final section discusses those applications which are still in the development stage within academic research but which hold forth the promise of becoming a part of financial practice in the future. As the reader will discover, the boundaries among these three temporal categories are both permeable and flexible. Given the enormous range of the subject, we cannot begin to cover all the uses of CCA here and those we do cover can be done in limited depth only. We therefore call special attention to the survey article by Smith (1976) and the forthcoming book by Cox and Rubenstein as concentrated sources for further exploration of the subject.

We begin our study with a brief review of basic option analysis. There are two basic types of options: the call option, which gives the owner the right to buy a specified asset at a specified price on or before a specified date and the put option, which gives its owner the right to sell a specified asset at a specified price on or before a specified date.[1] Recently, with IBM stock trading at $118 per share on the New York Stock Exchange (NYSE), the CBOE was trading both calls and puts written on 100 shares of IBM stock with an exercise price of $120 per share and a maturity of eight months. The calls were trading for $1150 and the puts for $750. These options have value because they are "rights," not obligations, to transact in the IBM stock. The owner of the IBM call options will exercise his right to purchase IBM stock in eight months only if the price then exceeds $120. The IBM put options owner will exercise his right to sell IBM stock in eight months only if the price is then below $120. The value of the options is contingent upon the value of IBM stock, i.e., the options are contingent claims.

To understand how the concept of contingent claims is related to corporate liabilities, imagine a firm's "economic" balance sheet. The left side of the balance sheet represents the economic value of the firm, whereas the right side lists the economic value of all of the firm's liabilities. For example, consider the simple firm which has only two classes of liabilities: equity and a zero-coupon bond which matures in one year with a promised principal of \$10 million. One year from now, if the value of the firm exceeds \$10 million, the firm will retire the debt and the equity will be worth the difference between the value of the firm and \$10 million. However, if the value of the firm is less than \$10 million, the firm will default. In such an event, the equity will be worth zero and the debt will be worth the value of the firm. Thus, the value of both the equity and debt is contingent upon the value of the firm; i.e., equity and debt are also contingent claims.

Black and Scholes (1973) demonstrate that corporate liabilities can be viewed as combinations of simple options contracts. The next section of this chapter demonstrates the generality of this insight and the important fact that this correspondence is not dependent on any particular option pricing model. Black and Scholes are able to derive their option pricing model because of the additional important observation that it is possible to replicate options using the underlying stock and the risk-free asset. A later section describes the replication argument and the Black and Scholes option pricing model. By combining the results of these two sections, it is possible to quantify the characterization of corporate liabilities as combinations of simple option contracts. The remaining sections describe CCA as a generalization of the Black and Scholes insights with a discussion of the pricing of several simple corporate securities, the potential role of CCA in capital budgeting decisions, and the characterization of a project's strategic value as a series of "operating options." Finally, in the appendix we present a detailed application of CCA to the analysis of large-scale investment projects that demonstrates the potential of this technique in solving complex capital budgeting and financing problems.

CORPORATE LIABILITIES AS OPTIONS: THE BASIC CONCEPTS

To see the correspondence between corporate liabilities and options, it is first necessary to understand the most fundamental options:

calls and puts. An American call option whose price we denote by $C(S,T,X)$ gives its owner the right to purchase one share of stock, with current price S, at an exercise price, X, on or before an expiration date which is T time periods from now. The call option owner will exercise his right to buy only if it is to his advantage. Figure 1 depicts the value of the call option as it depends on the stock price on the expiration date, when $T = 0$. Should the stock price on the expiration date be less than the exercise price, the call option owner will not exercise his right to purchase the stock and the option will expire worthless, i.e., $C = 0$. If, however, the stock price is greater than the exercise price, the call option will be worth $S - X$, the difference between the stock price and the exercise price. Thus, at the expiration date, the value of the call option is

$$C(S,0,X) = \text{Max}\,(S - X, 0) \tag{1}$$

Expression (1) says that the value of the call option at expiration, $T = 0$, is the maximum of $(S - X)$ and 0. Expression (1) is also true for European call options, $c(S,0,X) = \text{Max}\,(S - X,0)$, since at expiration an American and European option are identical. Furthermore, Merton (1973) demonstrates that American and European call options written on a nondividend-paying stock have the same value, $C(S,T,X) = c(S,T,X)$, i.e., the right to exercise prior to expiration has zero value for calls.[2]

An American put option, $P(S,T,X)$, gives its owner the right to sell one share of stock S, at an exercise price, X, on or before its ex-

FIGURE 1

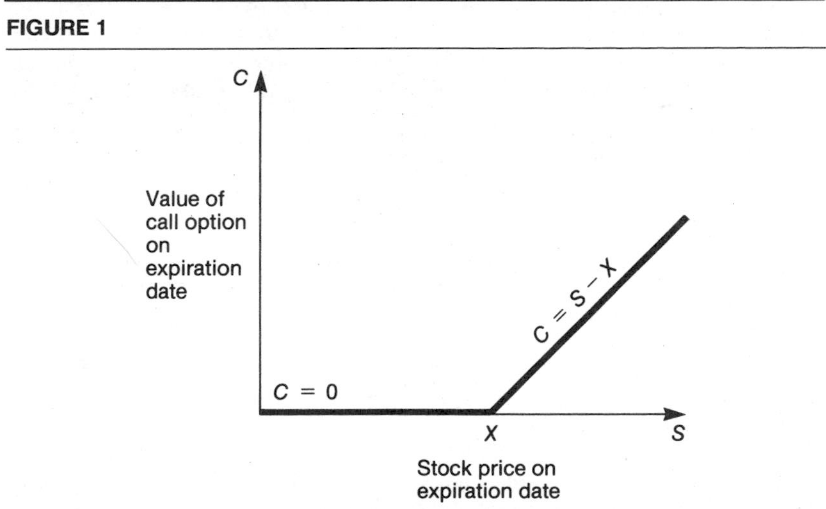

piration date T periods from now. Again, the put option owner will exercise his right to sell only if it is to his advantage. Figure 2 depicts the value of the put option on its expiration date. If the stock price on the expiration date is greater than the exercise price, the put option owner will not exercise his right to sell the stock and the put option will expire worthless, $P = 0$. However, should the stock price be less than the exercise price, the put option owner will exercise his right to sell the stock and the put option will be worth $X - S$, the difference between the exercise price and the stock price. Thus, at the expiration date the value of the put option is

$$P(S,0,X) = \text{Max}\ (X - S,0) \tag{2}$$

Expression (2) says that the value of the put option at expiration, $T = 0$, is the maximum of $(X - S)$ and 0. Figure 2 makes it clear why puts are often characterized as an insurance contract on the stock because they pay off when "things go badly," i.e., when stock price is low. Expression (2) is also true for European puts, $p(S,0,X) = \text{Max}\ (X - S,0)$, because American and European options have identical values at expiration. Unlike call options, however, Merton (1973) demonstrates that American puts are generally more valuable than European puts, $P(S,T,X) \geq p(S,T,X)$, because it sometimes pays to exercise the put before expiration, i.e., the right to exercise prior to expiration has value for puts.[3]

An important relationship between European call and put prices can be derived from Figures 1 and 2. Consider an investment posi-

FIGURE 2

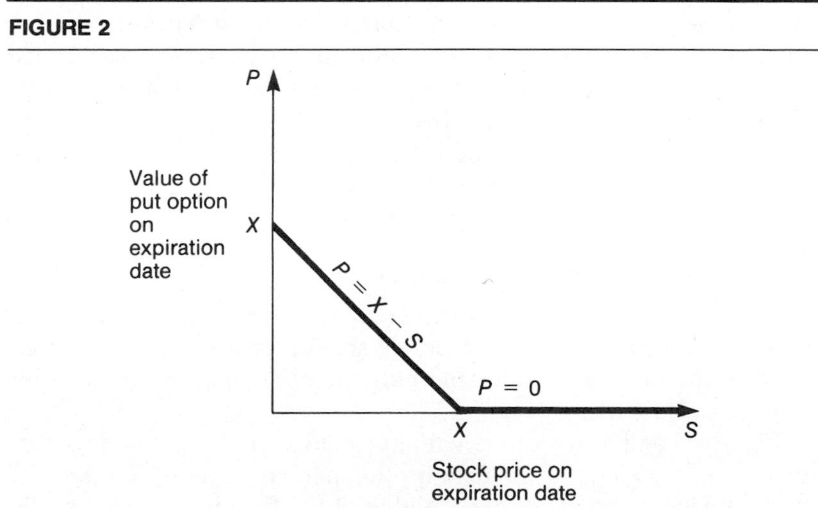

tion, I_1, which has purchased a European call and sold a European put on the same stock, with the same exercise price and expiration date. Therefore,

$$I_1 = c(S,T,X) - p(S,T,X) \tag{3}$$

The value of this investment position at expiration of the options is depicted in Figure 3. The value of the investment position on the expiration date is $S - X$, the difference between the stock price and the exercise price. The investment can have negative value if the stock price is below the exercise price because the call will expire worthless and the put will be exercised against its seller. However, there is another investment position, I_2, involving no options which can replicate the payoff depicted in Figure 3. Consider buying one share of stock, S, and borrowing on a discount basis X dollars for T time periods at rate r, i.e., the proceeds from the loan will be Xe^{-rT}, allowing for continuous discounting. Therefore

$$I_2 = S - Xe^{-rT} \tag{4}$$

In T periods the value of this position will be $I_2 = S - X$, since the position owns one share of stock and owes X dollars. But if these two positions have precisely the same value at $T = 0$, then it must be true that the initial net investment necessary to establish the positions will be the same.

$$c(S,T,X) - p(S,T,X) = S - Xe^{-rT} \tag{5}$$

Expression (5) is well known by professional traders as "put-call parity." The expression simply says that prices in the call, put, stock, and lending markets must be such that expression (5) is always true. If this were not the case, traders would simply buy the lower-priced alternative and sell the higher-priced alternative and earn an immediate riskless return on zero net investment.[4]

With these fundamental options properties as background, the correspondence between options and corporate liabilities can now be established. Consider Figure 4, the economic balance sheet of a simple firm which has only two liabilities, equity, E, and a single issue of zero-coupon debt, D, where the equity receives no dividends and the firm will issue no new securities while the debt is outstanding. The left side of the balance sheet represents the economic value of the firm. The right side lists the economic value of all the liabilities of the firm.

Figures 5 and 6 depict the value of equity and risky debt as they depend on the value of the firm on the maturity date of the debt. If, on the debt's maturity date, the value of the firm is greater than the

FIGURE 3

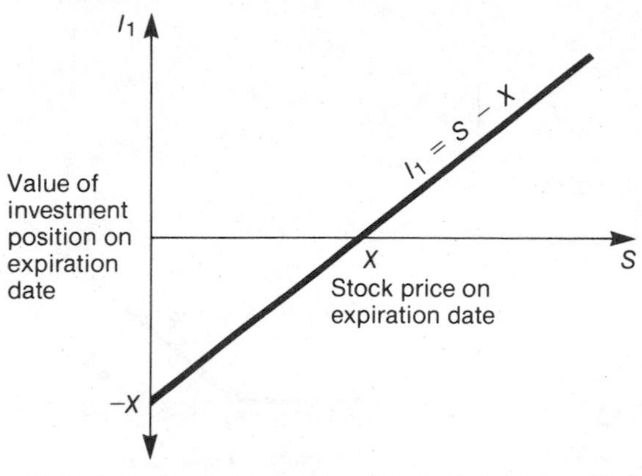

FIGURE 4

V	D
	E
V	V

promised principal, $V > B$, then the debt will be paid off, $D = B$, and the equity will be worth $V - B$. However, if the value of the firm is less than the promised principal, $V < B$, then the equity will be worthless, $E = 0$, since it is preferable to surrender the firm to the debtholders, $D = V$, then repay the debt. Thus, on the maturity date of the debt, the value of equity can be represented as

$$E(V,0,B) = \text{Max}(V - B,0) \tag{6}$$

Expression (6) says that the value of equity on the debt's maturity date, $T = 0$, is the maximum of the difference between the value of the firm and the promised principal payment, $(V - B)$, and zero. The value of the risky debt, D, on its maturity date can be represented as

$$D(V,0,B) = \text{Min}\ (V,B) \tag{7}$$

Expression (7) says that the value of the risky debt on its maturity date, $T = 0$, is the minimum of V and B. Both equity and risky debt

FIGURE 5

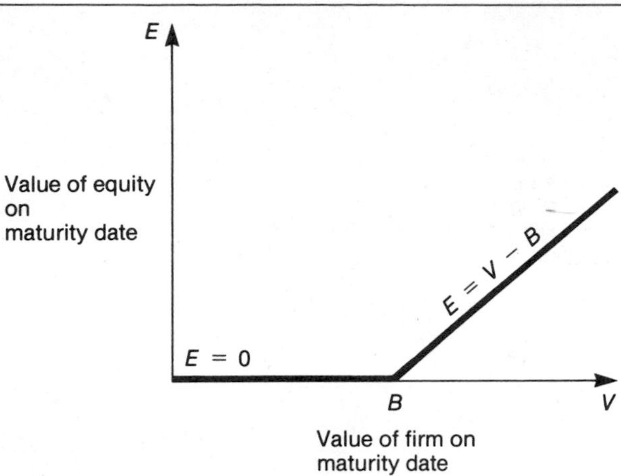

FIGURE 6

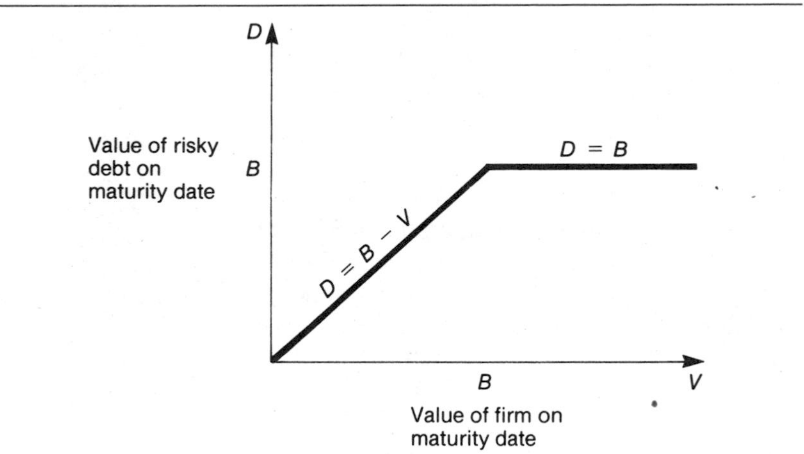

are contingent claim securities whose value is contingent on the value of the firm.

It follows immediately from the comparison of expressions (1) and (6) or by inspection of Figures 1 and 5 that equity in the presence of zero-coupon risky debt is directly analogous to a European call option written on the firm value, V, with an exercise price, B, equal to the debt's promised principal, and an expiration date equal to the maturity date of the debt.

$$E(V,T,B) = c(V,T,B) \tag{8}$$

In other words, equity can be viewed as a call option with the right to buy the firm for B dollars T time periods from now.

Now, return to the put-call parity result, expression (5), for options demonstrated earlier. In the characterization of corporate liabilities as options, the value of the firm, V, is the underlying asset on which the options are written; the debt's promised principal, B, is the exercise price; and the debt's maturity date is the option's expiration date. With this correspondence in mind, expression (5) can be rearranged and restated as

$$V = c(V,T,B) + Be^{-rT} - p(V,T,B) \tag{9}$$

But, since the value of the firm is the sum of the value of the equity and the value of the debt,

$$V = E + D \tag{10}$$

and since the value of the equity is given by expression (8), then it follows that

$$D(V,T,B) = Be^{-rT} - p(V,T,B) \tag{11}$$

The value of risky debt is equal to the price of a risk-free bond with the same terms minus the price of a put written on the value of the firm. Expression (11) has an intuitive interpretation. It is commonly understood that risky debt plus a loan guarantee has the same value as risk-free debt. The loan guarantee is like insurance, i.e., it will pay any shortfall in the value of the firm necessary to fully repay the debt. Figure 7 depicts the value of a loan guarantee, $G(V,T,B)$, on the maturity date, $T = 0$, of the risky debt. If on the maturity date of the debt the value of the firm is greater than the debt's promised principal, i.e., $V > B$, the guarantee will pay nothing since the firm is sufficiently valuable to retire the debt. However, if the value of the firm is less than the promised principal, $V < B$, the guarantor must pay the difference between the promised principal and the value of the firm, $B - V$, in order that the debt be fully repaid. Thus, on the maturity date of the debt, the value of the loan guarantee can be represented as

$$G(V,0,B) = \text{Max}(B - V,0) \tag{12}$$

Now compare either expressions (2) and (12) or Figures 2 and 7. It is evident that a loan guarantee is analogous to a European put option

FIGURE 7

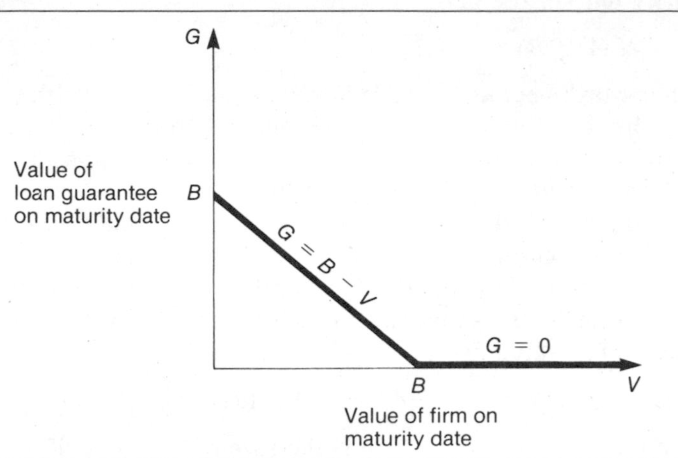

written on the value of the firm, i.e., $G(V,T,B) = p(V,T,B)$. And, therefore, expression (11) is simply the statement that risky debt plus a loan guarantee is equal to a risk-free bond.

To demonstrate that the characterization of corporate liabilities as options goes much deeper than the simple corporate securities studied so far, assume that the debt receives coupon payments, $\bar{c}$. Then equity can be thought of as analogous to a European call option on a dividend-paying stock where $\bar{c}$ is the "dividend." Now assume that the coupon bond is callable under a schedule of prices $K(T)$ where $K(0) = B$. The equity is now analogous to an American call option on a dividend-paying stock where the exercise price changes according to the schedule K(T). Furthermore, the value of the call provision can be characterized as the difference between the value of an American and European call option where the exercise price changes according to $K(T)$. The value of call protection against redemption for the first $T_1 < T$ time periods can be viewed as the difference between the values of two American call options on a dividend-paying stock where the first call can be exercised at any time according to $K(T)$ and the second call can be exercised only in the last $T - T_1$ time periods. As is evident from these examples, the correspondence between corporate liabilities and options extends to a wide variety of securities and covenants.

As shown, equity, zero-coupon debt, and loan guarantees can be represented as combinations of simple option contracts. The correspondence is, moreover, sufficiently robust that it is possible to characterize many of the complex securities and covenants encountered in practice by similar analogies to basic options. Note that this correspondence is not dependent upon any particular option pricing model but instead is a fundamental relationship which must hold independently of how options and corporate securities are assumed to be priced. Therefore, given any option pricing model with all its direct implications for pricing stock options, that same model has corresponding direct implications for the pricing of corporate liabilities. Black and Scholes have developed a particularly attractive option pricing model which provides the means for quantifying this qualitative characterization of corporate liabilities as options. The next section describes the Black and Scholes option pricing model and the following section make explicit the implications of the model for the pricing of corporate liabilities.

BLACK AND SCHOLES OPTION PRICING MODEL

Historically, option pricing models have fallen into two categories: (1) ad hoc models and (2) equilibrium models. Ad hoc models generally rely only upon empirical observation or curve fitting and, therefore, need not reflect any of the price restrictions imposed by economic equilibrium. Equilibrium models deduce option prices as the result of maximizing behavior on the part of market participants. This latter approach to option pricing dates back to the work of Bachelier (1900). Although the economics and mathematics of Bachelier's work are flawed, his research pointed the way for a number of attempts to describe an equilibrium theory of option pricing, including Sprenkle (1964), Boness (1964), and Samuelson (1965). All of these models essentially equate the value of an option to the discounted expected payoff to the option. The expected payoff to the option clearly depends on the assumed probability distribution of future stock prices. In addition, the proper rate to discount the expected payoff to the present must also be specified. Thus, to complete these models it is necessary to make specific and typically quite restrictive assumptions about individual risk preferences and/or the pricing structure in market equilibrium. These assumptions limit the generality (and practicality) of these early results.

Black and Scholes (1973) derive an equilibrium model of option pricing that avoids restrictive assumptions on individual risk references and market equilibrium price formation. This is made possible by their crucial insight that it is possible to replicate the payoff to options by following a prescribed investment strategy involving the underlying stock and the risk-free asset. Under the following assumptions:

A.1. There are no transaction costs or differential taxes.

A.2. Borrowing and lending, at the same rate of interest, are unrestricted.

A.3. The short-term risk-free rate of interest, r, is known and constant through time.

A.4. Short sales, with full use of proceeds, are unrestricted.

A.5. Trading takes place continuously in time.

A.6. The movement of the stock price can be described by a diffusion-type process

$$dS = \alpha S dt + \sigma S dz$$

where α is the instantaneous expected rate of return on the stock per unit time, σ is the assumed constant instantaneous standard deviation of the return on the stock per unit time, dz is a standard Gauss-Weiner process, and it is assumed the stock pays no dividends.

Black and Scholes demonstrate that it is possible to construct a portfolio involving positions in the stock and the risk-free asset where the return to the portfolio over a short time interval exactly replicates the return to the option. In addition, Black and Scholes show precisely how the composition of the portfolio must continually change in response to movements in the stock price and the passage of time such that the replication of the return to the option is maintained.

It is important to realize the implications of the fact that it is possible to replicate the return to options. The replication rules can be viewed as blueprints for a production technology which permits one to build synthetic options. As with any production technology, if the input markets are competitive and there is free entry into the industry, the price of the product must simply be the cost of production, i.e., there can be no excess profits. The fact that synthetic options can be constructed from existing securities does not imply that options contracts are redundant securities with no economic purpose. In the absence of options markets, individuals or institutions could achieve the desired pattern of returns only by attempting to create the options themselves using the Black-Scholes replication rules. The cost of this replication would necessarily exceed the price at which the options could be purchased if an option market existed because, in a competitive market, the price will equal the cost to the least-cost producers. Thus, all but the lowest-cost producers of options gain an economic benefit from availability of options through an organized market. Moreover, all that is necessary for the Black-Scholes pricing result to obtain is that there exist enough potential producers of options who can (to a reasonable approximation) trade continuously without significant costs or restrictions. Such a condition appears to be met by most large security-trading firms. Hence, the price at which an option trades should be well approximated by the Black-Scholes replication cost and it should not be sensitive to the specific economic reasons underlying the demand for option contracts by individuals or institutions.

The Black-Scholes option price is determined by the capital costs required to produce an identical payoff structure to the option by employing a dynamic portfolio strategy using other available securities. A general derivation of this blueprint for replicating the patterns of returns from options is given in Merton (1977). The continuous application of this replication argument results in a partial differential equation which must be satisfied by the price of the option. For example, the call option, $C(S,T,X)$ must satisfy

$$\tfrac{1}{2}\sigma^2 S^2 C_{SS} + rSC_S - C_T - rC = 0 \tag{13}$$

where subscripts denote partial derivatives. This equation can be thought of as the mathematical prescription, or "recipe," for the portfolio rules governing the replication of the option. To complete the specification of the call option pricing problem, boundary and terminal conditions must be appended to the partial differential equation.

$$C(0,T) = 0 \tag{13a}$$

$$C(S,T)/S \rightarrow 1 \text{ as } S \rightarrow \infty \tag{13b}$$

$$C(S,0) = \text{Max } (S - X, 0) \tag{13c}$$

Condition (13*a*) says that, should the stock become worthless, the call option becomes worthless. Condition (13*b*) says that, as the stock price becomes very large, the value of the call approaches the value of the stock. Condition (13*c*) is simply expression (1) which describes the value of the call option on the expiration date.

Black and Scholes solve equation (13), with appended conditions (13*a*), (13*b*), and (13*c*), for the value of a call option

$$C(S,T,X) = SN(d_1) - Xe^{-rT}N(d_2) \tag{14}$$

where

$$d_1 = \frac{\log(S/X) + (r + \tfrac{1}{2}\sigma^2)T}{\sigma T^{1/2}}$$

$$d_2 = \frac{\log(S/X) + (r - \frac{1}{2}\sigma^2)T}{\sigma T^{1/2}}$$

and N(•) is the standard cumulative normal distribution function.[5]

While the economic and mathematical arguments necessary to derive the option pricing result expression (14) are involved, the model has several attractive features which explain its widespread use by financial practitioners. One key feature is what the model does—or, more importantly, does not—require as data or inputs. The necessary inputs include the current stock price, S, the exercise price, X, the time to expiration, T, and the risk-free rate of interest, r, all of which are observable. The fifth input is the variance rate, σ^2, of the return to the stock which is relatively easy to estimate from historical data. The model does not depend on the expected rate of return, α, on the stock. This is an important and attractive feature of the Black-Scholes model because expected rates of return are not observable and, unlike variance rates, are not easily estimated from historical data. The model requires no assumptions about investor risk preferences. This characteristic of the model can be seen to follow from our production analogy where the price of the options is determined solely by the technology or production cost structure (i.e., the supply side) and is, therefore, not affected by investor preferences (i.e., the demand side).

The Black-Scholes formula can be used to demonstrate the qualitative impact on option prices of changes in the various inputs.

1. The higher the stock price, S, the higher the call price, i.e., $S \uparrow \Rightarrow C \uparrow$.
2. The later the expiration date, T, the higher the call price, i.e., $T \uparrow \Rightarrow C \uparrow$.
3. The higher the exercise price, E, the lower the call price, i.e., $E \uparrow \Rightarrow C \downarrow$.
4. The higher the variance, σ^2, of stock return, the higher the call price, i.e., $\sigma^2 \uparrow \Rightarrow C \uparrow$.
5. The higher the risk-free rate of interest, r, the higher the call price, i.e., $r \uparrow \Rightarrow C \uparrow$.

Property 1 follows from the fact that, if the stock price increases, the expected payoff to the call increases and thus the call price goes up. Property 2 is induced by two phenomena. First, if the expiration date increases, the present value of the expenditure of the exercise price goes down. Second, with a longer-lived call option the probability of the stock reaching very high levels increases. It is also true that the probability of the stock reaching very low levels increases, but the effect of downward moves on the option price are bounded, unlike upward moves, by zero, i.e., the option has limited liability. Property 3 says, if all things are the same, a call option with an exercise price of X_1 is worth less than a call option with an exercise price of X_2 where $X_1 > X_2$. Property 4 says that the more risky a stock the more valuable is a call option written on it. The more volatile a stock is, the higher the probability that the future stock price will be high and, therefore, the higher the probability that the payoff to the call option will be high. It is also true that increased volatility increases the probability that the future stock price will be low but, again, losses from downward moves are limited by zero. Property 5 says that, as interest rates go up, the present value today of the expenditure of the exercise price goes down.

Whether designed by practitioner or researcher, every pricing model makes abstractions from complex reality. The art of model building is to choose those abstractions which make the model tractable while capturing the essence of the real-world environment in which it is to be applied. As is evident from the discussion surrounding formula (14), the Black-Scholes option pricing model is certainly tractable. Because formula (14) follows directly from assumptions A.1–A.6, the effectiveness of the model can be judged in part by evaluating the reasonableness of those assumptions.

Assumptions A.1–A.5 are essentially institutional assumptions which imply that there are enough traders who can trade with about the same frequency as price changes at virtually zero marginal cost and without restrictions. As we have noted, these conditions appear to be met by the least-cost producers of options. A.6 is an assumption about the dynamic path followed by the price of the security underlying the option. The posited diffusion process implies that the time path of the stock price is continuous, which rules out the possibility that the stock price can "gap" or jump. It is, of course, a well-known empirical fact that the prices of individual stocks do (albeit, infrequently) exhibit large changes as in the case of tender offers, and the Black-Scholes formula, expression (14), does not capture that fact. Cox and Ross (1976), Merton (1976), and Jones (1983), however, have developed models along the lines of Black-Scholes which do allow for the possibility that stock prices can change in a discontinuous fashion.

The assumption of a constant variance rate in A.6 implies that the distribution of unanticipated stock price changes is log normal. The log normal distribution is the prototype distribution used in finance to model stock returns. Unlike, for example, the normal distribution, the log normal distribution (as depicted in Figure 8) captures the important limited liability property of securities by assigning a zero probability to negative stock prices. It is not, however, consistent with the established empirical fact that the variance rate of stock returns changes over time. Black (1975) finds that changes in this rate tend to be negatively correlated with changes in stock prices. As with jumps, this property of stock returns is not reflected in the Black-Scholes formula (expression (14)). Cox (1975) has derived a modified Black-Scholes formula for a class of stock price processes which exhibit a changing variance rate that is consistent with Black's empirical findings. Considering the importance of stock price volatility in the determination of option pricing, it is perhaps not surprising that both academics and practitioners are making a substantial research effort to understand the variance-rate process for stocks.

These analyses which take into account the jump component of stock returns and the stochastic variance rate, although important, are evolutionary—not revolutionary—steps in the further development of option pricing theory. As such, they exemplify the remarkable robustness of the Black-Scholes methodology. If, indeed, the practical significance of their model is measured only by its empirical accuracy in predicting option prices, then formula (14) does rather well even without correcting for the deviations between the posited and real-world stock price dynamics.

Black and Scholes (1972) test their model on price data gathered on options traded in the over-the-counter market from 1966 to 1969. Taking transaction costs into account, they demonstrate a close cor-

FIGURE 8

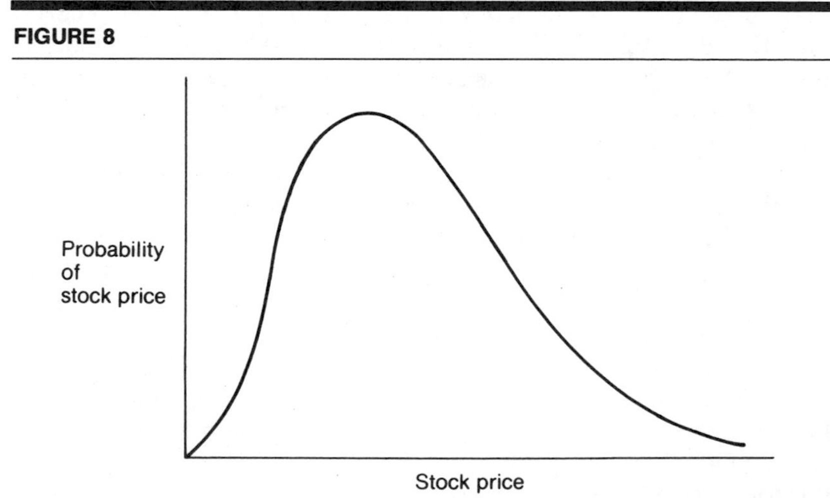

respondence between model and market prices. Galai (1977) replicates and extends the Black-Scholes test using data from the first seven months of trading on the CBOE. His results essentially reaffirm the findings of Black and Scholes (1972).

The same arguments used by Black and Scholes to solve for the value of call options can be used to solve for the value of put options.[6] Combining their model with the results derived earlier, the qualitative relationship between corporate liabilities and options can also be quantified. Merton (1974, 1977) formally sets forth the application of these same arguments to the problem of pricing corporate liabilities.

CONTINGENT CLAIM ANALYSIS AND THE PRICING OF CORPORATE LIABILITIES

The traditional approach to the pricing of corporate liabilities is exemplified by the organizational structure of a typical, vintage corporate finance textbook: a chapter on the pricing of equity, a chapter on long-term debt, a chapter on preferred stock, a chapter on warrants and convertible securities, etc. Each chapter employs a different valuation technique and rarely, if ever, are any attempts made to integrate the various components of the firm's capital structure as even a check on the internal consistency of these diverse valuation methodologies. In contrast, the contemporary CCA approach to the pricing of corporate liabilities begins with the firm's total capital structure and uses a single evaluation technique to simultaneously price each of the individual components of that structure. Thus, the CCA methodology takes into account the interactive effects of each of the securities on the prices of all the others and ensures a consistent evaluation procedure for the entire capital structure. In short, the pricing of corporate liabilities becomes a single, long chapter.

The development of the CCA approach began when it was first recognized that the payoff structures of risky pure-discount debt and corporate-levered equity are identical to the structure of simple call and put option strategies. These basic corporate liabilities can, therefore, be priced using the call and put option formulas derived by Black and Scholes. With this insight, further demonstrations followed rather rapidly showing that the same valuation procedure can be used to price multiple issues of coupon bonds as well as convertible securities and warrants. The procedure can, moreover, accommodate further refinements such as call provisions, sinking-fund requirements, and other covenants frequently required in the indentures of corporate securities.

As with the original Black-Scholes option pricing model, the CCA evaluation procedure does not require a past price history of similar-type corporate securities in order to price a particular security. Thus, unlike a statistical or regression model approach to valuation, the CCA model can price new types of corporate securities which have not been issued previously. This important characteristic of the approach greatly widens its range of application. One clear example is the private placement of debt with special terms where there is no observed market price. However, even in public offerings it is not uncommon to issue liabilities which are specifically linked to the asset characteristics of the firm. For example, Sunshine Mining Corporation issued a bond in the late 1970s which permits its holders to choose between receiving a specified amount of cash or a specified quantity of silver. Other bonds have been issued which are linked to oil prices and still others permit a choice of currencies.

The CCA technique can also be used to evaluate loan guarantees. Such guarantees are important in the oil pipeline industry where pipeline companies are typically financed almost entirely by debt which is guaranteed by the parent oil company. Federal deposit insurance and government guarantees of loans to private businesses can also be evaluated. With these examples as background, we now proceed with a more detailed discussion of the development of CCA.

Merton (1977) shows that the return to any corporate liability can be replicated using an investment strategy similar to the one employed by Black and Scholes. By adding the following assumption to the first five assumptions, A.1–A.5, of Black and Scholes,

> (A.6′) The movement of the firm value, V, through time can be described by a diffusion-type equation
>
> $$dV = (\alpha V - \overline{P})dt + \sigma V dz$$
>
> where α is the instantaneous expected rate of return to the firm per unit time, $\overline{P}$ is the known net total payout by the firm per unit time, and σ^2 is the variance of the return on the firm per unit time.[7]

Merton (1977) derives a dynamic portfolio strategy which involves mixing positions in the firm with the risk-free asset to produce a pattern of returns that exactly replicates the return to any given corporate liability of the firm. The replicating portfolio must be continually adjusted in response to changes in the value of the firm and the passage of time. The continuous application of this replication argument results in a fundamental partial differential equation which must be satisfied by the prices of all of the firm's liabilities.

For example, equity $E(V,T,B)$ must satisfy the fundamental partial differential equation

$$\tfrac{1}{2}\sigma^2V^2E_{VV} + (rV - \overline{P})E_V - E_T - rE + \overline{p} = 0 \tag{15}$$

where $\overline{p}$ is the payout per unit time from the firm to the equity. To solve for the value of equity, it is necessary to append boundary and terminal conditions to equation (15).

$$E(0,T) = 0 \tag{15a}$$

$$E(V,T,)/V \rightarrow 1 \text{ as } V \rightarrow \infty \tag{15b}$$

$$E(V,0) = \text{Max}(V - B,0) \tag{15c}$$

Condition (15*a*) says that when the firm is worthless the equity is worthless. Condition (15*b*) says that, as the value of the firm becomes very high, the value of the equity approaches the value of the firm. Condition (15*c*) is simply expression (6), the value of equity on the debt's maturity date.

For the case where the firm pays no dividends, $\overline{p} = 0$, and the debt is in the form of a zero-coupon bond, $\overline{P} = 0$, it is evident from inspection that the equity valuation problem, (15), (15*a*), (15*b*), (15*c*) is the same as the Black and Scholes call option problem (13), (13*a*), (13*b*), (13*c*). But this is precisely the general correspondence between equity and call options derived earlier. Thus, the value of equity is formally given by formula (14) for the value of a call option, where S is replaced by V, X is replaced by B, T is understood to be the maturity of the debt, and σ^2 is understood to be the variance of the return to the firm.

By the same replication argument, Merton (1974) shows that the value of the risky debt must satisfy the same fundamental partial differential equation,

$$\tfrac{1}{2}\sigma^2V^2D_{VV} + rVD_V - D_T - rD = 0 \tag{16}$$

where $\overline{P} = 0$ because the firm in this example is assumed to make no payouts and $\overline{p} = 0$ because the debt is a zero-coupon bond. To solve equation (16) for the value of the debt, it is necessary to specify boundary and terminal conditions.

$$D(0,T) = 0 \tag{16a}$$

$$D(V,T) \rightarrow Be^{-rT} \text{ as } V \rightarrow \infty \tag{16b}$$

$$D(V,0) = \text{Min}(V,B) \tag{16c}$$

Condition (16*a*) says that, when the firm is worthless, the debt is worthless. Condition (16*b*) says that, as the firm value becomes very large, the value of the risky debt approaches that of a riskless bond,

Be^{-rT}, with the same terms as the risky debt. Condition (16*c*) is a restatement of expression (7), the value of the debt on its maturity date. Merton (1974) presents the solution to the debt valuation problem, equations (16), (16*a*), (16*b*), (16*c*) as[8]

$$D(V,T,B) = Be^{-rT}N(h_1) + VN(h_2) \tag{17}$$

where

$$h_1 = \frac{\log(V/B) + (r - \frac{1}{2}\sigma^2)T}{\sigma T^{1/2}}$$

$$h_2 = \frac{\log(B/V) + (r - \frac{1}{2}\sigma^2)T}{\sigma T^{1/2}}$$

The response of the risky debt valuation, equation (17), to changes in the inputs gives some insight into the reasonableness of the CCA characterization of risky debt.

1. The higher the value of the firm, the higher the value of the risky debt, i.e., $V\uparrow \Rightarrow D\uparrow$.
2. The later the maturity of the debt, the lower the value of the risky debt, i.e., $T\uparrow \Rightarrow D\downarrow$.
3. The higher the promised principal, the higher the value of the risky debt, i.e., $B\uparrow \Rightarrow D\uparrow$.
4. The higher the volatility of the firm value, the lower the value of the risky debt, i.e., $\sigma^2\uparrow \Rightarrow D\downarrow$.
5. The higher the risk-free rate, the lower the value of the risky debt, i.e., $r\uparrow \Rightarrow D\downarrow$.

These derived properties are what one might expect from a reasonable model of risky debt valuation. As the value of the firm goes up, the debt becomes less risky and the value of the debt increases. As the maturity of the debt is lengthened, the present value of the receipt of the promised principal decreases; thus, the value of the debt falls. If all other things are the same, increasing the promised principal increases the debt value. If the risk of the firm increases, the value of the debt decreases because the expected losses to the debtholders from default increases. If riskless interest rates rise, the value of the debt falls.

Although the evaluation of levered equity and risky debt for the simple firm considered above is instructive, the more practical interest in CCA evolves from its ability to handle many of the complexities encountered with more realistic securities and capital structures. For example, consider a firm financed by equity, which receives dividends, and a callable coupon bond. The CCA characterization of the callable coupon bond, $F(V,T,B)$, as described in Merton (1974) can be written as

$$\tfrac{1}{2}\sigma^2V^2F_{VV} + (rV - \overline{c} - d)F_V - F_T - rF + \overline{c} = 0 \quad (18)$$

$$F(0,T) = 0 \quad (18a)$$

$$F(\overline{V}(T),T) = K(T) \quad (18b)$$

$$F(V,0) = \text{Min}(V,B) \quad (18c)$$

where $\overline{P} = \overline{c} + d$, $\overline{p} = \overline{c}$, $\overline{c}$ is the coupon on the debt, and d is the dollar dividend to the equity. Condition (18b) says that there is a schedule of firm values, $\overline{V}(T)$, at or above which it is optimal for the firm to call the debt at the call price, $K(T)$, where $K(0) = B$. The solution of this problem will provide both the value of the debt and the identification of $\overline{V}(T)$.

Another interesting application of CCA to complex securities is the evaluation of callable convertible debt, $H(V,T,X)$. The CCA formulation of this problem is due to Ingersoll (1976) and Brennen and Schwartz (1977a). The fundamental partial differential equation is the same as equations (18), (18a), (18b), and (18c), except that conditions (18b) and (18c) are replaced by

$$H(\overline{V}(T)T) = \gamma\overline{V}(T) \quad (18b')$$

$$H(V,0') = \text{Min }(V, \text{Max})\ (B,\gamma V) \quad (18c')$$

where γ is the fraction of the equity which would be held by owners of the convertible debt if all of the bonds were converted. The solution of equations (18), (18a), (18b'), and (18c') will not only give the value of the convertible bond but also the firm schedule, $\overline{V}(T)$, at or above which it is optimal to call the convertibles and force conversion. Ingersoll (1976) and Brennan and Schwartz (1977a) demonstrate that when equity receives no dividends, i.e., $d = 0$, CCA implies

$$\overline{V}(T) = K(T)/\gamma \quad (19)$$

That is, a convertible bond should be called the moment the bond's common stock value equals the call price. Ingersoll (1977) tests the implication of CCA for the optimal call policy against observed behavior. He finds that call policies of convertible-issuing corporations systematically differ from the optimal policy suggested by CCA. Even by taking the call notice and underwriting costs into account, Ingersoll (1977) is still unable to reconcile observed behavior with the model's prescription. He concludes that convertibles should sell for a premium over the model prices.

Other examples of CCA research include the work of Galai and Masulis (1976) on the effects of mergers, acquisitions, scale expansions, and spin-offs on the relative values of levered equity and risky debt; Black and Cox (1976) on the evaluation of specific bond indentures such as safety covenants, subordination agreements, and restrictions on the financing of payouts; and Jones, Mason, and Rosenfeld (1983) on the theory and empirical testing of the implications of CCA for the valuation of capital structures comprised of multiple callable coupon bonds with sinking funds.

Most of these more complex, and interesting, applications of CCA result in partial differential equations which cannot be solved for simple formulas. However, it is possible to approximate the solutions to these problems through numerical analysis on a computer. Techniques for performing the numerical analysis of CCA type problems are described in Parkinson (1977), Brennen and Schwartz (1978a), and Mason (1978). These numerical analysis techniques have been applied to many and diverse problems, including the evaluation of callable convertible debt (Brennan and Schwartz (1982)) and the pricing of loan guarantees (Jones and Mason (1980)).

The CCA model captures quantitatively what practitioners have long known to be the major determinants of value for corporate liabilities: (1) business risk, (2) financial risk, (3) level of interest rates, and (4) covenants. The notion of business risk is captured directly by σ^2, the variance of the rate of return to the firm. Clearly the value, and riskiness, of a firm's liabilities is in part driven by the riskiness of its assets. CCA captures financial risk through knowledge of the value of the firm, V, and the amount and timing of mandatory payouts. Two firms may have the same value and business risk, but the more levered firm's debt will be worth less. The model is given a direct indication of the level of interest rates through the specification of r, the riskless rate of interest. A security's covenants are reflected in the boundary conditions and the payout term, $\overline{p}$, as demonstrated in the callable coupon bond problem.

CCA, in its more general application, also provides many of the same advantages of the original Black-Scholes option pricing model in that many of the inputs required in the evaluation formula are directly observable. Mandatory payouts, maturities, and covenants are easily determined from indenture provisions. The risk-free rate, r, is also observable. The variance of the return to the firm, σ^2, can be estimated from a time series of firm values. Again, as with the Black-Scholes model, the CCA model does not depend on α, the expected rate of return on the firm, nor are any assumptions concerning individual risk preferences or market equilibrium necessary.

A major obstacle in applying CCA to practical corporate financial problems is the observability of V, the firm value. If the firm value can be observed in the form of all its liabilities trading, then the application goes through as described above. If, however, all of a firm's liabilities are not traded, then certain adjustments to the procedure are necessary. For example, if all of a firm's liabilities do not trade but there exists another traded asset which is assumed to move closely together with the unobserved firm value, the variance, σ^2, can be estimated from this traded asset. Then all that is necessary is that the firm has one traded claim. Since this traded claim must obey its own CCA partial differential equation, the unknown firm value can be inferred as that which gives a predicted price consistent with the observed price for the traded claim. With this knowledge of the implied firm value, the value of any other claim can then be determined. If the firm has no traded claims, but there is another traded asset which moves with the unobserved firm value, the variance can be estimated from this traded asset and a classical capital budgeting evaluation is necessary to determine the firm value. If the firm value is unobservable and there are no traded assets which move closely with the firm value, but the firm has at least two traded liabilities, then a firm value and variance rate which are consistent with observed prices can be inferred from the model.

As is evident from our examples, much research has been done with CCA in the area of pricing corporate liabilities. There is, however, still much development work to do before its full practical potential can be realized. To date, applications in the financial community have been focused on the pricing of convertible and other equity-type securities and on pricing the call option component of essentially default-free debt. Empirical testing of the model's accuracy in pricing complex capital structures is just beginning. As practical experience accumulates and the test results come in, there will undoubtedly be changes made in the detailed formulation of the pricing equations. As has been the experience with the Black-Scholes model in its application to option pricing, we expect, however, that these changes will be evolutionary and that the basic structure of the contingent claims analysis presented here will remain essentially intact.

With these developments, CCA will become an increasingly more useful tool for analyzing corporate liability strategy and planning. The capability to simulate a virtually unlimited range of financial packages presents the opportunity to determine the firm's most efficient capital structure. The cost in terms of reduced flexibility caused by the terms and covenants of financial instruments can be explicitly evaluated. The trade-offs between tax shields, financial distress, and the corporate need for additional funds under various contingencies can also be analyzed. Indeed, as we look to the future, perhaps the most important application of CCA will turn out to be in the strategy and planning activities surrounding the combined capital budgeting and financing decision problem. With this in mind, we explore briefly the potential of this application in our next and concluding section.

THE ROLE OF CCA IN CAPITAL BUDGETING DECISIONS

For more than a generation, finance academics have taught the net present value method as the correct procedure to use in making capital budgeting decisions. If recent survey statistics are accurate, this view is also widely shared in practice where apparently the majority of corporations now use some version of discounted cash flow analysis to evaluate their projects. Nevertheless, these capital budgeting techniques have their critics, with some of the sharpest criticisms coming from those in business policy and strategy. As a recent example, Hayes and Garvin (1982) assert that discounted cash flow methods cause a systematic undervaluation of projects because, among other reasons, the strategic value of projects is ignored. As an alternate and more direct remedy of this claimed undervaluation bias, Hayes and Garvin suggest that major investment decisions be made simply on the basis of judgment and strategic considerations, without subjecting them to the "distortions" of quantitative methods.

One does not have to embrace the suggested solutions of Hayes and Garvin to accept as a valid concern that current capital budgeting practices fail to properly account for all the important sources of value associated with a specific project. Such failures, when they occur, reflect the shortcomings of the particular evaluation technique used and not the quantitative approach itself. In this final section of the paper, we explore the potential of CCA to correct some of these shortcomings and conclude that it is especially well suited to the task of evaluating what strategists call the "flexibility" of a project.

Although not a precisely defined technical term, the flexibility of a project seems to us to be nothing more (or less) than a description of the options made available to management as part of the project. Baldwin, Mason, and Ruback (1983) call such options "operating options." As an example, the management of an electric utility faces a choice between building a power plant that burns only oil and one that can burn either oil or coal. Although the latter costs more to build, it also provides greater flexibility because management has the option to select which fuel to use and can switch back and forth, depending upon energy market conditions. In making its choice, management must, therefore, weigh the value of this operating option against its cost.

Operating facilities (such as oil refineries and chemical plants) which can use different mixes of inputs to produce the same output or the same inputs to produce various arrays of outputs, are general examples of this type of flexibility. That such options have value has, of course, long been recognized. As a practical matter, however, these option values are rarely incorporated into the capital budgeting process except, perhaps, in a qualitative fashion. With its proven record in valuing financial options, CCA shows great promise for providing the quantitative methods necessary to include explicitly the value of such options as part of the project evaluation procedure. Research along these lines is already underway, as is evident from the papers by Baldwin, Mason, and Ruback (1983). Brennan and Schwartz (1983a; 1983b), and Kester (1984). To provide a sense of the range of applications for this research, we present a brief catalog of examples of various operating options which could be evaluated by CCA.

Although a formula for the value of the option described in our electric utility example does not as yet appear in the CCA literature, there are published analyses which could be used to solve this problem. Three such papers are Margrade (1978) on the value of an option to exchange one risky asset for another; Stultz (1982) on pricing securities whose payoff is the maximum (or minimum) value of two assets; and Baldwin, and Ruback (1982) on the option value implicit in short-lived assets when prices are variable and uncertain.

Traditional capital budgeting procedures typically assume that a project will operate in each year of its anticipated lifetime. However, especially for projects involving production facilities, it may not be optimal to operate a plant in a given year because project revenue is not expected to cover variable cost. Explicit recognition of this type of management flexibility is particularly important when choosing among alternative production technologies with different ratios of variable-to-fixed costs. McDonald and Siegel (1981) use CCA to evaluate this option (not) to operate.

Another closely related type of flexibility is the option to expand or contract the scale of the project. Changes in the total output of the project can be achieved by changing the output rate per unit time or by changing the total length of time of the production run. Management may choose, for example, to build production capacity in excess of the expected level of output so that it can produce at a higher rate if the product is more successful than was originally anticipated.

Management can also choose to build a facility whose physical life exceeds the expected duration of its use, and thereby provide the firm with the option to produce more output over the life of the project by extending the production period. By choosing a plant with high maintenance costs relative to original construction costs, management gains the flexibility to reduce the life of the plant and contract the scale of the project by reducing expenditures for maintenance.

In addition to the option to temporarily shut down the project, management also has the option to terminate it. The value of this option can be substantial for large capital-intensive projects like nuclear power plants which have long construction periods. It is also important in the evaluation of projects involving new products where their acceptance in the market is uncertain. Myers and Majd (1983) provide a quantitative analysis of this option to abandon.

Just as the option to abandon can be an important source of flexibility in a project, so the option to choose when to initiate a project can be valuable. For example, the purchaser of an off-shore oil lease can choose when, if at all, during the lease period to develop the property. An analysis by Paddock, Siegel, and Smith (1982) suggests that this option can represent a significant part of the value of such leases. Their analysis implies, for example, that if the U.S. government were to require immediate development as a condition for granting such leases, then the prices paid for the leases would be considerably less than under current conditions, including, in some cases, no purchases at all.

Much the same analysis would apply to the evaluation of exploration activities. If natural resource companies were somehow committed to produce all resources discovered, then they would never explore in areas where the estimated development and extraction costs exceed the expected future price at which the resource could be sold. However, because they can choose when to initiate such development, it may pay to explore in high production cost areas in order to gain the option to produce if the price of the resource at some later date is higher than was expected. The value of the option associated with exploration has been formally analyzed by Tourinho (1979) using the Black-Scholes option pricing model.

As discussed in Kester (1984), an important strategic issue is the sequencing of investments in projects, and this, too, can be analyzed in an options-evaluation framework. Examples would be projects involving the production of basic consumer products like soap and light bulbs. In the successful marketing of such products, a brand name plays an important role, not only because of consumer recognition, but also because a brand name product is more likely to obtain "shelf space" from distributors such as supermarkets. For a firm evaluating projects to produce a number of consumer products, it may be advantageous to implement these projects sequentially rather than simultaneously. By developing a single product first, the firm can resolve at least some of the uncertainty surrounding its ability to establish a brand name and can determine the likelihood of obtaining the necessary shelf space for subsequent products. This resolved, management then has the option to proceed or not with the development of these other products. If, instead, these projects were undertaken in parallel, management would already have spent the resources and the value of the option not to spend them is lost.

Unlike the previous examples of intraproject options, the sequencing of projects involves the creation of options on one or more projects as the direct result of undertaking another project. Because the standard capital budgeting procedure is to evaluate a project on a "stand-alone" basis, the value of such interproject options can easily be missed. While neglecting such linkages may cause small errors in the evaluation of some projects, it can cause a significant undervaluation for others. Such a polar case would be research and development projects whose only source of value is the options they create to undertake other projects. More generally, interproject options are created whenever management makes an investment that places the firm in a position to use a new technology or to enter a different industry.

As discussed in Myers (1977), option analysis is important to the proper evaluation of a firm's "growth opportunities." As is well known in financial analysis, the value of a firm can exceed the market value of its projects currently in place because the firm may have the opportunity to earn a return in excess of the competitive rate on some of its future projects. The standard methodology for evaluating such projects is to discount back to the current time their net present values as of the anticipated implementation dates. This methodology implicitly assumes that the firm is committed to undertake the projects although, in fact, management need not make such a commitment before the implementation date. The standard method, therefore, neglects the value of the option not to go forward if conditions change before the implementation date.

Along with the options associated with growth opportunities, there are also "protective" or "strategic insurance" options which involve investments made by management to protect the value of current or planned future operations of the firm. An example with considerable public policy interest is the development of synthetic fuels as energy alternatives to oil. Consider the evaluation of a synthetic fuel alternative which, if developed, would provide an energy equivalent reserve of 10 billion barrels of oil. The project requires an immediate expenditure of $20 billion for development and the cost of production is $40 per equivalent barrel of oil. Suppose that the best available long-term forecast predicts that the price of oil will remain constant in real terms at $27 per barrel.

A standard capital budgeting analysis, which takes the expected future revenues (i.e., $27 per barrel) minus the expected future costs (i.e., $40 per barrel) and discounts it back to the present, would lead to the conclusion that the project should not be undertaken even if there were no development costs. Such a procedure assumes, however, that having once developed the project, the owner will produce the synthetic fuel independently of the price received for it and, therefore, the procedure neglects the option component of the project. By spending the money for development, the project owner acquires the option to produce energy at $40 per barrel, which also means that he has the option not to produce if the price is below $40. In a world of certainty, where future oil prices always turn out to follow their forecasted path, this option to produce would never be exercised and would, therefore, have no value. As we all know, however, the future course of energy costs is far from fully predictable. As long as there is some probability that oil prices will exceed $40 per barrel, the option has a positive value. As was previously shown for financial options, the value of this operating option and, hence, the value of the project, is an increasing function of the amount of uncertainty surrounding future energy prices. CCA can be used to evaluate this option and therefore help provide an answer to the strategic question, "Is $20 billion too much to pay to ensure that future energy costs will not exceed $40 per equivalent barrel of oil?"

We describe our hypothetical project as an "insurance" option because its manifest purpose is to protect the existing capital stock and consumption patterns of the economy from unanticipated and disruptively high energy prices. It also shares the characteristic common to most insurance arrangements that the insured is better off in those events where there is no need to collect on the policy. That is, a net energy-consuming economy is more likely to be better off if energy prices remain below $40 per barrel, in which case the option to produce is not exercised.

Throughout this sampler of operating options examples, we have repeatedly noted the failure of traditional capital budgeting techniques to properly take the value of these options into account. Although ignoring any single operating option may not introduce an important error in a project's evaluation, the cumulative error of ignoring all the operating options embedded in that project can cause a significant underestimate of its value. This is not, however, to say that standard techniques systematically and significantly undervalue *all* types of projects. Many classes of projects provide few, if any, operating options and, for others, the cumulative value of all such options will be small. Indeed, by neglecting the option components, these techniques may overestimate the values of some projects by failing to recognize the losses in flexibility to the firm caused by their implementation.

While rejecting the universal condemnation of current capital budgeting procedures expressed by some corporate strategists, we tend to agree with the more selective criticisms expressed by others in that community. As discussed in Myers (forthcoming), the focus of these criticisms is on the evaluation of long-horizon and broadly defined projects whose future profitabilities can only be imprecisely estimated. It is under just such conditions that taking account of the associated operating options is most important. As shown in our previous analyses, the value of an option is an increasing function of both the duration of the option and the amount of uncertainty surrounding the future value of the underlying asset. Hence, for projects of this sort, an evaluation technique which neglects these options can produce significant undervaluations. Moreover, as Myers (1977) has demonstrated, the choice of capital structure for the firm can also significantly affect the value of such projects. Although current capital budgeting procedures typically do make some provision for the tax deductibility of interest paid by the firm, they do not take into account the flexibility of its capital structure. Like operating flexibility, financial flexibility can be measured by the value of the financial options made available to the firm by its choice of capital structure. The interactive effects between financial and operating flexibility can be quite strong for major long-term investment projects involving considerable uncertainty. CCA would, therefore, appear to be a particularly useful tool to the corporate strategist because it provides an integrated analysis of both the operating and financial options associated with the combined investment and financing decision.

In this light, it is perhaps not surprising that the early capital budgeting applications of CCA concentrated on the evaluation of natural resource development and energy production types of projects where the scale of operations and financings is large and where the construction-development period and the production life are both long. As discussed in these analyses, the methods of financing these projects are important to their evaluation and the ones chosen are often complex. Nowhere is this more apparent than in project financings. We have resisted the temptation to accompany each of the specific applications of CCA with a technical development of the corresponding model. To have done otherwise would surely have defeated its manifest purpose as an expository overview. A survey on the application of CCA would, nevertheless, be incomplete without at least one such detailed demonstration. Therefore, in the appendix we develop a CCA model to analyze a generic large-scale project financing. Projects need not, of course, be of great complexity and size in order to justify the use of CCA. A project financing does, however, provide a rich setting for illustrating the wide variety of corporate finance issues to which CCA can be applied. To provide a real-world background for the analysis in the appendix, we briefly describe here a few examples of large project financings. These examples also serve to underscore the substantive importance of this type of financing.

The construction of the Trans Alaska Pipeline System (TAPS) required the expenditure of $10 billion, which at completion made it the single most expensive construction project ever undertaken. Owned by a consortium of major oil companies, TAPS was financed entirely by debt guaranteed by these companies. The proposed mining of the tar-sand deposits in the Athabasca region of Alberta, involved not only U.S. and Canadian private interest but also the federal and provincial governments of Canada. In this proposal, Gulf Oil's Alsands Project and Exxon's Cold Lake Project were each expected to cost between $10 and $15 billion and were to be financed by a complicated package of equity, debt, government-guaranteed debt, and tax concessions. The United States Synthetic Fuels Corporation (SFC) was established in 1980 to assist projects involving the development of commercially-viable alternative fuel technologies. SFC is empowered to provide loan guarantees, purchase commitments, price supports, direct loans, and joint venture participations as the means of extending subsidies to such energy projects. Financing packages such as these have principally been used in "hard asset" type projects and so the hypothetical project analyzed in the appendix is of this sort.

As discussed in the earlier sections, the fundamental evaluation equations of CCA are derived from arbitrage arguments involving portfolio strategies using traded securities. One might reasonably question, therefore, the validity of such equations for evaluating capital budgeting projects which are not traded. All capital budgeting procedures have as a common objective the estimation of the price that an asset or project would have if it *were* traded. Thus, for example, a standard discount cash flow analysis uses as a discount rate the equilibrium expected return required on a traded security in the same risk class as the nontraded project. Because the absence of arbitrage is a necessary condition for equilibrium prices, the no-arbitrage price of an option on a traded security must be the equilibrium price of an option on a corresponding nontraded project. If the undertaking of the project being evaluated would, however, significantly change the macroinvestment opportunity set available to capital market investors, then using either the equilibrium discount rate (absence this investment) or the option model (absence this investment) will lead to an error in the project's estimated value. Such "uniqueness" of a project is likely, as an empirical matter, to be rare. Moreover, the resulting error from using the option model in such rare cases would be no different from the one arising from the standard procedure.

There are, of course, other types of quantitative models for analyzing complex capital budgeting decisions. These typically fall into two classes: (1) Monte Carlo techniques and (2) hierarchical decision trees. Monte Carlo techniques, or simulation, as proposed by Hertz (1964), suffer from the problem that the output, i.e., a probability distribution, is not easily translated into a decision. The application of decision trees to capital budgeting, as described in Magee (1964), is hampered by ambiguity in the selection of a discount rate. The CCA model has the advantage over these alternative approaches that no matter how detailed and complex the interactions, the resulting evaluations are "consistent." That is, the derived values of all the component pieces are mutually consistent with an equilibrium price structure. Thus, CCA is particularly attractive for planning models because it can be used to simulate a variety of choices with the knowledge that any unusual characteristics which surface are likely to be "true" unanticipated consequences of actions and not simply the result of inconsistencies in the model's component equations.

In summary, it is unlikely that managers will ever rely entirely upon quantitative models in making major investment decisions. We do believe, however, that CCA will become as important and commonplace a tool for capital budgeting decisions in the future as it is for financial market decisions in the present.

APPENDIX: A CCA STUDY OF A PROJECT FINANCING

In this hypothetical example, a corporation has been invited to join a consortium of companies which has the opportunity to develop a natural resource base, e.g., coal, oil, minerals, etc. The project is to be financed by equity, senior debt, and subordinated debt guaranteed by the consortium members. In addition, the host government will provide a price guarantee for output over some early portion of the project's life. Therefore the project has three distinct phases: (1) construction, (2) operations with price guarantees, and (3) operations without price guarantees. Assume that the construction phase lasts until time T_c and the project produces no cash flows during construction. Total necessary investment in the project is assumed to cover the cost and repayment of financing during construction.

The project will produce according to a known production schedule and all its production is assumed to be sold at prevailing "spot" market prices which are assumed to fluctuate. As a means of partially reducing this price risk, the host government agrees to guarantee the price of output until time T_p. The productive life of the project is assumed to extend to at least time T_d, the maturity date of the longest-term bond. Therefore

$$T_c < T_p < T_d$$

After construction, the project generates cash flow, which is proportional to its current value at various discrete points in time and all debt service must be funded from this cash flow. If current cash flow is insufficient to cover mandatory payments, senior debt has first lien on the existing cash flow. If the cash flow is sufficient to cover senior debt payments, then the junior debt guarantee will make up the current cash flow shortfall to the junior debt and the project will continue. If the cash flow is insufficient to cover the senior debt payments then equityholders have the option of either contributing more cash to make up the shortfall in payments to the senior debt or abandoning the project. If equity chooses to make up the shortfall, then the guarantor will provide any currently due payment to the junior debt and the project will continue. If equity chooses not to make up the shortfall, then all debt is due immediately. Should the cash flow prove sufficient to cover all debt payments, the equity may declare a dividend equal to the surplus. The corporation's problem is to determine, given all the terms and conditions, whether or not membership in the consortium is an attractive investment opportunity. In this formulation of the problem, the value of equity, E, will be the corporation's share of total equity and the value of the project, V, will be taken to be the corporation's share of total project value as dictated by its interest in the consortium. As will be shown, it will prove to be illuminating if the analysis keeps separate the value of the loan guarantee from the value of equity even though the same entities provide both. As is often the case in these types of problems, the "trick" to solving this problem is to recognize that the solution can be derived in a recursive manner by working backward in time.

Thus, working backward, the "first phase" of interest is the operations phase without price guarantees. Table 1 sets forth the partial differential equations which must be satisfied by equity, E'', the senior debt, D'', and the loan guarantee, G'', in this regime. The guaranteed junior debt does not appear since its value is equal to that of a risk-free bond with the same terms. It is assumed that the junior debt's guarantors, the consortium members, are large enough that their guarantees are deemed to be risk-free. The price guarantee also does not appear because in this later phase it no longer exists.

TABLE 1

$$\tfrac{1}{2}\sigma^2V^2E''_{VV} + \Big(r - \sum_{j=m+1}^{mm} \delta(T - T_j)\gamma(T_j)\Big)VE''_V + E''_T - rE''$$
$$+ \sum_{j=m+1}^{mm} \delta(T - T_j)\mathrm{Max}(\mathrm{Min}(\gamma(T_j)V - DPS(T_j),0),\gamma(T_j)V - DP(T_j)) = 0 \qquad (20)$$
$$E''(\overline{V}(T),T) = \mathrm{Max}(\overline{V}(T) - DP(T) - BP(T),0) \qquad (20a)$$
$$E''(V,T)/V \rightarrow 1 \text{ as } V \rightarrow \infty \qquad (20b)$$
$$E''(V,T_d) = \mathrm{Max}(V - DP(T_d),0) \qquad (20c)$$

$$\tfrac{1}{2}\sigma^2V^2D''_{VV} + \Big(r - \sum_{j=m+1}^{mm} \delta(T - T_j)\gamma(T_j)\Big)VD''_V + D''_T - rd''$$
$$+ \sum_{j=m+1}^{mm} \delta(T - T_j)DPS(T_j) = 0 \qquad (21)$$
$$D''(\overline{V}(T),T) = \mathrm{Min}(\overline{V}(T),DPS(T) + BPS(T)) \qquad (21a)$$
$$D''(V,T)/V \rightarrow RBS(T) \text{ as } V \rightarrow \infty \qquad (21b)$$
$$D''(V,T_d) = \mathrm{Min}(V,DPS(T_d)) \qquad (21c)$$

$$\tfrac{1}{2}\sigma^2V^2G''_{VV} + \Big(r - \sum_{j=m+1}^{mm} \delta(T - T_j)\gamma(T_j)\Big)VG''_V + G''_T - rG''$$
$$+ \sum_{j=m+1}^{mm} \delta(T - T_j)\mathrm{Max}(\mathrm{Min}(DPJ(T_j),DPJ(T_j)$$
$$+ DPS(T_j) - \gamma(T_j)V, 0) = 0 \qquad (22)$$
$$G''(\overline{V}(T),T) = \mathrm{Max}(\mathrm{Min}(DPJ(T) + BPJ(T),DPS(T) + BPS(T) + DPJ(T)$$
$$+ BPJ(T) - \overline{V}(T)),0) \qquad (22a)$$
$$G''(V,T)/V \rightarrow 0 \text{ as } V \rightarrow \infty \qquad (22b)$$
$$G''(V,T_d) = \mathrm{Max}(\mathrm{Min}(DPJ(T_d),DPS(T_d) - V),0) \qquad (22c)$$

It is assumed that the variance rate of the project's return, σ^2, can be specified as a function of project value and time. It is also assumed that the risk-free rate of interest, r, is a deterministic function of time and that the cash flow proportionality factor, γ, can be specified as a function of project value and time. There are mm dates during production on which cash flow is realized from the project and the last $(mm - m)$ of these occurs during this last phase of production. The Dirac Delta function, $\delta(x) = 0$ for all x except $\delta(0) = 1$, is intended to capture the discrete nature of the cash flow. The debt payment currently due the senior debt is $DPS(T)$, the debt payment due the junior debt is $DPJ(T)$, and $DP(T)$ is the sum of $DPS(T)$ and $DPJ(T)$. The senior, junior, and total bond principal outstanding at any time, T, are given by $BPS(T)$, $BPJ(T)$, and $BP(T)$, respectively. Finally, $RBS(T)$ is the value of a risk-free bond with the same terms as the senior debt.

Although these equations are complicated, they all have the same structure, and this format is precisely the one described previously. For example, recall the fundamental partial differential equation, equation (15), which Merton (1974) demonstrates must be satisfied by all corporate liabilities. As illustrated by equation (15), the total payout from the project, $\overline{P}$, appears in the second term of the partial differential equation. Now examine each of the three equations in Table 1. In this case, the total payout from the project is the proportionality factor, $\gamma(T_j)$, multiplied times the project value and this same payout appears in the second term of each equation. Returning to the fundamental partial differential equation (equation (15)), the last term in the equation, $\overline{p}$, is the pay-out/pay-in term describing the distribution to or contribution from the security. In each of the equations in Table 1, the last term describes that security's unique payout/pay-in situation. For example, in the equation for equity, equation (20), the last term determines, as a function of project value and time, whether equity will receive a dividend or be required to make up a shortfall in the payment to the senior debt. Similarly, the last term in the equation for the guarantee, equation (22), determines, as a function of project value and time, whether the guarantor must make up any shortfall in a payment to the junior debt. Returning once again to the fundamental partial differential equation, equation (15), note the pattern of the three boundary conditions, (15a), (15b), and (15c). The first boundary condition gives the value that the security tends toward as project values become low. The second boundary condition gives the value that the security tends toward as project values become high. The last boundary condition gives the security's value at the end of the period of interest. This same pattern of boundary conditions is exhibited in Table 1. In the equation for equity, equation (20), boundary condition (20*a*) says that, as project values become low, there will come a point where the value of equity is less than the payment it is required to make to the senior debt if the project is to continue. At this point the equity will abandon the project. The schedule of project values at which this will happen is given by $\overline{V}(T)$. If $V(T) = \overline{V}(T)$, the value of equity is the maximum of the difference between the project value and the total payments due debt and zero. Of course, the decision to abandon by equity holders also affects the values of other securities. Note that $\overline{V}(T)$ appears in the first boundary condition of each of the other two security evaluation problems in Table 1. That is, the schedule $\overline{V}(T)$, determined in the solution to equation (20), becomes input data for the solution of equations (21) and (22). This interaction illustrates one of the many ways that the solutions to a set of CCA equations can be interrelated in a cross-sectional sense. The analysis of the next earlier production phase will demonstrate the backward recursive nature of the solution of the overall problem which causes the equations to be interrelated in an intertemporal sense.

Table 2 gives the equations which must hold in the production phase characterized by the presence of the price guarantee, S'. It is assumed here that the price guarantee takes the form of a schedule of guaranteed cash flows, $CF(T)$, which at all times during this phase equals or exceeds the schedule of payments due the senior debt. Note again that all of the equations in Table 2 have the same overall format as the fundamental partial differential equation (equation (15)). The presence of the price guarantee clearly affects the value of the securities at low project values; $PVE(T)$ is the present value of Max $(CF(T) - DP(T),0)$; $PVD(T)$ is the present value of $DPS(T)$ evaluated out to T_p. $PVG(T)$ is the present value of $\text{Max}(DP(T) - CF(T),0)$ evaluated out to T_p plus the present value of $BPJ(T_p)$, and $PVS(T)$ is the present value of $CF(T)$. These terms reflect the condition that no matter how low the project value becomes, the price guarantee continues to provide cash flow sufficient to ensure that equity holders will not abandon the project. Finally, take special note of the third boundary condition in each of the first three equations in Table 2. Here the recursive nature of the problem is made clear since, as an example, the solution to equation (20) is needed as a boundary condition for the solution of equation (23). This is caused by the requirement that the two solutions must match up at the time, T_p, when they meet.

Finally, Table 3 sets forth the equations for the construction phase, $T < T_c$. The schedule of total construction funds needed is

TABLE 2

$$\tfrac{1}{2}\sigma^2 V^2 E'_V + (r - \sum_{j=1}^{m} \delta(T - T_j)\gamma(T_j))VE'_V + E'_T - rE + \sum_{j=1}^{m} \delta(T - T_j)\text{Max}(\text{Max}(\gamma(T_j)V, CF(T_j)) - DP(T_j), 0) = 0 \quad (23)$$

$$E'(0,T) = PVE(T) \quad (23a)$$

$$E'(V,T)/V \to 1 \text{ as } V \to \infty \quad (23b)$$

$$E'(V,T_p) = E''(V,T_p) \quad (23c)$$

$$\tfrac{1}{2}\sigma^2 V^2 D'_{VV} + (r - \sum_{j=1}^{m} \delta(T - T_j)\gamma(T_j))VD'_V + D'_t - rD' + \sum_{j=1}^{m} \delta(T - T_j)DPS(T_j) = 0 \quad (24)$$

$$D'(0,T) = PVCD(T) \quad (24a)$$

$$D'(V,T)/V \to RBS(T) \text{ as } V \to \infty \quad (24b)$$

$$D'(V,T_p) = D''(V,T_p) \quad (24c)$$

$$\tfrac{1}{2}\sigma^2 V^2 G'_{VV} + (r - \sum_{j=1}^{m} \delta(T - T_j)\gamma(T_j))VG'_V + G'_t - rG' + \sum_{j=1}^{m} \delta(T - T_j)\text{Max}(DP(T_j) - \text{Max}(CF(T_j), \gamma(T_j)V), 0) = 0 \quad (25)$$

$$G'(0,T) = PVG(T) \quad (25a)$$

$$G'(V,T)/V \to 0 \text{ as } V \to \infty \quad (25b)$$

$$G'(V,T_p) = G''(V,T_p) \quad (25c)$$

$$\tfrac{1}{2}\sigma^2 V^2 S'_{VV} + (r - \sum_{j=1}^{m} \delta(T - T_j)\gamma(T_j))VS'_V + S'_T - rS' + \sum_{j=1}^{m} \delta(T - T_j)\text{Max}(CF(T_j) - \gamma(T_j)V, 0) = 0 \quad (26)$$

$$S'(0,T) = PVS(T) \quad (26a)$$

$$S'(V,T)/V \to 0 \text{ as } V \to \infty \quad (26b)$$

$$S'(V,T_p) = 0 \quad (26c)$$

given by $I(T_k)$, where T_k are the dates on which investment funds are committed and debt payments made and $k = 1, 2, \ldots, n$. The schedule of equity investment is given by $I_E(T_k)$. Recall that it is assumed that the consortium members guarantee the junior debt. Assume further that the junior debt is issued and the guarantees are provided according to a schedule such that G^k is the value of that

TABLE 3

$$\tfrac{1}{2}\sigma^2V^2W_{VV} + rVW + W_T - rW - \sum_{k=1}^{n} \delta(T - T_k)I(T_k) = 0 \quad (27)$$
$$W(\bar{V}(T),T) = 0 \quad (27a)$$
$$W(V,T)/V \to 1 \text{ as } V \to \infty \quad (27b)$$
$$W(V,T_c) = V \quad (27c)$$

$$\tfrac{1}{2}\sigma^2V^2E_{VV} + rVE_V + E_T - rE - \sum_{k=1}^{n} \delta(T - T_k)(I_E(T_k) + G^k) = 0 \quad (28)$$
$$E(\bar{V}(T),T)) = \text{Max}(W(\bar{V}(T)) - BPS(T) - BPJ(T) - DPS(T) - DPJ(T),0) \quad (28a)$$
$$E(V,T)/V \to 1 \text{ as } V \to \infty \quad (28b)$$
$$E(V,T_c) = E'(V,T_c) \quad (28c)$$

$$\tfrac{1}{2}\sigma^2V^2D_{VV} + rVD + D_T - rD + \sum_{k=1}^{n} \delta(T - T_k)DPS(T_k) = 0 \quad (29)$$
$$D(\bar{V}(T),T) = \text{Min}(W(\bar{V}(T)),BPS(T) + DPS(T)) \quad (29a)$$
$$D(V,T)/V \to RBS(T) \text{ as } V \to \infty \quad (29b)$$
$$D(V,T_c) = D'(V,T_c) \quad (29c)$$

$$\tfrac{1}{2}\sigma^2V^2G_{VV} + rVG_V + G_T - rG = 0 \quad (30)$$
$$G(\bar{V}(T),T) = \text{Max}(\text{Min}(DPJ(T) + BPJ(T), DPJ(T) + BPJ(T) + DPS(T) + BPS(T) - W(\bar{V}(T)),0) \quad (30a)$$
$$G(V,T)/V \to 0 \text{ as } V \to \infty \quad (30b)$$
$$G(V,T_c) = G'(V,T_c) \quad (30c)$$

$$\tfrac{1}{2}\sigma^2V^2V_{VV} + rVS + S_T - rS = 0 \quad (31)$$
$$S(\bar{V}(T),T) = 0 \quad (31a)$$
$$S(V,T)/V \to 0 \text{ as } V \to \infty \quad (31b)$$
$$S(V,T_c) = S'(V,T_c) \quad (31c)$$

portion of the total guarantee let at time T_k. Therefore, the value of the guarantee appears as a payout term for the equity. An alternative way to interpret this condition is to think of the equityholders as having purchased the guarantees from a third-party guarantor at a price of G^k. Notice that the total payout term for the project is equal to zero in each of the equations since it is assumed that the project makes no net cash distributions during construction. Of course the project value can drop to a sufficiently low level during construction that the equityholders will optimally abandon the project. The schedule of firm values at which this takes place during construction is given by $\bar{V}(T)$. If the equityholders choose to abandon, it is assumed that the project is sold, all debt is immediately due, and the offer of a price guarantee is withdrawn. The value of the project to another investor, W, during construction, $T \leq T_c$, is given by equation (27), where $\bar{V}(T)$ is the schedule of project values at which the new owner would abandon. In this analysis, it is assumed that ownership of the project is transferred to the host government.

Having developed the three sets of equations, Tables 1–3, it is now possible to describe the solution procedure for determining (1) investment value, (2) traded securities prices, (3) nontraded securities values, (4) the effects of bond covenants, and (5) the value of operating options. The investment value to the corporation is the value of the equity, E, or the solution to equation (28). Note, however, that in order to solve equation (28) it is first necessary to solve equations (20), (22), (23), (25), (27), and (30). Thus, it is not only necessary to solve recursively for the value of equity, but also for the value of the guarantee. In addition, the value of the abandoned project during construction, $W(V,T)$, must be determined to complete the boundary conditions for equation (28). While the solution of this problem may appear formidable, there are computer programs which will perform the necessary numerical computations. Indeed, the authors have applied CCA to problems of this complexity in practice.

It is perhaps appropriate to summarize what data are needed in addition to the numerical analysis computer programs to actually carry out the solution to equation (28). The necessary data are (1) interest-rate data, (2) variance-rate data, (3) covenant descriptions, and (4) project value. Some estimate of the time path of interest rates over the life of the project is needed in order to specify $r(T)$. One possibility for the latter is to infer a series of forward rates from the term structure of interest rates which is observed at the time of analysis. To estimate the variance of project returns, σ^2, it is helpful if a traded asset can be found which has volatility characteristics similar to those of the nontraded project. Alternatively, if the source of volatility in the value of the project can be attributed primarily to a single commodity, then the volatility of that commodity's price could serve as an estimate for the project's volatility. A description of the covenants (for example, coupon rates or sinking funds) can be found readily in the indentures. These data are needed to properly specify the boundary conditions and the pay-out/pay-in terms in each problem. The cash flow proportionality factor, $\gamma(V,T)$, must also be estimated. It is assumed in this example that $\gamma(V,T)$ is a specified function which describes the changes in the size of the natural resource base and the production schedule in response to the stochastic passage of time and changes in the level of the project value. Finally, the value of the project, V, which is measured gross of investment must be estimated. It may perhaps appear circular that it is necessary to estimate the *gross* value of the project in order to estimate the *investment* value of the project. However, the pertinent decision problem for the corporation is not simply the valuation of the project but the valuation of the terms and conditions surrounding its opportunity to "buy into" the project. To make the point in a less complex example, knowing the price of IBM stock is not sufficient to deduce the value of a call option on IBM stock. The value of the call option will also depend on its terms and conditions, e.g., exercise price and maturity. The project value can be estimated as the value today of a fully operational project available at time T_c. This project value can be determined by discounting expected cash flows by a risk-adjusted discount rate using standard capital budgeting procedures.

To illustrate how a change in the terms and conditions surrounding the opportunity affect the analysis, consider the case where the loan guarantees on the junior debt are provided by the host government instead of by members of the consortium. The valuation of equity proceeds as before except that the G^k term is now deleted from the pay-in/pay-out term of equation (28). This illustrates one of the reasons why it is convenient to separate the valuation of the guarantee from the valuation of the equity. In any negotiations between the consortium and the host government, the value of the loan guarantee and the price guarantee would be of significant interest to both in arriving at the form of subsidy to be selected. The value of the loan guarantee, G, is the solution to equation (29), which in turn depends on the solution to equations (20), (22), (23), (25), (27), and (30). The value of the price guaranteed, S, is the solution to equation (31), which depends on the solutions to equations (20), (23), (26), (27), and (28). Note that both of these problems exhibit the same recursive and interdependent nature as the equity valuation problem. The ability to price these nontraded contracts would not only permit both the consortium and the host government to negotiate in a more enlightened manner, but also to determine the impact on the value of these financial incentives caused by changes in their terms (e.g., the amount of debt guaranteed, level of the price guarantee, maturity of the guaranteed debt, and length of the price guarantee) which might arise during the negotiations. Thus, the system of equations can be solved for many different sets of terms and the impact on the value of the equity, loan guarantee, or price guarantee can be determined.

Another set of issues of interest to the project equityholders is the set of terms at which the nonguaranteed senior debt could be issued. Since it is the convention to issue debt at par, it is possible to test directly whether a specific combination of maturity, coupon, and sinking fund will result in equation (25) predicting a par price for the senior debt. To do so, it is necessary to first solve equations (20), (21), (22), (23), (24), (25), (27), (28), and (30) before solving equation (29). The trade-offs among different maturities, coupons, and sinking funds can be determined by simulating various combinations of these components. It is also possible to estimate the value of seniority status for nonguaranteed debt, by adjusting the pay-out/pay-in terms and boundary conditions to reflect the condition that the unguaranteed debt and the guaranteed debt are of the same rank if seniority rights are eliminated.

The model can also be used to solve for the value of the project's operating options. As an example, suppose that the host government requires that the consortium post a surety bond in the amount of the present value of equity's contribution to construction costs in return for the host government providing loan guarantees. The requirement takes away the owner's operating option to abandon the project during construction and thus ensures the completion of the project. The impact of this condition on the value of equity can be readily computed as the difference between the solution to equation (28) as originally posed and the solution to equation (28) with the new boundary condition

$$E(0,T) = -PVI(T) \tag{28'a}$$

where $PVI(T)$ is the present value of the mandatory contribution of construction funds by the equity. Condition (28′*a*) is simply a formal statement of the owner's obligation to contribute the necessary construction funds, independently of the project's economic values.

As another example of an operating option, consider an offer by the host government to make available to the consortium enough of the natural resource that the scale of the project could be doubled at time T_d at a cost of I_d to each consortium member. The value of this option is the difference between the solution to equation (28), where condition (20*c*) has been replaced by

$$E'''(V,T_d) = \text{Max}(\text{Max}(V - I_d,0) + V - DP(T_d)) \tag{20'c}$$

and the solution to equation (28) as posed.

The other classes of operating options discussed in our examples in the text can be evaluated in a similar manner using CCA. In our hypothetical project, for example, the option to initiate would apply to the consortium having the choice to begin construction at any time during a specified period. By adjusting the boundary conditions to reflect this option, CCA can estimate the value of this flexibility to delay construction.

Notes

1. Options can be of either American or European type. An American-type option allows exercise on or before the expiration date, whereas a European-type option allows exercise only on the expiration date.
2. See Merton, (1973), p. 144.
3. See Merton, (1973), pp. 156–60.
4. Expression (5) is true only for European options. Merton pp. 158–59.
5. Recall from the second section that $C(S,T,X) = c(S,T,X)$ and therefore expression (14) must hold for a European call option also.
6. Alternatively, given the Black and Scholes value of a European call option, (equation (14)), the value of a European put option follows immediately from equation (5), the put-call parity result.
7. It is important to note that $\overline{P}$ is the *known net* flows out of the firm. Examples of outflows would be dividends, coupon payments, sinking-fund payments, and principal repayments. Examples of inflows would be the future issuance of new securities, e.g., equity or debt, where the timing, terms, and proceeds are known for certain.
8. Instead of formally solving equations (16), (16*a*), (16*b*), (16*c*) for the value of risky debt, the same result could be achieved in two other ways. First, since the value of the firm is the sum of the value of the equity and debt, $V = E + D$, the value of equity gotten from equations (15), (15*a*), (15*b*), and (15*c*) could simply be subtracted from V. Second, given expression (11), the value of a put or loan guarantee on the firm could be computed and subtracted from the value of a risk-free bond, $Be^{-r\tau}$.

REFERENCES

Ananthanarayanan, A. L. and E. S. Schwartz. "Retractable and Extendible Bonds." *Journal of Finance* 35, No. 1 (1980), pp. 31–47.

Bachelier, L. "Theory of Speculation" (1900) (translation), reprinted in *Cootner* (1967).

Baldwin, C. Y.; S. P. Mason, and R. S. Ruback. "Evaluation of Government Subsidies to Large Scale Energy Projects: A Contingent Claims Approach," Harvard Business School Working Paper, (1983), pp. 83–66.

Banz, R. and M. Miller. "Prices for State Contingent Claims: Some Estimates and Applications." *Journal of Business* 51, No. 4 (1978), pp. 653–72.

Bhattacharya, M. "Empirical Properties of the Black-Scholes Formula Under Ideal Conditions." *Journal of Financial and Quantitative Analysis* 15, (1980), pp. 1081–1105.

Bhattacharya, S. "Notes on Multiperiod Valuation and the Pricing of Options." *Journal of Finance* 36, No. 1 (1981), pp. 163–180.

Black, F. "How to Use the Option Formula in Pricing Corporate Bonds." *Proceedings of the Seminar on the Analysis of Security Prices*. November 1974.

Black, F., "More on the Pricing of Corporate Bonds." *Proceedings of the Seminar on the Analysis of Security Prices*. May 1975.

Black, F., "Studies of Stock Price Volatility Changes," *Proceedings of the* 1976 *Meetings of Business and Economic Statistics Section*, American Statistical Association, 1976, pp. 177–181.

Black, F. and J. C. Cox. "Valuing Corporate Securities: Some Effects of Bond Indenture Provisions." *Journal of Finance* 17, No. 2 (1976), pp. 351–67.

Black, F. and M. Scholes. "The Valuation of Option Contracts and a Test of Market Efficiency." *Journal of Finance* 27, No. 2 (1972), pp. 399–417.

Black, F. and M. Scholes. "The Pricing of Options and Corporate Liabilities." *Journal of Political Economy* 81 (1973), pp. 637–59.

Boness, A. J. "Elements of a Theory of Stock-Option Values." *Journal of Political Economy*. 72, No. 2 (1964), pp. 163–75.

Boyle, P. and D. Emanuel. "Discretely Adjusted Option Hedges." *Journal of Financial Economics* 8, No. 3 (1980), pp. 259–82.

Boyle, P. and E. Schwartz. "Equilibrium Prices of Guarantees Under Equity-Linked Contracts." *Journal of Risk and Insurance* 44 (December 1977), pp. 639–80.

Brennan, M. J. and E. S. Schwartz. "Convertible Bonds: Valuation and Optimal Strategies for Call and Conversion." *Journal of Finance* 32, No. 5 (1977*a*), pp. 1699–1715.

Brennan, M. J. and E. S. Schwartz. "Savings Bonds, Retractable Bonds and Callable Bonds." *Journal of Financial Economics* 5, No. 1 (1977*b*), pp. 67–88.

Brennan, M. J. and E. S. Schwartz. "Corporate Income Taxes, Valuation and the Problem of Optimal Capital Structure." *Journal of Business* 51, No. 1 (1978*a*).

Brennan, M. J. and E. S. Schwartz. "Finite Difference Methods and Jump Processes Arising in the Pricing of Contingent Claims: A Synthesis." *Journal of Financial and Quantitative Analysis* (September 1978*b*), pp. 461–74.

Brennan, M. J. and E. S. Schwartz. "An Equilibrium Model of Bond Pricing and a Test of Market Efficiency." *Journal of Financial and Quantitative Analysis* 17 (September 1982), pp. 301–29.

Brennan, M. J. and E. S. Schwartz. "Evaluating Natural Resource Investments." Report prepared for the Division of Corporate Finance, Department of Finance, Ottawa (1983*b*).

Brennan, M. J. and E. S. Schwartz. "Optimal Financial Policy and Firm Valuation," Unpublished manuscript, University of British Columbia, 1983*b*.

Brennan, M. J. and E. S. Schwartz. "The Pricing of Equity-Linked Life Insurance Policies with Asset Value Guarantee." *Journal of Financial Economics* 3 (June 1976) pp. 195–214.

Cootner, P. H., ed. "The Random Character of Stock Market Prices." Cambridge, Mass.: MIT Press, 1967.

Cox, J. S. "Notes on Option Pricing 1: Constant Elasticity of Variance Diffusions." Unpublished manuscript, Stanford University, 1975.

Cox, J. C. and M. Rubinstein. *Options Markets* Englewood Cliffs, N.J.: Prentice-Hall, 1984.

Cox, J. C. and S. A. Ross. "The Valuation of Options for Alternative Stochastic Processes." *Journal of Financial Economics* 3 (1976), pp. 145–66.

Cox, J. C., J. E. Ingersoll, and S. A. Ross. "The Theory of the Term Structure of Interest Rates." *Econometrica* (forthcoming).

Cox, J. S., S. A. Ross, and M. Rubinstein. "Option Pricing: A Simplified Approach." *Journal of Financial Economics* 7 (1979), pp. 229–63.

Emanuel, D. "Warrant Valuation and Exercise Strategy." *Journal of Financial Economics* 12, No. 2 (1983), pp. 211–36.

Emanuel, D. "A Theoretical Model for Valuing Preferred Stock." Unpublished Working Paper, University of Texas at Dallas.

Galai, D. "Corporate Income Taxes and the Valuation of Claims on the Corporation." U.C.L.A. Working Paper No. 9–83 (1983).

Galai, D. "Pricing of Options and the Efficiency of the Chicago Board Options Exchange." *Journal of Business* 50, No. 2 (1977), pp. 167–97.

Galai, D. and R. W. Masulis. "The Option Pricing Model and the Risk Factor of Stock." *Journal of Financial Economics* 3 (1976), pp. 53–81.

Garman, M. "A General Theory of Asset Valuation Under Diffusion Processes." Working Paper No. 50, Research Program in Finance, Institute of Business and Economic Research, University of California, Berkeley, 1977.

Geske, R. and H. E. Johnson. "The American Put Valued Analytically." Graduate School of Management Working Paper 17–82, U.C.L.A., 1982.

Geske, R. "The Valuation of Corporate Liabilities as Compound Options." *Journal of Financial and Quantitative Analysis* 4 (May 1977), pp. 269–322.

Geske, R. "The Valuation of Corporate Liabilities as Compound Options." *Journal of Financial and Quantitative Analysis* 4 (November 1977), pp. 541–52.

Hayes, R. H. and D. A. Garvin. "Managing as If Tomorrow Mattered." *Harvard Business Review* 50, No. 3 (1982), pp. 70–79.

Hertz, D. B. "Risk Analysis in Capital Investment." *Harvard Business Review* 42, No. 1 (1964), pp. 95–106.

Ingersoll, J. E. "A Theoretical and Empirical Investigation of the Dual Purpose Funds: An Application of Contingent Claims Analysis." *Journal of Financial Economics* 3, No. 1/2 (1976), pp. 83–123.

Ingersoll, J. E. "A Contingent Claims Valuation of Convertible Securities." *Journal of Financial Economics* 4, No. 3 (1977), pp. 269–322.

Ingersoll, J. E. "An Examination of Corporate Call Policies on Convertible Securities." *Journal of Finance* 32 (1977), pp. 463–78.

Jones, E. P. "Option Arbitrage with Large Price Jumps." Working Paper No. 83–09, Harvard Business School, 1983.

Jones, E. P. and S. P. Mason. "Valuation of Loan Guarantees." *Journal of Banking and Finance* 4 (1980), pp. 89–107.

Jones, E. P., S. P. Mason, and E. Rosenfeld. "Contingent Claims Valuation of Corporate Liabilities: Theory and Empirical Tests." Working Paper No. 1143, National Bureau of Economic Research, Inc., Cambridge, Mass., 1983.

Kester, C. "Growth Options and Investment: Reducing the Guesswork in Strategic Capital Budgeting." *Harvard Business Review* (March/April 1984), pp.

Magee, J. F. "How to Use Decision Trees in Capital Investment." *Harvard Business Review* (September/October 1964).

Majd, S. and S. C. Myers. "Valuing the Government's Tax Claim on Risky Assets." Unpublished manuscript, Sloan School of Management, MIT 1983.

Margrabe, W. "The Value of an Option to Exchange One Asset for Another." *Journal of Finance* 33, No. 1 (1978), pp. 177–86.

Mason, S. P. "The Numerical Analysis of Certain Free Boundary Problems Arising in Financial Economics." Working Paper No. 78–52, Harvard Business School, 1978.

Mason, S. P. "The Numerical Analysis of Risky Bond Contracts." Working Paper No. 79–35 Harvard Business School, 1978.

Mason, S. P. and S. Bhattacharya. "Risky Debt, Jump Processes and Safety Covenants." *Journal of Financial Economics* 9, No. 3 (1981), pp. 281–307.

Mason, S. P. "Call Provisions and Protection Against Redemption and Refunding." Working Paper No. 80–26, Harvard Business School, 1980.

McDonald, R. L. and D. R. Siegel. "Options and the Valuation of Risky Projects." Unpublished Working Paper, Boston University, 1981.

Merton, R. C. "On the Cost of Deposit Insurance When There are Surveillance Costs." *Journal of Business* 51, No. 3 (1978), pp. 439–52.

Merton, R. C. "Option Pricing When Underlying Stock Returns are Discontinuous." *Journal of Financial Economics* 3 (1976*a*), pp. 125–44.

Merton, R. C. "The Impact on Option Pricing of Specification Error in the Underlying Stock Price Returns." *Journal of Finance* 31, No. 2 (1976*b*), pp. 333–50.

Merton, R. C. "The Theory of Rational Option Pricing." *Bell Journal of Economics and Management Science* 4, No. 1 (1973), pp. 141–83.

Merton, R. C. "On the Pricing of Corporate Debt: The Risk Structure of Interest Rates." *Journal of Finance* 19, No. 2 (1974), pp. 449–70.

Merton, R. C. "Option Pricing When Underlying Stock Returns Are Discontinuous." *Journal of Financial Economics* 3, No. 1/2 (1976), pp. 125–44.

Merton, R. C. "An Analytic Derivation of the Cost of Deposit Insurance and Loan Guarantees: An Application of Modern Option Pricing Theory." *Journal of Banking and Finance* 1 (1977*a*), pp. 3–12.

Merton, R. C. "On the Pricing of Contingent Claims and the Modigliani-Miller Theorem." *Journal of Financial Economics* 15, No. 2 (1977*b*), pp. 241–50.

Myers, S. C. "Determinants of Corporate Borrowing." *Journal of Financial Econmics* 5, No. 2 (1977), pp. 147–75.

Myers, S. C. "Finance Theory and Financial Strategy." *Interfaces* 14, No. 1, (January–February 1984), pp. 126–37.

Myers, S. C. and S. Majd. "Calculating Abandonment Value Using Option Pricing Theory." Working Paper, Alfred P. Sloan School of Management, MIT, 1983.

Paddock, J. L., D. Siegel, and J. L. Smith. "Valuation of Corporate Bids for Hydrocarbon Leases." Working Paper, Alfred P. Sloan School of Management, MIT, 1982.

Parkinson, M. "Option Pricing: The American Put." *Journal of Business* 5 (1977), pp. 21–36.

Roll, R. "An Analytic Valuation Formula for Unprotected Call Options on Stocks with Known Dividends." *Journal of Financial Economics* 5 (1977).

Ross, S. A. "A Simple Approach to the Valuation of Risky Streams." *Journal of Business* 51, No. 3 (1978), pp. 453–75.

Samuelson, P. A. "Rational Theory of Warrant Pricing." *Industrial Management Review* 6 (Spring 1965), pp. 13–31. Reprinted in Cootner (1967), pp. 506–32.

Sandler, L. "The Surge in Nonrecourse Financing." *Institutional Investor* (April 1982), pp. 149–61.

Schwartz, E. S. "The Pricing of Commodity-linked Bonds." *Journal of Finance* 37, No. 2 (1982), pp. 525–39.

Smith, C. W. "Option Pricing: A Review." *Journal of Financial Economics* 3, No. 1/2 (1976), pp. 3–51.

Smith, C. W. "Alternative Methods for Raising Capital: Rights Versus Underwritten Offerings." *Journal of Financial Economics* 5, No. 3 (1977), pp. 273–307.

Smith, C. W. "Applications of Option Pricing Analysis." In *Handbook of Financial Economics*, ed. J. L. Bicksler. Amsterdam: North-Holland Publishing Company, 1979, pp. 80–121.

Sosin, H. W. "On the Valuation of Federal Loan Guarantees to Corporations." *Journal of Finance* 35, No. 5 (1980), pp. 1209–21.

Sprenkle, C. M. "Warrant Prices as Indicators of Expectations and Preferences." Reprinted in Cootner (1967), pp. 412–74.

Stultz, R. "Options on the Minimum of Maximum of Two Risky Assets: Analysis and Applications." *Journal of Finance* 10, No. 2 (1982), pp. 161–85.

Tourinho, O.A.F. "The Option Value of Reserves of Natural Resources." Unpublished Working Paper, University of California, Berkeley, 1979.

Turnbull, S. M. "Debt Capacity." *Journal of Finance* 34, No. 4 (1979), pp. 931–40.

2

The Value of a Sinking Fund Provision under Interest-Rate Risk

Thomas S. Y. Ho*
Associate Professor of Finance
New York University

Most corporate bonds have sinking-fund provisions. When the bonds are subjected to interest-rate risks, and when the bond market is competitive, the provisions offer a valuable delivery option to the issuer. This paper studies the behavior of this delivery option, and the impact of the option value on the sinking-fund bond pricing.

The paper shows that issuing a sinking-fund bond is equivalent to issuing a nonsinking-fund bond and holding European interest-rate call options. Alternatively, an issuer of a sinking-fund bond may be viewed as an issuer of a nonsinking-fund serial bond, holding interest-rate put options. Further, the paper shows that the sinking-fund provision always increases the bond yield (relative to the nonsinking-fund bond). This increment should depend on the slope of the yield curve, without assuming a pure expectation theory. As long as trading is permitted, we should find the delivery option value to be low when the yield curve is upward-sloping and the option value to be high when the yield curve is downward sloping. Finally, the paper presents some empirical evidence showing that the bond market is competitive for Aa-industrial bonds at issuance and, therefore, put options associated with sinking-fund provisions are valuable.

The Value of a Sinking Fund Provision under Interest-Rate Risk

INTRODUCTION

Most industrial bond issues carry a sinking-fund provision that requires the issuers to retire a portion of the bond issue prior to maturity. The proportion to be retired is specified at issuance, and is redeemed over a period of time according to a prespecified *amortization schedule*.

The amortization schedule shortens the effective maturity of the issue, and affects the bond value at issuance. The sinking-fund provision has a second feature in that it offers the issuers an option to retire the debt either at the sinking-fund call price (usually at par) or at the market price. That is, the corporation may retire the portion of the bonds at par and call them on a lottery basis, or it may purchase the required portion of the bonds on the open market and deliver them to the trustee. This option to the issuer is called the *delivery option*.

As a consequence of the amortized retirement and the delivery option, the impact of a sinking-fund provision on the bond value can be substantial, even more so in recent years since we have been experiencing high interest rates in conjunction with high volatility. Moreover, we are also in a period when an increased number of the corporate bonds are subject to significant default risk. Both amortized retirement and delivery options should be more valuable as a result of these recent developments and, therefore, it has become more important to analyze the value of a sinking-fund provision.

There have been few theoretical studies on sinking-fund bonds, and most of these studies focus only on the impact of default risk, abstracted from interest-rate risk. Geske (1977), viewing a sinking-fund bond as a serial bond, derives a valuation model of the sinking-fund provision. Ho and Singer (1982), under a similar framework, show that early retirement is valuable under default risk. In a later paper, Ho and Singer (1984) analyze the delivery option under default risk, and show how the delivery option is related to the firm's risk, capital structure, and the debt refinancing policy. These studies assume that the interest rate is known and constant. Jen and Wert (1966) note the importance of interest-rate risk, but then go on to assume that sinking-fund bonds are equivalent to serial bonds. That is, they ignore the delivery option.

The purpose of this paper is to value the sinking-fund provision and to study the combined effect of the amortization schedule and the delivery option under interest-rate risks.[1] The approach taken is similar to that utilized in recent literature on the term structure of interest rates. The interest-rate generating process is assumed, and models of sinking-fund bonds and of nonsinking-fund bonds are derived. The value of the sinking-fund provision is shown to be related to the shape of the term structure of interest rates and to the variability of interest rates. Some empirical evidence consistent with the model is presented.

The next section presents a model which shows that issuing a sinking-fund bond is equivalent to issuing a discount bond and purchasing interest-rate European call options or, alternatively, issuing a serial bond and purchasing interest-rate European put options (Proposition 1). Then the effects of the sinking-fund provision on the nominal yield spread when the bond market is competitive (Proposition 2) and when the market is noncompetitive (Proposition 3) are shown. Utilizing a continuous-trading argument, the relationship between the term structure of interest rates and the yield spread (between sinking-fund bond and nonsinking-fund bond) is derived. This relationship shows that the yield spread may be formulated by assuming that the expectations hypothesis holds (Proposition 4). In the following section, some empirical evidence is presented. It shows that the Aa-industrial bond yield spread depends on both the values of the call provision and the delivery option of the sinking-fund provision. The observations suggest that the sinking-fund bonds may not be viewed as serial bonds, and that the market is not noncompetitive. The final section contains the conclusions.

DEFAULT-FREE BONDS WITH SINKING-FUND PROVISIONS

In this section, the model of a sinking-fund bond is presented. Utilizing an arbitrage argument, the sinking-fund bond is priced relative to the corresponding discount bond and to the corresponding serial bond. The impact of the sinking-fund provision on the yield spread between a sinking-fund bond and a nonsinking-fund bond is also investigated.

Assumptions

We make the following assumptions:

A.1. There are no transaction costs. Agents can issue or retire bonds without cost. There are no taxes, no short-selling constraints, or other frictions. All participants have equal access to information and, therefore, there is no problem of asymmetric information between bond issuers and investors. For the time being, we do not require the markets to open continuously. For simplicity, we may assume that all agents make their decisions and transact at times T_0, T_1, and T_2, although the model does not require them to do so.

A.2. All securities are infinitely divisible. The bond market is competitive and each investor holds a small proportion of any bond issue. This assumption eliminates the possibility that a single investor can accumulate an entire sinking-fund bond, so that the issuer must call back the bonds to satisfy the sinking-fund requirement.

A.3. The following default-free basic security types are defined:

a. *Short-term discount bonds*. Each bond pays \$1 at time T_1, and its value is B_1 at T_0.

b. *Long-term discount bonds*. Each bond pays \$1 at time T_2, and is valued at B_2 at T_0. We let $T_1 < T_2$.

c. *Sinking-fund bonds*. Each sinking-fund bond issue consists of $(1 + S)$ long-term discount bonds (for some $S > 0$). At T_1, the time of the sinking-fund operation, the issuer is required to retire a portion $[S/(1 + S)]$ of the face amount of the sinking-fund bond issue. The agent can retire the bonds in one of two ways. First, he may call the S long-term discount bonds by lottery at a fixed price, X. Second, he may purchase the required proportion of the sinking-fund bond issue in the open market. The portion of the issue not retired at T_1 is to be retired at T_2. The sinking-fund bond value at T_0 is denoted by B_{SF}.

d. *Corresponding discount bonds*. Each bond is a portfolio of $(1 + S)$ long-term discount bonds. The arbitrage conditions require the bond value to be

$$B = (1 + S)B_2 \tag{1}$$

e. *Corresponding serial bonds*.[2] Each bond is a portfolio of one long-term discount bond and SX short-term discount bonds. Similarly, by arbitrage conditions, the bond value B_S must be

$$B_S = (SXB_1 + B_2) \tag{2}$$

f. *Corresponding Call Options*. Each option is a European call option to buy a long-term discount bond at time T_1, with the exercise price, X. Therefore it is an interest-rate call option. Its value at T_0 is denoted by C.

g. *Corresponding Put Options*. The corresponding put option is defined analogously. It is a European put option to sell a long-term discount bond at time T_1, with the exercise price, X. Its value at time T_0 is denoted by P.

Arbitrage and sinking-fund bond pricing

We now show that issuing a sinking-fund bond is identical to selling a corresponding discount bond and simultaneously buying S corresponding options. Consider the two possible states at time T_1: (*a*) the long-term discount bond value is greater than the exercise price, $[B_2(T_1) > X]$, and (*b*) the long-term discount bond value is less than or equal to the exercise price, $[B_2(T_1) < X]$.

In state (*a*), the sinking-fund bond issuer would retire the sinking fund by calling the bonds. Therefore, the issuer spends SX in redeeming the bonds. Together with the remaining bonds outstanding, the agent owes a total amount of $[SX + B_2(T_1)]$ to the investors of the bond. Alternatively, if he had issued a long-term discount bond and purchased the option, the issuer would exercise his option in state (*a*), and receive $S[B_2(T_1) - X]$. Recall that the firm would also owe an amount $B(T_1)$ to the bondholders and, therefore, would owe in total $B(T_1) - S[B_2(T_1) - X]$. Equation (1), however, gives $[SX + B_2(T_1)]$. Hence, the issuer's position is the same in both cases.

In state (*b*), the sinking-fund bond issuer would redeem the sinking fund in the open market. Since the bond investors know that the firm would not call the bonds, and since, by assumption 2 they are atomistic, it follows that they would consider their bonds as equivalent to long-term discount bonds. Therefore, the bond issuer owes the investors $(1 + S)B_2(T_1)$ in market value. Alternatively, if the agent had issued a corresponding long-term bond and bought S corresponding options at T_0, his options would be valueless, and he would owe the bondholders $B(T_1)$. By equation (1), therefore, the agent's position would be the same in both cases. Hence, we have the following proposition.

Proposition 1. For a firm, issuing a sinking-fund bond is equivalent to issuing a corresponding discount bond and buying S corresponding options. At market equilibrium, equation (3) specifies that the relative pricing of a sinking-fund bond must hold:

$$B_{SF} = (B - SC) \tag{3}$$

Proof. We need to derive the equilibrium condition of equation (3). If $B_{SF} < (B - SC)$, the issuer of the sinking-fund bond would sell a corresponding discount bond, buy S corresponding options, and retire all of the outstanding sinking-fund bonds. The firm would realize net proceeds of

$$(B - SC - B_{SF}) > 0$$

As a consequence, there will be no sinking-fund bonds in the market.

Conversely, if we allow

$$B_{SF} > (B - SC)$$

the discount bonds issuers would issue a sinking-fund bond, realizing B_{SF}, buy back a corresponding discount bond, and write S corresponding options. The firm would realize net proceeds of

$$(B_{SF} - B + SC) > 0$$

and there will be no discount bonds. Therefore, equation (3) represents the equilibrium condition, QED.

Corollary. The sinking-fund bond may be priced relative to the corresponding serial bond. It is given by

$$(B_S - B_{SF}) = SP \tag{4}$$

where P is the value of a European put option on a long-term discount bond with exercise price X and expiration date T_1.

Proof. Equations (2) and (3) give

$$(B_S - B_{SF}) = (XSB_1 + B_2 - B - SC) \tag{5}$$

From equation (1), we note

$$(B_2 - B) = -SB_2$$

Hence, from equation (5), and applying put-call parity, we obtain equation (4), QED.

Indeed, by applying a similar argument to the proof of Proposition 1, it can be shown that issuing a sinking-fund bond is identical to issuing a corresponding serial bond and buying S European put options. It is in this sense that a sinking-fund bond has a delivery option. Relative to a discount bond, it grants the option to deliver a fixed payment. Meanwhile, relative to a serial bond, it grants the option to deliver the underlying bonds. Utilizing equations (3) and (4), we may compare the value of a sinking-fund bond with the values of the corresponding serial bond and the corresponding discount bond for different long-term bond values. This comparison is depicted in Figure 1.

The line *AB* represents the formula price of the interest-rate option. Therefore, by standard option pricing theory, the interest-rate option value is given by a curve *OC* which lies above the line *AB* such that it is asymptotic to the formula price as B_2 increases. The line *OD* represents the value of the corresponding discount bond. It is a straight line with slope $(1 + S)$. By equation (3), the sinking-fund

FIGURE 1 Relative Pricing of Sinking Fund Bond

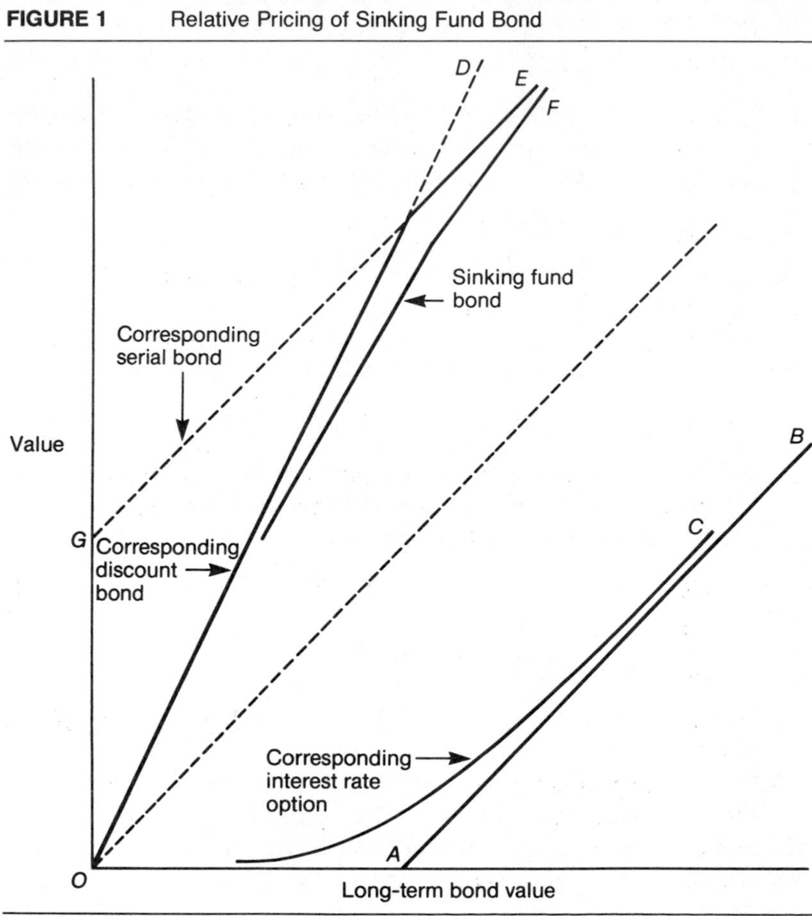

bond value can be constructed from the curve *OC* and the line *OD*. The curve of the sinking-fund bond value (*OF*) must increase and be asymptotic to a straight line (45°), with *Y* intercept being B_1X. This line is denoted by *GE*. But the line *GE*, by equation (4), is precisely the value of the corresponding serial bond.

Several interesting observations can be made from Figure 1.

First, the sinking-bond value must be less than both the corresponding serial bond value and the corresponding discount bond value. That is,

$$B_{SF} < \text{Min}(B_S,B)$$

This result can be explained intuitively. Relative to the discount bond, the sinking fund gives the option to the firm to redeem the bond at par in the sinking-fund operation. Therefore, the sinking-fund bond must be priced lower than the discount bond. On the other hand, relative to the serial bond, the sinking-fund bond gives the firm an option to redeem the sinking fund at the market price. Therefore, we should price the bond below the corresponding serial bond value.

Second, when the price level of the discount bond is low, the sinking-fund bond value would approximate the corresponding discount bond value. When the price level of the discount bond is high, however, the sinking-fund bond value would approximate the corresponding serial bond value. The explanation of this result is clear. When the bond value is low, the issuer expects, in all likelihood, to buy the bonds back in the market and, therefore, the sinking-fund bond is priced as if it were a corresponding discount bond. On the other hand, when the long-term bond price is high, the sinking-fund bond would in all likelihood be called and, therefore, the bond would be priced similarly to the corresponding serial bond.

Finally, the sinking-fund bond is affected by the interest-rate risk. If we assume that interest-rate volatility increases, but that interest-rate levels remain unchanged, the sinking-fund bond value would decrease. This change in the bond price is the direct result of the increase in the option values.

The sinking-fund provision and the yield spread

Define the *yield spread* to be the difference between the yield-to-maturity of the sinking-fund bond and that of the long-term discount bond. If we denote the yield-to-maturity of a sinking-fund bond by r_{SF}, then r_{SF} must be related to the bond price, B_{SF}, by[3]

$$B_{SF} = (1 + S)e^{-r_{SF}T_2} \tag{6}$$

Similarly, denoting the yield-to-maturity of the corresponding discount bond by r_D, we have

$$B_2 = e^{-r_D T_2} \tag{7}$$

Then, the yield spread is

$$\Delta = (r_{SF} - r_D) \tag{8}$$

We have shown that the sinking-fund provision affects the bond value. The yield spread would be an alternative way to measure this effect. The result is stated in the following proposition.

Proposition 2. The yield-to-maturity of a sinking-fund bond is strictly greater than that of the corresponding discount bond. The difference is positively and monotonically related to SC/B (i.e., the ratio between the corresponding option and the corresponding discount bond value), and it is bounded above by

$$\ln (1 + S)/T_2$$

Proof. Substituting equations (6) and (7) into equation (3), we get

$$(1 + S)e^{-r_{SF}T_2} + SC = (1 + S)e^{-r_D T_2}$$

Rearranging, we get

$$-(r_{SF} - r_D)T_2 = \ln [1 - (SC/B)]$$

That is,

$$(r_{SF} - r_D) = \frac{\{\ln [1 - (SC/B)]\}}{T_2} \tag{8}$$

Since the option value must be less than the underlying asset value, we have

$$0 < C < B_2$$

Hence we have

$$0 < (SC/B) < [S/(1 + S)] < 1 \tag{9}$$

Now $\ln (x) < 0$ for $0 < x < 1$, and, therefore, inequality (9) shows that the spread is always positive. Furthermore, since $\ln (x)$ is a monotonically increasing function, we have proved the first part of the proposition. For the second part, substituting equation (9) into (8) gives

$$(r_{SF} - r_D) < \frac{-\ln \{1 - [S/(1 + S)]\}}{T_2} = \frac{\ln (1 + S)}{T_2} \qquad \text{QED}$$

It is interesting to note that formulation of the sinking-fund bond depends crucially on the bond market being competitive. When the sinking-fund bond is privately placed or is fully accumulated, the bond should be viewed as the corresponding serial bond because the holder will not sell the bond back to the issuer at a price below the call price. In this case the yield spread may be negative. That is, define the yield of the serial bond, r_s, by

$$B_S = (1 + S)e^{-r_S T_2}$$

By equation (2) we can determine the yield spread to be:

$$\begin{aligned}\Delta' &= (r_S - r_D)\\ &= -(1/T_2)\ \ln\left[\frac{XSB_1}{(1+S)B_2} + \frac{1}{(1+S)}\right]\end{aligned}$$

Hence, $(r_S - r_D) < 0$ if and only if

$$\frac{XSB_1}{(1+S)B_2} + \frac{1}{1+S} > 1$$

or

$$(B_2/B_1 < X) \tag{10}$$

Note that B_2/B_1 is the implied forward (discount bond) price. Therefore, the following proposition may be stated.

Proposition 3. When a sinking-fund bond is the corresponding serial bond (as in the case of a private placement or a fully accumulated bond), and when the yield curve is sufficiently upward-sloping that the call price X is greater than the implied forward price B_2/B_1, then the yield spread would be negative.

We now compare our results with those of Jen and Wert (1966). They argue that, because of the amortization schedule, a sinking-fund bond should be more appropriately viewed as a serial bond, and they proceed to show how the bond yield would then be affected. In this paper, it is shown that, if the bond market is competitive and subject only to interest-rate risk, it is no better or worse to view a sinking-fund bond as a serial bond than as a discount bond. This is because the delivery option allows the sinking fund to behave either as a discount bond or as a serial bond (Proposition 1).

Sinking-fund bonds and the price dynamics of discount bonds

Thus far, we have expressed the value of a sinking-fund bond in terms of the corresponding discount bond, B, the serial bond, B_S, and the option, C. However, these asset values may not be independent of each other. Indeed, they must all be dependent on the price dynamics of the short-term and long-term discount bonds. For this reason, we shall in this section express the sinking-fund bond value only in terms of the dynamics of these bond prices. In addition to the previous assumptions, we now assume:

A.4. Continuous trading is allowed. At any time instant, t, the short-term and long-term discount bond prices are denoted by B_{1t} and B_{2t}, and they are generated by the following processes:

$$dB_1 = \mu_1 B_1 dt + \delta_1 B_1 dz_1 \tag{11}$$

$$dB_2 = \mu_2 B_2 dt + \delta_2 B_2 dz_2 \tag{12}$$

where μ_1, μ_2 are instantaneous expected rates of return of the bonds. They may be functions of time and the bonds' values, and other parameters, such as a liquidity premium. The dz_1, dz_2 are normalized Wiener processes and, in general, correlated. We assume that $dz_1 dz_2 = \rho\ dt$, where ρ is not assumed to be constant; δ_1 and δ_2 are functions of the time parameter but they are not functions of any stochastic variables.

This assumption is consistent with the model in Merton (1973). Equations (11) and (12) require that the bond prices follow some stochastic processes. We may view the price uncertainties as generated by the short-rate and the long-rate risks. Although the short and long rates may follow some Ito processes, we do not require the exact specification of the processes at this point. They are related to the bond's instantaneous expected rates of return μ_1 and μ_2. For our purpose, however, we need not specify these relationships. The additional assumption allows us to derive an alternative valuation model of a sinking-fund bond, giving us additional insight into bond pricing.

Proposition 4. Under assumptions (A.1)–(A.4), the yield spread (between the sinking-fund bond and the long-term discount bond) is

$$\Delta = (r_{SF} - r_D) = -\frac{1}{T_2}\ \ln\ \left\{1 - \frac{S}{1+S}\left[N(\mathrm{h}_1) - \frac{XB_1}{B_2}N(h_2)\right]\right\} \tag{13}$$

where $N(\cdot)$ is the cumulative normal distribution function.

$$h_1 = \frac{\ln(B_2/XB_1) + \frac{1}{2}T}{\sqrt{T}}$$

$$h_2 = h_1 - \sqrt{T}$$

$$T = \int_0^{T_1} [(\delta_1^2 - 2\rho\delta_1\delta_2 + \delta_2^2)]dt$$

(Note: δ_1 and δ_2 are functions of time t.)

Proof. We derive equation (13) by first pricing the corresponding call option. A detailed derivation of the valuation model can be found in Merton (1973). Just the basic steps are presented here. First note that, since the option is a contingent claim, we write

$$C = C(B_1, B_2, t) \tag{4.1}$$

Applying Ito's lemma to equation (4.1), we get

$$dC = \mu C dt + \sigma_1 C dz_1 + \sigma_2 C dz_2$$

where

$$\begin{aligned} \mu C &= C_t + B_1 C_{B_1}\mu_1 + B_2 C_{B_2}\mu_2 + \tfrac{1}{2}\delta_1^2 C_{B_1B_1}B_1^2 \\ &\quad + \rho\delta_1\delta_2 C_{B_1B_2}B_1B_2 + \tfrac{1}{2}\delta_2^2 C_{B_2B_2}B_2^2 \\ \sigma_1 C &= B_1\delta_1 C_{B_1} \\ \sigma_2 C &= B_2\delta_2 C_{B_2} \end{aligned} \tag{4.2}$$

Now, we invest W_1, W_2, and W_3 in the long-term bond, the option, and the short-term bond, respectively, and portfolio which is formed has no risk and no investment outlay. We require, therefore, that

$$\begin{aligned} &W_1 + W_2 + W_3 = 0 \\ &W_1\frac{dB_2}{B_2} + W_2\frac{dC}{C} + W_3\frac{dB_1}{B_1} = 0 \end{aligned} \tag{4.3}$$

Using conditions (4.3), together with the specifications on μ, σ_1, and σ_2 by equation (4.2), the option value must be determined by

$$\tfrac{1}{2}\delta_1^2 B_1^2 C_{B_1B_1} + \rho\delta_1\delta_2 B_1B_2 C_{B_1B_2} + \tfrac{1}{2}\delta_2^2 B_2^2 C_{B_2B_2} + C_t = 0 \tag{4.4}$$

where $C(B_1, B_2, T) = \text{Max}(0, B_2 - X)$

While both B_1 and B_2 are stochastic variables, the call option is closely related as an option on an index

$$y = (B_2/XB_1)$$

Specifically, define

$$h(y, t) = [C(B_2, B_1, t)/XB_1] \tag{4.5}$$

then, by equation (4.4), $h(y,t)$ must satisfy

$$\tfrac{1}{2}(\delta_2^2 - 2\rho\delta_1\delta_2 + \delta_2^2)y^2 h_{yy} + h_t = 0 \tag{4.6}$$

with $h(y, T) = \text{Max}(0, y - 1)$

In comparing equation (4.5) with the Black and Scholes equation, $h(y,t)$ is an option on y, with exercise price of \$1, on the underlying index with unit instantaneous variance of return, risk-free rate zero, and the time-to-expiration T, where

$$T = \int_0^{T_1} (\delta_1^2 - 2\rho\delta_1\delta_2 + \delta_2^2)dt \tag{4.7}$$

Hence, by the Black and Scholes model,

$$h = [yN(d_1) - N(d_2)]$$

where

$$\begin{aligned} d_1 &= (1ny + \tfrac{1}{2}T)/\sqrt{T} \\ d_2 &= (d_1 - \sqrt{T}) \end{aligned} \tag{4.8}$$

Combining equations (4.5), (4.6), and (4.8), we get

$$C = XB_1\left[\frac{B_2}{XB_1}N(d_1) - N(d_2)\right]$$

or (4.9)

$$C = B_2N(d_1) - XB_1N(d_2)$$

Substituting equation (4.9) into equation (8), we get the desired result, QED.

Let r be defined by the equation

$$B_1/B_2 = e^{r\tau} \tag{14}$$

where $\tau = (T_2 - T_1)$. Then r is the implied forward rate. Since a sinking fund is usually called at book value, we shall define c by

$$X = e^{-c\tau} \tag{15}$$

and we shall call c the bond discount rate.

Substituting equations (14) and (15) into equation (13), we get

$$\Delta = -\frac{1}{T_2}\ln\left\{1 - \frac{S}{1+S}[N(h_1) - e^{(c-r)\tau}N(h_2)]\right\} \tag{16}$$

$$h_1 = \frac{(c-r)\tau + \tfrac{1}{2}T}{\sqrt{T}}$$

$$h_2 = h_1 - \sqrt{T}$$

It is interesting to note that the yield spread is completely defined by the time-to-maturity T_2, the amortization schedule S, the difference between the coupon rate and the implied forward rate $(c - r)$, and the amount of interest-rate risk T. It is, however, independent of the level of interest rates explicitly (i.e., independent of B_1 and B_2).

The interest-rate level may affect the yield spread only to the extent that in a high-interest-rate regime, we may anticipate high-interest-rate risk, resulting in a high value of T.

It is also interesting to note that the spread is not explicitly dependent on the liquidity premium that may be priced in the term structure of interest rates. That is, in a regime with a steeply upward-sloping yield curve, the implied forward rate would be high. However, this could be the result of a high liquidity premium, combined with an expected spot rate at T_1 which is sufficiently low that the issuer does expect to call back the bonds. Yet, according to equation (16), the bond is priced as if there were no liquidity premium and as if the interest rate is expected to be high, so that the bonds would be purchased in the open market.

Differentiating equation (16) with respect to S, $(c - r)$, and T, we can show that:

$$\frac{\partial \Delta}{\partial S} > 0, \frac{\partial \Delta}{\partial (c - r)} > 0, \text{ and } \frac{\partial \Delta}{\partial T} > 0$$

In summary, comparative statics show that the yield spread depends primarily on three economic parameters. They are:

1. The amortization schedule, S.
   An increase in the amortization rate would lead to a higher option value, and therefore a wider spread.
2. The interest-rate risks T.
   Similarly, an increase in the interest-rate risk would result in an increase in the call option value. Therefore, the yield spread is positively related to interest-rate risk.
3. The relationship of the coupon rate and the implied forward rate $[(c - r)\tau]$. This relationship depends on the coupon rate as well as the implied forward rate. The impact of each can be analyzed separately. The spread is positively related to the coupon rate and negatively related to the implied forward rate.

EMPIRICAL REGULARITY

Proposition 4 shows that, for newly issued sinking-fund bonds, the yield spread should be related to the shape of the yield curve. When the yield curve is steeply downward-sloping, the implied forward rate would be low relative to the discount rate and, therefore, the spread would be large. Conversely, in a regime when the yield curve is steeply upward-sloping, the implied forward rate would be high relative to the discount rate. Then the spread would be low. In both cases, the spread is positive.

The above results were used to study the intertemporal variations of the yield spreads (*Corpsp*) between newly issued long term Aa-industrial bonds and government bonds of the same maturity. Observations of the yield spread are obtained from the *Analytical Record of Yields and Yield Spreads*. The newly issued bond yields are Salomon Brothers estimates as of the first day of each month. Monthly observations are obtained for a 12-year period between 1969 and 1980. Corporate bonds are priced differently from government bonds for several reasons; the yield spread should capture these differences. The magnitude of the yield spread should depend primarily on the default risk premium, marketability premium, and the values of the call provision and the sinking-fund provisions.

It seems reasonable to assume that default risk and marketability premiums do not vary on a monthly basis, and are not systematically related to the slope of the yield curve. Thus, by relating the monthly variations of the yield spreads and the yield curve slopes, we should observe the effects of the call provision and the sinking-fund provisions on corporate bond pricing. Specifically, because of these provisions for corporate bonds, yield spreads should be negatively correlated to the slopes of the yield curve. Furthermore, the previous analysis suggests the following hypothesis: If the bond market is competitive, the yield spread is always positive; otherwise, the yield spread may become negative when the yield curve is steeply upward-sloping. Note that, although the model has not incorporated the call provision, the above hypothesis still holds in the presence of the call provision. This is because the call provision and the corresponding option would both have negligible values when the yield curve is steeply upward-sloping in a competitive market, and the corporate bond would behave like a discount bond. However, given the same term structure of interest rates, in a noncompetitive market, the amortization schedule of the sinking-fund provision would result in the bond behaving like a serial bond. Therefore, the yield spread in this case may become negative.

To investigate the above hypotheses, compare the yield spread with the slope of the yield curve over time. The parameter $(Govsp)_t$ is used to measure the slope of the yield curve, and is defined by:

$$(Govsp)_t = (Yd_{30t} - Yd_{5t})$$

where t is defined over the same sample period as $(Govsp)$ and Yd_{30}, Yd_5 are the yield-to-maturity of the newly issued 30-year government bond and 5-year government bond, respectively.

To compare (*Govsp*) and (*Corpsp*), both parameters are plotted against time in Figure 2. The negative correlation between the two parameters is evident. In the periods when the yield curve is mostly downward-sloping (1969–72 and 1978–81) the yield spread remains high, above 60 basis points. However, during 1973–77, when the yield curve is mostly upward-sloping, the yield spread is low, mostly below 60 basis points. Further, Figure 2 shows that the variables are also negatively related to each other on a monthly basis. More interestingly, during the period 1968–72, the yield curve becomes increasingly upward-sloping, and the yield spread steadily decreases in value. However, during 1973–77, while the yield curve continues to become more upward-sloping, reaching the peak at the end of 1976, the yield spread at the same time stabilizes in value, remaining at the value roughly 20 basis points over the period 1976–77. This observation indicates that a sinking-fund bond may not be viewed as a serial bond.

There is further evidence that the sinking-fund bonds may not be viewed as serial bonds. If the bonds were priced as serial bonds and, if the observations of the slope of the yield curve are evenly distributed around the mean, then the observed yield spreads would also be evenly distributed around the mean. But the distributions of our sample observations do not support this view. Referring to Figure 3, it is evident that there is a significant skewness in the distribution of the corporate bond yield spreads, although the observations of the yield curve slope are roughly symmetrically distributed.[5]

The hypothesis is formulated under a set of restrictive assumptions. The validity of the model must be discussed to explain the observations depicted in Figures 2 and 3. Maybe other factors, not considered in the model, can also explain the empirical observations.

One possible explanation is the tax effect on the corporate and government bond pricing. Yet, considering that all of the observations in the sample are made on recently issued bonds, the built-in capital gain (loss) on the bonds is minimized, and therefore the tax effect would have a minimal impact on the observations. Another effect the model has ignored is the coupon effect. Since both government bonds and corporate bonds have coupons, one should compare the yield of bonds with the same duration, as opposed to the same maturity, because of the coupon effect. However, the bonds considered for the yield spreads are long-term bonds and, since government bond yields have similar values for long-term maturities, the yield curve becomes relatively flat for long-term maturities; hence, such misspecifications would also have a minimal impact on the results.

FIGURE 2 Corporate Bond Spread and Slope of the Yield Curve

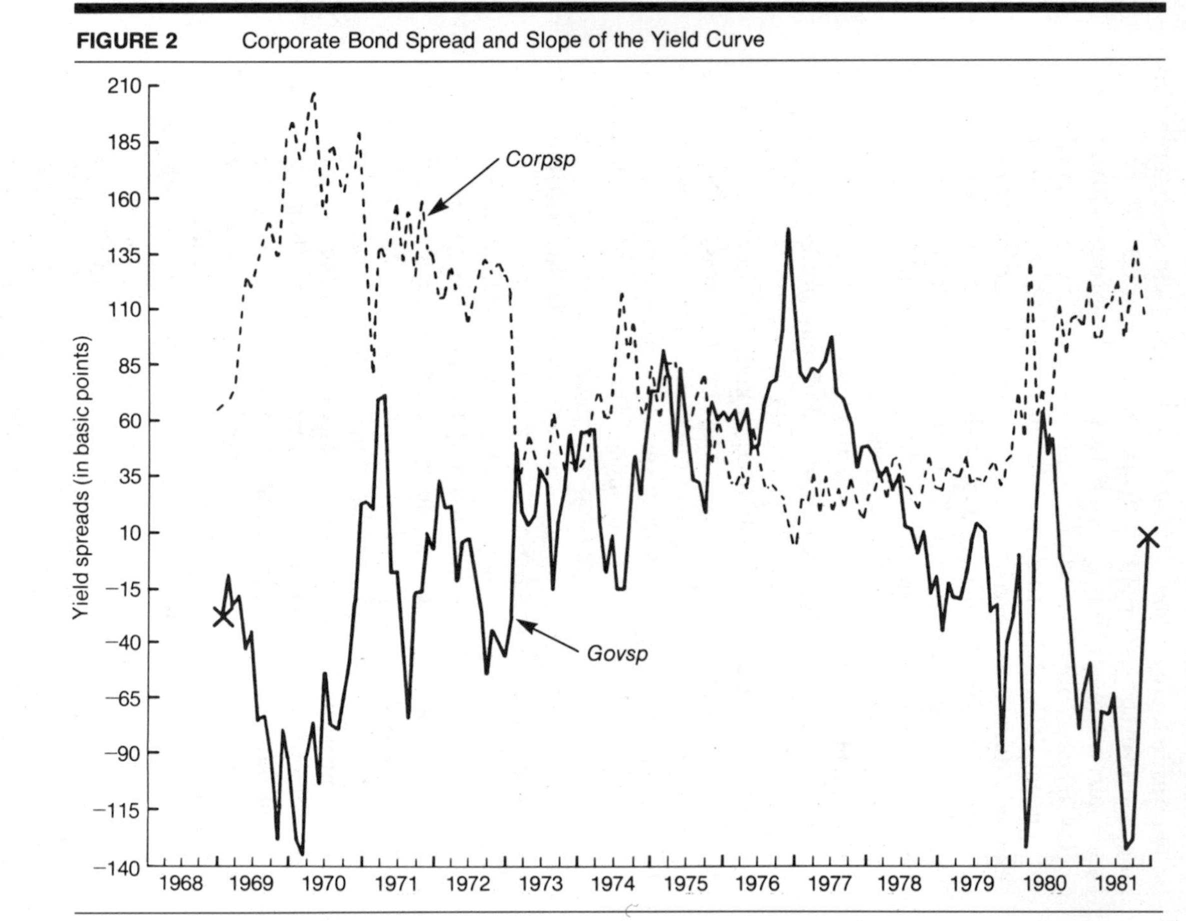

FIGURE 3 A Comparison of the Frequency Distributions of Corpsp and Govsp

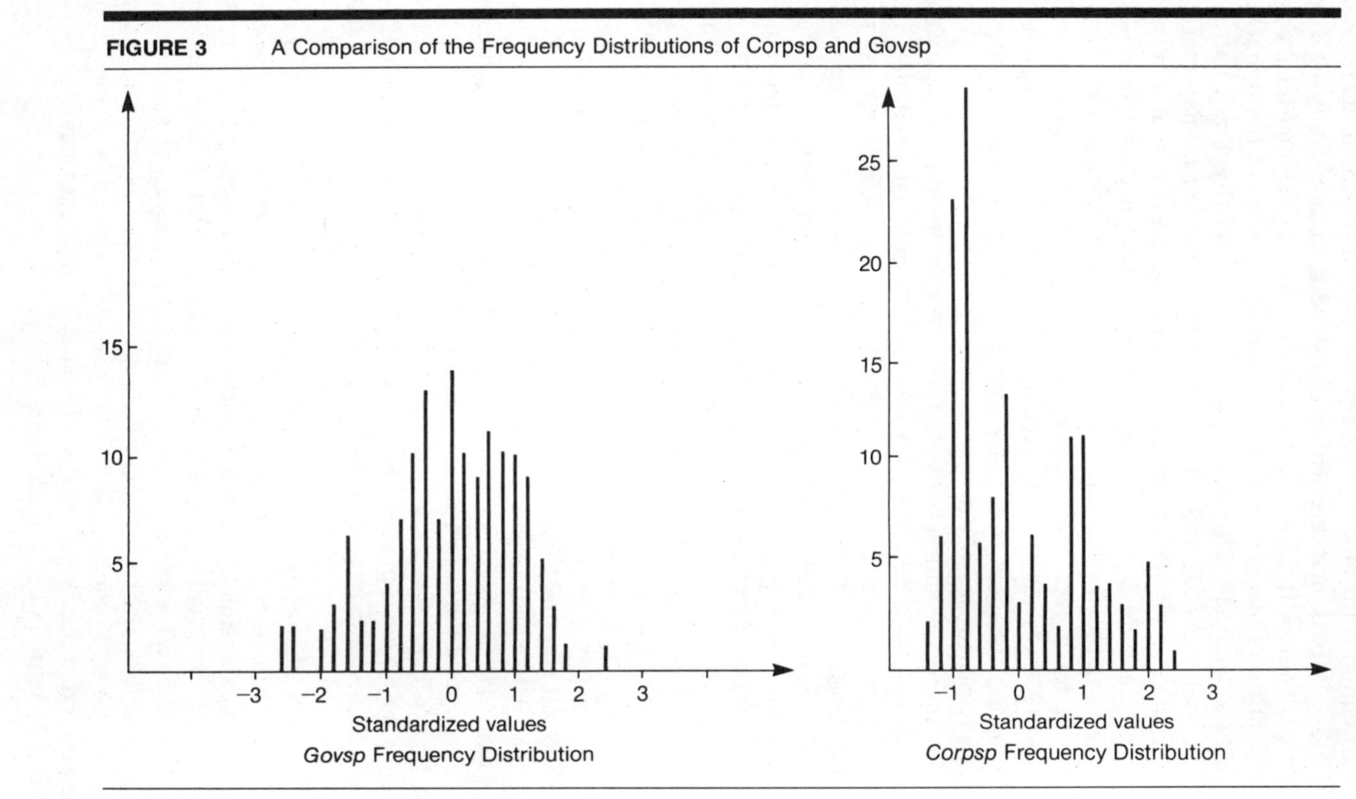

An equilibrium model has been developed in which agents can arbitrage across markets without cost. But markets may be segmented. That is, the Aa-industrial bond market, the short-term government bond market, and the long-term government bond market may be segmented. Therefore, the observed (negative) correlations of the yield spreads and the slopes of the yield curve may merely reflect the correlations of imbalances in supply and demand in each market. Such an argument, based on the possibility of market disequilibrium, may perhaps hold for intramonth yield variations, However, we have seen that the corporate bonds were "underpriced" during 1969–71 and "overpriced" during 1975–77. It is less than convincing to argue that a disequilibrium situation would persist over such extended periods.

Another explanation of the observed regularity may be that yield spread variations reflect variations in the default risk premium. Default risk should be related to the slope of the yield curve, as the interest-rate structure is closely related to the underlying economic outlook. Studies have shown that risk premiums narrow during periods of prosperity and widen during recessions. Since the yield curve slope is also related to the state of the economy, this cyclical behavior may explain some of the correlations of our observations. However, the empirical results show that the negative correlation of the yield spread and the slope of the yield curve is evident on a monthly basis and over all periods, including periods other than the peaks and the troughs of investment cycles. Therefore, default risk premiums cannot satisfactorily explain the results. Moreover, the observations of the yield spreads are confined to bonds rated Aa. Therefore, variations in default risk premiums cannot account for the significant intertemporal variations of the yield spread. For example, referring to Figure 2, we see that, over the sample period, the mean of the yields is 81.5 basis points. During April 1970, it reached a high of 210 basis points. Meanwhile, in January 1977, it reached a low of 10 basis points.

Finally, changes in interest-rate volatility may explain part of the yield spreads since the interest-rate risk level should affect the call provision and sinking-fund provision values. The higher the interest-rate risk, the higher would be call provision and delivery option values, thus affecting the yield spread. Nonetheless, we see that, in the late 1960s, the term structure of interest rates was relatively calm as compared to the late 1970s. Yet the yield spread is wider in the latter than in the former period. Therefore, this reason cannot satisfactorily explain our observations.

In conclusion, the empirical results show that the yield spread (between the Aa-industrial bonds and government bonds of the same maturity) is negatively correlated with the slope of the yield curve and, also, that even when the yield curve is steeply upward-sloping, the yield spread would remain positive. We argue that these observations demonstrate the significant effect of the call provision[6] and the sinking-fund provision on corporate bond values, and that they further demonstrate that the bond market is competitive and that it is inappropriate to view sinking-fund bonds as serial bonds.

CONCLUSIONS

Studies on the value of a sinking-fund provision under interest-rate uncertainty have been presented. It has been shown that issuing a default-free sinking-fund bond is equivalent to either issuing a discount bond and buying interest-rate call options or issuing a serial bond and buying interest-rate put options. Therefore, a sinking-fund bond may be better approximated by the discount bond than by the serial bond when the call option is out of the money. Conversely, when the put option is out of the money (the call option is in the money), the sinking-fund bond would be more analogous to a serial bond. Hence, a duration measure of a sinking-fund bond must depend on the term structure of interest rate. This paper also shows that the yield spread between a sinking-fund bond and nonsinking-fund bond is always positive when the bond market is competitive. But if the bond market is not competitive, the yield spread may become negative when the yield curve is steeply upward-sloping. The paper also shows that, when we allow continous trading between a sinking-fund bond and a nonsinking-fund bond, the yield spread is negatively correlated to the slope of the yield curve. This result does not depend on any expectations hypothesis. Finally, some empirical evidence is presented showing that the call provision and the sinking-fund provision can be valuable, and that it is inappropriate to view Aa-industrial bonds as serial bonds.

The paper results may be related to Dyl and Joehnk's (1979) empirical results. They have found that the sinking-fund provision reduces the yield of a bond. They argue that the reduction may be explained by the amortization schedule of the sinking-fund provision. When sinking-fund bonds are viewed as serial bonds, the appropriate bond yield would be determined by the effective maturity of the corresponding serial bond. In an upward-sloping yield curve regime, the sinking-fund bond would then have a lower yield. We argue that this may be erroneous. In an upward-sloping yield-curve regime, the corresponding call option of the sinking fund may have less value, but the option is always valuable. And, therefore, given interest-rate uncertainty alone, the sinking-fund provision should always *increase* the bond yield. In fact, in such a regime, the sinking-fund bond should behave like the corresponding discount bond, because the corresponding option would be out of the money. Thus, the bond duration (in terms of price elasticity) should approximate that of the discount bond, not that of the corresponding serial bond.

Notes

1. It is important to study the sinking-fund provision even without default risk. This is because a large portion of the industrial bonds is investment-grade, and most of these bonds have sinking-fund provisions. See Thompson and Norgaard (1967) and McKeon (1980).
2. These bonds may be more appropriately called pro-rata bonds. The term "serial bond" is used here for consistency with previous sinking-fund bond literature.
3. This definition of yield-to-maturity is used because this would be the nominal yield-to-maturity of a sinking-fund bond, when the bond market is noncompetitive and when the sinking-fund obligation is not considered in calculating the yield.
4. This specification of the bond return generating process implicitly assumes a certain type of interest rate process which permits interest rates to be negative. For this reason, this specification is somewhat undesirable. But this model does permit simple, intuitive explanations of the results, and the main conclusions of the paper should not be affected by using a more complicated (but more realistic) bond return generating process. This is because the major results of the paper depend on continuous pricing, not on the price distribution.
5. This empirical evidence suggests that the yield spreads between private placements and government securities should behave quite differently than those between industrial bonds and government securities. This is because the private placements market is noncompetitive and, therefore, the associated put option is valueless.
6. For a discussion of the value of the call provision of a corporate bond, see Pye (1967).

REFERENCES

Dyl, E. and M.C. Joehnk. "Sinking Funds and the Cost of Corporate Debt." *Journal of Finance* 34, No. 4, (September 1979), pp. 887–98.

Geske, R. "The Valuation of Corporate Liabilities as Compound Options." *Journal of Financial and Quantitative Analysis* 12, No. 4, (November 1977), pp. 541–52.

———. "The Valuation of Compound Options." *Journal of Financial Economics* (March 1979), pp. 63–82.

Ho, T. and R. F. Singer. "Bond Indenture Provisions and the Risk of Corporate Debt." *Journal of Financial Economics* (December 1982), pp. 375–406.

——— and ———. "The Value of Corporate Debt with a Sinking Fund Provision." *Journal of Business* 57, No. 3 (July 1984).

Jen, F. C. and J. E. Wert. "Imputed Yields of a Sinking Fund Bond and the Term Structure of Interest Rates." *Journal of Finance* (December 1966), pp. 697–713.

Kalotay, A. "The Effect of Sinking Funds on the Cost of Debt." Salomon Brothers, Inc., September 1981.

MeKeon, J. "The Anatomy of the Secondary Market in Corporate Bonds: Year-End, 1979 Update." Salomon Brothers, Memorandum to Portfolio Managers, April 1980.

Merton, R. "The Theory of Rational Option Pricing." *Bell Journal of Economics* 4, No. 1 (Spring 1973), pp. 141–83.

Pye, G. "The Value of a Call Deferment on a Bond: Some Empirical Evidence." *Journal of Finance* (December 1967), pp. 623–37.

Thompson, F. C. and R. L. Norgaard. *Sinking Funds*: *Their Use and Value* New York: Financial Executives Research Foundation, 1967.

---

* The paper was completed while visiting the Owen Graduate School of Management, Vanderbilt University. I would like to thank the participants of the Research Seminar at Vanderbilt University for their helpful comments.

3

Valuation of Corporate Securities: Applications of Contingent Claims Analysis

Martin L. Leibowitz
Managing Director
Salomon Brothers Inc.

Andrew J. Kalotay
Vice President
Salomon Brothers Inc.

Valuation of Corporate Securities: Applications of Contingent Claims Analysis

COMMENTS OF MARTIN L. LEIBOWITZ

The contingent claims approach provides a useful framework for gaining fresh insights into complex and tradition-encrusted problems. Where it borders on well-priced market securities, there is, of course, a cross interface with option theory and it has direct utility as a quantitative tool. However, as a framework, the concept applies not just at the financial level but extends into many areas of economic activity, e.g., capital budgeting, entrepreneurial processes, etc. In a certain sense, all entrepreneurial investment derives from a search for asymmetric reward situations. Just as the investment manager dreams of, and is always searching for, situations where he can achieve relatively unlimited return with limited risk, so there are many analogies on the side of corporate activity. The ideal capital project is one which is assured of producing a certain minimum level of expected profits, but which has an open-ended upside potential that could spark the development of whole new businesses.

In this connection, I must compliment Professors Mason and Merton on their suggestion that the option value of various capital projects may prove critical to their overall worth. Many of these options are unstated or at least unformalized—the option to stop, the option to sell off at an early stage, the option to take new directions under an increasing information framework, the options that relate to having a shot at all the opportunities that may arise when one enters the game but that will surely be foreclosed if one elects not to, etc. This recognition of the positive value in the implicit options associated with a capital project may be the key to putting it over the DCF hurdle.

The abbreviation, DCF, discounted cash flows, is far more common in the London markets than it is in the United States. This reminds me of an article that appeared a few years ago on the front page of the *London Financial Times*. The article described an internal corporate report prepared by the staff which had repeatedly referred to the DCF of a particular project. However, the project was being presented to the board by the Chief financial officer who evidently was not as familiar as his staff with this particular terminology. When a board member asked him what DCF meant, he responded without batting an eye, "Why, discontinued cash flows, of course!"

In terms of the corporate financial structure, although the debt option model is intriguing, it must be stated that few financial structuring decisions will ever be made with this construct as a primary consideration. Obviously, the threat of bankruptcy lurks somewhere beyond the horizon and does impact these decisions in a number of ways, most of which are indirect. This is an important distinction. In some ways, the corporate officer goes to great lengths to establish protective barriers that shield the corporation from being viewed in this rather harsh debt options context. Basically, his intent, as a practical matter, is to so structure the company finances that these bankruptcy options are so far out-of-the-money that the company can continue to operate as a creditworthy concern on an ongoing basis.

Thus, while the use of option theory as a quantitative tool has proved itself in well-defined and well-priced markets, many of its applications in corporate finance seem to be at the framework stage. This is not to demean the theory. On the contrary, the qualitative theoretic framework can prove a very useful and very enlightening corporate finance *weltanschauung*. By trying to identify and characterize the contingent claims features in corporate situations—such as the capital project problem discussed earlier—much light and an important sense of real option values can be uncovered, even at a qualitative level. Of course, this does not satisfy the natural desire of the quantifier to bring everything to the numerical level. However, overquantification may sever the essential ingredients of the problem from the quantitative solution that is ultimately (and often painfully) obtained. Therefore, I would like to suggest that applications of the contingent claims approach be encouraged even in this framework context without saddling all its practical applications with the need to solve partial differential equations and obtain quantifiable results.

Finally, it seems somewhat unfortunate that the choice of terms for this broad approach—contingent claims—has such a negative connotation. It has overtones that remind one of the Internal Revenue Service. It might be more upbeat to refer to the area as the theory of contingent opportunities.

COMMENTS OF ANDREW J. KALOTAY

The discussion about the applicability of contingent claims to corporate finance reminds me of a telephone call I received a couple of years ago from the manager of a midwestern corporation. He had recently read *Finance as a Dynamic Process*, and he was deeply impressed by the wide-range applicability of analytical methods to corporate finance. So he contacted Professor Elton (one of the authors) and asked about actual case studies, but he was surprised to learn that there were very few applications. This man was obviously delighted to hear from me when I was able to assure him that my colleagues and I had actually applied stochastic dynamic programming to bond refunding. Clearly, his somewhat shaken faith in the applicability of quantitative techniques was restored. The rather limited use of these techniques in corporate finance is obviously a concern to all practitioners and some academics.

The paper by Mason and Merton was a pleasure to read, at least up to the differential equations. After being puzzled for years by fragmented statements such as "equity can be viewed as a call option," it was enlightening to find out how the pieces fit together. A universal approach which attempts to capture all interactions, whether right or wrong, is always intellectually stimulating.

Since, to my knowledge, few financial managers have ever heard of contingent claims analysis (CCA), I assume that the approach is still waiting for its first application. The important question is whether it should be used and, if so, how it could be made palatable to practitioners. I will confine my comments to the second question.

A PROBLEM WITH CCA

I would like to discuss what I perceive to be a major obstacle in the acceptance of the CCA framework in practice. Let me say at the outset that I am *not* concerned with the complexity of the numerical computations, formidable as they may be. My concern is that, to a practitioner, a general theory is only as strong as its *weakest* link. I know that in the analysis of a bond portfolio, the mispricing of a single issue is sufficient to discredit the entire study, and I believe that financial managers will apply the same scrutiny to CCA. Financial managers will accept the overall approach only when they are comfortable with every one of its recommendations. My own lack of comfort with CCA stems not from any perceived deficiency of the general model—although I would like to see the explicit incorporation of taxes—but from the failure of the model to explain managerial behavior in specific instances related to the calling of bonds, which is a subject very familiar to me. As the paper indicates, the theory recommends that a convertible bond should be called when the conversion value equals the call price. The paper also points out that, when Professor Ingersoll tested this model, he found that it had virtually no predictive power. More recently, I had an opportunity to read a related study based upon a Ph.D thesis at the University of Chicago by Joesph Vu, who researched the calling of nonconvertible bonds. In the case of nonconvertible bonds, the recommendation is to call when the market price of the bond reaches the call price. However, Dr. Vu found the predictive power of this rule to be equally poor. Nevertheless, this recommendation has already found its way into a standard textbook by Brealey and Myers (*Principles of Corporate Finance*, 1984). I consider this somewhat premature.

Note that in the CCA framework the call is triggered by the market price. The manager only has to watch his QUOTRON, and mail out the call notices the moment the market price reaches a particular level. But clearly this is *not* the way decisions are made today. Either the theory is deficient or the managers are acting irrationally. I would like to offer some evidence that the traditional corporate approach to the calling of bonds has been quite reasonable. At this point, I would like to briefly review the methodology that Dr. William Boyce and I developed to assist with the refunding decisions that various Bell System companies were facing in 1976 and 1977.

The basic problem we perceived was that managers seemed to be anxious to call too early, without extracting the time value of the call option. Due to the call premium, the break-even rate on a typical 9 percent long-term issue (these were high-coupon bonds in 1976) is about 50 basis points (b.p.) below the coupon rate. There was a rule of thumb that a bond should be called when the spread between the coupon rate and the refunding rate widens to 100 basis points (1 percent). Our concern was that some treasurers might call at a narrower spread; say at 80 b.p., which is only 30 b.p. below the break-even rate. It seemed to us that, at such a narrow spread, the realized value of the call option would be much lower than its theoretical value.

Our fundamental assumption was that long-term interest rates follow a geometric random walk without a trend and with historical volatility. I might mention that practitioners generally find this model of interest rates more appealing than estimates derived from the term structure. Dr. Boyce and I always pointed out that the model would handle any interest-rate scenario, but nobody ever objected to the random-walk assumption.

Our analysis was heavily *cash flow* oriented. We incorporated into it taxes (which turned out to have a significant effect upon the optimum policy) and transaction costs (which had an insignificant effect).

To make a long story short, we found that, for the particular parameters in question, the optimum policy was to call at 125 b.p. below the coupon, but a call at a 100 b.p. spread would still capture more than 85 percent of the theoretical option value. So, with the use of standard, rather intuitive analytical techniques, we were able to establish that the "100 b.p. rule" was extremely reasonable although it is obviously not applicable in today's market. This concept suggested that we define the notion of *efficiency* (realized value/theoretical value), which subsequently became a basis for valuing not only calls, but also tender offers.

The 85 percent efficiency corresponding to a 100 b.p. spread is considered to be acceptable by most managers. In contrast, at an 80 b.p. spread, the efficiency would be reduced to about 50 percent. This would appear to be unacceptably low.

Two curious facts should be pointed out:

1. In the absence of taxes, the optimum call point would occur about 200 b.p. below the coupon, rather than at a 125 b.p. spread.
2. The market price is not an input to this analysis (except in the case of market purchases and tender offers).

COMPARISON

Let me try to abstract what I perceive to be three major differences between the "financial theory" approach, such as CCA, and the "financial/practice engineering" approach, such as the one just described.

1. The theoreticians' base of reference is a macro model of general equilibrium theory; practitioners are satisfied as long as they can identify the relevant features of the particular micro problem. The latter is essentially an operations research approach.
2. The emphasis in financial theory is upon optimality; practitioners are more concerned with reasonable rules, i.e., with

efficiency. I might add that I have found, not only in bond refunding but also in various engineering studies, that large deviations from the theoretically optimal policy often result in surprisingly little loss of efficiency.

3. Finally, theoreticians understandably tend to be committed to a particular approach and look for applications. Practitioners, on the other hand, have to be pragmatic. For them, the applications are given; their challenge is to use the optimal tools—analytical or not.

I have already alluded to the direction in which, in my opinion, academics will have to move to narrow the gap between theory and practice. They should be fully aware of the relevant institutional aspects of the problem—taxes and cash flows in general are certainly important, and accounting consequences should also be considered. And, recognizing that any mathematical model, by its very nature, provides only an incomplete description of the actual process, the emphasis should be on efficiency, not on optimality.

Part II

Agency Theory and Analysis: Introduction

In the early literature on corporate finance, much of the analysis was carried out in a context where all market participants have the same information. Since all agents had identical expectations about the future in this idealized full-information world, it was also implicitly assumed that participants had the opportunity to observe each others' actions and take decisions which protected their respective interests. The classical objective of maximization of stockholders' wealth, which was the cornerstone of much of the analysis, could therefore be justified easily since there would be no conflict of interest between the various ownership and management participants. One could also extend this to a third group of interested parties, namely the firm's creditors.

Unfortunately, many of the conclusions of the analysis based on a full-information world did not accord well with the observed actions of firms. For instance, the theoretical conclusion of irrelevance of the debt-equity mix when there are no corporate taxes, was not in line with actual corporate decisions—firms employed differing amounts of debt depending, for example, on the industry in which they operated, even in the precorporate tax era. Similarly, the logical prescription of "zero dividends," when dividends are taxed at a higher rate than capital gains, did not seem to be followed by most firms. Obviously, there were important elements missing from the earlier literature, which caused problems for the applicability of the conclusions. Perhaps the most important of these elements was the simplistic modeling of the information available to various market participants.

An important thrust in the recent academic literature has been the recognition of the asymmetry of information available to the various participants in a firm's ownership and management. Specifically, if the action of one of the participants, say the manager, are not directly observable by others, i.e., the stockholders, there is a potential conflict of interest between them, given that each of these groups pursues its individual self-interest. This characterization of the owner as a principal and the manager as an agent who acts on his behalf, but pursues his own interest, has been employed in the economics literature for a long time. However, the formal analysis of the problem is of more recent vintage. Early work in this area was done by Robert Wilson in an article in *Econometrica* (36, No. 1, pp. 119–32) in 1968 on "syndicates" of individuals who are constrained to make decisions in common, and also by Steven Ross, who presented a formal analysis of the so-called "principal-agent" problem in an article in the *American Economic Review* (63, pp. 134–39) in 1973. The burgeoning literature on the principal-agent problem in economics initially emphasized the sharing of risk and subsequently the formulation of optimal contracting arrangements between the two parties, given that observed data, e.g., output and profits, provide, at best, imperfect information about the agent's efforts and, at worst, misleading information.

A related development in the literature addressed the question of how the asymmetry of information can be, at least partially, redressed. The agents have a stake in this since, as George Akerlof pointed out in his paper in the *Quarterly Journal of Economics* (87, No. 3, pp. 488–500) in 1970, that in the absence of specific information about a product's quality, outsiders (i.e., principals) will tar all products (i.e., managers) with the same brush. The incentive for "poorer" agents to pass themselves off as "better" ones will cause the truly better managers to leave the market, in turn causing the average quality of agents in the market to deteriorate. Michael Spence, in subsequent work published in the *Quarterly Journal of Economics* (88, pp. 355–74) in 1973 pointed out that, under certain circumstances, it is possible for agents to "signal" their true quality. More importantly, there is an equilibrium relation between the signal and true quality such that it does not pay for poorer quality agents to pass themselves off as better quality ones. The signaling approach to the problem of information asymmetry has several applications in corporate finance, such as providing explanations for the debt-equity choice and the dividend policies of firms.

A particular strand of the agency-theoretic literature, which has become popular in analyzing corporate financial problems, emphasizes the costs of the relationships between the principal and the agent and the specific contractual arrangements that minimize this cost. This approach, pioneered by Michael Jensen and William Meckling in an article in the *Journal of Financial Economics* (23, pp. 371–407) in 1976, has been elaborated upon by several researchers and applied to a wide variety of corporate financial problems, ranging from analysis of covenants on corporate debt instruments to managerial compensation. It is useful to highlight the specific features of this approach in contrast to the general principal-agent problem in the economics literature. First, the approach in the finance literature has focused mostly on positive predictions of firm and investor behavior rather than the normative design of contracts. Since, in financial problems, one has the advantage of market valuation of corporate claims, it is not necessary to go into the details of the preferences of the principal and the agent or the specific aspects of the asymmetry of information between them. All that is required is to impose the restriction that the outside owners of corporate claims (usually the principals) earn at least the market opportunity rate of return on their investments. Note that this is in contrast to the classical principal-agent problem in economics, where the restriction imposed is that the *agent* earns at least his market opportunity wage rate. In essence, their roles are reversed.

The Jensen-Meckling paper, and others that draw from it, emphasize the costs of the agency relationship. Other than the obvious costs of structuring the contract, there are costs involved in enforcing the contract. They can be further categorized as costs of monitoring (i.e., ensuring that the terms of the contract are adhered to) and bonding (i.e., steps taken by the agent to restrict his ability to act against the principal's interests). If the contract design is not optimized or the firm is forced to undertake nonoptimal courses of action as a result of the agency relationship, there will be an additional residual loss as well. Of course, it pays to invest in bonding or monitoring arrangements only to the point where the benefits from enforcement just outweigh the costs. The key insight in this approach is that, since the principal earns the market opportunity rate of return on his investment in the firm, all agency costs are borne by the agent. It pays for the agent and the principal to write contracts that minimize the total costs of the agency relationship.

In this Part of the book, Michael Jensen and Clifford Smith survey the positive theory of agency that has found wide application in corporate financial problems. They examine the conflicts of interest between residual claimants (equityholders) and managers. They look at alternative forms of organization and analyze the risk-bearing efficiencies of the corporate form of organization and contrast them with the agency costs entailed. They then look at mechanisms to reduce the agency costs of the relationship through managerial compensation. The next step in their analysis is to examine the market for corporate control and to attempt to put the disparate empirical evidence in this area of research into a common framework.

The next section of their survey examines the conflict of interest between stockholders and bondholders. The potential mechanisms for transfer of wealth to stockholders are payment of dividends, dilution of claims by those with higher priority, investment in high-risk assets, and underinvestment in new projects. The authors look at these incentives and restrictive covenants imposed by bondholders that reduce their magnitude and consequent agency costs. They then examine observed practice in the context of this framework and also look at alternative forms of debt in terms of their potential agency costs. Finally, they look at debt substitutes, such as leasing, as well as related claims, such as insurance contracts, in the agency-theoretic framework.

In the research paper in this Part, Kose John and Avner Kalay attempt to integrate the signaling and agency approaches into a common framework. They start with the stockholders' incentive to underinvest in new projects and consequent agency costs which they bear. Therefore, it pays for the stockholders to reduce the agency costs by precommitting themselves to a minimal level of investment. The signaling equilibrium emerges from the fact that the costs of a higher level of precommitted investment are greater for poorer quality firms (i.e., those with poorer investment projects), and hence it does not pay for them to mimic the better quality firms. The agency costs, which are endogenous to the model, directly motivate the use of a signaling framework and, in particular, precommitted investment or its counterpart, dividends, as a signal. Based on their model, John and Kalay explain empirical evidence such as the behavior of security prices (both stocks and bonds) around the announcement dates of dividend and new equity issues.

In their critiques of the academic papers, practitioners John Hackett and Robert Kay are sympathetic to the basic framework of agency theory. However, they have several comments and criticisms to make based mainly on real-world considerations. Kay makes a plea for recognition of the vast spectrum of securities actually issued by firms rather than the strait-jacket categories of "debt" and "equity" employed in the literature. He also calls for more attention to be devoted to the relationships between academic research and actual rules for accounting practice. Hackett, while basically in agreement with the agency view of the firms, finds the description of the firm used in the literature somewhat limited. He finds the approach lacking in the attention paid to environmental issues such as pollution control regulations and labor legislation. He argues that the number of agents in a realistic situation is much greater than is visualized in the literature. Hackett also questions Jensen and Smith's view of the corporate form of organization and the checks and balances employed therein. He then elaborates on his view using the regulated electric utility industry in the United States as a case study. He points out that, in the regulated context, the traditional view that the equity investor is the residual claimant is open to question and the roles of principal and agent may at times be reversed.

4

Stockholder, Manager, and Creditor Interests: Applications of Agency Theory

Michael C. Jensen
Professor and Director
Managerial Economics Research Center
University of Rochester

Clifford W. Smith, Jr.
Associate Professor
Graduate School of Management
University of Rochester

We review some of the recent work in agency theory that has implications for the structure of the corporation, in particular the resolution of conflicts of interest among stockholders, managers, and creditors. We analyze the nature of residual claims and the separation of management and risk bearing in the corporation. This analysis provides a theory based on trade-offs of the risk sharing and other advantages of the corporate form with its agency costs to explain the survival of the corporate form in large-scale, complex, nonfinancial activities. We then discuss the structure of corporate bond, lease, and insurance contracts, and show how agency theory can be used to analyze contractual provisions for monitoring and bonding to help control the conflicts of interest between these fixed claimholders and stockholders.

Stockholder, Manager, and Creditor Interests: Applications of Agency Theory

INTRODUCTION

The modern corporate form of organization is a highly productive social invention. It accounts for a large fraction of nonagricultural output and employment in the Western world. Despite the importance of the corporation, it has been only within the last 10 years that scholars have begun to develop knowledge of the factors that make it so productive. Our purpose here is to review some of the recent work in agency theory that has implications for the structure of the corporation, in particular the resolution of conflicts of interest among stockholders, managers, and creditors.

We view the corporation as a legal entity that serves as a nexus for a complex set of explicit and implicit contracts among disparate individuals (Jensen and Meckling (1976, 310 ff.)). The nexus-of-contracts view provides useful insights. For example, it helps to dispel the tendency to treat organizations as if they were persons; organizations do not have preferences and they do not choose in the conscious and rational sense that we attribute to people. Instead, the behavior of an organization is the equilibrium behavior of a complex contractual system made up of maximizing agents with diverse and conflicting objectives. In this sense, the behavior of the organization is like the equilibrium behavior of a market.

Construction of a theory of organizations involves describing the equilibrium behavior of these complex contractual systems where the individual agent is the elementary unit of analysis. In such a theory the exogenous variables are individuals' preferences and opportunity sets, including the impact of the contracting technology on opportunity sets. The structure of contracts, the forms of institutions, and the firm's investment, financing, dividend, insurance, accounting, production, and marketing policies are all endogenous, that is, determined within the system.

Agency theory

Narrowly defined, an agency relationship is a contract in which one or more persons (the principal(s)) engage another person (the agent) to take actions on behalf of the principal(s) which involves the delegation of some decision-making authority to the agent. Spence and Zeckhauser (1971) and Ross (1973) provide early formal analyses of the problems associated with structuring the agent's compensation to align his incentives with the interest of the principal. Jensen and Meckling (1976) argue that agency problems emanating from conflicts of interest are general to virtually all cooperative activity among individuals, whether or not they occur in the hierarchial fashion suggested by the principal-agent analogy.

The substantial attention devoted to developing a theory of agency has resulted in two approaches, which we refer to as the "positive theory of agency" and the "principal-agent" literatures. Although they differ in many respects, both literatures address the contracting problem among self-interested individuals and assume that in any contracting relationship total agency costs are minimized. The principal-agent literature is generally mathematical and non-empirically oriented, whereas the positive-agency literature is generally nonmathematical and empirically oriented. The principal-agent literature has concentrated more on analysis of the effects of preferences and asymmetric information and less on the effects of the technology of contracting and control. We focus on the positive-agency-theory literature. Jensen (1983) provides additional comparison of the two approaches.

Jensen and Meckling (1976) define agency costs as the sum of the out-of-pocket costs of structuring, administering, and enforcing contracts (both formal and informal) plus the residual loss. Enforcement costs include both monitoring and bonding costs, that is, the resources expended by the principal and agent, respectively, to ensure contract enforcement. It pays to expend resources on enforcement only to the point where the reduction in the loss from noncompliance equals the increase in enforcement costs. The residual loss represents the opportunity loss remaining when contracts are optimally but imperfectly enforced. Thus agency costs include all costs frequently referred to as contracting costs, transactions costs, moral-hazard costs, and information costs.

The key to understanding the agency problem is recognition that the parties to a contract bear the agency costs of the relationship. Therefore, for any given scale of activity, self-interested maximizing agents minimize the agency costs in any contracting relationship.

Incentives exist to write contracts that provide monitoring and bonding activities to the point where their marginal cost equals the marginal gains from reducing the residual loss. Specifically, parties to a contract can make themselves better off by forecasting the activities to be accomplished and structuring contracts to facilitate the anticipated activities. This means that, in the absence of externalities, incentives exist within the contracting process to produce an efficient utilization of resources. By externalities we mean situations in which the actions of one party have a physical effect on others and the acting party does not have to pay for costs imposed on others or cannot charge for benefits granted to others. Air and water pollution are examples.

Competition, contracts, survival, and efficiency

Competition is as pervasive a phenomenon among agents in the social and economic sphere as among species in nature. Long ago, Alchian (1950, p. 218) argued that success is associated with relative superiority and that "whenever successful enterprises are observed, the elements common to those observed successes will be associated with success and copied by others in their pursuit of profits or success." Since most goods and services can be produced by any form of organization, different organizational forms compete for survival in any activity just as different species compete for survival in nature. Competition among organizational forms occurs in numerous dimensions, not only in their pricing and other marketing policies but also, for example, in their investment, financing, compensation, dividend, leasing, insurance, and accounting policies. Fama and Jensen (1983a, b) define the survival criterion by which the economic environment chooses among organizational forms as follows: Absent fiat, the form of organization that survives in an activity, is the one that can deliver the product demanded by consumers at the lowest price while covering costs. Under general conditions, competition and survivorship produce an efficient utilization of resources.

Overview

In the next section, we examine the conflicts between residual claimants and managers. This leads to examination of the theory of the determination of organizational forms. We analyze the nature of residual claims and the separation of management and risk bearing in the corporation. This analysis provides a theory based on trade-offs of the risk sharing and other advantages of the corporate form with its agency costs to explain the survival of the corporate form in large-scale, complex, nonfinancial activities. In such activities, the corporation tends to dominate other organizational forms such as nonprofits, proprietorships, partnerships, and mutuals. Since the primary characteristic distinguishing among alternative organizational forms is the nature of their residual or equity claims, analysis of the survival of alternative organizational forms addresses the question: What type of equity claim should an organization issue? Although this question has not been widely examined in the literature, determination of the nature of the equity claim is a natural predecessor to the determination of the optimal quantity of debt relative to equity—the capital structure issue—that has long been discussed in finance. We also examine how managerial compensation contracts, labor markets, and the market for corporate control help to control the conflicts of interest between managers and stockholders in corporations.

In the following section, the conflicts of interest between creditors and stockholders are examined. We discuss the structure of corporate bond, lease, and insurance contracts, and show how agency theory can be used to analyze contractual provisions for monitoring and bonding to help control the conflicts of interest between these fixed claimholders and stockholders.

Other factors are important to a complete understanding of organizational structure and practices. We focus on the positive-agency literature to the exclusion of both tax and signaling issues. Hamada and Scholes (1984) review a major part of the literature on the effect of taxes on the structure of corporate contracts. The signaling literature focuses on the implications of asymmetric costs of information. Important papers include Ross (1977) and Bhattacharya (1979).

RESIDUAL CLAIMANT INTERESTS AND AGENCY PROBLEMS WITH MANAGERS

Contract structures of organizations limit risks undertaken by most agents through contractual specification of payoffs that are either fixed or vary with specific measures of performance. Residual claims are claims to net cash flows that result from differences between inflows and promised payments to other claimholders. The risks of residual claims are restricted only by limited-liability provisions, but even these provisions are not universal.

Conflicts of interest generate agency problems between managers and residual claimants when risk bearing is separated from management—in the language of Berle and Means (1932), when "ownership" is separated from "control." Such agency costs can be reduced by the multitude of control procedures discussed in the accounting and control literatures. Fama and Jensen (1983a) analyze ways of controlling these costs by imposing restrictions on residual claims; for example, restricting their ownership to one or more of the major decision agents. This restriction ensures that such decision agents bear the wealth effects of their decisions and therefore reduces the agency costs associated with outside ownership of residual claims.

Fama and Jensen (1983a) emphasize that such restrictions on residual claims are the distinguishing characteristic among alternative organizational forms. A proprietorship is characterized by 100 percent ownership of the residual claims by the top-level decision agent, whereas partnerships and closed corporations generally restrict residual-claim ownership to major internal decision agents. In contrast, mutuals restrict residual-claim ownership to customers, nonprofits have no residual claims, and open corporations place no restrictions on ownership of their residual claims.

In the extreme, agency problems in the open corporation between managers and common stockholders can be eliminated by combining the two functions, that is, by abandoning the open corporate form. Thus, it is useful to begin our analysis of corporations by analyzing the reasons why this organizational form survives.

Advantages of common stock residual claims: Risk-bearing efficiencies

Fama and Jensen (1983a) emphasize that common stock residual claims of open corporations are unrestricted in the sense that (1) stockholders are not required to have any other role in the organization, (2) their residual claims are freely tradable, and (3) the residual claims are rights in net cash flows for the life of the organization. The unrestricted nature of the residual claims of open corporations allows almost complete separation and specialization of decision functions and residual risk bearing.

Activities of large, open, nonfinancial corporations are typically complicated. They involve contractually specified payoffs to many agents in the production process. Contracting costs with these agents increase if there is significant variation through time in the probability of contract default because such variation makes it necessary to reprice contracts. Concentrating much of this risk on a specific group of claimants can create efficiencies by reducing substantially the duplication of information costs incurred by all other contracting parties in the organization. However, specialized risk bearing by common stockholders is effective only if they bond their contractual risk-bearing obligation. This is accomplished by having common stockholders put up wealth used to purchase assets to bond payments promised to other agents. When the wealth required to bond promised payments exceeds the value of inputs optimally purchased rather than leased, common stock proceeds can be used to purchase liquid assets that have no function except to bond specialization of risk bearing by common stockholders.

In addition, the common stock of open corporations allows more efficient risk sharing among individuals than residual claims that are not separable from other roles in the enterprise. Nonseparable residual claims characterize financial mutuals, where the customers are the residual riskbearers, and proprietorships and partnerships, where the primary decision makers are the residual riskbearers. Since employees and managers develop firm-specific human capital, risk aversion generally causes them to charge more for the risk they bear compared to that charged by common stockholders. Unrestricted common stock allows residual risk to be spread across many residual claimants who each choose the extent to which he or she bears risk and who can diversify across organizations offering such claims. The separability and tradability of common stock are critical to realization of the efficiencies in risk bearing through diversification in the capital markets. Other things being equal, portfolio theory tells us that such unrestricted risk sharing lowers the price of risk-bearing services. (For example, see Arrow (1964).) Thus, efficient large-scale specialized risk bearing by residual claimants is the major advantage of corporate common stock.

To summarize, the efficiencies in risk bearing offered by common stock residual claims imply that corporations will tend to survive and dominate in activities where the gains from specialization of risk bearing are large. This tends to occur in activities involving economies of scale where there are large aggregate risks to be borne.

Although complete markets for state-contingent claims as envisioned by Arrow (1964) and Debreu (1959) would allow more specialization in risk bearing than common stock residual claims, it would be too expensive to pre-specify all future states and payoffs in those states. However, it does pay to define a partial set of contingent claims such as insurance contracts, forward contracts, and futures contracts that permit additional specialization of risk bearing. They facilitate the shifting of risk in specified dimensions from stockholders. (See Mayers and Smith (1982a, 1982b) and Smith and Stulz (1983).)

Disadvantages of common stock residual claims: Agency costs

Agency costs and the separation of decision control from decision management. The unrestricted nature of the common stock residual claims of open corporations leads to an important agency problem between residual claimants and the agents in the decision process, the professional managers, whose interests are not identical to those of residual claimants. This problem of separation of "ownership" from "control"—more precisely, the separation of residual risk bearing from decision functions—has long troubled students of open corporations. (See, for example, Adam Smith (1776) and Berle and Means (1932).) Fama and Jensen (1982b) argue that this agency problem is controlled by decision systems that separate the management (initiation and implementation) and control (ratification and monitoring) of important decisions at all levels of the organization. Effective separation means that no manager has control rights over decisions for which he has management rights.

Devices for separating management and control include (1) hierarchical structures in which the decision initiatives of lower-level agents are passed on to agents above them in the hierarchy, first for ratification and then for monitoring; (2) boards of directors that ratify and monitor the organization's most important decisions and hire, fire, and compensate top-level decision managers; and (3) incentive structures which encourage mutual monitoring among decision agents. The cost of such mechanisms to separate decision management from decision control is the price that open corporations pay for the benefits of unrestricted common stock residual claims.

The implications of specific knowledge. Specific knowledge is knowledge that is transmitted between agents only at high cost. When an organization's activities are such that specific knowledge relevant for decisions is widely diffused among agents, efficiencies in decision making are accomplished by delegating decision-management rights to the agents with the specific knowledge valuable to those decisions. When such decision rights are diffused among agents throughout the organization, control of agency problems with managers who can benefit by using those rights in their own interests requires the separation of decision-management and decision-control rights. In this situation the net additional cost of achieving the separation of management and control rights required to realize the benefits of specialized risk bearing through common stock residual claims is smaller. Thus, the value of the corporation is higher and the survival of corporations tends to be encouraged in activities where specific knowledge relevant for decisions is widely diffused among agents. Activities that are complex and subject to large economies of scale tend to satisfy these conditions and therefore tend to be dominated by the corporate form.

Control of the conflict between managers and stockholders

The structure of the corporation. The use of hierarchical control mechanisms in corporations is commonly recognized. Less generally recognized, however, is the use of mutual monitoring or "bottom up" monitoring in corporations. Many aspects of the administration of the corporation and the structures for monitoring managerial decisions are consistent with recognition and use of mutual monitoring to control conflicts between managers and the firm's other claimholders. For example, managers other than the president or chief executive officer often serve on the board of directors. Competition among vice presidents for recognition and advancement provides an important source of information to the board-level control mechanism and reduces the likelihood that top-level managers will take actions in conflict with maximization of firm value.

The general administration of executive compensation plans reflects the separation of decision management and decision control, thereby enhancing the corporation's chances of survival. Executive compensation plans are administered by the compensation committee of the board of directors. Membership on this committee is typically restricted to outside members of the board and inside members not covered by the plan. This committee's primary function is to monitor and evaluate the inside board members' performance and determine inside board members' compensation.

Monitoring by the compensation committee is augmented by incentives for managers to monitor other managers, not only from the top of the organization to the bottom, but also at the same level and above (see Alchian and Demsetz (1972), Zimmerman (1979), Fama (1980), and Fama and Jensen (1982b)). Lower-level managers have an incentive to monitor managers above them because of the interdependence of their productivities, as well as the direct gains from successfully stepping over less competent managers.

Management compensation contracts and conflict resolution

Sources of conflict. Three sources of conflict of interest between the firm's managers and other claimholders arise because managers are risk-averse individuals who invest in significant firm-specific capital that must be amortized over their careers: (1) Choice of effort—additional effort by the manager generally increases the value of the firm, but to the manager effort is a "bad." (See Ross (1973).) (2) Differential risk exposure—managers typically have a nontrivial fraction of their wealth in firm-specific human capital and thus are concerned about the variability of total firm value, including that portion of firm risk that can be eliminated through diversification by the firm's stockholders. (See Reagan and Stulz (1983) for a detailed discussion of risk-bearing incentives between residual claimants and employees, and references to the related literature.) (3) Differential horizons—the manager's claim on the corporation is generally limited to his tenure with the firm. The corporation, on the other hand, has an indefinite life, and stockholder claims are tradable claims on the entire future stream of residual cash flows. Managers therefore have incentives to place lower values on cash flows occurring beyond their horizon than is implied by the market values of these cash flows. (See Furubotn and Pejovich (1973) or Jensen and Meckling (1979) for a detailed discussion of this problem.)

Control mechanisms in compensation plans. Smith and Watts (1982, 1983) offer detailed descriptions of typical provisions of compensation plans and analyze ways these provisions help control costs arising from conflicts of interest between managers and other claimholders. They group observed components of compensation plans into three categories: (1) compensation that does not depend on firm performance (salary, pensions, and insurance), (2) compensation that depends on market measures of firm performance (restricted and phantom stock, stock options, and stock appreciation rights), and (3) compensation that depends on accounting measures of performance (bonus, performance units, and performance shares).

Compensation in the form of salary payments fixed at the beginning of the period controls the major sources of conflict, primarily through future adjustments in salary. Salary renegotiation will be most effective in controlling younger managers where the present value of future salary subject to renegotiation is large. However, for managers closer to retirement, the control afforded by adjustment in future salary is less; in the extreme case, for a 64-year-old manager scheduled to retire at 65, future salary changes provide no control of the effort problem.

Compensation by salaries fixed at the beginning of the period leads to three additional sources of conflict of interest between residual claimants and managers because of the structure of the payoffs. They are: (1) Asset substitution—when compensated with fixed claims that depend only on corporate solvency, the manager will want to reduce the variance of cash flows because his expected payoff increases as cash-flow risk and the probability of default decline. (2) Overretention—managers compensated with fixed claims on the corporation have incentives to retain funds within the firm to increase the coverage on their fixed claims. (3) Underleverage—managers compensated with fixed claims have incentives to reduce debt and other fixed claims on the firm, even when such reductions adversely affect firm value.

Market-based compensation provisions are well suited to control the effort and horizon problems, since the market value of the stock reflects the present value of the entire future stream of expected cash flows. Market-based compensation provisions include stock options, stock appreciation rights (similar to stock options but upon exercise the holder receives cash rather than shares), restricted stock (common stock that carries restrictions on transferability for a stated period of time), and phantom stock (like restricted stock, but at expiration of the restrictions the manager receives the cash value of shares rather than common stock). Because the expected payoff to stock options increases with stock price variance, options provide the manager with incentives to invest in projects which increase the riskiness of the firm's cash flows. Options thus help to control the managers' incentives to take too little risk. Stock options also help control the underleverage problem. Higher leverage becomes more attractive to the manager since it increases the variance of the equity and thus the value of the options. However, unless options are adjusted for dividends paid, they reinforce the overretention incentive associated with fixed claims.

Because use of accounting-based performance measures allows disaggregation of the firm's total performance among divisions, accounting-based compensation provisions will be relatively more important in compensating middle managers than market-based measures of performance. Bonus plans explicitly tie managers' compensation to an accounting measure of the change in the value of the firm. This formal tie to performance reduces the costs resulting from conflicts over the effort and horizon problems. For example, a bonus plan causes a 64-year-old manager's compensation to depend on his performance during his last year. Finally, part of the manager's compensation can be deferred to the retirement period in a nonvested program that makes receipt of the deferred compensation contingent on satisfactory current performance. (See Becker and Stigler (1974) for a detailed discussion of this solution.)

Stock price effects of compensation plan announcements. Larcker (1983) and Brickley, Bhagat, and Lease (1983a, b) examine stock price changes associated with the announcement of the initiation of compensation schemes. Brickley, Bhagat, and Lease (1983a) focus on the announcement of stock option, stock appreciation right, restricted stock, phantom stock, and performance plans. They find statistically significant abnormal returns of approximately 3.5 percent over the period between the board of directors' approval date and the stockholder meeting date, a period of approximately 60 trading days. Larcker (1983) finds a statistically significant two-day abnormal stock return of 0.8 percent associated with the announcement of the adoption of performance plans. Finally, Brickley, Bhagat, and Lease (1985b) examine returns at the announcement of stock purchase plans. They find two-day abnormal returns associated with the announcement date of these plans (which they take to be the proxy mailing date) of 3.4 percent. These stock price increases appear to be due to expected productivity increases rather than tax effects because these plans do not affect tax payments.

Management compensation and corporate accounting policy. Using accounting measures of performance to determine payments to managers gives managers a direct interest in the choice among alternative accounting techniques since such choices can affect the bonus calculation. This means that compensation policy will affect the choice of accounting policy. The evidence of Healy (1985) indicates that the firm's choice of accounting-accrual policy is influenced by the effects of those policies on bonuses awarded to managers. Other studies (Hagerman and Zmijewski (1979), Zmijewski and Hagerman (1981), Dhaliwal, Salamon, and Smith (1982)) find that bonus plans increase the probability of choice of corporate accounting procedures which shift accounting earnings from future periods to current periods.

Market control mechanisms. The degree to which top managements' behavior can diverge from value-maximizing behavior is limited by the managerial-labor market and the capital markets (see Jensen and Meckling (1976, pp. 328–29) and Fama (1980)). Competition in the labor market tends to ensure that the manager receives only a competitive level of compensation. Reputation effects cause the value of a manager's human capital to depend on his performance inside the firm. In addition, when pricing the firm's traded claims, investors have incentives to anticipate the actions of managers which diverge from the interests of shareholders. All of these forces provide incentives for the parties to construct procedures to reduce managers' divergence from value-maximizing behavior, but they seldom will eliminate the problem.

Another factor contributing to survival of the corporation is the constraint imposed on managerial investment, financing, and dividend decisions by what Manne (1965) calls the market for corporate control. Jensen and Ruback (1983) argue that this market is the arena in which alternative management teams compete for the rights to manage corporate resources, with stockholders playing the relatively passive role of accepting or rejecting offers from competing management teams.

Unrestricted transferability of common stock residual claims of open corporations makes possible a stock market that provides low-cost transfer and accurate valuation of claims. Low-cost transferability makes it possible for competing outside managers to bypass the current management and board of directors to acquire the rights to manage the corporation's resources. These rights can be acquired by direct solicitation of stockholders, either through tender offers or proxy solicitation. Alternatively, outside management teams can also acquire the management rights by merger negotiations with the target's management and board, subject to ratification by vote of the stockholders.

The corporation's internal-control system has its foundation in the corporate charter. The effectiveness of this control system is affected by operating practices and procedures and by the quality of the individuals who hold board seats and management positions. Competition from alternative management teams in the market for corporate control serves as a source of external checks on the internal-control system of the corporation. Thus the conflict in the control market is not between powerful entrenched managers and weak stockholders as it is often characterized. Rather it is between internal managers and the managers of other corporations that wish to take over the company and perhaps replace them.

When a breakdown of the corporation's internal-control system imposes large costs on shareholders from incompetent, lazy, or dishonest managers, takeover bids in the market for corporate control provide a vehicle for replacing the entire internal-control system. Competing managers who perceive the opportunity to eliminate the inefficiencies can offer target shareholders a higher-valued alternative than current management while benefiting their own shareholders and themselves. Similar incentives come into play when the acquisition of substantial synergy gains requires displacement of an efficient current management team.

Other institutional forms such as partnerships, nonprofit organizations, and mutuals do not receive the benefits of competition from alternative management teams in an external control market. Fama and Jensen (1983a,b, 1984) provide an analysis of these alternative organizational forms and their survival properties. Wolfson (1983) provides analysis and empirical evidence on the agency problems in various forms of oil and gas limited partnerships and how the resulting agency costs are reduced. Mayers and Smith (1981, 1983) and Smith (1982) analyze the choice of organizational form in the insurance and thrift industries. Of course, internal competition in each of these organizations and the external regulatory environment (such as in insurance or banking) contribute to the control function. But because of their structure, only the corporation benefits from the augmentation of its internal control mechanisms by the private external control market.

Evidence from the market for corporate control

Mergers, tender offers, and proxy contests. Numerous studies estimate the effects of mergers on the stock prices of the participating firms. Table 1 presents a summary of stock price changes (measured net of marketwide price movements) for successful and unsuccessful takeovers in these studies. The returns reported in the table are the Jensen and Ruback (1983, Tables 1 and 2) synthesis of the evidence reported in the 13 studies noted in the footnotes to the tables.

Table 1 shows that target firms in successful takeovers experience statistically significant abnormal stock price increases of 20 percent in mergers and 30 percent in tender offers. Bidding firms realize statistically significant abnormal gains of 4 percent in tender offers and zero in mergers. Both bidders and targets suffer small negative abnormal stock price changes in unsuccessful mergers and tender offers, although only the −5 percent return to unsuccessful bidders in mergers is significantly different from zero. Stockholders in com-

TABLE 1 Abnormal percentage stock price changes associated with successful and unsuccessful corporate takeovers found by 13 studies of such transactions as summarized by Jensen and Ruback (1983, tables 1 and 2)[a]

Takeover	*Targets*		*Bidders*	
Technique	*Successful*	*Unsuccessful*	*Successful*	*Unsuccessful*
Tender offers[b]	30%	−3%[e]	4%	−1%[e]
Mergers[c]	20	−3	0[e]	−5
Proxy contests[d]	8	8	n.a.[f]	n.a.

[a] Abnormal price changes are price changes adjusted for the effects of marketwide price changes.

[b] Sources: Dodd and Ruback (1977), Kummer and Hoffmeister (1978), Bradley (1980), Jarrell and Bradley (1980), Bradley, Desai, and Kim (1983), Ruback (1983).

[c] Sources: Dodd (1980), Asquith (1983), Eckbo (1983), Asquith, Brunner, and Mullins (1983), Malatesta (1983), Wier (1983).

[d] Source: Dodd and Warner (1983).

[e] Not statistically significantly different from zero.

[f] n.a. = not applicable.

panies that experience control-related proxy contests earn statistically significant average abnormal returns of about 8 percent. These returns are not substantially lower when the insurgent group loses the contest.

The contrast between the large stock price increases for successful targets and insignificant stock price changes for unsuccessful targets indicates that the benefits of mergers and tender offers are realized only when control of the target firm's assets is transferred. This suggests that stockholders of potential target firms are harmed when target managers oppose takeover bids or take other actions that reduce the probability of successful acquisition. Moreover, since target managers are frequently replaced after takeovers, they have incentives to oppose takeover bids even though, if they were successful, shareholders might benefit substantially. However, management opposition to a bid benefits stockholders if it leads to a higher takeover price. Thus, the effect on shareholder wealth of management opposition to takeovers is an empirical matter. It is interesting to note that in their study of the announcement of special termination agreements in executive compensation contracts typically called "golden parachutes," Lambert and Larcker (1985) find statistically significant positive abnormal returns to shareholders of 2.4 percent. Since these provisions provide substantial compensation to executives if they leave the corporation subsequent to a control change, they are likely to reduce managers' incentives to oppose takeovers.

The evidence indicates that the effect of unsuccessful takeover attempts varies across takeover techniques. In unsuccessful mergers, the target's stock price falls to about its preoffer level. In unsuccessful tender offers the target's stock price remains substantially above its preoffer level, unless a subsequent bid does not occur in the two years following the initial offer. If such a subsequent bid does not occur, the target's stock price reverts to its preoffer level. Finally, in proxy contests the 8 percent increase in equity values does not depend on the outcome of the contest.

While the numbers in Table 1 suggest that merger bids are, on average, unprofitable for bidding firms, estimation of the appropriate return measure is more difficult for bidders than targets. Since stock price changes reflect changes in expectations, a merger announcement will not affect prices if it is fully anticipated. Since bidders can engage in prolonged acquisition programs, the present value of the expected benefits will be incorporated in the share price when the program is announced or becomes apparent. (See Schipper and Thompson (1983).) The returns reported in Table 1 measure only the incremental value change of each acquisition and are thus potentially incomplete measures of merger gains to bidders.

Spin-offs and divestitures. In a spin-off, corporate assets are divested and shares in the newly created entity are distributed to the original shareholders of the divesting firm. These transactions are in many ways the mirror image of a merger. The empirical studies of spin-offs (Hite and Owers (1983), Schipper and Smith (1983), Miles and Rosenfeld (1983)), indicate that stockholders of the firms receive a statistically significant 3 percent return on the announcement of the event and senior, nonconvertible security holders receive returns that appear to be positive but are insignificantly different from zero. This indicates that stockholder gains from spin-offs are not due to wealth transfers from senior security holders.

In a divestiture, assets of one firm are sold to another firm. Klein (1983) examines price effects of voluntary divestitures and finds 1 percent abnormal returns to shareholders of divesting firms. In the cases where returns to divesting and acquiring firms are both available, she finds positive but statistically insignificant gains to both divesting and acquiring firm stockholders. Wier (1983) examines price effects of involuntary divestitures ordered by the Federal Trade Commission and the Justice Department for violations of Section 7 to the Clayton Act. For firms that are subsequently convicted, she finds a 2 percent abnormal loss associated with the announcement of the complaint, followed by an additional 2 percent loss on the announcement of the conviction. These losses appear to eliminate the gains from the original acquisition.

Corporate charter changes. Corporate charters specify governance rules for corporations. They contain, for example, rules that establish conditions for mergers—such as the percentage of stockholders that must vote approval for a merger to take effect. Individual states specify constraints on charter rules and these constraints differ from state to state. This variation across states means that changing the state of incorporation affects the constraints on contractual arrangements among shareholders that are imposed through the corporate charter. Differences in state rules can affect the probability that a firm will become a takeover target. It is alleged that some states, desiring to increase their corporate charter revenues, compete to make their statutes appealing to corporate management. In doing so, it is argued, they provide management with great freedom from stockholder control and little shareholder protection. Delaware provides few constraints on corporate charter rules and therefore great corporate contractual freedom. William Cary (1974), the former Chairman of the Securities and Exchange Commission, criticizes Delaware, arguing that it is leading a "movement towards the least common denominator" and "winning" a "race for the bottom." In a sample of 140 firms that switched their state of incorporation, most of them to Delaware, Dodd and Leftwich (1980) find no evidence of stock price declines at the time of the switch and some indication of small abnormal price increases. This is inconsistent with the notion that changes in the state of incorporation are motivated by managerial exploitation of shareholders.

Firms can amend their charters to make the conditions for shareholder approval of mergers more stringent. Such antitakeover amendments include supermajority provisions and provisions for the staggered election of board members. By increasing the stringency of takeover conditions, these amendments can reduce the probability of being a takeover target and therefore reduce shareholder wealth. However, by increasing the plurality required for takeover approval, the amendments could benefit shareholders by enabling target management to better represent their common interests in the merger negotiations. Studies by DeAngelo and Rice (1983) and Linn and McConnell (1983) of the stockprice effects associated with the passage of antitakeover amendments indicate no negative effect on shareholder wealth, although it is possible that when new supermajority provisions grant a manager-stockholder effective blocking power there are negative effects. This can happen, for example, if a manager holds 21 percent of the stock when an 80 percent supermajority provision is enacted.

Corporate charters also specify voting rights of the firm's shareholders in elections to determine the board of directors. Some firms provide cumulative voting which allows a group of minority shareholders to elect directors even if the majority of shareholders oppose their election. Bhagat and Brickley (1984) examine abnormal returns to stockholders around management-sponsored proposals that either eliminate cumulative voting or provide for staggered election of the members of the board of directors, thus reducing the effect of cumulative voting rights of shareholders. They find statistically significant negative returns of approximately -1% associated with proposals to reduce the effect of cumulative voting. Bhagat (1983) also examines the effects of elimination of the preemptive right in the corporate charter. This provision gives existing shareholders the prior right to purchase new equity offered by the firm in proportion to their current holdings. For a sample of 211 firms which eliminated the preemptive right from the corporate charter, he finds statistically significant negative abnormal returns to stockholders of approximately -0.5 percent. The results of both of these studies are inconsistent with the hypothesis that these management proposals are in the shareholders' best interests.

CREDITOR INTERESTS AND AGENCY PROBLEMS

Bondholder-Stockholder Conflict

A number of authors have discussed the conflict of interest between the firm's bondholders and stockholders. (See, for example, Modigliani and Miller (1958), Fama and Miller (1972), Black and Cox (1976), Jensen and Meckling (1976), Myers (1977), Black, Miller, and Posner (1978), and Smith and Warner (1979).) An extreme example of this conflict is offered by Black (1976) who points out that "there is no easier way for a company to escape the burden of a debt than to pay out all of its assets in the form of a dividend, and leave the creditors holding an empty shell."

Sources of the conflict. Some corporate decisions increase the wealth of stockholders while reducing the wealth of bondholders and, in cases where the wealth transfers are large enough, stock prices can rise from decisions that reduce the value of the firm. Smith and Warner identify four major sources of conflict between bondholders and stockholders: (1) Dividend payout—if bonds are priced assuming that the firm will maintain its dividend policy, their value is reduced by unexpected dividend increases financed either by reductions in investments or by the sale of debt. (See Kalay (1982).) (2) Claim dilution—if bonds are priced assuming that additional debt of the same or higher priority will not be issued, the value of the bondholders' claims is reduced by issuing such additional debt. (3) Asset substitution—the value of the stockholders' equity rises and the value of the bondholders' claim is reduced when the firm substitutes high-risk for low-risk projects. (See Jensen and Meckling (1976) or Green (1984).) (4) Underinvestment—when a substantial portion of the value of the firm is composed of future investment opportunities, a firm with outstanding risky bonds can have incentives to reject positive net present value projects if the benefit from accepting the project accrues to the bondholders. (See Myers (1977).)

Rational bondholders recognize incentives faced by stockholders in each of these four dimensions. When bonds are sold, bondholders forecast the value effects of future decisions. They understand that, after issuance, any action which increases the wealth of the stockholders will be taken. Therefore, on average, bondholders will not suffer losses unless they systematically underestimate effects of such future actions. But the firm (and hence its stockholders) suffers losses, agency costs, from all nonoptimal decisions motivated by wealth transfers from debtholders. Therefore, by reducing these agency costs, contractual control of the bondholder-stockholder conflict can increase the value of the firm.

Bond covenants constraining activities such as asset sales or mergers are examples of voluntary contracts that can reduce agency costs generated when stockholders of a levered firm follow a policy which deviates from firm-value maximization. The cost-reducing benefits of the covenants accrue to the firm's owners through the higher price the bond issue commands at the time the bonds are issued. Furthermore, if covenants lower the costs which bondholders incur in monitoring stockholders, these reductions in agency costs are also passed on to stockholders through higher bond prices at issuance. For example, Asquith and Kim (1982) examine bond returns around the announcement dates of merger bids for a sample of conglomerate mergers. They find that abnormal returns to bondholders are insignificantly different from zero at times of merger bids. This suggests that bondholders on average are effectively protected from potential wealth transfers in mergers.

Note that the bondholder-stockholder conflict would not be solved by giving the bondholders control of the firm; bondholders would have incentives to pay too few dividends, issue too little debt, and choose projects with too little risk. Moreover, the degree of control that can be given to bondholders is limited by Rule 10b–5 of Section 10 of the Securities Act of 1934 and by the Trust Indenture Act of 1939. See Smith and Warner (1979, Section 3) for a discussion of these legal constraints.

Empirical evidence from financial restructuring

Exchange offers, calls, and new security issues. Financial restructuring can be accomplished in many ways, for example, through issues of new securities, through retirement of securities by exercising call provisions, or through exchange offers. Table 2 summarizes the evidence from 13 studies of the abnormal stock price changes associated with the announcement of various transactions which change corporate capital structure. The upper panel of Table 2 summarizes leverage-increasing transactions, for example, new issues of debt and convertible debt, common stock repurchases, and exchange offers in which debt is issued and common stock is retired, debt issued and preferred retired, preferred issued and common retired, and income bonds issued and preferred retired. Leverage-reducing transactions such as new issues of common stock, calls of convertible bonds, and preferred stock forcing conversion into common stock and the reverse of the exchanges listed in the upper panel of the table are grouped together in the lower panel of the table.

Examination of the upper and lower panels of Table 2 indicates that leverage-increasing capital market transactions are generally associated with significantly positive abnormal returns to common stockholders, and leverage-reducing transactions are associated with significantly negative abnormal returns to common stockholders. The exceptions are new debt issues and convertible debt issues that are leverage-increasing and yet are associated with, respectively, insignificantly negative returns of −0.4 percent, and significantly negative returns of −2.3 percent. The interpretation of the significantly negative returns associated with the issuance of con-

TABLE 2 Summary of common stock price effects associated with various leverage-increasing and leverage-decreasing capital market transactions found by 13 studies.

Type of Transaction	*Security Issued*	*Security Retired*	*Average Sample Size*	*Two-Day Announcement Period Return*
Leverage-Increasing Transactions				
Exchange offer[a]	Debt	Common	52	14.0%
Exchange offer[a]	Preferred	Common	9	8.3
Exchange offer[a]	Debt	Preferred	24	3.5
Exchange offer[b]	Income bonds	Preferred	24	2.2
Repurchase[c]	none	Common	413	6.4
Security issue[d]	Debt	none	150	−0.4[g]
Security issue[d]	Convertible debt	none	132	−2.3
Leverage-Reducing Transactions				
Exchange offer[a]	Common	Debt	20	−9.9
Exchange offer[a]	Common	Preferred	30	−2.6
Exchange offer[a]	Preferred	Debt	9	−7.7
Security issue[e]	Common	none	408	−2.1
Conversion-forcing call[f]	Common	Convertible bond	113	−2.1
Conversion-forcing call[f]	Common	Convertible preferred	57	−0.4[g]

[a] Source: Masulis (1983). (Note: These returns include announcement days of both the original offer and, for about 40 percent of the sample, a second announcement of specific terms of the exchange.)

[b] Source: McConnell and Schlarbaum (1981).

[c] Source: Weighted average (by sample size) of the returns reported in the seven studies summarized in column 5 of Table 3.

[d] Source: Dann and Mikkelson (1984).

[e] Sources: Korwar (1983)—examined 424 firms; Asquith and Mullins (1985)—examined 128 industrials and 264 utilities. (Note: The reported sample size and returns are averages of the two studies, with no attempt to correct for overlap in observations.)

[f] Source: Mikkelson (1981).

[g] Not statistically different from zero.

vertible debt is problematical because, while they initially increase leverage, their eventual conversion into common stock reduces leverage.

Masulis (1980b, 1983) argues that, since exchange offers are simply a swap of one class of securities for another, the transaction has no effect on the firm's investment policy and, thus, if the Modigliani-Miller (1958) capital structure irrelevance proposition is applicable, they should have no effect on firm value. As Table 2 shows, the evidence from each of the exchange offers studied by Masulis is inconsistent with the Modigliani-Miller financial structure irrelevance propositions. In fact, the evidence presented in all 13 studies summarized in Table 2 is inconsistent with the irrelevance propositions. Each of the studies documents statistically significant equity value changes associated with changes in corporate leverage, and only 2 of 13 events examined are associated with insignificant equity value changes.

Masulis (1980b, 1983) attempts to separate value effects attributable to wealth redistribution among classes of securityholders, bankruptcy cost effects, and the effects of corporate and personal taxes. His data provide evidence of tax shields from corporate debt around the date of announcement of exchange offers. As Table 2 shows, average common stock returns are 14.0 percent in debt-for-common exchanges, where tax-deductible interest expense is increased, but only 8.3 percent in preferred-for-common exchanges, where there should be no corporate tax effect for the issuing corporation. In Masulis (1980b), he finds evidence of wealth transfers from debtholders to stockholders. For example, in exchange offers where debt is issued and common is retired, stockholders gain and bondholders lose; common stock returns are significantly positive at 9.8 percent, and straight debt returns are significantly negative at −0.3 percent (not shown in Table 2). However, Mikkelson (1981) finds no such evidence of wealth transfers in his examination of calls of convertible bonds.

The generally significant negative stock price effects associated with the six leverage-reducing transactions shown in the lower panel of Table 2 and the issuance of convertible debt shown in the upper panel of Table 2 present a puzzle. There is no convincing explanation for why firms voluntarily take such actions that consistently harm stockholders. These transactions might represent agency problems between stockholders and managers but, given the costs to stockholders, it is difficult to believe that managers gain enough from them to make the transactions worth the effort. In addition, it is possible that leverage-decreasing transactions are optimal responses to negative changes in the firm's fortunes and that the negative stock price changes are due to the factors causing the hard times. The leverage reduction, while beneficial itself, might well signal information to market participants that the firm has received bad news. In this situation the incremental value effects of the leverage reduction could be positive but our empirical methods do not allow separation of this component from the value decrease caused by the bad news.

Stock repurchases. In the upper panel of Table 2, we have aggregated the results associated with repurchases of common stock reported by seven studies. However, since corporations repurchase their own shares in a number of different ways, it is worthwhile to examine the stock price effects associated with different forms of repurchase. The different forms include tender offers, simple repurchases in the open market, negotiated repurchases of large blocks, targeted repurchases of small holdings, repurchase of all publicly held shares in going-private transactions, and repurchase of all shares in mutualization transactions. Table 3 summarizes the evidence from nine studies of these various methods of repurchasing the firm's stock. The table reports by method of repurchase the premium offered, the fraction of shares repurchased, the predicted stock price change for the remaining shares given no change in firm value, and the actual stock price change for the remaining shares. As Table 3 shows, evidence on the stock price changes associated with common stock repurchases is consistent with that from exchange offers; leverage-increasing events are generally associated with positive stockholder returns.

In tender-offer repurchases of corporate stock, the average premium above the preoffer market price of the stock offered to selling shareholders is approximately 23 percent (column 3). If there is no change in overall firm value, the premium paid to selling shareholders represents a loss to the remaining shareholders, and this predicted loss is on average −4 percent in tender offers (column 5). Thus the 15 percent actual average stock price increase for the remaining shares (column 6) indicates that tender-offer repurchases of common stock are associated with positive changes in total firm value. These figures for intrafirm tender offers should be contrasted with those that occur when a corporation buys its stock through open-market purchases at a zero premium; remaining stockholders earn average abnormal returns of approximately 4 percent (column 6).

In a negotiated large-block repurchase, a firm buys a block of its common stock from an individual holder at an average 10 percent premium over market price (column 3). Remaining stockholders of

TABLE 3 Summary of average repurchase premiums and price effects of common stock repurchases for various repurchase methods found by nine studies

Repurchase Method (1)	Average Sample Size (2)	Premium Offered (3)	Fraction of Shares Repurchased (4)	Predicted Stock Price Change for Remaining Shares[a] (5)	Actual Stock Price Change for Remaining Shares[b] (6)
Tender offer[c]	148	23%	15%	−4%	15%
Open market repurchase[d]	182	0	4	0	4
Negotiated large blocks[e]	68	10	11	−2	−5
Targeted small holdings[f]	15	13	under 1	slightly negative	2
Going private[g]	81	56	54	−35	n.a.[i]
Mutualization[h]	29	54[j]	100	n.a.[i]	n.a.[i]

[a] This assumes no change in firm value and is calculated as minus the premium times the fraction of shares repurchased divided by one minus the fraction of shares repurchased.
[b] Abnormal price changes are price changes adjusted for marketwide price changes.
[c] Sources: Dann (1981), Masulis (1980a), Vermaelen (1981), Rosenfeld (1982).
[d] Sources: Dann (1980), Vermaelen (1981).
[e] Sources: Dann and DeAngelo (1983), Bradley and Wakeman (1983).
[f] Source: Bradley and Wakeman (1983).
[g] Source: DeAngelo, DeAngelo, and Rice (1984). Note: The abnormal stock price changes on announcement of the going-private transaction is 30 percent.
[h] Source: Mayers and Smith (1983).
[i] n.a. = not applicable.
[j] Measured by abnormal stock price change, not the premuim offered to selling shareholders.

the repurchasing firm realize statistically significant losses of approximately 5 percent (column 6) on the announcement of such privately negotiated large-block repurchases. Since large-block sellers in negotiated repurchases are frequently actual or potential takeover bidders, the premium can be interpreted as payment to the holder to cease takeover activity. Moreover, takeover offers are frequently cancelled at the time of negotiated repurchases. Therefore, one explanation for the losses to remaining stockholders in negotiated repurchases, in contrast to the gains in tender-offer and open-market repurchases, is that they reflect the loss of expected benefits of takeovers to the repurchasing firm.

In repurchase offers targeted only for small shareholdings (generally odd lots), the average premium paid to sellers is about 13 percent (column 3), and remaining stockholders earn average abnormal returns of approximately 2 percent. This value increase apparently reflects the savings in administrative expenses associated with servicing small accounts.

Going-private transactions represent an extreme case of stock repurchases. In these transactions public stock ownership is replaced with full equity ownership by an incumbent management group and the stock is delisted. In some cases, generally called leveraged buyouts, management shares the equity with private outside investors. On average, 54 percent of the total shares are held by the public and repurchased in these transactions (column 4). It is often argued that conflicts of interest between incumbent managers as buyers of the stock and outside shareholders as sellers of the stock result in exploitation of outside shareholders. Hence, these transactions are frequently labeled "minority freezeouts." There is, however, no evidence that outside shareholders are harmed in these minority freezeouts. In fact the announcement by management of the going-private repurchase offer at an average premium of 56 percent (column 3) is associated with a 30 percent average abnormal stock price increase. DeAngelo, DeAngelo, and Rice (1984) conjecture that the gains are due to improved incentives for corporate decision makers under private ownership, as well as savings of registration and other public-ownership expenses.

The average premium received by stockholders' life insurance companies when their shares were repurchased in order to switch to a mutual ownership structure was 54 percent (column 3). Mayers and Smith (1983) conclude that the premium arises from the increased efficiency of the mutual ownership form for this group of life insurance firms.

The structure of creditor contracts

Corporate bonds. Smith and Warner (1979) analyze the role of bond covenants in the control of bondholder-stockholder conflicts. They group covenants into four categories: production-investment covenants, dividend covenants, financing covenants, and bonding covenants. The fact that investment equals net cash flow plus net proceeds from new financing minus dividends means that investment, financing, and dividend policies are interrelated. This implies that covenants which restrict dividend and financing policies also restrict investment policy. Smith and Warner argue that bond contracts are structured to maximize the value of the firm. This analysis yields a substantial body of theory describing the contracting incentives associated with the choice of provisions in corporate bond contracts.

Convertible versus straight debt. A convertible bond is one which gives the holder the right to exchange the bond for the firm's common stock. Jensen and Meckling (1976), Smith and Warner (1979), Mikkelson (1981), and Green (1984) discuss the use of convertible debt to control the asset substitution problem, that is, the stockholders' incentive to have the firm take some unprofitable but variance-increasing projects. With convertible debt, risk-increasing activities increase the value of the conversion option, and thus reduce the gains to stockholders from taking high-risk projects by transferring part of the gains to convertible bondholders. This lowers agency costs by reducing incentives for the firm to take highly risky negative net present value projects. Issuance of warrants also has some of these effects.

Secured versus unsecured debt. Secured debt gives the bondholders title to pledged assets until the bonds are paid in full. Smith and Warner (1979) argue that security provisions control the asset substitution problem and lower administrative and enforcement costs by ensuring that the lender has clear title to the assets and by restricting the firm's disposition of assets. Stulz and Johnson (1983) suggest that the option to issue secured debt controls the underinvestment problem. They show that secured debt allows stockholders to sell claims to the payoffs of a new project which otherwise would accrue as a windfall to holders of previously issued debt. Thus, some new positive net-present-value projects can increase the value of equity if financed with secured debt, but not with unsecured debt.

Short-term versus long-term debt. Myers (1977) argues that a corporation's future investment opportunities can be viewed as call options. The value of such options depends on whether the firm is expected to optimally exercise them. But, with risky debt outstanding, situations can arise in which stockholders do not benefit from even highly profitable investment decisions because the benefits go primarily to the debtholders. In these cases the value of the investment options is zero because they are unlikely to be exercised and this lowers the value of the firm. With longer-lived debt claims in a firm's capital structure, the conflict between debtholders and stockholders over the exercise of investment options is greater, and without resolution the value of the firm is lower. Myers argues that firms can control these incentive problems by matching effective maturities of assets and liabilities. Mayers and Smith (1981) note that the incentive to match maturities of assets and liabilities is easily observable in the insurance industry and is consistent with Myers' proposition. Life insurance companies purchase more long-lived assets, such as privately placed loans and mortgages, than casualty insurers that have much shorter effective maturities of their outstanding liabilities.

Dividend covenants and dividend policy. The standard bond covenant restricting the payment of dividends specifies that the maximum allowable dividend payment is a positive function of both accounting earnings and the proceeds from the sale of new equity. Since dividend and investment policy are interdependent, specification of a maximum on dividends imposes a minimum on the fraction of earnings retained in the firm. Increased earnings retention generated by lower dividend constraints, however, imposes overinvestment costs in a firm that expects few profitable projects over the life of the bonds. Thus, the theory predicts that an unregulated firm which expects recurring profitable future investment projects will set a low maximum on dividends, and therefore a high minimum on retentions. This reduces both the requirements for externally raised equity capital and the associated equity flotation costs, as well as the present value of agency costs.

Rozeff (1982) and Easterbrook (1984) note that a policy of paying dividends increases the frequency with which the corporation's managers go to the capital markets to obtain new equity. This policy subjects the firm more frequently to the intensive capital market monitoring and discipline that occurs at the time new funds are raised and lowers agency costs. They also argue that dividend payments to stockholders allow the firm to raise its debt-equity ratio without requiring the firm to increase its assets by issuing debt. Their arguments predict that firms with high growth rates and high demand for new capital will have less reason to pay high dividends because they are going to the capital markets frequently anyway. Consistent with this prediction, such firms generally have low dividends.

In contrast, utilities have historically had high demands for new capital and high dividend payout rates. Smith (1983) argues that utility stockholders are likely to fare less well in the rate-regulation process if the dividend rate is lowered to reduce the frequency and costs of floating new equity in the capital markets. By paying high dividends, the regulated firm subjects both itself and its regulatory body to the discipline of the marketplace more frequently. Stockholders are less likely to suffer expropriation through low rates set in the adversarial regulatory setting when the regulatory body is more frequently policed by the capital markets. Giving suppliers of debt and equity capital an opportunity to signal their dissatisfaction with confiscatorily low rates through low prices, or perhaps through denial of funds required to maintain service, accomplishes this. Thus, high dividends are a way of bonding to stockholders that they will receive a normal rate of return on the capital invested in the corporation.

Kalay (1982) has examined corporate dividend covenants and finds that firms do not pay all dividends allowed under the contract. If firms are behaving optimally, this implies that there are benefits from maintaining a reservoir that gives the firm the right to pay dividends. These benefits could come from avoiding forced investment at low returns when no profitable projects are available.

Handjinicolaou and Kalay (1984) examine returns to both stockholders and bondholders to distinguish between two potential explanations of positive stockholder returns associated with the announcement of dividend changes. One hypothesis is that dividend increases are associated with higher expected cash flows and thus higher firm value; the other is that higher dividends transfer wealth from bondholders to stockholders. They find that bonds of firms with low leverage show no significant reaction to announcements of dividend changes and that stockholders of such firms receive statistically significant abnormal returns of the same sign as the dividend change. However, for high-leverage firms, dividend increases are associated with significantly positive stockholder returns and insignificant bondholder returns; but for dividend decreases, bondholders receive significant negative returns while stockholders' returns are insignificantly different from zero. Handjinicolaou and Kalay suggest that this asymmetry in response is due to the structure of the typical dividend constraint which allows the stockholders to capture the value implications of positive information through higher dividends. Interestingly, their evidence indicates that stockholders of high-leverage firms do not share the losses that bondholders experience in association with unexpected dividend decreases.

The major weakness in all of the agency hypotheses about dividend policy is that they only explain distributions to stockholders, they do not explain why they take the form of cash dividends. Bond dividend covenants reflect an understanding of the availability of substitute forms of distributions. They universally restrict "all distributions on account of or in respect of capital stock . . . whether they be dividends, redemptions, purchases, retirements, partial liquidations or capital reductions, and whether in cash, in kind, or in the form of debt obligations of the company." (American Bar Foundation (1971, p. 405).) Stock repurchases and exchange offers accomplish many of the same ends as cash dividend payments and do so at potentially lower tax costs. Thus, we still do not have a satisfactory explanation of why firms pay cash dividends.

Public versus private placements. Section 4(2) of the Securities Act of 1933 provides that a sale of securities not involving a public offering is exempt from registration. Such exempt issues are referred to as private placements or direct placements and represent an alternative to publicly placed debt. Because of the legal limitations on the discretion allowed a trustee, the modification of tightly restrictive covenants for a public debt issue requires a supplemental indenture approved by a majority of the bondholders. Therefore, the benefit from private rather than public placement of the firm's debt can be substantial when it is anticipated that such renegotiations will be desirable in the future. This implies that riskier debt issues are more likely to be privately placed because they require modification more frequently. The argument also implies that private placements will include more detailed restrictions on the firm's behavior than do public issues because change is less costly.

Leftwich (1981) compares the specification of covenants in public versus privately placed bond issues. He finds that privately placed bonds include more frequent use of constraints on investment and financing policy as well as more frequent specification of the accounting methods to be used. He finds that the accounting procedures required for use in calculating constraints on financing, dividend, and investment policies usually differs from generally accepted accounting procedures (GAAP) by eliminating noncash items.

Bonding covenants and corporate accounting policy. Other covenants specify that various bonding activities be performed by the firm to help control the bondholder-stockholder conflict. These activities include requirements for the provision of audited financial statements, the use of specified accounting techniques, and periodic provision of a statement, signed by the firm's officers, indicating compliance with the covenants.

Covenant-imposed constraints are typically specified in terms of accounting numbers. Since different accounting techniques imply different accounting numbers, firms have incentives to relax onerous constraints through the choice of accounting techniques. Bowen, Noreen, and Lacey (1981), Deakin (1979), Dhaliwal (1980), Dhaliwal, Salamon, and Smith (1982), Lilien and Pastena (1982), and Zmijewski and Hagerman (1981) have examined corporations' accounting choices. All find that the structure of corporate bond contracts establishes incentives that are consistent with the evidence on choices of accounting techniques by corporations.

Intrabondholder conflict and restrictions on debt. We have discussed the bondholder-stockholder conflict as if there were only two homogeneous classes of capital claims on the corporation. In fact, the typical corporation has multiple classes of debt claims outstanding which can differ in dimensions such as coupon, maturity, and priority. Intradebtholder conflicts over wealth transfers are highly visible in bankruptcy proceedings. The conflict is exacerbated by the deviations from absolute priority in court decisions documented by Warner (1977). He shows that junior claimholders systematically receive higher-valued claims in corporate reorganizations under the bankruptcy code than a literal application of absolute priority would imply. Smith and Warner (1979) note that bond covenants frequently restrict the issuance of new debt, not only of the same and higher priority, but the issuance of debt of any priority. The Ho and Singer (1982) analysis of the risk of corporate debt helps explain such puzzling restrictions. Restriction of the issuance of junior debt is consistent with the fact that junior debt that matures earlier than a senior debt issue has effective priority in payment as long as the firm is not in bankruptcy.

Leases. A lease is a substitute for secured debt. It is a contractual arrangement in which a firm acquires the services of an asset for a specified time period as an alternative to purchasing the asset. In a secured debt contract, the user owns the asset but the bondholder has a lien that allows seizure of the asset if the borrower defaults. In a lease contract, the lessor keeps title to the asset and the lessee (borrower) uses the asset as long as he does not default on the lease. Thus, leases help control the asset substitution and underinvestment problems in the same ways as secured debt.

Leasing, however, also generates conflicts of interest and therefore agency costs. For example, consider organization-specific assets. They are assets that are more highly valued within the organization than in their best alternative use; for example, crude-oil-gathering pipelines have little alternative-use value and are therefore specific to the oil fields they serve. Lease of organization-specific assets generates agency costs in the form of significant additional negotiation, administration, and contract enforcement costs due to conflicts between lessor and lessee. These conflicts arise over the division of the value in excess of the alternative-use value of the asset. Klein, Crawford, and Alchian (1978) argue that agency costs are reduced when such organization-specific assets are owned rather than leased.

In addition, since the lessee does not have claim to the residual value of the asset at the end of the lease, the lessee has limited incentives to maintain the asset or to limit abuse in other ways, and this generates agency costs. Damage from inappropriate asset use and maintenance will be reflected in the lease price. Smith and Wakeman (1983) argue that this leads to a tendency to lease assets whose value is less sensitive to abuse. (For example, the furnishings in a rental unit will generally be more durable and less sensitive to abuse than furnishings in owner-occupied dwellings.) The additional abuse problems in lease contracts mean that, if they are leased at all, assets whose use is difficult to monitor but are easily abused will have rental rates for short periods that are a high fraction of the purchase price. Lessee bonding through large damage deposits should also be more frequently observed in these situations. Service leases that include prepaid maintenance contracts are a way for the lessee to bond a promise that he will not abuse the asset by failing to maintain it. These arguments imply that financial leases will generally be used only for assets where the costs of undermaintenance are low.

Smith and Wakeman also argue that the higher the ratio of the term of the lease to the asset's usable life, the less severe are the perverse use and maintenance incentives. Thus long-term leases, options to extend the life of the lease, and options to purchase the asset at the end of the lease are contractual mechanisms which can reduce the agency costs of leasing. They all give the lessee a greater financial interest in the future value of the asset. In contrast, Flath (1980) analyzes situations where there are advantages to leasing because the useful life of the asset is significantly longer than the period over which a particular company or individual expects to use the asset. He analyzes arrangements which reduce contracting costs of short-term leases, focusing on reductions in monitoring costs and the costs of transferring ownership that are available through specialized leasing contracts rather than ownership. (Thus, for a week at the beach, one is more likely to rent a room than to buy a condominium.)

Insurance contracts. Bond indentures frequently contain covenants requiring the firm to maintain certain types of insurance coverage. These provisions reduce the firm's incentives to reject certain variance-reducing positive net present value safety projects. For example, if an uninsured firm invests in an unanticipated safety project, such as a sprinkler system, that reduces the variance of corporate cash flows, wealth is transferred to bondholders. However, if the firm has previously purchased full-coverage fire insurance, the risk of corporate cash flows, including indemnity payments from the policy, is unchanged. In this situation there are no wealth transfers to bondholders and the firm need only compare the cost of the safety project with the present value of the reduction in insurance premiums. In addition, insurance companies, because of economies of scale and specialization, develop a comparative advantage in claims administration. In fact, claims-only contracts exist wherein the insurance company provides only claim management services, and the corporation pays the claims. These contracts reduce the administrative costs of self-insurance programs.

CONCLUSIONS

Agency theory has provided a useful tool for detailed analysis of the determinants of the complex contractual arrangement called the modern corporation. Our purpose here has been to survey the applications of this theory to the conflicts of interest between corporate managers, stockholders, and creditors. The analysis of these conflicts and their resolution increases our understanding of the survival of many contractual practices that heretofore have either been taken for granted or viewed with great suspicion. It also illustrates the often close relation between financial and organizational practices. Future work promises even greater increases in our knowledge of organizational and contracting practices.

REFERENCES

Alchian, Armen A. "Uncertainty, Evolution and Economic Theory." *Journal of Political Economy* 58 (1950) pp. 211–21.

Alchian, Armen A. and Harold Demsetz. "Production, Information Costs, and Economic Organization." *American Economic Review* 62 (1972) pp. 777–95.

American Bar Foundation. Commentaries on Model Debenture Indenture Provisions (Chicago, 1971).

Arrow, Kenneth J. "Control in Large Organizations." *Management Science* 10 (1964) pp. 397–408.

Asquith, Paul. "Merger Bids, Uncertainty, and Stockholder Returns." *Journal of Financial Economics* 11 (1983) pp. 51–83.

Asquith, Paul, Robert F. Bruner, and David W. Mullins, Jr. "The Gains to Bidding Firms from Merger." *Journal of Financial Economics* 11 (1983) pp. 121–39.

Asquith, Paul and E. Han Kim. "The Impact of Merger Bids on the Participating Firms' Security Holders." *Journal of Finance* 37 (1982) pp. 1209–28.

Asquith, Paul and David W. Mullins. "Equity Issues and Stock Price Dilution." *Journal of Financial Economics* 14, (1985) forthcoming.

Becker, Gary S. and George L. Stigler. "Law Enforcement, Malfeasance, and Compensation of Enforcers." *Journal of Legal Studies* 3 (1974) pp.1–18.

Berle, A. A. and Gardner C. Means. *The Modern Corporation and Private Property*. New York: Macmillan, 1932.

Bhagat, Sanjai. "The Effect of Pre-Emptive Right Amendments on Shareholder Wealth." *Journal of Financial Economics* 12 (1983) pp.289–310.

Bhagat, Sanjai and James A. Brickley. "Cumulative Voting: The Value of Minority Shareholder Voting Rights." *Journal of Law and Economics*, (1984).

Bhattacharya, Sudipto. "Imperfect Information, Dividend Policy, and 'The Bird-in-the Hand' Fallacy." *Bell Journal of Economics* 10, No. 1 (1979) pp. 259–70.

Black, Fischer. "The Dividend Puzzle." *Journal of Portfolio Management* 2 (1976) pp. 5–8.

Black, Fischer and John Cox. "Valuing Corporate Securities: Some Effects of Bond Indenture Provisions." *Journal of Finance* 31 (1976) pp. 351–67.

Black, Fischer, Merton Miller, and Richard Posner. "An Approach to the Regulation of Bank Holding Companies." *Journal of Business* 51 (1978) pp. 379–412.

Bowen, Robert M., Eric W. Noreen, and John M. Lacey. "Determinants of the Decision by Firms to Capitalize Interest Costs." *Journal of Accounting and Economics* 3 (1981) pp. 151–79.

Bradley, Michael. "Interfirm Tender Offers and the Market for Corporate Control." *Journal of Business* 53 (1980) pp. 345–76.

Bradley, Michael, Anand Desai, and E. Han Kim. "The Rationale Behind Interfirm Tender Offers: Information or Synergy?" *Journal of Financial Economics* 11 (1983) pp. 183–206.

Bradley, Michael and L. M. Wakeman. "The Wealth Effects of Targeted Share Repurchases." *Journal of Financial Economics* 11 (1983) pp. 301–28.

Brickley, James A., Sanjai Bhagat, and Ronald C. Lease. "The Impact of Long-Range Managerial Compensation Plans on Shareholder Wealth." *Journal of Accounting & Economics* 7 (1985a) forthcoming.

Brickley, James A., Sanjai Bhagat, and Ronald C. Lease. "Incentive Effects of Stock Purchase Plans." *Journal of Financial Economics* 14 (1985b) forthcoming.

Carey, W. L. "Federalism and Corporate Law: Reflections upon Delaware." *Yale Law Journal* 83 (1974) pp. 663–707.

Dann, Larry. "The Effect of Common Stock Repurchase on Stockholder Returns." Unpublished dissertation, University of California, Los Angeles, 1980.

Dann, Larry. "Common Stock Repurchases: An Analysis of Returns to Bondholders and Stockholders." *Journal of Financial Economics* 9 (1981) pp. 113–38.

Dann, Larry and Harry DeAngelo. "Standstill Agreements, Privately Negotiated Stock Repurchases and the Market for Corporate Control." *Journal of Financial Economics* 11 (1983) pp. 275–300.

Dann, Larry Y. and Wayne H. Mikkelson. "Convertible Debt Issuance, Capital Structure Change and Financing-Related Information: Some New Evidence." *Journal of Financial Economics* 13 (1984) pp. 157–86.

Deakin, E. B. "An Analysis of Differences Between Non-Major Oil Firms Using Successful Efforts and Full Cost Methods." *The Accounting Review* 54 (1979) pp. 722–34.

DeAngelo, Harry, Linda DeAngelo, and Edward M. Rice. "Going Private: Minority Freezeouts and Shareholder Wealth." *Journal of Law and Economics* 27 (1984) forthcoming.

DeAngelo, Harry and Edward M. Rice. "Antitakeover Charter Amendments and Stockholder Wealth." *Journal of Financial Economics* 11 (1983) pp. 329–60.

Debreu, Gerard. *Theory of Value*. New York: John Wiley & Sons, 1959.

Dhaliwal, D. "The Effect of the Firm's Capital Structure on the Choice of Accounting Methods." *The Accounting Review* 55 (1980) pp. 78–84.

Dhaliwal, Dan S., Gerald Salamon, and E. Dan Smith. "The Effect of Owner versus Management Control on the Choice of Accounting Methods." *Journal of Accounting and Economics* 4 (1982) pp. 41–53.

Dodd, Peter. "Merger Proposals, Management Discretion and Stockholder Wealth." *Journal of Financial Economics* 8 (1980) pp. 105–38.

Dodd, Peter and Richard Leftwich. "The Market for Corporate Charters: 'Unhealthy Competition' versus Federal Regulation." *Journal of Business* 53 (1980) pp. 259–83.

Dodd, Peter and Richard S. Ruback. "Tender Offers and Stockholder Returns: An Empirical Analysis." *Journal of Financial Economics* 5 (1977) pp. 351–74.

Dodd, Peter and Jerold B. Warner. "On Corporate Governance: A Study of Proxy Contests." *Journal of Financial Economics* 11 (1983) pp. 401–38.

Eckbo, B. Espen. "Horizontal Mergers, Collusion, and Stockholder Wealth." *Journal of Financial Economics* 11 (1983) pp. 241–73.

Easterbrook, Frank H. "Two Agency-Cost Explanations of Dividends." *American Economic Review* 74 (1984) pp. 650–59.

Fama, Eugene F. "Agency Problems and the Theory of the Firm." *Journal of Political Economy* 88 (1980) pp. 288–307.

Fama, Eugene F. and Michael C. Jensen. "Agency Problems and Residual Claims." *Journal of Law and Economics* 26 (1983a) pp. 327–49.

Fama, Eugene F. and Michael C. Jensen. "Separation of Ownership and Control." *Journal of Law and Economics* 26 (1983b) 301–25.

Fama, Eugene F. and Michael C. Jensen. "Residual Claims and Investment Decisions." *Journal of Financial Economics* 14 (1985) forthcoming.

Fama, Eugene F. and Merton H. Miller. *The Theory of Finance*. New York: Holt, Rinehart and Winston; 1972.

Flath, David. "The Economics of Short-Term Leasing." *Economic Inquiry* 18 (1980) pp. 247–59.

Furubotn, Eirik and Steven Pejovich. "Property Rights, Economic Decentralization and the Evolution of the Yugoslav Firm, 1965–1972." *Journal of Law and Economics* 16 (1973) pp. 275–307.

Green, Richard C. "Investment Incentives, Debt and Warrants." *Journal of Financial Economics* 13 (1984) pp. 115–36.

Hagerman, Robert L. and Mark E. Zmijewski. "Some Economic Determinants of Accounting Policy Choice." *Journal of Accounting and Economics* 1 (1979) pp. 141–61.

Hamada, Robert S. and Myron S. Scholes. "Taxes and Corporate Financial Management" (1985) this volume.

Handjinicolaou, G. and Avner Kalay. "Wealth Redistributions or Changes in Firm Value: An Analysis of Returns to the Bondholders and to the Stockholders Around Dividend Announcements." *Journal of Financial Economics* 13 (1984) pp. 35–63.

Healy, Paul. "The Impact of Bonus Schemes on Accounting Choices." *Journal of Accounting and Economics* 7 (1985) forthcoming.

Hite, Gailen L. and James E. Owers. "Security Price Reactions Around Corporate Spin-Off Announcements." *Journal of Financial Economics* 12 (1983) pp. 407–33.

Ho, Thomas S. Y. and Ronald F. Singer. "Bond Indenture Provisions and the Risk of Corporate Debt." *Journal of Financial Economics* 10 (1982) pp. 375–406.

Jarrell, Gregg and Michael Bradley. "The Economic Effects of Federal and State Regulations of Cash Tender Offers." *Journal of Law and Economics* 23 (1980) pp. 371–407.

Jensen, Michael C. "Organization Theory and Methodology." *Accounting Review* 58 (1983) pp. 319–39.

Jensen, Michael C. and William H. Meckling. "Theory of the Firm: Managerial Behavior Agency Costs and Ownership Structure." *Journal of Financial Economics* 3 (1976) pp. 305–60.

Jensen, Michael C. and William H. Meckling. "Rights and Production Functions: An Application to Labor-Managed Firms and Codetermination." *Journal of Business* 52 (1979) pp. 469–506.

Jensen, Michael C. and Richard Ruback. "The Market for Corporate Control: The Scientific Evidence." *Journal of Financial Economics* 11 (1983) pp. 5–50.

Kalay, Avner. "Stockholder-Bondholder Conflict and Dividend Constraints." *Journal of Financial Economics* 10 (1982) pp. 211–33.

Klein, April. "The Information Content of Voluntary Corporate Divestitures." Unpublished working paper, 1983.

Klein, Benjamin, Robert Crawford, and Armen A. Alchian. "Vertical Integration, Appropriable Rents and the Competitive Contracting Process." *Journal of Law and Economics* 21 (1978) pp. 297–326.

Korwar, A. N. "The Effect of New Issues of Equity: An Empirical Investigation." Unpublished manuscript, University of Iowa, 1983.

Kummer, D. and R. Hoffmeister. "Valuation Consequences of Cash Tender Offers." *Journal of Finance* 33 (1978) pp. 505–16.

Lambert, Richard A. and David F. Larcker. ' "Golden Parachutes,' Executive Decision-Making and Shareholder Wealth." *Journal of Accounting and Economics* 7 (1985) forthcoming.

Larcker, David F. "The Association Between Performance Plan Adoption and Corporate Capital Investment." *Journal of Accounting and Economics* 5 (1983) pp. 3–30.

Leftwich, Richard. "Evidence of the Impact of Mandatory Changes in Accounting Principles on Corporate Loan Agreements." *Journal of Accounting and Economics* 3 (1981) pp. 3–36.

Lilien, Steven and Victor Pastena. "Determinants of Intra-Method Choice in the Oil and Gas Industry." *Journal of Accounting and Economics* 4 (1982) pp. 145–70.

Linn, Scott C. and John J. McConnell. "An Empirical Investigation of the Impact of 'Antitakeover' Amendments on Common Stock Prices." *Journal of Financial Economics* 11 (1983) pp. 361–99.

Malatesta, Paul H. "The Wealth Effect of Merger Activity and the Objective Functions of Merging Firms." *Journal of Financial Economics* 11 (1983) pp. 155–81.

Manne, Henry. "Mergers and the Market for Corporate Control." *Journal of Political Economy* 74 (1965) pp. 110–20.

Masulis, Ronald. "Stock Repurchase by Tender Offer: An Analysis of the Causes of Common Stock Price Changes." *Journal of Finance* 35 (1980a) pp. 305–19.

Masulis, Ronald. "The Effect of Capital Structure Change on Security Prices: A Study of Exchange Offers." *Journal of Financial Economics* 8 (1980b) pp. 139–77.

Masulis, Ronald. "The Impact of Capital Structure Change on Firm Value: Some Estimates." *Journal of Finance* 38 (1983) pp. 107–26.

Mayers, David and Clifford Smith. "Contractual Provisions, Organizational Structure, and Conflict Control in Insurance Markets." *Journal of Business* 54 (1981) pp. 407–34.

Mayers, David and Clifford Smith. "Toward A Positive Theory of Insurance." *Monograph Series in Economics and Finance*. New York University Salomon Brothers Center for the Study of Financial Institutions (1982a) pp. 1–48.

Mayers, David and Clifford Smith. "On the Corporate Demand for Insurance." *Journal of Business* 55 (1982b) pp. 281–96.

Mayers, David and Clifford Smith. "Ownership Structure and Control: The Mutualization of Stock Life Insurance Companies." Unpublished manuscript, 1983.

McConnell, John J. and Gary G. Schlarbaum. "Evidence on the Impact of Exchange Offers on Security Prices: The Case of Income Bonds." *Journal of Business* 54 (1981) pp. 65–85.

Mikkelson, Wayne. "Convertible Calls and Security Returns." *Journal of Financial Economics* 9 (1981) pp. 237–64.

Miles, J. and J. Rosenfeld. "An Empirical Analysis of the Effects of Spin-Off Announcements on Shareholder Wealth." *Journal of Finance* 38 (1983) pp. 1597–1606.

Miller, Merton. "Debt and Taxes." *Journal of Finance* 32 (1977) pp. 261–76.

Modigliani, Franco and Merton Miller. "The Cost of Capital, Corporation Finance and the Theory of Investment." *American Economic Review* 48 (1958) pp. 261–97.

Modigliani, Franco and Merton H. Miller. "Corporate Income Taxes and the Cost of Capital: A Correction." *American Economic Review* 53 (1963) pp. 433–43.

Myers, Stewart. "The Determinants of Corporate Borrowing." *Journal of Financial Economics* 5 (1977) pp. 147–75.

Reagan, Patricia B. and Rene M. Stulz. "Risk Sharing, Labor Contracts and Capital Markets." Unpublished manuscript, University of Rochester, 1983.

Rosenfeld, Ahron "Repurchase Offers: Information Adjusted Premiums and Shareholders' Response." *Monograph Series in Economics and Finance*. University of Rochester, 1982.

Ross, Stephen. "The Economic Theory of Agency: The Principal's Problem." *American Economic Review* 63 (1973) pp. 134–39.

Ross, Steven. "The Determination of Financial Structure: The Incentive-Signalling Approach." *Bell Journal of Economics* 8 (1977) pp. 23–40.

Rozeff, Michael. "Growth, Beta and Agency Costs As Determinants of Dividend Payout Ratios." *Journal of Financial Research* 5 (1982) pp. 249–59.

Ruback, Richard S. "Assessing Competition in the Market for Corporate Acquisitions." *Journal of Financial Economics* 11 (1983) pp. 141–53.

Schipper, Katherine and Abbie Smith. "Effects of Recontracting on Shareholder Wealth: The Case of Voluntary Spin-Offs." *Journal of Financial Economics* 12 (1983) pp. 434–66.

Schipper, Katherine and Rex Thompson. "Evidence on the Capitalized Value of Merger Activity for Acquiring Firms." *Journal of Financial Economics* 11 (1983) pp. 85–119.

Scholes, Myron. "Market for Securities: Substitution versus Price Pressure and the Effects of Information on Share Prices." *Journal of Business* 45 (1972) pp. 179–211.

Smith, Adam. (1776) *The Wealth of Nations*. Canaan ed. New York: Modern Library, 1937.

Smith, Clifford. "Alternative Methods for Raising Capital: Rights versus Underwritten Offerings." *Journal of Financial Economics* 5 (1977) pp. 273–307.

Smith, Clifford. "Pricing Mortgage Originations." *American Real Estate and Urban Economics Association Journal* 10 (1982) pp. 313–30.

Smith, Clifford. "Corporate Dividend Policy: An Analysis of Dividend Reinvestment Plans." Unpublished manuscript, University of Rochester, 1983.

Smith, Clifford and Rene Stulz. "Determinants of Firm's Hedging Policies." Unpublished manuscript, University of Rochester, 1983.

Smith, Clifford and Lee Wakeman. "An Analysis of the Provisions of Lease Contracts." Unpublished manuscript, University of Rochester, 1983.

Smith, Clifford and Jerold Warner. "On Financial Contracting: An Analysis of Bond Covenants." *Journal of Financial Economics* 7 (1979) pp. 117–61.

Smith, Clifford and Ross Watts. "Incentive and Tax Effects of Executive Compensation Plans." *Australian Journal of Management* 7 (1982) pp. 139–57

Smith, Clifford and Ross Watts. "The Structure of Executive Compensation Contracts and the Control of Management." Unpublished manuscript, University of Rochester, 1983.

Spence, Michael and Richard Zeckhauser. "Insurance, Information, and Individual Action." *American Economic Review* 61 (1971) pp. 119–132.

Stulz, Rene M. and Herb Johnson. "An Analysis of Secured Debt." Unpublished manuscript, University of Rochester, 1983.

Vermaelen, Theo. "Common Stock Repurchases and Market Signalling." *Journal of Financial Economics* 9 (1981) pp. 139–83.

Warner, Jerold. "Bankruptcy, Absolute Priority and the Pricing of Risky Debt Claims." *Journal of Financial Economics* 4 (1977) pp. 239–76.

Wier, Peggy. "The Costs of Antimerger Lawsuits: Evidence from the Stock Market." *Journal of Financial Economics* 11 (1983) pp. 207–24.

Wolfson, Mark A. "Empirical Evidence of Incentive Problems and Their Mitigation in Oil and Gas Tax Shelter Programs." Unpublished manuscript, Stanford University, 1983.

Zimmerman, Jerold L. "The Costs and Benefits of Cost Allocations." *The Accounting Review* 54 (1979) pp. 504–21.

Zmijewski, Mark E. and Robert L. Hagerman. "An Income Strategy Approach to the Positive Theory of Accounting Standard Setting/Choice." *Journal of Accounting and Economics* 3 (1981) pp. 129–49.

* This research was supported by the Managerial Economics Research Center, Graduate School of Management, University of Rochester, and the Salomon Brothers Center for the Study of Financial Institutions, Graduate School of Business Administration, New York University. We are indebted to Edward Altman and Marti Subrahmanyam for helpful comments and suggestions and to William H. Meckling for many stimulating discussions on the material discussed here.

5

Informational Content of Optimal Debt Contracts*

Kose John
Avner Kalay
Graduate School of Business
New York University

This paper examines conditions under which optimally specified dividend constraints included in debt contracts would act as a reliable signaling device. The implications of such a signaling equilibrium are used to investigate the following apparent paradox: The commonly observed empirical regularity is that announcements of cash dividends increases are associated with positive stock price reactions, whereas its reductions are associated with negative stock price responses. That is, cash dividend reductions seem to be bad signals. On the other hand, if outside financing is costly, cash dividend reductions can be the result of good investment opportunities, thereby serving as good *signals.*

The underlying model used is that of John and Kalay (1982), augmented to include asymmetry of information about the exogenously given "type" of a firm's investment opportunities. To solve the underinvestment problem, the stockholders self-impose "optimal" constraints on their future investments through appropriate dividend constraints. This optimal precommitment made by the better firm results in a larger minimum investment than that of the poorer firm. If the poor firm mimics the precommitment of the better firm it would have to overinvest. These costs of overinvestment, which are endogenous to the model, constitute the costs of false signaling. The resulting signaling equilibrium has several empirical implications. Documented evidence on the behavior of security prices (stocks and bonds) around dividend announcements, share repurchases, and announcements of new equity issues are examined and shown to be consistent with the predictions of our model.

Informational Content of Optimal Debt Contracts

INTRODUCTION

We seek to accomplish two objectives in this paper. First, we show that optimally specified payout constraints included in debt indentures can serve as a signaling device, i.e., in the identified signaling equilibrium they correctly communicate to the market the quality of the investment opportunities, which differ across firms. Second, we examine a large body of documented empirical evidence on the "information content" of cash dividends, share repurchases, and issues of new equity in the light of the implications of our model. In particular, we address the following apparent incongruity: On one hand there are a large number of studies documenting that announcement of payout increases (cash dividend increases and share repurchases) are associated with positive stock price reactions, whereas its reductions (cash dividend reductions and issues of new equity) are associated with negative stock price responses[1]; that is, payout reductions seem to convey *bad* news. On the other hand, if outside financing is costly, payout reductions can be the result of good investment opportunities, thereby serving as *good* signals. Our model seems to provide a reconciliation of these apparently opposing views on the information content of payouts.

We model the firm in the context of the conflict of interest between the stockholders (insiders, who have control over the firm) and bondholders.[2] When risky debt is outstanding, the stockholders could attempt to transfer wealth from the bondholders even by rejecting profitable investment projects.[3] Constraints on dividend payouts,[4] self-imposed by stockholders, are a possible solution to the problem of underinvestment. John and Kalay (1982) derive an optimal set of such contraints. These constraints form the basis of the nondissipative signaling equilibrium described in this paper.[5]

Our economy extends through two periods (three dates). At $t = 0$, stockholders issue a pure discount bond which matures at $t = 2$. At contracting time ($t = 0$), stockholders have better information than the market, i.e., they know the type of investment opportunities (which will be available to them at $t = 1$), while the market does not. Investment opportunities available (at $t = 0$ and $t = 1$) are characterized by a limited supply of nonnegative net present value projects. To solve the underinvestment problem, the stockholders self-impose, at $t = 0$, "optimal" constraints on their future (at $t = 1$) ability to pay dividends. These precommitments to minimum investment at $t = 1$ can serve as a separating signaling schedule. The optimal precommitment made by the better firm results in a larger minimum investment than that of the poorer firm. If the poor firm mimics the precommitment of the better firm it would have to overinvest. These costs of overinvestment, which are *endogenous* to our model, constitute the costs of false signaling. If these costs are high enough, a separating signaling equilibrium results.

The signaling equilibrium of our model differs from the existing signaling models in several ways. In most of the existing models of informational equilibria (e.g., labor market model of Spence (1973), insurance market model of Rothschild and Stiglitz (1976), capital structure models of Leland and Pyle (1977) and John and Williams (1982a) and the dividends signaling models of Bhattacharya (1979), Miller and Rock (1982), and John and Williams (1982b)) the informed party incurs some deadweight loss in the signaling equilibrium in comparison to the full-information equilibrium. In contrast to the models mentioned above, the signaling equilibrium in our model is nondissipative. With a finite number of firms, when the debt level is within the admissible range (to be specified formally) the signaling equilibrium is characterized by firms adopting their own full-information optimal dividend constraints.[6]

Another distinctive feature of our model is that the signal is productive. The signaling instrument is chosen based on an optimal activity choice. In other finance models, e.g., Ross (1977) and Bhattacharya (1980), the sole purpose of the signaling activity (debt in the Ross models and dividends in the Bhattacharya model) is the resolution of the informational asymmetry, i.e., debt and dividends would have had no role in a symmetric information setting. In this paper, the signaling activity can be viewed as arising from optimally solving the underinvestment problem. In other words, the optimal payout constraints which serve as signals would have had a purpose even in a symmetric information scenario to solve the underinvestment problem.

Our signaling equilibrium implies that firms having better investment opportunities would signal them by choosing a tighter dividend constraint, i.e., a low *expected dividend* is a good signal. Nevertheless, for a given set of contracts prescribed at time 0, high future dividends will be associated with good realized states of the world as uncertainty resolves.[7] Therefore, announcement of dividend increases can convey good news as well. Notice that share repurchases (and new issues of equity) play a role similar to cash dividends in the context of the conflict of interest between the bondholders and the stockholders. Therefore, the empirical implication derived for dividends follows just as well for cash dividends and share repurchases, i.e., unexpected changes in each of them can be positively correlated with stock price response.

Almost all existing studies on the information content of dividend have focused on the effects of unexpected changes in the magnitude of cash dividends and share repurchases. Our model suggests that expected dividends serve as a signaling device. Moreover, such a measure of expected dividend (based on the optimal contracts) can serve as the proper benchmark for further studies of the announcements effects of unexpected changes in payouts.

The paper is organized as follows. In the next section, the essential idea of our signaling equilibrium through optimally specified constraints is presented in a simple scenario. A full-fledged description of our economy follows. The conditions for the existence of a nondissipative signaling schedule are formalized in the next section, followed by an example of nondissipative signaling for a class of investment opportunity sets. Empirical implications of our theory and its relation to a large body of existing empirical evidence on the information content of cash dividends, share repurchases, and new equity issues are presented next and, finally, conclusions and a summary of the results are presented.

THE BASIC IDEA

Before we embark on a full-fledged model, it is useful to demonstrate our main idea in a simple scenario. Let the investment opportunities facing our firm be such that they result in the end of period (i.e., $t = 1$) market value of the firm being $V(s)$ where s, $s \epsilon (\underline{s}, \overline{s})$, is the realized state of the world at $t = 1$. The investment's outlays, I, are made at $t = 1$, after the state of the world has been revealed. In other words, at time $t = 0$ the firm "owns" options on projects, some of which have positive net present value. The firm has initial capital, of present value Q.

$$Q = I \int_{\underline{s}}^{\overline{s}} q(s) ds$$

where $q(s)$ is the time 0 market value of \$1 delivered if state s occurred.

Figure 1 describes the investment opportunities. The stockholders would choose to invest as long as $V(s) \geq I$ (i.e., for all $s \geq s_a$) and would choose not to invest (i.e., pay I as a dividend when $V(s) < I$ (i.e., in all $s < s_a$). The present value of dividends at time 1, D_1, is therefore,

$$D_1 = I \int_{\underline{s}}^{s_a} q(s)ds$$

and stockholders' wealth at $t = 0$ is

$$W_0 = I \int_{\underline{s}}^{s_a} q(s)ds + \int_{s_a}^{\bar{s}} V(s)q(s)ds \qquad (1)$$

Now suppose the firm issues debt which matures at $t = 1$ with face value F and pays out the proceeds $B_0(F)$ as dividends at $t = 0$. If stockholders' future ability to pay out dividends is unconstrained, they will choose to invest at $t = 1$ only when $V(s) \geq I + F$(i.e., for all $s \geq s_b$). With the debt outstanding, the present value of time 1 dividends, $D_1(F)$, would be

$$D_1(F) = I \int_{\underline{s}}^{s_b} q(s)ds \qquad (2)$$

These incentives are known to the potential bondholders who would pay for the bond,

$$B_0(F) = F \int_{s_b}^{\bar{s}} q(s)ds \qquad (3)$$

and stockholders' wealth is

$$W_0(F) = B_0(F) + D_1(F) + \int_{s_b}^{\bar{s}} [V(s) - F]q(s)ds \qquad (4)$$

Substituting for $D_1(F)$ from equation (2) and $B_0(F)$ from equation (3),

$$\begin{aligned} W_0(F) &= I \int_{\underline{s}}^{s_b} q(s)ds + \int_{s_b}^{\bar{s}} V(s)q(s)ds \\ &= W_0 - \underbrace{\int_{s_a}^{s_b} [V(s) - I]q(s)ds}_{L} \end{aligned}$$

where L is the loss due to the underinvestment problem (compare with equation (1)).

The presence of risky debt induces stockholders to underinvest.[8] Stockholders can avoid the losses associated with underinvestment by constraining their future ability to pay out funds while contracting at $t = 0$, i.e., on the debt's issuance date. In our simple scenario, if stockholders can write enforceable state contingent contracts, they would precommit to pay no dividends at all in states $s > s_a$. Given this constraint on stockholders' future freedom of choice (denoted as K), the bondholders would pay

FIGURE 1 The investment opportunity of a firm as a function of the states of the world, s. The investment outlays are I and F is the face value of its debt.

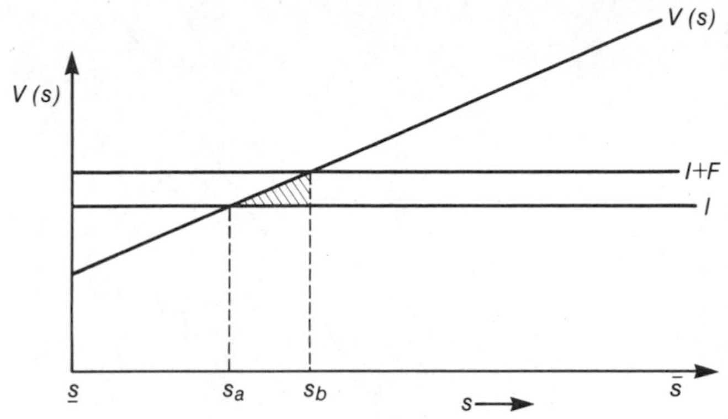

$$B_0(F,K) = F\int_{s_a}^{\bar{s}} q(s)ds$$

and stockholders' wealth can be shown to be

$$W_0(F,K) = W_0$$

Hence, by self-imposing constraints on their future ability to pay dividends, the stockholders can avoid the losses associated with underinvestment. The question posed in this paper is: Can optimally specified dividend constraints included in the debt indentures be used as a signaling device when stockholders have better information than the bond market at contracting time? If so, what implications would it have for the information content of dividends?

Now we proceed to model asymmetry of information about the investment opportunity of the firm between insiders and the market.[9] Suppose there are two types of firms (G and N) whose investment opportunities are described in Figure 2. In any state of the world, $V_G(s) > V_N(s)$ for the same investment outlays, I. Further, the type of firm is unknown to the market. Assuming risk neutrality, an uninformed investor would pay the average price for the claims of either firm, say B_0, where

$$B_0 = \alpha B_G + (1 - \alpha)B_N \qquad (5)$$

and α is the probability of a type G firm.

FIGURE 2 The investment opportunities of two firms (G and N) as a function of the states of the world, s. The investments outlay required is I. F is the face value of the debt.

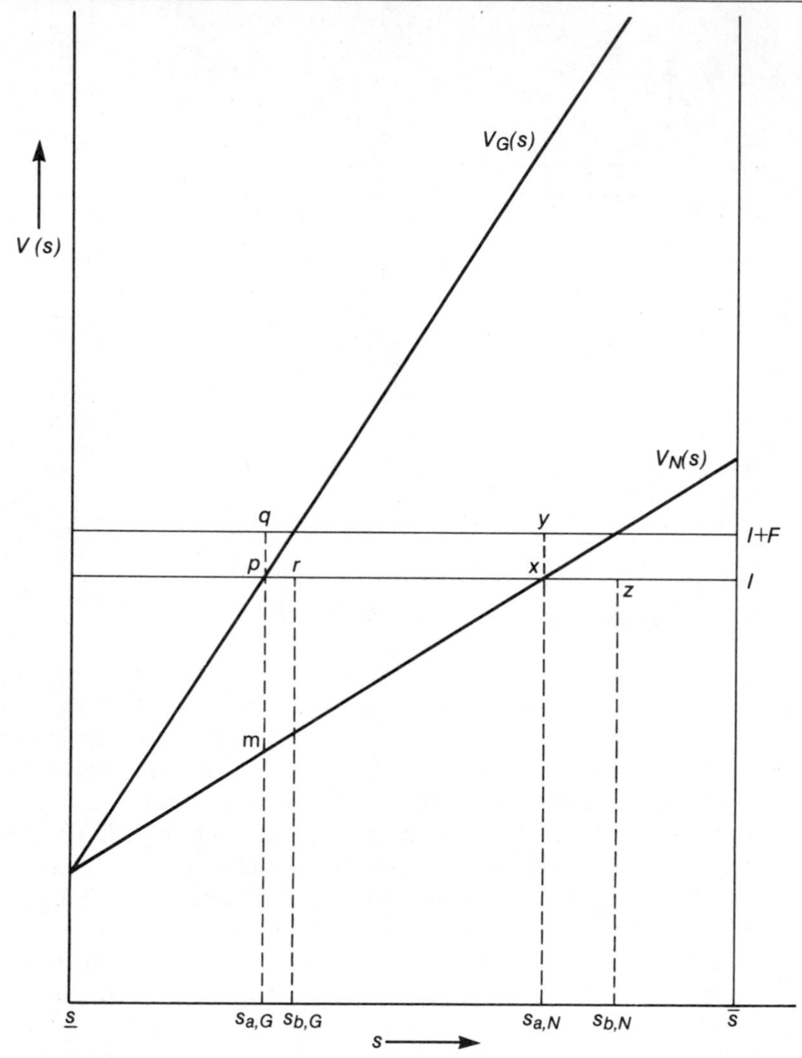

The managers of the good firms, i.e., G-type firms, have incentives to signal the "true" value of their firm to the market. They can do it by raising debt and precommiting to pay no dividends at all for the states of the world in which $V_G(s) > I$. By writing such a constraint, call it K_G, they would solve the underinvestment problem.

Moreover, they would differentiate their firms from the N-type firms. If the manager of an N firm would issue the same amount of debt (i.e., the same F) and include the same dividend constraints, K_G, in its debt indentures, he would be forced to overinvest in some states of the world. The costs of false signaling would, therefore, be

$$\phi = \int_{s_{a,G}}^{s_{a,N}} [I - V(s)]q(s)ds \tag{6}$$

while the benefits are the increased value of the bonds sold, which are:

$$\beta = F\int_{s_{a,G}}^{s_{a,N}} q(s)ds \tag{7}$$

In Figure 2, ϕ is represented by area (pmx) and β by $(pqyx)$. If $\phi > \beta$, the N-type firm has no incentive to mimic the constraints of the G-type firm. Then a nondissipative signaling equilibrium exists. In this equilibrium a precommitment to pay *less* in dividends serves as a good signal. The expected dividends of a G-type firm under its optimal dividend constraint, K_G is:

$$D_1(F,K_G,G) = I\int_{0}^{s_{a,G}} q(s)ds \tag{8}$$

which would be less than that of an N-type firm under its optimal constraint, K_N, i.e.,

$$D_1(F,K_N,N) = I\int_{0}^{s_{a,N}} q(s)ds \tag{9}$$

In other words, firms with better investment opportunities would precommit to a larger minimum investment (i.e., smaller payout). The above analysis demonstrates the essential features of our signaling equilibrium. In the next section the full-fledged model is presented.

THE MODEL

Description of the economy

The economy is described by the following set of assumptions:

A.1. The economy extends through three dates, $t = 0$, $t = 1$, and $t = 2$.

A.2. The insiders of each firm control the investment, financing, and dividend decisions of the firm acting in the interests of the current shareholders. They possess superior information compared to the market participants (as detailed in A.4).[9]

A.3. The uncertainty in the economy is represented by an Arrow-Debreu state preference model, where $\omega \epsilon \Omega$ indexes the eventual states of the world to be realized at $t = 2$. There is partial resolution of uncertainty at time $t = 1$, where the event η (a subset of Ω) will be realized.

A.4. The firms in the economy are indexed by an exogenous-type variable $\theta \epsilon \Theta$ based on the investment opportunities available to it at time $t = 1$. This parameter θ is known to the insiders precisely but it is unknown to the market. Thus, at contracting time $t = 0$, there is asymmetry of information between the insiders and the market (including prospective bondholders). Θ is assumed to be of finite cardinality, say $|\Theta| = n$, in this paper.[10]

A.5. Corporations are subject to income tax, τ_C, and their payments to the bondholders are fully tax-deductible. The firm gets the depreciation tax credits at the time the investment is made. Personal income taxes are assumed to be zero for all agents in the economy.[11]

A.6. The insiders issue a pure discount bond with a payment F promised at maturity $t = 2$, for which the bondholders pay a price B at $t = 0$. The optimal level of F used by each firm is determined outside the model by trading off the benefits and costs of leverage.

A.7. Renegotiation between the bondholders and the stockholders is prohibitively costly. Hence, any contract between the bondholders and the stockholders is written at time 0 and expires at time 2. Possible market mechanisms (like takeovers and recapitalizations at $t = 1$) which might resolve an effective conflict between stockholders and bondholders are also assumed to be too costly.

A.8. The agents in the economy behave as if they are risk-neutral and the risk-free rate is assumed to be zero.[12]

A.9. For a given set of constraints, which are included in the debt indentures (if there are any), the insiders who control the firm take investment and financing decisions which maximize stockholders' wealth. The investment opportunities facing a firm at time $t = 0$ are represented by $f(I_0, \eta)$ and those at time $t = 1$ by $\bar{f}(I_1, \omega:\theta)$. $f(I_0,\eta)$ represents the total payoffs at time $t = 1$ in state η from investment I_0 made at $t = 0$. For convenience, we assume that $f(I_0, \eta)$ is the same for all firms. For the θ-type firm, $\bar{f}(I_1, \omega:\theta)$ represents the total terminal payoffs at time 2 in state ω resulting from investment of $I_1(\theta)$ in time $t = 1$.

Both f and $\bar{f}$ have the usual properties of production functions,[13] that is:

$$\frac{\partial f}{\partial I_0}, \frac{\partial \bar{f}}{\partial I_1} > 0 \text{ and } \frac{\partial^2 f}{\partial I_0^2}, \frac{\partial^2 \bar{f}}{\partial I_1^2} < 0$$

Further,

$$f(0,\eta) = 0, \bar{f}(0, \omega{:}\theta) = 0, \text{ for all } \theta, \omega, \eta$$
$$f(I_0,\eta) \geq 0, \bar{f}(I_1, \omega{:}\theta) \geq 0, \text{ for all } \theta, \omega, I_0, I_1, \eta$$

Insiders invest at times $t = 0$ and $t = 1$ and liquidation takes place at $t = 2$. The value of stockholders' claims on the firm can, therefore, be represented as the present value of their expected dividend stream; D_t, $t = 0, 1, 2$, where D_2 is a liquidating dividend. Hence, insiders would choose the investment policy which maximizes

$$\overline{D} = E_\eta E_{\omega/\theta} \left[D_0 + D_1(\eta) + D_2(\omega{:}\theta)\right] \tag{10}$$

which is the NPV of their investment, for the θ-type firm.

The insider's problem

In this section we formalize the problem of the insiders who have to choose at time $t = 0$ the optimal contractual arrangements, faced with the underinvestment problem (indicated in the previous section) and an asymmetry of information with the bond market about their type $\theta \epsilon \Theta$. The insiders start at time $t = 0$ with the objective of extracting the maximum value from the firm's investment opportunities represented by $f(I_0, \eta)$ and $\bar{f}(I_1, \omega{:}\theta)$. They issue a pure discount bond with a payment F promised at maturity $t = 2$, for which the bondholders pay B at $t = 0$.

Thus the insiders solve the following problem (P)

$$\begin{aligned} &\underset{I_0 \epsilon K_0}{\text{Max}}\ B - I_0 (1 - \tau_C) + E_\eta f(I_0,\eta) (1 - \tau_C) \\ &\quad + \underset{I_1(\theta) \epsilon K_1(\theta)}{\text{Max}} \{-I_1(\theta)(1 - \tau_C) + E_{\omega/\theta}[\bar{f}(I_1, \omega{:}\theta) \\ &\quad - \text{Min}\{\bar{f}(I_1, \omega{:}\theta), F\}] (1 - \tau_C)]\} \end{aligned} \tag{11}$$

where K_0 is the feasible set of I_0 as stipulated by any dividend constraint, $K_1(\theta)$ is the feasible set of $I_1(\theta)$ as stipulated by any dividend constraint relevant for time $t = 1$, for the θ-type firm, and E_η and $E_{\omega/\theta}$ are the expectation operators over η and ω, respectively, for the θ-type firm.

The net equity raised by the stockholders $D_0 = B - I_0 (1 - \tau_C)$ can be thought of as a negative dividend at $t = 0$.

The problem facing the insiders is to solve for the optimal constraints (specifying feasible sets K_0 and $K_1(\theta)$) such that the resulting investments and the bondholders' pricing of the bonds results in the maximal value for the stockholders' claims, as specified in equation (1).

Clearly the price B paid by the bondholders is their time $t = 0$ valuation of its payoffs at time $t = 2$; namely, $\text{Min}\{\bar{f}(I_1, \omega:\theta), F\}$. Now, if the market cannot distinguish between the different θ types the price imputed to the bonds (including that of type θ) is

$$B = E_\theta E_{\omega/\theta} \text{ Min}[\bar{f}(I_1,\omega:\theta),F)] \tag{12}$$

for any level of investment I_1 anticipated.

On the other hand, if the insiders of the θ-type firm successfully fully signal their firm type, the bonds will be priced at

$$B = E_{\omega/\theta} \text{ min}[\bar{f}(I_1,\omega:\theta),F] \tag{13}$$

Substituting equation (13) into equation (11), we have

$$\begin{aligned}&\underset{I_0 \epsilon K_0}{\text{Max}} - I_0(1-\tau_C) + E_\eta f(I_0,\eta)(1-\tau_C) + \underset{I_1(\theta)\epsilon K_1(\theta)}{\text{Max}} \\ &\{-I_1(\theta)(1-\tau_C) + E_{\omega/\theta}[\bar{f}(I_1,\omega:\theta)(1-\tau_C) \\ &\quad + \tau_C \text{ Min}\{F, \bar{f}(I_1,\omega:\theta)\}]\}\end{aligned} \tag{14}$$

Equation (14) is nothing but the combined value of the firm, say $V(I_0,I_1(\theta))$. Thus if the insiders can precommit themselves to investment levels I_0 and $I_1(\theta)$ they would, in fact, maximize $\bar{D}$ in equation (10). Clearly I_0^C and $I_1^C(\theta)$, which maximize the combined wealth given in equation (14), are given by the appropriate first-order conditions,

$$E_\eta f'(I_0^C, \eta) = 1 \tag{15}$$

$$-1 + E_{\omega/\theta} \bar{f}'(I_1^C,\omega:\theta) + \frac{\tau_C}{(1-\tau_C)} \underset{\omega\epsilon\Delta(I_1^C)}{E} \bar{f}'(I_1^C,\omega:\theta) = 0 \tag{16}$$

where $\underset{\omega\epsilon\Delta(I_1)}{E}$ denotes integration only over the insolvency states, i.e.,

$$\Delta(I_1) \equiv \Delta(I_1(\theta)) = \{\omega:\bar{f}(I_1(\theta),\omega:\theta) \leqq F\}, \text{ for any value } I_1(\theta) \tag{17}$$

Since the objective in equation (3) is concave, the first-order conditions are also sufficient. Thus I_0^C and $I_1^C(\theta)$ are the optimal levels of investments to which the insiders of a θ-type firm will precommit themselves contractually. At $t = 0$, they would invest I_0^C and offer a precommitting constraint $K_1(\theta)$, which would induce an investment $I_1^C(\theta)$ at $t = 1$.

If insiders can signal their firm type by writing an enforceable precommitment to undertake investment levels I_0^C and $I_1^C(\theta)$ such that the bondholders would price it correctly in B, stockholders' wealth and the combined wealth of the bondholders and the stockholders would be maximized. The precommitment to undertake $I_1^C(\theta)$ at $t = 1$ implies that insiders are constrained to pay stockholders no more than $(1 - \tau_C)\ (f(I_0,\eta) - I_1^C(\theta)\ )$ as dividends at $t = 1$. Moreover, if $(1 - \tau_C)(f(I_0,\ \eta) - I_1^C(\theta)) < 0$, the stockholders are *forced* to issue new equity to meet their obligations. Any other precommitment by the insiders would reduce stockholders' dividend wealth (as given in their objective function, equation (14)).[14] The economy described in this paper allows stockholders to solve the underinvestment problem without cost. This is true only because we assume symmetry of information structures between insiders and the bond market after contracting, so that we can focus on the precontractual informational asymmetry and the signaling aspects of the problem.[15]

OPTIMAL CONTRACTS AND SIGNALING

In the previous section, we examined how the insiders of the θ-type firm would include, in the debt covenants, constraints precommitting themselves to certain levels of investment I_0 at $t = 0$ and $I_1(\theta)$ at $t = 1$ as an optimal solution to their problem (P). Note that I_0^C is the same for all firms (since $f(I_0,\eta)$ is). But different firms will specify $K_1(\theta)$, precommitting different levels of $I_1^C(\theta)$. $K_1(\theta)$ simply specifies the minimum level of investment $I_1^C(\theta)$ (determined by equation (16) for the θ-type firm). The issue examined in this section is whether the optimal contracts $K_1(\theta)$ specified by the different firms can give rise to an equilibrium signaling structure for the θ-type firm. If all firms correctly precommit themselves to the proper level of $I_1^C(\theta)$, can that serve as an equilibrium schedule to signal the θ-type correctly?

Before we examine this, it is useful to clarify the following issues in the environment of our model where the θ type of the firm is unknown to the market.

At time $t = 0$, it is optimal for all firms to invest $I_0(1 - \tau_C)$; therefore, the net amount of equity raised by the θ-type firm is $I_0(1 - \tau_C) - B(\theta)$ if the type is correctly signaled to the market. The cash flow at $t = 1$ is $(1 - \tau_C)f(I_0,\ \eta)$, from which the precommitted amount $(1 - \tau_C)I_1(\theta)$ is invested. The residual amount, $[f(I_0,\ \eta)\ -\ I_0(\theta)]\ (1 - \tau_C)$ is paid out as dividends by the θ-type firm. At time $t = 2$, the liquidating payments, $\text{Min}[F, \bar{f}(I_1(\theta),\omega{:}\theta)]$ are paid to the bondholders and $\{\bar{f}[I_1(\theta,\ \omega{:}\theta) - \text{Min}(F, \bar{f})]\ (1 - \tau_C\}$ to the stockholders. Now we characterize the conditions under which a signaling equilibrium exists such that the firms can successfully signal their θ type to the market through the self-imposed dividend constraints.

Before we develop the general conditions, it would be useful to motivate the reasoning through a simple case where there are only two types of firms, $\Theta = \{a, b\}$. Assume that $\bar{f}(I_1,\omega:a)$ represents better investment opportunities than $\bar{f}(I_1,\omega:b)$ with $I_1^C(a) > I_1^C(b)$. The condition for a firms to signal themselves to be better by precommiting themselves to their optimal investment level $I_1^C(a)$ is as follows: The costs of overinvestment for the b firm are larger than the gains from false signaling through overpriced bonds. This can be written explicitly as follows:

G, the gains from false signaling is given by,

$$G = \Delta B + \Delta S + \Delta I \tag{18}$$

where $\Delta B = B(I_1^C(a)) - B(I_1^C(b))$

$$\Delta B = E_{\omega/a}\,\text{Min}\{\bar{f}(I_1^C(a),a),F\} - E_{\omega/b}\,\text{Min}\{\bar{f}(I_1^C(b),b),F\} \tag{19}$$

and

$$\begin{aligned}\Delta S = {} & E_{\omega/b}\,[\bar{f}(I_1^C(a),b) - \text{Min}\{\bar{f}(I_1^C(a),b),F\}]\,(1 - \tau_C) \\ & - E_{\omega/b}\,[\bar{f}(I_1^C(b),b) - \text{Min}\{\bar{f}(I_1^C(b),b),F\}]\,(1 - \tau_C)\end{aligned} \tag{20}$$

and

$$\Delta I = [I_1^C(b) - I_1^C(a)](1 - \tau_C) \tag{21}$$

Clearly, if $G < 0$, a signaling equilibrium can exist. Such a signaling equilibrium is nondissipative because each firm optimally invests the levels it would have invested in a full-information scenario. Investors simply observe the investment precommitment levels I_1^C and impute the true θ and therefore the correct prices $B(\theta)$ for the bonds.

Sufficient conditions for such a signaling equilibrium can be collected below.

Let $\Theta = \{\theta_1,\theta_2, \ldots, \theta_n\}$ be the index set of firm types. For any given value of F (which is commonly observed by all market participants), if the following conditions are satisfied, there is a signaling equilibrium (conditional on that value of F) in which the market participants can impute the correct θ from the I_1^C levels optimally precommitted by the firms. For a given set Θ of firm types, let us define $\bar{F}$ as the set of F levels such that, conditional on F, there exists a signaling equilibrium. It will be shown that $\bar{F}$ is always nonempty and contains an interval of the form $[0, \bar{F}]$.

A set of sufficient conditions is:

C.1. The true value of debt $B(\theta)$ is increasing in θ.

C.2. The optimal investment $I_1^C(\theta)$ which would be undertaken by the firms in a full-information scenario is increasing in θ.

C.3. The net gains for a θ-type firm from implementing any other investment policy (say $I_1^C(\theta')$, which is optimal for firm $\theta' \neq \theta$) should be negative.

The monotonicity in the first condition simply formalizes the attractiveness of increasing θ; i.e., the higher-θ firms have bonds of larger true value. The second condition ensures that abiding by the minimum-investment precommitment of a higher-θ-type firm would impose costs of overinvestment, which is the potential costs of false signaling in the model.

To formalize the third condition, let us write down the net gains of a θ-type firm from signaling a type θ' (by precommitting a level of investment $I_1^C(\theta')$ instead of $I_1^C(\theta)$).

$$\begin{aligned}\psi(\theta,\theta') = (1-\tau_C)\,[&-I_1^C(\theta') + E_{\omega:\theta}[\bar{f}(I_1^C(\theta'),\omega{:}\theta)\\ &- \text{Min}\{\bar{f}(I_1^C(\theta'),\omega{:}\theta),F\}]]\\ &+ E_{\omega/\theta'}\,\text{Min}\{\bar{f}(I_1^C(\theta'),\omega{:}\theta'),F\} - (1-\tau_C)[-I_1^C(\theta)\\ &+ E_{\omega/\theta}\,[\bar{f}(I_1^C(\theta),\omega{:}\theta) - \text{Min}\{\bar{f}(I_1^C(\theta),\omega{:}\theta),\,F\}]]\\ &+ E_{\omega/\theta}\,\text{Min}\{f(I_1^C(\theta),\omega{:}\theta),F\}\end{aligned} \tag{22}$$

Clearly, the $I_1^C(\theta)$ is an incentive-compatible equilibrium schedule for the stockholders (insiders) only if

$$\underset{\theta'}{\text{Max}}\ \psi(\theta,\theta') = \psi(\theta,\theta) \tag{23}$$

i.e., a θ firm cannot improve its gains from false signaling. Equivalently,

$$\psi(\theta,\theta') < \psi(\theta,\theta) \qquad \text{for all } \theta' \neq \theta \tag{24}$$

For any value of F such that the conditions C.1 to C.3 are satisfied, there exists a nondissipative signaling equilibrium. Let $\overline{F}$ be the set of such values of F. It can be easily shown that $\overline{F}$ is nonempty and includes an interval of the form $[0,\overline{F}]$.

We can rewrite equation (22) as:

$$\begin{aligned}\psi(\theta,\theta':F) &= \lambda(\theta,\theta':F) + \rho(\theta,\theta':F)\\ \lambda(\theta,\theta':F) &= (1-\tau_C)\,[I_1^C(\theta') + E_{\omega/\theta}(\bar{f}(I_1^C(\theta'),\omega{:}\theta)]\\ &\quad + \tau_C E_{\omega/\theta}\,\text{Min}\{\bar{f}(I_1^C(\theta'),\omega{:}\theta),\,F\}\\ &\quad - [(1-\tau_C)[-I_1^C(\theta) + E_{\omega/\theta}(\bar{f}(I_1^C(\theta),\omega{:}\theta)]\\ &\quad + \tau_C E_{\omega/\theta}\,\text{Min}\{f(I_1^C(\theta),\omega{:}\theta,\,F\}]\\ \rho(\theta,\theta':F) &= E_{\omega/\theta'}\,\text{Min}\{\bar{f}(I_1^C(\theta'),\omega{:}\theta'),\,F\}\\ &\quad - E_{\omega/\theta}\,\text{Min}\{\bar{f}(I_{,1}^{\,C}(\theta'),\omega{:}\theta'),F\}\end{aligned}$$

Since $\lambda(\theta,\theta':F)$ is the change in with-tax-shield firm value resulting from implementing the suboptimal investment $I_1^C(\theta')$ rather than $I_1^C(\theta)$ for the θ-type firm, it is negative for any value of F. Now, for all values of F for which $\rho(\theta,\theta':F)$ is nonpositive, $\psi(\theta,\theta':F) < 0$ such that a signaling equilbrium exists. It is clear that for all values of $F \leq F_R$, where F_R is the riskless level of debt conditional on the investment of the constrained amounts, i.e.,

$$F_R = \omega \text{ Min}\{\bar{f}(I_1^C(\theta'),\omega{:}\theta),\ \bar{f}(I_1^C(\theta'),\omega{:}\theta')\}$$

$\rho(\theta,\theta'{:}F) = 0$ and a signaling equilibrium exists because $\psi(\theta, \theta'{:}F) < 0$. Now, by continuity of ψ in F it follows that there is some value of F, say $\bar{F} > F_R$ such that $\psi(\theta,\theta'{:}F) < 0$ for all $F \leq \bar{F}$. Clearly, if the symmetric information optimal choice of F, say F^0 of all firms falls within the range $[0,\bar{F}]$ in the signaling equilibrium no firm has an incentive to choose a level of F different from F^0.[16]

In our model, the signal involves no deadweight loss, and it results in pareto efficient levels of investments. Thus, the optimal solution to the agency problem by the stockholders in the form of optimally specified contracts would also result in resolving the precontractual informational asymmetry about the firm type.

In the next section, we present a detailed example to illustrate the above conditions. We limit our attention to production technologies with multiplicative uncertainty. We are also able to characterize the largest level of F, say $\bar{F}$, which allows such an equilibrium in terms of the dispersion of the firm types in Θ.

AN EXAMPLE OF NONDISSIPATIVE SIGNALING

Having discussed the general structure of the model and the costs that permit optimal contractual precommitments to function as a signal, we now use a simple example to examine in more detail the nature of the equilibrium and its properties. Since corporate taxes were used in our full-fledged model only to provide one possible advantage of leverage, we set $\tau_C = 0$ in the following model.

Let $\bar{f}(I_1,\ \omega{:}\theta) = \bar{f}(I_1,\ \theta)g(\omega)$, i.e., the uncertainty involved is multiplicative. Further assume that the distribution of ω for all firms $\theta \epsilon \Theta$ is the same, a uniform distribution over interval $[0,h]$. Also take $g(\omega) \equiv \omega$. Then the gains from false signaling

$$\psi(\theta,\theta') = \frac{F^2}{2h}\left[\frac{1}{\bar{f}(I_1^C(\theta'),\ \theta)} - \frac{1}{\bar{f}(I_1^C(\theta'),\theta')}\right] \tag{25}$$

$$+ \left\{\left[\frac{h}{2}\ \bar{f}(I_1^C(\theta'),\ \theta) - I_1^C(\theta')\right] - \left[\frac{h}{2}\ \bar{f}(I_1^C(\theta),\ \theta) - I_1^C(\theta)\right]\right\}$$

When $\theta' > \theta$, the first term represents the benefits from false signaling via the overpricing of bonds. The second term represents the costs of (suboptimal) overinvestment and is negative, i.e.,

$$-I_1^C(\theta) + \frac{h}{2}\bar{f}(I_1^C(\theta), \theta) > -I_1^C(\theta') + \frac{h}{2}\bar{f}(I_1^C(\theta'), \theta)$$

since $I_1^C(\theta)$ is the optimum for the combined value of the θ-type firm. Clearly, for large values of F, the gains from false signaling are larger, ceteris paribus. On the other hand the curvature of the production function and the overinvestment $I_1^C(\theta') - I_1^C(\theta)$ determine the costs of false signals.

It would be useful to explicitly work out the above model, where $\bar{f}(I_1, \theta) = \sqrt{\theta I_1}$

It is easily seen that $I_1^C(\theta) = h^2\theta/16$. Further, for any level of investment I_1, the bond price is monotonically increasing in θ.

$$B(\theta) = F - \frac{F^2}{2h}\frac{1}{\sqrt{\theta I_1}} \tag{26}$$

$$\frac{\partial B}{\partial \theta} = \frac{F^2}{4h}\frac{\theta^{-3/2}}{\sqrt{I_1}} > 0 \tag{27}$$

Further, note that $I_1^C(\theta)$ is monotonically increasing in θ. Now, to establish condition C.3, we can compute,

$$\psi(\theta,\theta') = \frac{2F^2}{h^2}\left(\frac{1}{\sqrt{\theta\theta'}} - \frac{1}{\theta'}\right) + \frac{h^2}{16}[2\sqrt{\theta\theta'} - \theta' - \theta] \tag{28}$$

To show $\psi(\theta,\theta) \geq \psi(\theta,\theta')$ for all θ, θ' it is enough to show that $\psi(\theta,\theta') < 0$ for all $\theta' > \theta$.

Simplifying,

$$\psi(\theta, \theta') = \frac{2F^2}{h^2\,\theta'\sqrt{\theta}}(\sqrt{\theta'} - \sqrt{\theta}) - \frac{h^2}{16}(\sqrt{\theta'} - \sqrt{\theta})$$

Assuming $\theta_1 = \underset{\theta}{\text{Min}}\Theta > 0$, and given $\theta' > \theta$, we have that $\psi(\theta,\theta) < 0$ if and only if,

$$(32F^2/h^4\theta\theta') < \sqrt{\theta'/\theta} - 1 \tag{29}$$

Define $k^2 = \underset{\theta,\theta' \epsilon \Theta}{\text{Min}} \sqrt{\frac{\theta'}{\theta}} - 1.$ Then equation (29) is true if

$$F < (kh^2\theta_1/4\sqrt{2}) = \overline{F} \tag{30}$$

Note that $\overline{F}$ is increasing in k, which is a measure of how far apart the quality of the different firms are. It is also increasing in θ_1, the minimum quality in the market.

Let $\Theta = \{100, 110, 120, 130\}$, $h = 10$.

Clearly $k^2 = \sqrt{130/120} - 1 = 0.041$
$\bar{F} = 2020$

If $\Theta = \{100, 130\}$, then $\bar{F} = 3744$.

Thus the disparity in firm quality allows a signaling equilibrium, supporting a larger range of debt. Therefore, if the face value of debt is anywhere in the range $[0, (kh^2\theta_1/4\sqrt{2})]$, a signaling equilibrium exists. The resolution of the signaling equilibrium is increasing in h and decreasing in F, the face value.

EVIDENCE AND IMPLICATIONS

Empirical implications

Our theory provides a possible explanation for the following apparent incongruity: The commonly observed empirical regularity is that announcements of payout increases are associated with positive stock price reaction, whereas payout reduction is associated with negative stock price reaction. This empirical regularity is consistent with the implications of recent theoretical studies, e.g., Bhattacharya (1979), John and Williams (1982), Miller and Rock (1982). That is, *high* cash-dividend payout seems to be a *good* signal. On the other hand, if outside financing is costly, payout reductions can be the result of good investment opportunities. Consequently, *low* payout can serve as a *good* signal.

Our theory suggests that a signaling equilibrium in which a precommitment to pay less in dividends (i.e., to choose a lower payout ratio) signals that good investment opportunities can exist. In our model, firms have the same investment opportunities at $t = 0$, $f(I_0,\eta)$, but the better firms are precommiting to a larger minimum investment at $t = 1$. In the simple case where there are only two types of firms, $\theta = a$ and $\theta = b$, $\bar{f}(I_1(a), \omega{:}a)$ is better than $\bar{f}(I_1(b), \omega{:}b)$ and $I_1^C(a) > I_1^C(b)$; the better firm, a, is expected to pay less in dividends. This can be written explicitly as follows:

$$\overline{D}_1(a) = E_\eta f(I_0,\eta) - I_1^C(a) < \overline{D}_1(b) = E_\eta f(I_0,\eta) - I_1^C(b)$$

where $\overline{D}_1(\theta)$ is the expected dividend paid by a θ-type firm at time 1, $\theta = a,b$. That is, a smaller *expected dividend* serves as a good signal since it implies a larger minimum investment and, therefore, better investment opportunities. Nevertheless, for a given set of contracts prescribed at time 0, higher dividends at time 1 are associated with good realized states of the world as uncertainty resolves. At time $t = 1$, stockholders have the incentive to pay themselves all of the unconstrained portions of the realized cash flows, $f(I_0,\eta)$.[17] Since in the better states $f(I_0,\eta)$ is larger and the precommited investment $I_1^C(\theta)$ is unchanged, less would be paid in dividends. Therefore, announcements of unexpectedly large (small) dividends can be correlated with positive (negative) stock price responses.[18] It is important to note that no signaling activity takes place at $t = 1$. The payout announcement in itself conveys no additional information to the market than that provided by the realized state.[19]

An important implication of our model is in providing a new measure of expected dividends that can be used as a benchmark in future studies of payout announcement effects.

Notice that, when viewed in the context of the conflict of interests between the bondholders and the stockholders, cash dividends and share repurchases serve similar functions. Indeed, dividends in our model are defined to include all forms of payments to the stockholders and, in particular, to include share repurchases. The empirical implications derived for dividends follow just as well for cash dividends and share repurchases. That is, unexpected increases (decreases) in each of them are associated with good (bad) realized states of the world.

Empirical evidence

To date, empirical research has focused almost exclusively on the effects of unexpected changes in the magnitude of *cash dividends* and *share repurchases*. This section demonstrates that the empirical evidence is consistent with our theory. At this juncture, the signaling value of *expected dividends* has not been tested. However, indirect evidence on this implication of our model has been documented recently. Better firms (other things being constant) have been shown to choose "tighter" dividend constraints. This empirical regularity is consistent with our model, which suggests that better firms would find it optimal to precommit to smaller *expected dividends*. Below we survey the existing empirical evidence and examine its relationship to our model.

Evidence on the information content of unexpected cash dividend changes. In our model, stockholders of θ-type firms have precommited themselves to invest $I_1^C(\theta)$, irrespective of the realized state η. They also have the incentive to pay themselves any excess after-tax cash flows, $(1 - \tau_c)(f(I_0,\eta) - I_1^C(\theta))$, as dividends. Paying *less* than they are allowed to by the constraints would amount to redistributing wealth *to* the bondholders. Consequently unexpectedly large (small) cash dividends are associated with good (bad) realized states of the world. Indeed, a large body of empirical evidence documents positive (negative) stock price reaction to announcements of unexpectedly large (small) dividends (see footnote 1).

The net effect of announcements of unexpectedly large cash dividends on the market value of the outstanding bonds is less clear. These payments are associated with the good states of the world, but at the same time they also reduce the ex-dividend market value of the firm. In our model, all the after-tax excess cash flows are paid out. By doing that, the stockholders prevent the bondholders from participating in the gains which are associated with the good realized states of the world. Notice, however, that our model allows the stockholders to forego their legal right for limited liability, without cost. If such were the world, the stockholders of a θ-type firm have incentives to precommit at $t = 0$ to undertake the optimal $I_1^C(\theta)$ even in states of the world in which the realized new equity required, $I_1^C(\theta) - f(I_0,\eta)$, is very large. It follows that, in the environment of costless contracting described in our model, bond prices would not be affected by dividend reductions as well. However, typically stockholders would find it contractually costly to give up their legal right of limited liability. Consequently, a precommitment at time $t = 0$ to a large issue of new equity at $t = 1$ becomes infeasible (i.e., it is not incentive-compatible). As a result, a small realized cash flow which would require a large issue of new equity would result in underinvestment. Therefore, typically bond prices are expected to fall when dividends are unexpectedly reduced. Recent empirical evidence (see Woolridge (1983) and Handjinicolaou and Kalay (1984)) is consistent with these predictions. When dividends are unexpectedly reduced, bond prices fall, whereas there is no effect on bond prices when dividends are unexpectedly increased.

Evidence on the informational content of share repurchases. A common share repurchase is a substitute for cash dividends in that the repurchasing firm distributes cash to some of its stockholders to acquire a part of the outstanding equity. The firm can repurchase its own shares in the open market via a broker like any other investor. Alternatively, it could attempt to buy the stocks via a tender offer in which it specifies the tender price, the number of shares which are to be repurchased, and the period of time during which the offer is outstanding. Open-market repurchases differ from cash dividends by being smaller, infrequent, and usually not disclosed to the public. Stock repurchases via tender offer, in contrast, are announced and data on price response to them are available. Thus, recent research has focused on the behavior of security prices around tender offers.

The behavior of stock prices around and during the period of a tender offer have been recently documented by Masulis (1980), Dann (1981), Rosenfeld (1982), Dann and DeAngelo (1983) and Bradley and Wakeman (1983). The mean tender offer premium is 22.46 percent, whereas the mean postexpiration price drop is much smaller. Notice that the payment of the premium should have resulted in a postexpiration price which is lower than the preannouncement price. The documented permanent price increase suggests a reevaluation of the stock associated with the tender offer to repurchase it.

The effects of stock repurchases on the market value of the outstanding debt have been investigated by Dann (1981). He reports that bond prices are not affected by the announcements of share repurchases. These empirical regularities are consistent with our theory.[20] For a given firm, a share repurchase is an infrequent and unpredictable event. Therefore, announcements of a share repurchase can be viewed as an *unexpected increase in dividends*. As argued above, our theory predicts that such announcements would lead to stock price increases and would not affect bond prices. The empirical evidence on the effects of share repurchases is consistent with this prediciton. It is also very similar to the evidence on the effects of announcements of unexpected cash dividend changes presented by Handjinicoloau and Kalay (1984).

Notice that, similarly to share repurchases which are substitutes for unexpected cash dividend increases, new issues of equity are substitutes for unexpected dividend reductions. New issues of equity are essentially negative dividends and in our model are associated with bad realized states of the world. This prediction is consistent with recently documented empirical evidence. Korwar (1980) and Asquith and Mullins (1983) find that stock prices react negatively to announcements of new issues of equity. Thus, consistent with our theory, new issues of equity seem like a substitute for unexpected cash dividend reductions and have similar effects on stock prices.

Indirect evidence on the signaling value of "expected dividends". Recent empirical research on the informational content of cash dividends and share repurchases has focused almost exclusively on the effects of unexpected changes in their magnitude on security prices. In the case of cash dividends, a dividend expectation model is typically estimated. The actual cash dividends at time t are then subtracted from the expected cash dividends at this time (as viewed from time $t - 1$). The effect of the unexpected change is then estimated. In the case of share repurchases, the implicit assumption is that the market expects none. Therefore, the total amount is considered to be unexpected.

Our theory predicts that the insiders can use optimal precommitments of minimum investments to convey their firm type to the market. In particular, the firms with the "better" investment opportunities would choose a more binding dividend constraint. By doing so they are precommitted to a lower *expected payout*. An indirect test of this empirical implication is contained in Kalay (1979) who found that firms with (other things being constant) larger growth potential (i.e., larger supply of non-negative NPV projects) choose a "tighter" dividend constraint. This evidence is consistent with our theory, which suggests that smaller *expected dividends* resulting from tighter dividend constraints are good signals.

CONCLUSION

When risky debt is outstanding, the stockholders of a levered firm (modeled as insiders) have incentives to underinvest. It is in their own best interest to precommit to minimum levels of investments by self-imposing constraints on their future ability to pay dividends. This is true even in an environment where the firms type is known to the market. In this paper we show that, when there is precontractual information asymmetry, the optimal constraints chosen by the stockholders can correctly signal its type to the market. The optimal precommitment made by the better firms implies a large minimum investment in the future. If the poor firms were to choose the same precommitment they would have to overinvest. The resulting (endogenous) costs of overinvestment constitute a penalty for false signaling. A nondissapative signaling equilibrium would result if these costs were large enough. In other words, the optimal constraints chosen to solve the underinvestment problem (in a world with symmetric information) can serve as a signaling device as well in a world with asymmetric information.

The signaling equilibrium derived in this paper implies that firms with better investment opportunities would choose tighter dividend constraints. The lower *expected dividends* which are implied by the tighter constraints would serve as good signals. However, under a given set of constraints prescribed at the contracting time, it is in stockholders' best interests to pay out any unexpected increase in the realized cash flows at $t = 1$. Paying less than anticipated by the bondholders would amount to redistributing wealth to them. Therefore, announcements of unexpected dividend increases can be associated with good states of the world.

Our theory predicts that the insiders can use optimal precommitments of minimum investments to convey their firm type to the market. A direct implication is that, for the same face value, bonds of firms with tighter constraints will have a higher market value. This result derives from the association between a tighter constraint and a superior technology in the signaling equilibrium. Needless to say, a direct test of this relationship is difficult.

The signaling equilibrium of our model further yields a new measure of expected dividends based on the optimal payout constraints. These expected dividends can be used as a proper benchmark in future studies of announcement effects of unexpected changes in payout. In fact, in past studies attention has been focused on these announcement effects (see footnote 1). Although our model does not focus on these announcement effects, we survey the existing empirical evidence and point out that it is consistent with our model.

Notes

1. The effects of unexpected changes in cash dividends on security prices were examined in Fama, Fischer, Jensen, and Roll (1969), Pettit (1972), Charest (1978), Aharony and Swary (1980), Penman (1983), Woolridge (1983), Handjinicolaou and Kalay (1984). Evidence on the effects of share repurchases can be found in Masulis (1980), Dann (1981), Vermaelen (1981), Bradley and Wakeman (1983), Rosenfeld (1982), and Dann and DeAngelo (1983). Finally, evidence on new issues of equity is documented by Korwar (1980) and Asquith and Mullins (1983).
2. Motivated by the assumption of perfect capital markets, the firm has been traditionally viewed as a homogeneous unit whose clear objective is to maximize its market value. However, in an environment of costly contracting, some recent research, (e.g., Black and Scholes (1973), Fama and Miller (1972), Galai and Masulis (1975), Jensen and Meckling (1976), John and Kalay (1982), John and Williams (1982a, b), Kalay (1979, 1982), Myers (1977), and Smith and Warner (1979) has portrayed the firm as a collection of competing groups whose interests can conflict.
3. See Myers (1977), Jensen and Meckling (1976), and Smith and Warner (1979).
4. Throughout the paper we define dividends to include share repurchases and all other cash payments to the stockholders. Hence the words "payout" and "dividends" are used interchangeably.
5. The signaling mechanism is said to be nondissipative if the signaling equilibrium involves no deadweight loss, i.e., there is no loss of welfare in comparison to a symmetric information equilibrium. Our

usage of the word "nondissipative" is in the same sense as in Rothschild and Stiglitz (1976).

6. In this paper we consider only the case of a finite number of firms. The existence of a separating signaling equilibrium can be proved for the case of a continuum of firms, but the equilibrium may not be nondissipative. See also footnote 10.
7. Under a given set of constraints, the bondholders would correctly anticipate the implied future dividends and price the bonds accordingly. Therefore, it is in the interest of the stockholders to pay out any unexpected increase in the realized cash flows at $t = 1$. Paying less than that would amount to redistributing wealth to the bondholders.
8. Myers (1977) was the first to demonstrate this incentive. In this section we employ a scenario similar to his to demonstrate our basic idea.
9. Our model does not distinguish between inside and outside equity. In particular we assume that the insider—manager maximizes stockholders' wealth. Therefore, the informational asymmetry will have an impact on the pricing of external claims, namely, the bonds.
10. The extension to the case when Θ is a continuum, say $\Theta = [\underline{\theta},\overline{\theta}]$ can be done by verifying a set of sufficient conditions given in Riley (1979, p. 334–35). It does not seem to yield any new insights to the problem studied here. Moreover, Θ being finite does not seem to be an unnatural restriction.
11. This assumption details a tax structure which is consistent with the equilibrium described in DeAngelo and Masulis (1980), i.e., the marginal tax the bondholders are paying on income is less than the corporate tax rate. For simplicity (and without loss of generality) we choose the case where personal taxes are zero. This tax structure provides a leverage-related benefit; however, it is not crucial to our analysis. As it will be clear to the reader, debt in our model has signaling value.
12. The assumption of risk neutrality is made only for convenience. More generally in a risk-averse economy, pricing of claims in the complete market setting can be accomplished by calculating expectations with respect to a market-determined, unique, state-price density function. See Ross (1978) for details.
13. The corporation is assumed to have a finite number of positive NPV projects. In equilibrium, investment in financial claims which are traded in a perfect capital market provides the investor zero NPV. In our economy, however, given assumption A.5, investment in the financial markets by the corporation for its claimholders would provide a negative NPV. Thus, our firm has a limited supply of projects with nonnegative NPV. Taxes, however, provide only one rationale for limiting the supply of nonnegative NPV projects. Agency costs of outside funds would make investment in the financial market by the corporation (which has zero NPV to a regular investor) of negative NPV. The assumption that the supply of nonnegative NPV projects is limited has some additional real-world basis. The tax on "improper profit accumulation" can affect the supply of zero net present value

projects. By retaining earnings beyond the "reasonable needs of business" the corporation is providing evidence of its intent to avoid income tax paid by its stockholders. Among the major elements determining whether the tax avoidance purpose is present are the corporation's dividend history and investment of undistributed earnings in assets unrelated to the corporation's business. Investment in the financial market is viewed as investment not related to the purpose of the business. Hence, including the expected costs due to the accumulated earnings' tax, those projects can have negative net present value. Admittedly, very few publicly held corporations have been prosecuted under this law. However, this can be an equilibrium result; firms can avoid this cost by paying dividends. Moreover, investing in assets having no reasonable connection with the purpose of the business can bring on a searching enquiry. Thus, costs can be imposed even without actual prosecution.

14. As stated, the optimal precommitment contract forces the stockholders to gain enough equity at time t = 1 to undertake $I_1^C(\theta)$. For low levels of realized after-tax cash flows at $t = 1$, $(1 - \tau_C)f(I_0,\eta)$, stockholders can have the incentive to default on the contract and turn over the firm to the bondholders, rather than to raise the required equity. If stockholders retain their right to do so, the effective investment would be less than $I_1^C(\theta)$ in some realized states, η. Since this is correctly incorporated in the pricing of the bonds, it would reduce stockholders' wealth. The stockholders can solve this problem in two ways. First, when allowed by the legal environment, they would give up their right to default on the contracts (i.e., many loan agreements include collateralization of personal wealth). Second, in our model the optimal face value of the debt, F, might be such that it will always be in the interest of insiders at $t = 1$ to undertake the optimal investment, $I_1^C(\theta)$.

15. John and Kalay (1982) derive optimal payout constraints in an environment of costly contracting induced by postcontractual informational asymmetry. The cost of contracting is introduced by requiring that all contracts offered by the stockholders have to be measurable with respect to the coarser information structure of the bondholders. In particular, the information structure in the economy is represented by a sequence of refining partitions of Ω, $\{F_t : t = 0, 1, 2\}$. $\{F_t^s : t = 0, 1, 2\}$ denotes the information structure of the stockholders and $\{F_t^B : t = 0, 1, 2\}$ that of the bond market. At contracting time ($t = 0$) the bondholders and the stockholders have the same information; without loss of generality, $F_0^s = F_0^B = \{\{\Omega\}\}$, the trivial partition. However, at $t = 1$, there is a partial resolution of uncertainty and the stockholders' information is better than that of the bondholders, i.e., F_1^s is strictly finer than F_1^B. η denotes the generic element of $F_1^s = \{\eta_1, \eta_2, \ldots, \eta_n\}$ and ϕ the generic element of $F_1^B\{\phi_1, \phi_2, \ldots\ldots, \phi_m\}$. Each ϕ_1 may be thought of as a meta state (lumpy state) containing many η_s. One interpretation of the coarser information structure of the bondholders is that the bondholders observe the true level of aggregate cash flows, say X_1, at time $t = 1$ and identify the meta state, say ϕ_i of ηs which could have generated it. But it is prohibitively costly for them to resolve ϕ_i any finer. On the other hand, stockholders

know exactly what $\eta\epsilon\phi_i$ is realized (i.e., $\eta\epsilon F_1^S$) and can make their contingent investment decisions appropriately. Since the optimal contracts are measurable with respect to F_1^B, they result in underinvestment or overinvestment in various states of the world. The solution to the conflict of interest between the bondholders and the stockholders is, therefore, *costly*. Even under the optimal package of constraints, there are residual agency costs.

16. We do not model the specific choice of F^0. As it is known, the tax-related benefits of debt could be optimally offset by some cost of having debt.
17. Empirical examination of the self-binding dividend constraints which are included in the bond indentures (Kalay (1979, 1982)) shows that stockholders do not pay themselves the maximum allowed dividend. In other words, they maintain a reservoir of payable funds which are available for debt and investment-financed dividends under the most restrictive constraint. Potential explanations for the existence of these reservoirs are analyzed in John and Kalay (1982). Briefly stated, the existence of the reservoirs provides optimal flexibility in an environment of costly contracting. The economy described in this paper allows the stockholders (based on the information they have at contracting time) to specify the optimal level of investment appropriate for their firm type, i.e., $I_1^C(\theta)$ via the optimal payout constraint. As a result, stockholders do not have an incentive to maintain reservoirs. However, modeling the economy such that stockholders would have the incentive to maintain reservoirs would not change the empirical implications detailed in this section.
18. Our model assumes that the optimal investment at time 1, $I_1^C(\theta)$, depends only on firm type, θ. A simple extension would allow this investment to depend on the realized cash flow as well. As long as the correlation between the realized cash flow and the future investment opportunities is negative, zero or even positive but small, unexpectedly large (small) dividends would be associated with good (bad) realized states of the world.
19. Note that, in this model, once the precontractual asymmetry of information is resolved through the signal (debt contracts) there is no further asymmetry of information between insiders and the market. Thus the market and the insiders are equally informed about any resolution of uncertainty at $t = 1$. Higher realization of earnings is associated with higher stock prices. For reasons mentioned, higher earnings states are also characterized by higher payouts and thus the observed positive correlation between payouts and stock price response. For some patterns of resolution of uncertainty (e.g., smoothly over time) not in phase with the payout announcement dates, the explanation of announcement effects might not be clear-cut in a symmetric information setting.
20. Several explanations of this empirical evidence have been suggested. Vermaelen (1982) argues that a tender offer to repurchase stocks serves as a signaling device. When the "true" value of the stock is higher than the market price, managers can offer to buy back stocks at a premium. A signaling equilibrium can exist because signaling

falsely (i.e., offering to buy back stocks at a premium when the "true" value is not higher than the market price) is costly. Alternative explanations of the observed behavior of security prices around share repurchases have been suggested. First, by repurchasing a significant fraction of the equity outstanding, the leverage ratio increases. This increment in the leverage ratio can have two effects on stockholders' wealth. First, it increases the per-share tax shield. Second, it can redistribute wealth from the bondholders. Alternatively, stock repurchases can cause a "permanent" stock price increase if the effective tax on cash dividends is higher than that of realized long-term capital gains and share repurchases are substitutes for cash dividends.

REFERENCES

Aharony J. and I. Swary. "Quarterly Dividend and Earnings Announcements and Stockholders' Returns: An Empirical Analysis." *Journal of Finance* 35 (1980), pp. 1–12.

Asquith R. and D. W. Mullins. "The Impact of Initiating Dividend Payments on Shareholders' Wealth." *Journal of Business*, 56, No. 1 (1983), pp. 78–96.

Asquith P. and D. W. Mullins. "Equity Issues and Stock Price Dilutions." Working Paper, Harvard Business School, 1983.

Bhattacharya S. "Imperfect Information, Dividend Policy," and "The Bird in the Hand Fallacy." *Bell Journal of Economics* 10, No. 1 (1979).

Bhattacharya S. "Nondissipative Signaling Structures and Dividend Policy." *Quarterly Journal of Economics*, 95 (1980), pp. 1–24.

Black F. and M. Scholes. "The Pricing of Options and Corporate Liabilities." *Journal of Political Economy* 81 (1973), pp. 637–59.

Bradley M. and L. Wakeman. "The Wealth Effects of Targeted Share Repurchases." *Journal of Financial Economic* 11 (1983), pp. 301–28.

Charest G. "Dividend Information, Stock Returns and Market Efficiency, II." *Journal of Financial Economics* 6 (1978), pp. 297–330.

Dann L. "The Effect of Common Stock Repurchases on Securityholders' Returns." *Journal of Financial Economics* 9 (1981), pp. 113–38.

Dann L. and H. DeAngelo. "Standstill Agreements, Privately Negotiated Stock Repurchases, and the Market for Corporate Control." *Journal of Financial Economics* 11 (1983), pp. 275–300.

DeAngelo H., and R. Masulis. "Optimal Capital Structure Under Corporate and Personal Taxation." *Journal of Financial Economics* 8 (1980), pp. 3–29.

Fama E. and M. Miller. *The Theory of Finance*, New York: Holt, Rinehart & Winston, 1972.

Fama E., L. Fisher, M. Jensen, and R. Roll. "The Adjustment of Stock

Prices to New Information." *International Economic Review* 10 (1969), pp. 1–21.

Galai D. and R. Masulis. "The Option Pricing Model and The Risk Factor of Stocks." *Journal of Financial Economics* 3 (1976), pp. 53–82.

Handjinicolaou G. and A. Kalay. "Wealth Redistribution Changes in Firm Value: An Analysis of Returns to the Bondholders and to the Stockholders." *Journal of Financial Economics*, forthcoming.

Jensen M. and W. Meckling. "Theory of the Firm: Management Behavior, Agency Costs and Capital Structure." *Journal of Financial Economics* 3 (1976), pp. 305–60.

John K. and A. Kalay. "Costly Contracting and Optimal Payout Constraints." *Journal of Finance* 37, No. 2 (1982), pp. 457–70.

John K. and J. Williams. "Financial Signaling with Agency Costs." Working paper, New York University, 1982a.

John K. and J. Williams. "Dividends, Dilution and Taxes: A Signaling Equilibrium." Working paper, New York University, 1982b.

Kalay A. "Corporate Dividend Policy: A Collection of Related Essays." Ph.D Thesis, University of Rochester, Graduate School of Management, 1979.

Kalay A. "Stockholder-Bondholder Conflict and Dividend Constraints." *Journal of Financial Economics* No. 10 1982.

Korwar A. N. "The Effect of New Issues of Equity." Unpublished manuscript, University of California, Los Angeles, 1980.

Leland H. and D. Pyle. "Information Asymmetry, Financial Structure and Financial Intermediation." *Journal of Finance* 22 (1977), pp. 371–87.

Masulis R. "Stock Repurchases by Tender Offer: An Analysis of the Causes of Common Stock Price Changes." *The Journal of Finance* 35, No. 2 (1980), pp. 305–19.

Miller M. and F. Modigliani. "Dividend Policy, Growth and the Valuation of Shares." *Journal of Business* 4 (1961), pp. 411–33.

Miller M. and K. Rock. "Dividend Policy under Asymmetric Information." Unpublished manuscript, University of Chicago, 1982.

Myers S. "Determinants of Corporate Borrowing." *Journal of Financial Economics* 5 (1977), pp. 147–75.

Penman S. H. "The Predictive Content of Earnings Forecasts and Dividends." *Journal of Finance* 38, No. 4 (1983), pp. 1181–99.

Pettit R. "Dividend Announcements, Security Performance and Capital Market Efficiency." *Journal of Finance* 27, No. 2 (1972), pp. 993–1008.

Riley J. "Informational Equilibrium." *Econometrica* 47 (1979), pp. 331–59.

Rosenfeld A. "Information Adjusted Premiums and Stockholders Response to Stock Repurchases Tenders." Working paper, Purdue University, 1982.

Ross S. "The Determination of Financial Structure: The Incentive Signaling Approach." *The Bell Journal of Economics* 8 (1977), pp. 23–40.

Ross S. "A Simple Approach to the Valuation of Risky Streams." *Journal of Business* 51 (1978), pp. 453–76.

Rothschild M. and J. Stiglitz. "Equilibrium in Competitive Insurance Markets: An Essay on the Economics of Imperfect Information." *Quarterly Journal of Economics* 91 (1976), pp. 629–49.

Smith C. and J. Warner. "On Financial Contracting: An Analysis of Bond Covenants." *Journal of Financial Economics* 7, No. 2 (1979), pp. 117–61.

Spence M. "Job Market Signaling." *Quarterly Journal of Economics* 88 (1973), pp. 355–74.

Vermaelen T. "Common Stock Repurchases and Market Signaling." *Journal of Financial Economics* 9 (1981), pp. 139–83.

Watts R. "The Information Content of Dividends." *Journal of Business* 46 (1973), pp. 191–211.

Woolridge J. R. "Dividend Changes and Security Prices." *Journal of Finance* 38, No. 5 (1983), pp. 1607–15.

---

* This research was supported by a Presidential Research Fellowship and a summer research grant from New York University. This project was completed during 1983–84 when Kose John was an awardee of the Battery march Fellowship. We also gratefully acknowledge the helpful comments of Amir Barnea, Alan Kraus, Uri Loewenstein, Bani Mishra, David Nachman, Sang Park, Ramasastry Ambarish, Marti Subrahmanyam, Joseph Williams, and participants in seminars at New York University, Western Finance Association, Eastern Finance Association, and European Finance Association meetings where earlier versions of this paper were presented.

6

Concepts and Practice of Agency Theory within the Corporation

John T. Hackett
Executive Vice President
and Chief Financial Officer
Cummins Engine Company

Concepts and Practice of Agency Theory within the Corporation

Professors Michael Jensen and Clifford Smith have presented an interesting analysis of the application of agency theory to the complex relationships between shareholders, managers, and creditors of publicly owned business corporations.

Although the term *agency theory* or *agency problems* is not commonly used in corporate lexicon, the concept of divergent claims on the resources and behavior of corporations has received increasing attention during the past 20 years. Thus, corporate managers have been required to devote greater attention to the resulting conflicts and complexities associated with an increasing number of petitioners who wish to participate in corporate decision making.

But it is unrealistic to assume that the agency problems of corporations are limited to the conflicting claims of shareholders, managers, and creditors. The inherent interests of the labor force, suppliers, customers, and the organized societies in which corporations operate must also be included among the agency claimants, and managers have realized limited success in attempting to reconcile the myriad of requests for representation and participation among these corporate stakeholders.

Moreover, the existing body of economic and business theory provides little assistance to managers who seek to achieve an appropriate balance between the conflicting claims. Economic theory addresses the problem of maximization and distribution of economic wealth in a relatively short time period. Business theory concentrates on achieving optimal profit performance in an equally short time. There is no established theory that addresses the conflicts that may arise between maximization of wealth for shareholders and the protection of the environment. Nor have economists provided much assistance to managers who must achieve a compromise between the conflicting demands of those who seek a faster pace of economic growth and others who wish to protect limited natural resources.

Consequently, corporate stakeholders whose interests are not recognized in economic theory and business practice seek representation by other means; for example, the passage of labor legislation and more rigorous regulation of financial institutions during the 1930s and the establishment of environmental legislation in the 1970s. In addition, the recent passage of legislation by several states restricting the export of employment, the inclusion of labor union representatives on the board of directors of European corporations, and the current revaluation of public utility regulation and management practices represent techniques by which corporate stakeholders influence the behavior of corporations and gain greater representation in decision making.

Jensen and Smith argue, and I quote directly from their paper,

> Construction of a theory of organizations involves describing the equilibrium behavior of these complex contractual systems where the individual agent is the elementary unit of analysis in that system and the exogenous variables are individual's preferences and opportunity sets. (Jensen and Smith, pp. 1 and 2 of the first draft of the survey paper which appears in this volume.)

Although I agree with their thesis, I believe that current economic and business theory is an inadequate explanation of the financial and organizational behavior of publicly held corporations because it considers only a narrow and traditional group of agents. In addition, current theory also fails to recognize the impact of institutional changes on the behavior of even traditional agents.

Many of the underlying assumptions in the theory of financial and organizational behavior regarding management techniques employed by large, publicly owned corporations are inaccurate and unrealistic and, therefore, render the theory inadequate. For example, Jensen and Smith argue in their section on control and conflict between managers and stockholders that:

> Competition among vice presidents for recognition and advancement provides an important source of information to the board level control mechanism and reduces the likelihood that top level managers will take actions in conflict with maximization of the value of the firm. (Jensen and Smith, Chapter 4 of this volume).

There are several specious assumptions in this argument. First, I disagree that all decisions proposed by senior management and approved by the board of directors are intended to maximize the value of the firm. Second, I question the assumption that members of boards of directors of large corporations have, or even desire to establish, sufficient contact with upper middle management so as to provide a means of monitoring the decisions of senior management. Finally, I cannot be convinced that the upper middle management of large corporations believe that decisions regarding their individual promotions and advancement are initiated by the board of directors.

Jensen and Smith also suggest that differences in attitudes regarding time horizons create conflicts between the objectives of managers and other financial claimholders, namely shareholders.

> The manager's claim on the corporation is generally limited to his tenure with the firm. The corporation, on the other hand, has an indefinite life, and stockholder claims are tradeable claims of the entire future stream of residual cash flows. Managers therefore have incentives to place lower values on cash flows occurring beyond their horizon than is implied by the values of these cash flows.

If I interpret the authors correctly, they suggest that current shareholders of large corporations have a greater interest in long-term cash flows and earnings than management, because an individual manager's interest does not extend beyond his tenure.

The internal rate of return techniques taught at graduate schools of business and employed by most large corporations and the portfolio investment analysis used by institutional investors challenge the author's assumptions. My experience suggests that management's time horizon is usually much longer than that of the institutional shareholder. Therefore, if a conflict exists between management and shareholders regarding the time horizon used in developing an investment strategy, it centers around the conflict between the intermediate term outlook of management and the institutional investor's preoccupation with current-year earnings estimates.

Perhaps no clearer illustration of the conflicting objectives of agents of corporations exists than the problems that have beset the electric power industry. Throughout the 1960s and early 1970s the industry benefited from what has been described as "regulatory lag." As the demand for electric power increased, public utilities were able to realize lower costs per unit of power produced by constructing new and more efficient power generation facilities, but public utility commissions were slow to require the utilities to reduce their rates to reflect the lower operating costs. Thus, the companies promoted the use of electric power and undertook massive capital expenditure programs to increase their production capacity and achieve further cost reductions. The profitability and cash flow of electric public utilities reflected these favorable conditions.

However, after 1974 the cost of fuel increased rapidly and power companies discovered that regulatory lag worked to their disadvantage. As the cost of fuel rose the operating costs of electric utilities advanced dramatically, but the public utility regulatory agencies were equally slow to approve rate increases. Thus, the cash flow and profits of the utilities were depressed, and rapid price inflation resulted in higher construction costs and interest rates which further damaged their financial performance.

Nevertheless, as the economy expanded in the 1970s, so did the demand for electricity, and the utilities continued to plan for additional power-generating capacity. Their assumptions regarding future demand were based largely on their collective experience of the previous decade. They failed to foresee that a reduction in the rate of economic growth, coupled with substantial increases in the cost of electricity, would result in a reduction in demand. In addition, public utility managers, like other corporate managements, underestimated increases in construction costs and interest rates. Finally, assuming that the cost of fossil fuels would continue to increase (we all remember the $5 per gallon gasoline price forecast) a significant number of utilities decided to undertake construction of nuclear power-generating facilities to achieve lower operating costs.

The cumulative effect of these decisions resulted in critical financial problems for many of the nation's electric utilities, and these problems have been further complicated by massive cost overruns in power plant construction, growing resistance to nuclear power, and refusal of public utility commissions to permit financial relief to the utilities by allowing construction and interest costs to be included in the rate base before power-generating facilities are actually in operation.

There are many agency issues involved in this dilemma. Perhaps the most controversial revolves around who will be required to pay for the excess power-generating capacity and the construction cost overruns.

The companies and their shareholders argue that the generating facilities were created to serve the consumer, and the excess capacity ensures that there will be no service interruptions. Therefore, the additional cost of creating these facilities should be recaptured through rate increases. If the shareholder is required to absorb the cost of these miscalculations, the ability of the utilities to raise additional equity capital needed to build additional power-generating facilities to replace those built during the 1950s and 1960s will be impeded.

Consumer advocates and ratepayer organizations reject these arguments. They contend that consumers have already absorbed enormous rate increases as a result of higher fuel and capital costs passed on by the utilities, and they insist that the utilities should not be allowed to recover the costs of management errors by including them in the rate base.

The creditors and bondholders are concerned about the deterioration in credit ratings among electric utilities. The adjustment of bond ratings has resulted in declines in market value of many utility bonds. Lending institutions and individual bondholders want to be assured that the utilities will be granted sufficient rate increases to adequately cover the payment of interest and principal, and they are also concerned about the companies' ability to sustain sufficient equity capital to protect the creditors.

Conservationists assert that nuclear power plants are unsafe and will cause permanent damage to the environment. They cite the Three Mile Island incident and other regulatory violations by nuclear power plant operators as evidence of the inherent danger associated with nuclear power. At the same time, growing concern regarding the harmful effects of acid rain from coal burning has generated resistance toward additional coal-fired plants. Yet, coal represents the most cost-effective alternative to nuclear power.

Proponents of economic growth and expansion argue that we must maintain the capacity to produce large amounts of electrical power at competitive rates to bolster our position in regional and world trade. Therefore, they campaign for new power capacity to replace older, less efficient plants and reduce the cost of electric power.

Finally, the public utility regualtory agencies are expected to resolve these conflicting objectives by applying legislation and regulations that were written many years ago and have little relevance to the problems they are attempting to solve.

The current problems of the electric power industry also reveal another interesting development in the relationship between corporate stakeholders. Investor-owned utilities that have encountered financial difficulties and have petitioned for higher rates have frequently been challenged regarding their capital structure and dividend policies. In the negotiations between the utilities and the regulatory agencies, management's arguments regarding the role of the equity investor frequently diverge from traditional financial theory.

Utility managements submit that the dividend payments to common shareholders must be treated in much the same fashion as interest on debt or dividends on preferred shares. The "residual concept," usually assigned to common shareholders, is rejected. They assert that, unless the payment of dividends to common shareholders can be ensured, the availability of additional equity to finance future capital requirements will be in jeopardy.

Thus, it can be argued that the ratepayer is being asked to assume the traditional role of the equity investor by absorbing rate increases sufficient to ensure that the common shareholders receive an uninterrupted and increasing stream of dividend payments. In addition, the reported profits of many utilities contain an accounting fiction referred to as "allowance for funds used during construction" (AFUDC), a theoretical rate of return on the funds invested in construction, assuming the construction were complete and could be included in the rate base. It is not uncommon among utilities engaged in nuclear power plant construction for more than one half of the reported earnings to be comprised of AFUDC. Although there is no cash inflow associated with the AFUDC portion of reported earnings, electric utilities continue to pay out high proportions of reported earnings as dividends to shareholders. Consequently, some utilities have been required to use borrowing capacity to maintain their dividend payments to shareholders.

If utility managers' arguments are accepted and we assume that the ratepayer is the equity investor, then wouldn't the ratepayer be better served if the utilities maintained a capital structure comprised entirely of debt, thereby gaining the leverage and tax advantage for the ratepayer that normally accrues to equity investors?

In addition, the traditional objection of bondholders regarding the loss of protection by eliminating equity investors is invalid if management insists that, regardless of operating performance or the quality of management, the equity investor should receive a competitive rate of return. Protection to secured and senior creditors could be established by substituting subordinated debt for equity.

Thus, an alternative solution would treat all investors as creditors and the ratepayer would assume the role of equity investor. In other words, investor-owned utilities become cooperatives. The utility rate-making process could ensure that the ratepayer received the benefits and assumed the risks normally associated with equity investors. This approach might also ensure that electric utilities are able to retain a larger proportion of their earnings for reinvestment purposes which may better serve the ratepayer.

The current problems of the electric power industry provide examples of the complex problems associated with corporate stakeholders. The deregulation of the airline and trucking industries provides yet another, as does the current restructuring of American Telephone and Telegraph Company and its operating subsidiaries.

The foregoing examples also demonstrate that the traditional role and relationships between corporate agents can be altered significantly as a result of unusual and unique circumstances, and they are frequently shaped and influenced by forces and special-interest groups that are not recognized in traditional economic and business theory.

My minor criticisms of the Jensen and Smith paper are not intended to detract from the importance of the research and thought the authors provide regarding agency theory. We should encourage research that examines the problems associated with corporate stakeholders. However, it is important that we approach the problem from a broader perspective than that associated with traditional economic theory. In our society, a list of corporate stakeholders includes far more participants than just those who furnish economic resources.

7

Stockholder, Manager, and Creditor Interests: Applications of Agency Theory and Informational Content of Optimal Dividend Constraints

Robert S. Kay
Partner
Touche Ross & Co.

Stockholder, Manager, and Creditor Interests: Applications of Agency Theory and Informational Content of Optimal Dividend Constraints

INTRODUCTION

As a practicing accountant, I'd like to give a well-reasoned accounting commentary on the papers. As so often is the case, however, economics and finance theories are slow to be recognized by the accounting profession. We're light years away from any semblance of recordkeeping for the countless nuances of each single transaction; yet the papers I am asked to critique have a strong focus on some of these nuances. Accordingly, I am here more to learn than to preach, and I will make only a few points.

Robert Jensen in the October 1975 *Accounting Review* (pp. 871–73) presented an anecdote regarding "Truth versus Fiction versus Something." This good-natured polemic on academic research not only scored the Greek alphabet, it challenged much research as "paddling powerfully toward the white cliffs of the obvious." I never learned lower case Greek, and therefore I could easily relate to Bob Jensen's criticism of much published research whose formulas frightened many of the intended readers. Let me suggest early on that this will be my excuse for a limited analysis of the second paper by John and Kalay.

As to the "white cliffs" part, neither paper presents information that is obvious—at least not to me. However, some of their points seem intuitive, and it's helpful to have support for intuition.

Stockholder, manager and creditor interests: applications of agency theory, by Michael C. Jensen and Clifford W. Smith, Jr.

I read the Jensen and Smith paper once, twice, a third time. It seemed to grow on me each time I read it. The explanation and presentation of agency theory is a structured explanation of learned phenomena, more communicative than I have generally seen. For the most part I agree with what is said, as the paper is up-to-date and consistent with my observed world of financial accounting and reporting practice.

My complaint is that "life isn't nearly so simple," and "people and organizations are not limited-option machines." The paper focuses on the specific areas of stockholders versus managers and creditors versus stockholders. To deal with possible diversities in interests, the paper seems to require the reader to infer assumptions about the lack of extraneous and interrelated influences. Clearing away these "obstacles" to pinpoint analysis may be necessary, but as an impatient accounting practitioner I want all the answers at once, and not a narrow and deep review of a few aspects. This complaint is, of course, exaggerated, but academia so often dismisses it as rhetoric.

The research in this paper clearly is simplified in relation to reality, but I recognize that we can't understand the complex without first understanding the basics.

Informational content of optimal dividend constraints, by Kose John and Avner Kalay

Although the John and Kalay paper is written mostly in Greek, I cannot argue with the logic to the extent that I have assimilated it. From my perspective, I think the paper neglects the manager aspect of a business organization, so thoroughly explored by Jensen and Smith; and it sets up only owners ("modeled" as insiders) and lenders. The reader is asked, for purposes of the paper, to ignore the overwhelming reality of absentee ownership.

The premise of this paper is that growth firms will or should pay less (dividends) to their owners, because they have better (reinvestment) uses for their cash flow. I think most pay no dividends because creditors won't allow them, as a practical matter. Although the authors' view seems incongruent with reality, their bridging is found in the "reservoir fund" of amounts usable either for dividends or investment.

A few additional "real-world" observations seem under-recognized in the paper:

1. It is true that overpayment of dividends can destroy a firm. By the same token, underpayment can be just as fatal, and perhaps just as subtle.
2. Just how important are dividends? Growth companies don't pay them. High-tech companies are not likely to be "cash cows." While some mature companies (old Ma Bell, for example) feel they must pay a dividend because their shareholders really look upon the investment as if it were an indexed fixed-income security, the market seems to better reward growth and future prospects. This results in an increase in the market value of the security, generating an ability for owners to obtain cash flow through sale of the investment, rather than through dividends.
3. A firm's future prospects are determinative of its ability to float equity or debt. The creditworthiness (i.e., desirability as an investment) of the company is heavily dependent on an assessment of its future.

Overall commentary

My comments regarding the two papers admittedly have not been penetrating but, having provided them, I am now entitled to expostulate.

The authors tend to characterize investments as "only this" or "only that," like "equity" or "debt." There are in fact only gradations of investments in corporate entities, ranging downward from off-balance sheet contracts such as project financings and leases, to recognized debt secured by property having a value clearly equal to the present value of the debt at current rates at any point in time, to purely speculative residual holders who get whatever's left—if anything.

To attract investors who begin at the spectrum of total security working downward, there is a negotiated cost, all factors discussed by the authors and many more being involved. To attract investors who are as far down on the totem pole as speculative residual holders, they must have an expectation of dividends and increase in the market value of their residual equity. In between there are endless varieties of hybrids, some of them exotic. To name a few:

1. Capital leases.
2. Property use under tolling agreements.
3. Product financings.

4. Project financings.
5. Adjustable-rate convertible notes.
6. Adjustable-rate preferred stocks.
7. Mandatory-redemption preferred stocks.
8. Mortgage-backed preferred stocks.
9. Convertible and exchangable debt.
10. Warrants—real and synthetic.
11. Commodity-backed bonds.
12. Publicly traded limited partnership units.
    And on and on. . . .

In addition, there are variations in markets in which these investments trade—for example, the United States, Europe, the Far East. Cross-currency swaps, foreign-currency placements, arbitrage, and the like take advantage of different perceptions by investors in different countries.

In accounting research we find that theory takes roughly 15 to 20 years to make it into the accounting rule books. I don't know how long it takes in economics and finance, but the proliferation of exotic instruments today suggests that the time frame is not much shorter. All manner of practice turns up in between to deal with real transactions, without waiting for the research verities.

Some transactions are so "voguish" that differing firms (as referred to by John and Kalay) seem indistinguishable. The rating agencies help sort them out, but not always that well, as they too can be misled by ersatz that looks like collateral.

It is interesting to note that accountants and tax regulators have not coped easily with these new instrument phenomena. Accountants tend to create neat compartments such as leases, debt, and equity; and nothing currently seems to fit to them well. The Financial Accounting Standards Board hasn't figured out what debt is, and therefore is probably unjustified in charging ahead to define what constitutes its extinguishment (as in "in-substance defeasance").

In the tax area, debt-equity rules were proposed many years ago, but never finally enacted. This has caused much consternation in the investment community, because it is often hard to know whether the treasury will swiftly come down hard on a new innovative instrument, as they did on adjustable-rate convertible notes (ARCNs). (These notes were 55 percent debt and 45 percent equity, designed to fit long-outstanding proposed regulations which the IRS then decided to withdraw because the IRS didn't like ARCNs. The several issues that were marketed might require litigation to straighten out the interest deductibility issue.)

I have more than used up my time and I know that these remarks have been disjointed. Let me try to pull it all together: We ought to figure out how to get all of this research conveyed much more quickly to people who make the rules regarding our accounting and tax treatments. The simple fact that accountants and other regulators will try to shoe-horn a financial instrument into a mold not made for it diverts their efforts away from developing good, solid approaches for financing the needs of our economic system. We seem to resort to much game playing strictly to fit within rules that are not responsive. The authors should recognize that much of what is done in the name of financing is unduly influenced by lagging rule setting and by vogues—and not by a cold analysis of what's needed.

Part III

Taxes and Corporate Financial Management: Introduction

INTRODUCTION

Taxation of corporate income reduces the amount of cash flow available for distribution to a firm's shareholders. The amounts paid by the firm to its shareholders are further reduced by personal taxation of shareholder income. Since the amounts available for consumption and reinvestment by shareholders are greatly affected by taxation at both corporate and personal levels, a firm seeking to maximize the welfare of its shareholders should take these into account in its financial decisions. Financial managers are constantly aware of tax considerations in their day-to-day decisions and, indeed, spend a considerable part of their managerial effort in attempting to reduce the impact of taxes on their firms' shareholders.

Academics in financial economics are keenly interested in the impact of taxes on a firm's cash flow. This interest is, of course, reflected in the teaching of finance courses in business schools. More fundamentally, taxes are an important factor in many valuation models developed in academic research. Perhaps the earliest effort to explicitly model corporate taxation in a valuation setting is the paper on capital structure by Franco Modigliani and Merton Miller in the *American Economic Review* (No. 3, June 1958). They argued that debt financing enjoys a tax advantage due to the deductibility of interest as an expense for tax purposes. Thus, in the absence of other considerations such as the possibility of financial distress or agency costs (see Part II of this book), it pays for the firm to increase its leverage indefinitely. Subsequent work by other researchers showed that this tax advantage of debt may be diminished by the impact of personal taxation.

The role of taxation is important in a related financing decision—the payment of dividends to shareholders, or equivalently, the amount retained by the firm for additional investment. Here, it is personal rather then corporate taxation that is relevant because of the differential taxation of dividend income versus capital gains.

The joint impact of corporate and personal taxation on the valuation of firms in equilibrium was first analyzed by Merton Miller in his presidential address to the American Finance Association in 1976 (*Journal of Finance*, May 1977). Miller emphasized that the corporate tax advantage on debt financing may be outweighed by its personal tax disadvantage since income from equity ownership is, in most cases, taxed at a lower rate than income from debt. In particular, firms have to woo investors in higher and higher tax brackets to hold their debt as they increase the total supply of debt, by offering higher and higher interest rates so that the after-tax rate of return does not fall. Equilibrium is reached when the corporate tax advantage of debt just matches the personal tax disadvantage of the marginal investor. In the simplified Miller model where equity income is taxed at a zero rate, the marginal investor in corportate debt instruments has a marginal tax rate equal to the corporate tax rate.

The basic Miller model has since been elaborated upon and extended to incorporate other factors such as the specifics of taxation of equity income and the availability of other tax shields such as depreciation and the effect of default. While the detailed conclusions of these various extensions differ, the basic Miller conclusion holds—the interaction of corporate and personal taxation tends to reduce the tax advantage of debt, in equilibrium.

Around the same time as this development, Merton Miller and Myron Scholes pointed out in an article in the *Journal of Financial Economics* (December 1978) that several provisions of the U.S. Tax Code reduce the impact of personal taxation on equity income. On the one hand, tax deductibility of the interest expense incurred by investors on their personal borrowings reduces the impact of taxation on the dividend income they receive. On the other, the possibility of investing in tax free assets, such as insurance annuities and Individual Retirement Accounts, allows investors to earn the pre-tax return on their riskless investments.

In terms of implications for practice, much of the discussion on taxes and financing policy in the academic literature can be reduced to two questions:

1. In equilibrium, what is the marginal corporate tax advantage of debt financing?
2. In equilibrium, what is the marginal rate of taxation of dividend income received by shareholders?

These questions, answered in both theoretical and empirical terms, are of considerable interest to financial managers as they constitute the crux of financial strategy. While other factors such as default risk and asymmetry of information between the various constituents of a firm also have ramifications for financing policy, the tax issue is of crucial importance.

In their survey paper in this part, Robert Hamada and Myron Scholes examine the equilibrium implications of the key provisions of the tax code. They consider the impact of features such as corporate versus partnership taxes, progressivity in the personal tax structure, the tax deductibility of interest expense, the existence of tax-free forms of wealth accumulation as well as tax-free debt instruments such as municipal bonds in the United States, and differential taxation of income versus capital gains. The method of analysis they employ, very much in the Miller tradition, is to examine the supply and demand for the various securities in light of the tax provisions in order to characterize the equilibrium in the securities market. In turn, this discussion clarifies issues such as the classification of investors into inframarginal and marginal. The latter investors are those who, at equilibrium prices, are indifferent to the choice between buying and not buying the security in question. The former are those who may obtain a tax gain from buying or selling the security in the absence of constraints preventing them from doing so. Hamada and Scholes emphasize the role of the inframarginal investors in relation to the market constraints they face in determining the actual equilibrium that results.

Hamada and Scholes contrast two competing approaches to financial equilibrium: one that incorporates all relevant tax effects (the after tax model) and the other that basically assumes away any tax effects as a result of tax avoidance (the before-tax model). The two theories, which are difficult to reconcile in a common framework, have different implications for managerial decision making regarding capital structure, dividends, the cost of capital and corporate pension funds.

Finally, Hamada and Scholes discuss the effect of increasing "completeness" of financial markets through the creation of new securities such as options, futures, and forward contracts. To the extent that these new instruments remove some of the constraints that the inframarginal investors face, they move the equilibrium closer to the before-tax model.

Empirical evidence, to date, does not clearly support the before- or after-tax models. Indeed, there may be shifts in the support given to the alternative hypotheses as tax laws change over time. The two approaches proposed provide a broad framework for planning corporate strategy rather than a specific blueprint for action.

In the next paper in this part, Michel Levasseur examines the relationship between capital structure, dividend policy, and taxes under the various tax regimes prevailing in the United States and Europe. He analyzes the issue by looking at the tax advantage of debt versus retained earnings after taking account both personal and corporate income taxes. As the tax systems in operation in the various countries vary in terms of (1) their treatment of capital gains, (2) the credit given to shareholders for corporate taxes paid, (the imputation system) and (3) the relative taxation of debt versus equity income besides the actual rates of taxation, the prescriptions for capital structure policy vary from country to country. The Levasseur paper thus provides many examples supporting the general observation made by Hamada and Scholes that the nature of the tax regime and the constraints imposed on investors have a major impact on the equilibrium value of securities.

The presentation by Jean-Paul Valles focuses on the specifics of current tax provisions of interest to financial managers. In contrast with the academic papers, the emphasis here is more on tax aspects of investment rather than financing decisions. We also find this to be true in Richard Goeltz's discussion of the impact of inflation on corporate financial management in part IV of this book. Thus, Valles deals with tax considerations in location of new plants, research and development, inventory control, exports, etc. Of course, he does mention issues of dividend policy and capital structure from a practitioner viewpoint, although in less detail. The discussion by Valles points out, in his opinion, the unrealistic assumptions incorporated by Hamada and Scholes in their paper and questions the final contribution of academic theory. The value of a good framework for assessing the impact of taxes is noted, however.

Two other papers in this section deal with the specifics of the tax regimes in two foreign countries, Israel and Great Britain, and their impact on financing decisions. These are of more than passing interest to both academics and practitioners in other countries since they deal with two general aspects of tax systems—the treatment of inflation (the Israeli case) and the taxation of dividends under the imputation system (the British case). Both of these papers also have relevance to the inflation discussion of Part IV of this book.

The paper by Saul Bronfeld and Itzhak Swary points out the biases that arise in a nominal system of taxation in a period of inflation. Two of these biases increase the effective taxation of corporate income. Depreciation allowances based on historic costs underestimates economic depreciation and provides a lower tax shield in an inflationary context. Taxation of capital gains tends to be higher in a period of inflation simply because the nominal value of assets rises to keep pace with inflation. In the former case, the expenses allowed for tax purposes are diminished in real terms, while in the latter case, taxable income is exaggerated, due to inflation. The third tax effect of inflation is due to the deductibility of interest payments for tax purposes. A rise in the rate of inflation leads to an increase in the nominal interest rate on debt, in order to preserve the real value of the principal owed. Since, under the nominal tax regime, the entire nominal interest payment is tax deductible, debt financing becomes even cheaper than equity financing under inflation.

Bronfeld and Swary trace through the details of the tax effects of inflation in a nominal tax system and then discuss the specifics of the Israeli tax reform. The distortionary effects of inflation through the tax system are obviously considerable when the inflation rate is at triple digit levels. However, while the sources of the distortion are identifiable in principle, there are problems of measurement and administrative costs that force one to make some compromises in translating the tax system in real terms. In principle, it would be necessary to identify every transaction and compute its inflationary component, obviously a Herculean task. Further, inflation indexes are computed only at monthly intervals, making the inflation adjustment difficult and inprecise. In addition, there are financial arrangements that have an indirect financing element to them such as leasing, where the interest element has to be imputed.

In order to simplify the tax of separating the real from the inflationary components of income, the Israeli tax reform, with which the authors were associated, classified assets into *protected* and *unprotected assets*. Protected assets are basically indexed against inflation. For these assets, the depreciation allowance and capital gains are adjusted for inflation. Unprotected assets are those that do not have a built-in hedge and are therefore taxed as in the nominal-based system. On the financing side, only the real component of interest is tax deductible. Based on this classification, the authors present the details of the new Israeli tax system and the implications of the system for optimal financial decisions.

The other paper on foreign tax regimes by James Poterba and Lawrence Summers deals with the British system of taxation of dividend income. They consider the effect of dividend taxation in the context of what Hamada and Scholes call the before-tax versus after-tax models. The before-tax model, in the context of dividends, has two variants. One version holds, as in the Hamada and Scholes paper, that investors are able to completely avoid taxes on dividends. The other, less restrictive hypothesis, is that while taxes on dividends reduce equity values, they do not distort a firm's incentive to invest, at the margin. Thus, dividend taxation is merely a lump-sum transfer and has no distortionary effect on real decisions. By contrast, if the after-tax model holds, taxation of dividends does distort the returns to shareholders, and thus, changes in the taxation of dividends do affect real decisions by firms.

The authors chose Britain as a case study because the substantial changes in the British tax regime over the recent past gave them the opportunity to observe the effect of changes in dividend taxation, in a controlled experiment. The British tax system has had differential *corporate* taxation of retained versus unretained earnings, the imputation system, the classicial tax system, and other variants among its tax regimes in the postwar years. Using data on the ex-dividend day behavior of share prices, they conclude that the valuation of dividends and capital gains have changed substantially in response to the tax regime in force.

Poterba and Summers then use the "event study" methodology commonly employed in financial economics to investigate the "information effect" of changes in the tax regime. Again, they find evidence in support of their hypothesis that changes in tax rules affect the market valuation of dividends. Other indirect evidence reported by these authors is the observed change in dividend payout ratios and aggregate corporate investment.

To summarize, this section provides a broad framework for analyzing the effect of taxation on corporate financing decisions. While no single model emerges as the "correct" one on either theoretical or empirical grounds, there is enough here to help one, be he or she an academic or a practitioner, to ask the right questions about the impact of taxes on corporate financial decisions.

8

Taxes and Corporate Financial Management

Robert S. Hamada*
Professor of Finance and
Director, Center for Research in Security Prices
Graduate School of Business
University of Chicago

Myron S. Scholes
Frank E. Buck Professor of Finance
Graduate School of Business
Professor of Law
Stanford University

Taxes and Corporate Financial Management

INTRODUCTION

Taxes and corporate financial management is an enormous and evolving subject. We will approach this subject by categorizing the tax and corporate financial management issues using the tax "equilibrium" models that have already been developed by Modigliani and Miller (1963) and Miller (1977). These two models seem to be considered, at least by academic financial economists, the purest tax models, the most promising, and without doubt, the most widely accepted at this time. We will label them, respectively, the "before-tax" and "after-tax" equilibriums.

The reason for this approach is that our world is extremely complex and becoming increasingly more so. It currently has a multitude of different tax provisions for a given individual or corporation, many different markets for the many different securities that currently exist or can potentially exist, and the various individuals or actors can switch from one market to another and can have different tax liabilities and rules as a result. In addition, the same actors can either supply or demand these different securities in various markets if they recognize an after-tax profit opportunity. Because of this complexity, what is most important is to consider *simultaneously* the effects of seemingly many different tax provisions and the equilibrium requirements across many different markets. There already exists a multitude of differential taxes, some on the suppliers of securities, some on the investors. A partial list would include: corporate income taxes versus partnership taxes, progressive personal taxes on interest income versus equity income, the corporate tax deductibility for interest expense versus equity payments, the existence of (and relative ease in expanding) many tax-free methods to accumulate wealth, for example, through pension funds and single-premium life insurance annuities, the existence of tax-exempt municipal bonds, differences in definition between ordinary income and capital gain (which lead to strategies of converting one type of income to another and strategies of realizing capital losses and accruing capital gains), ... Given these differential taxes, we wish to explore how the adjustment in the demand for, and supply of, these differentially taxed securities affects the resulting set of *equilibrium* prices (or rates of return).

We consider the determination of this set of relative equilibrium rates of return for the various securities in various markets to be the single most important issue. Without knowing or understanding how taxes affect these relative prices or rates of return facing an individual corporation, prescriptions for what a corporate financial manager ought to do could hardly be forthcoming. What set of rates of return will clear the market such that there is no more incentive to supply any more of a given security and that someone is willing to hold every outstanding security?

Realizing that equilibrium prices may imply that some securities may be dominated by other securities for some investors, who are the marginal investors for the various securities? What are the investment strategies that are available for the inframarginal investors? The "marginal" investors are defined as the class of investors setting the relative prices at the margin in the sense that they are indifferent to purchasing or to supplying any more of those securities at those prices and after having considered all the tax implications. There is no more tax gain nor tax loss for the marginal investor at the given relative prices. Conversely, an "inframarginal" investor will have a tax gain or tax loss by purchasing or selling more of those securities at the given relative prices, unless there are regulatory or tax constraints that prohibit such tax gaming. Clearly, the big-dollar managerial implications come about when a firm or individual can be safely assumed to be inframarginal. The problem is even more complex in that if these inframarginal investors have no binding constraints, their actions in a particular security and/or market (or combination of markets) may actually change the relative equilibrium rates of return so that they would instead become the marginal investors and others the inframarginal investors.

We strongly believe that this approach to summarizing the existing literature on "taxes and corporate financial management" is much superior to the alternative of starting this paper by defining what is included among the topics in "corporate financial management" and defining what "taxes" should be considered. For example, corporate financial management would then have to include among its topics the management decision on debt versus equity; the amount and timing of cash and stock dividends; the maturity and coupon level of its bonds and debt; the structure and level of leasing decisions (as a lessee and/or lessor); long-term asset management (capital budgeting); issuance and pricing of hybrid securities such as convertibles, warrants, and preferreds; short-term asset management; the theoretical and estimation issues relating to the cost of capital, insurance, and executive compensation; pension fund management; merger, acquisition, tender offer, and divestiture policy; international financial management; and on and on. A single paper (as opposed to a textbook) must somehow logically define the boundaries of its coverage. Likewise, the scope of "taxes," the other word in our title, can be enormous, as the partial list of differential taxes mentioned above should have indicated.

Our first decision on narrowing the scope of this paper is to focus primarily on the two "major" corporate financing decisions: the capital structure and dividend decisions. The reason is simple. With two major existing tax theories of equilibrium relative rates of return, coverage must be manageable. The effects of the two tax equilibriums on the firm's many investment decisions will not be considered in detail, other than to discuss the implications on two illustrative examples—the corporation's pension fund policy and the cost of capital issue.

Our second decision on narrowing the scope of this paper is to impose another requirement for systematizing the method of analyzing tax effects on corporate financial management. As physical scientists have approached this subject for years—by first hypothesizing about equilibrium and the cause and effect of marginal perturbations—in an idealized world (for example, in a perfect vacuum), academic financial economists have now emulated their approach. We will carry on this tradition in this paper, by postulating the conventional academic idealized world for our field: a perfectly competitive capital market. This idealized world literally requires no transaction costs of any kind in purchasing and selling existing securities (so that the seller receives what the buyer pays) nor in creating new securities (so that the capital markets are complete), no costs for obtaining information so that no actor in the capital markets has an advantage or monopoly in information over others at any time (so that asymmetric information issues can be ignored), and that there are enough actual and potential participants in the capital markets so that no single individual participant (demander or supplier) can affect the price.

This perfectly competitive capital market will serve as our benchmark. After quickly summarizing the managerial implications in this "idealized" world in the next section, this benchmark will be employed as our launching pad for all of the subsequent sections dealing with the marginal impact of taxes—which is the major focus of this paper, rather than the numerous other kinds of market imperfections.

In the third section, the two major existing market equilibrium tax theories will be outlined. The following section highlights the managerial implications of these two major tax theories.

Next, we intend to come back full circle to address what we already indicated to be the single most important issue on this topic: the interaction of markets, securities, actors, and tax provisions in arriving at the set of equilibrium relative rates of return facing individual corporations. There are many different markets (such as the equity, taxable and nontaxable bond, futures, options, etc.) and many different investors and demanders of capital (such as corporations, partnerships, broker-dealers, commercial banks, pension funds, estates, etc.) who are taxed differently. The relation—if there even exists one—among all these investors and markets must then be considered in that it is through this interdependency that a set of "equilibrium" relative rates of return emerge. Most of the equilibrium models in finance assume that the marginal investor setting equilibrium prices is holding securities to meet future consumption needs. Some papers, however, such as Miller and Scholes (1982) describe how broker-dealers have the potential to profit from differences in relative prices arising from differential taxation of dividends and capital gains. This profit potential arises because for them all trading gains and losses are similar to the profits and losses of any taxable corporation. If, however, they incur trading costs, costs associated with regulatory restrictions, and face costs of raising equity capital, tax-induced differences in relative prices could still exist.

We extend this line of analysis to the capital structure and dividend decisions by introducing the effects of new markets in financial futures and options. Their introduction has the potential to reduce the costs of eliminating differentials in relative prices, especially for these broker-dealers. Trading partners can be found at low cost by using these new instruments to hedge security positions. Therefore, an important part of our task will be to analyze how the advent of these low-cost hedging instruments affects the important capital structure and dividend equilibrium.

Finally, the paper closes with a few concluding remarks and observations, especially those that naturally emanate from consideration of the new markets and securities.

THE PERFECTLY COMPETITIVE CAPITAL MARKET WORLD AS A BENCHMARK

Under these conditions, it is well known that shareholders interested in maximizing their utility (and therefore, their wealth or current market value), should be indifferent to the firm's capital structure and dividend policies. The production-investment decisions in both short- and long-term real assets, as well as other real decisions affecting the present and future stream of cash flows (before financing costs) are all that matter if the goal is to maximize current value. Given these decisions and the resulting current market value of these present and future cash flows, the owners of the firm should be indifferent to the financing of these investments with different proportions of debt and equity; see Modigliani and Miller (1958). The basic argument boils down to a conservation of value condition: The past, present, and future production-investment decisions determine the entity's total value and that total cannot be affected by how it is split between the various owners or claimants (debt, preferred, convertibles, or equity) as there are no leakages (due to the assumptions underlying a perfectly competitive market) and each of the various claimants or securities are pricing their respective products to protect themselves in a no-transaction-cost (including no bankruptcy, monitoring, and contracting costs), perfectly competitive market; see Fama and Miller (1972) Chapter 4.

Similarly, given a perfectly competitive capital market and given the real production-investment decisions made by the managers, the second classic paper by Miller and Modigliani (1961) clearly shows that the dividend policy selected by a firm's manager is of no consequence to the wealth of any of its owners. Again, only "real" asset decisions will determine the present and future stream of cash flows (before financing costs) and the current value of the firm. In a perfectly competitive capital market, new shares can always be issued at a competitive price and dividends can be converted into capital gains without friction, or vice versa.

THE TWO MAJOR EQUILIBRIUM TAX THEORIES

Currently, assuming that capital market imperfections other than taxes are ignored, there are two major models of equilibrium, each with differing implications for managerial decision making because each predicts different relative prices (or rates of return) on bonds versus stocks.[1] The first, which we shall label the *after-tax theory*, is most frequently associated with Miller's presidential address to the American Finance Association, entitled "Debt and Taxes" (1977); the second model, which we shall call the *before-tax theory*, is associated with Modigliani and Miller (1963) and Miller and Scholes (1978).

To present these two theories, we shall need the following definitions in this section:

r_B = Before-tax rate of interest on taxable government and private bonds
r_c = Rate of return, *before* all taxes on a 100 percent equity-financed investment in the corporate sector
r_p = Rate of return, before all taxes, on a 100 percent equity-financed investment in the partnership sector
r_0 = Municipal bond interest rate
τ_c = Marginal corporate income tax rate
τ_B = Marginal personal income tax rate to the marginal bondholder
τ_s = Marginal personal income tax rate on capital gains and dividends to the marginal shareholder
τ_p = Marginal personal income tax rate for a marginal partner

All rates of return are certainty-equivalents; risky securities are adjusted for differences in risk so that only the risk-free equivalent rate of return will be discussed subsequently, unless otherwise noted.

The after-tax theory

A summary of the aggregate taxable corporate bond market equilibrium in Miller's after-tax theory (1977) is presented in Figure 1. Once differences in risk have been eliminated, all investors are interested ultimately in after-tax returns and, therefore, the tax-exempt municipal bond rate, r_0, must, in equilibrium, be equal to the after-corporate and after-personal tax rate of return on a pure equity investment, $(1 - \tau_s)(1 - \tau_c)r_c$. Either of these after-tax returns establishes the anchor, the point on the vertical axis in Figure 1, which is the minimum after-tax rate of return obtainable by every investor. Miller observes that the U.S. tax code allows τ_s to be much less than τ_B and he, for simplicity, assumes τ_s to be zero. We will keep τ_s in our presentation but assume it to be small and constant.

Corporations issuing bonds must attract bondholders. After exhausting the funds of the nontaxable investors (such as pension funds and the funds of nonprofit institutions), corporations must offer a higher before-tax interest rate on their bonds so that investors, after paying personal taxes, will realize an *after-tax* return at least equal to r_0. If more and more corporate bonds are issued, the demand curve slopes upward as higher and higher marginal tax bracket bondholders must be enticed to hold these taxable bonds, relative to municipals or common shares.

FIGURE 1 The aggregate corporate bond market in the "after-tax theory"

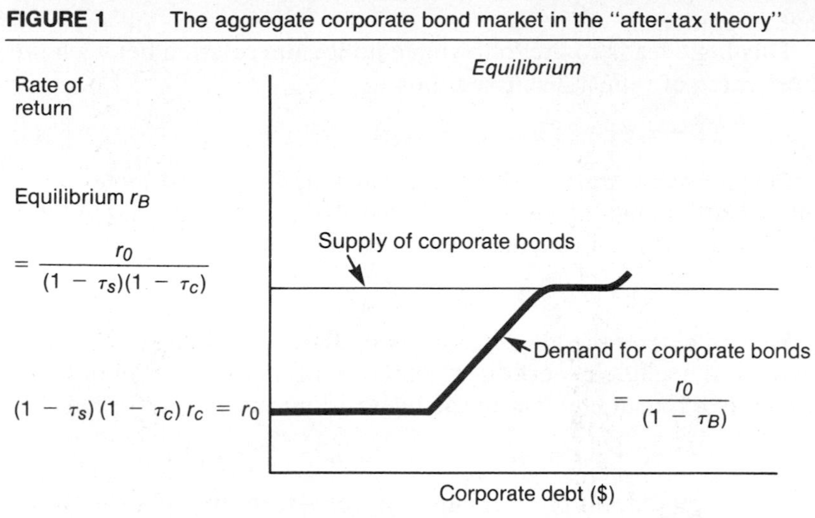

On the supply side, corporate taxable firms should be willing to issue only bonds (relative to equity) as long as the before-tax interest rate is below the "grossed up" after-tax cost of equity, $(1 - \tau_s)(1 - \tau_c)r_c$, or the equivalent municipal bond rate, r_0. The factor to "gross up" either one of these latter two rates is $(1 - \tau_s)(1 - \tau_c)$, to reflect the well-known fact that corporate debt interest is corporate-tax-deductible. This deductibility feature for corporate debt financing (relative to equity financing) induces corporations, in the aggregate, to supply more and more debt as long as the before-tax interest rate on this debt is below $[r_0/(1 - \tau_s)(1 - \tau_c)]$. For this reason, the supply curve is drawn at this horizontal level in Figure 1.

Equilibrium in the corporate bond market, then, is established where supply is equal to demand, i.e., when the before-tax interest rate on corporate bonds, r_B, is equal to $[r_0/(1 - \tau_s)(1 - \tau_c)]$. Because of the interaction of all of these taxes, the aggregate quantity of taxable bonds supplied (and held) in equilibrium is undoubtedly greater than what would have been supplied in a no-tax world.[2] Nevertheless, once this equilibrium has been established, the capital structure decision at the level of an individual taxable corporation is irrelevant. Assuming no capital market imperfection other than taxes, and after abstracting from differences in risk, the corporation can issue equity at an after-tax cost of $(1 - \tau_s)(1 - \tau_c)r_c$, or it can issue debt at a higher before-tax cost of r_B, but receive the tax deduction for interest paid such that the after-tax cost is identical to that of equity.

This logic leads to the following equilibrium relation between the three rates of return discussed thus far:

$$(1 - \tau_s)(1 - \tau_c)r_c = (1 - \tau_B)r_B = r_0 \tag{1}$$

and in terms of marginal tax rates for the marginal investors in stocks and taxable bonds, equation (1) implies (by setting the supply and demand equations in Figure 1 equal to each other):

$$(1 - \tau_s)(1 - \tau_c) = (1 - \tau_B)$$

We can extend the above analysis to include the partnership sector (a nonnegligible portion of the U.S. economy), and add this sector as a fourth element in the equilibrium market condition:

$$r_0 = (1 - \tau_p)r_p = (1 - \tau_s)(1 - \tau_c)r_c = (1 - \tau_B)r_B \tag{1a}$$

In this model, all partnership and corporate projects should be evaluated with a discount rate of r_0 (a unique, observable, after-tax, market-required rate of return), and the capital structure decision will be irrelevant for both the marginal owners of partnership or corporate shares. These marginal owners have tax rates such that:

$$(1 - \tau_p) = (1 - \tau_s)(1 - \tau_c) = (1 - \tau_B) \tag{1b}$$

or

$$\tau_p = \tau_s + \tau_c - \tau_s\tau_c = \tau_B \tag{1c}$$

An interesting implication of equation (1*a*) is that there is an economy-wide equilibrium after-tax rate of return, r_0, which somehow results from more general macroequilibrium considerations (for our purposes, it is like a numeraire). For capital structure decisions, the partner whose τ_p is greater than $\tau_c + \tau_s - \tau_s\tau_c$ would prefer debt financing, and the partner whose τ_p is less than $\tau_c + \tau_s - \tau_s\tau_c$ would prefer no partnership debt as long as equation (1*a*) holds. Partners with a tax rate as given in equation (1*c*) would be indifferent—the partnership equity taxes saved exactly cancel out the higher bond interest.

Nonprofit institutions, thus, are just a special case of a partnership whose $\tau_p = 0$. They should never borrow and pay interest at the rate r_B, receive no tax deduction for interest paid, and invest in anything earning at the rate r_0, like corporate equities.

The equilibrium of equation (1*a*) can arise in the same manner as in Miller's "Debt and Taxes." Because corporations have supplied so much debt that r_B is much larger than r_0, low-taxed partnerships in the aggregate would be induced to supply much more equity (relative to debt) to other low-taxed partners.

One would expect, then, an equilibrium in the partnership equity market to look like Figure 2. This partnership equity market equilibrium implies an aggregate debt (partnership, government, and corporate) market equilibrium as shown in Figure 3.

Similar tax considerations as were used to find a market equilibrium for the organization of partnerships lead corporations to establish entities in foreign countries to minimize corporate taxes; highly taxed subsidiaries and DISCs are set up and such noted low-taxed havens as Ireland or Puerto Rico are used, until marginal benefits potentially decrease as more firms race to do this or costs of far-flung operations increase. Organizations such as trusts, subchapter S corporations, and large limited partnerships taking on many of the forms of a corporation, are used to sell tax benefits to highly taxed entities or individuals from low-taxed entities or individuals. As these examples illustrate, the form of the organization can be motivated, in part, by tax considerations.

The before-tax theory

The before-tax theory essentially concludes that all personal income taxes—to bondholders, shareholders, and partners of businesses—can be effectively laundered. For example, in the Miller and Scholes' "Dividends and Taxes" (1978) argument, they claim that, because the federal tax statutes established so many easily accessible ways to save and invest at before-tax rates of return, the effective personal tax rate applicable on a dollar of dividends[3] is essentially zero (this would hold for any shareholder in any and all marginal tax brackets, assuming that his effective tax rate on marginal capital gains is approximately zero). The procedure required to avoid paying personal taxes on dividends is to borrow on a personal account, ensuring that the interest expense on this personal debt equals the dividends received. As dividends are taxable but interest expense is tax-deductible, they cancel out. The proceeds of the loan can then be invested in one of the many vehicles that are allowed to earn at a *before*-tax rate of return in one form or another (like pension, Keogh and IRA plans, single-premium life insurance annuities, etc.). Most of these methods to earn a before-tax rate of return are highly elastic and flexible. Also, these methods do not require that individuals violate tax rules that limit the deductibility of interest payments, nor on net do they affect the individual's personal capital structure (the individual's personal debt is offset against the bonds held in the

FIGURE 2 Equilibrium in the partnership equity market in the "after-tax theory"

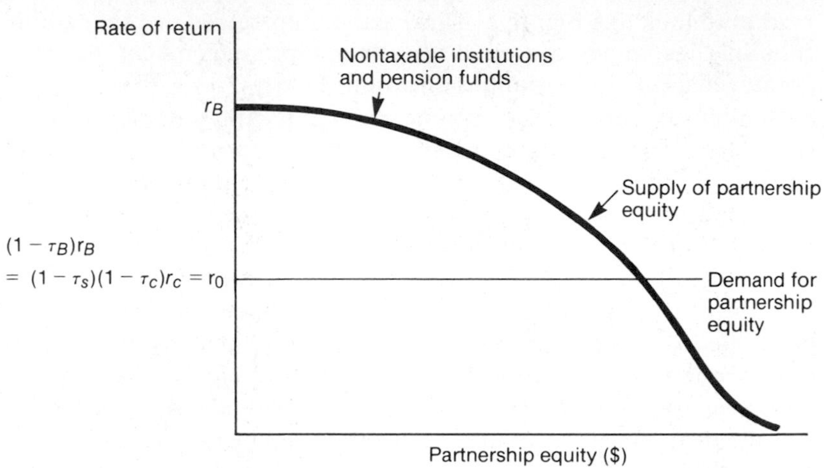

FIGURE 3 Equilibrium in the aggregate taxable debt market in the "after-tax theory"

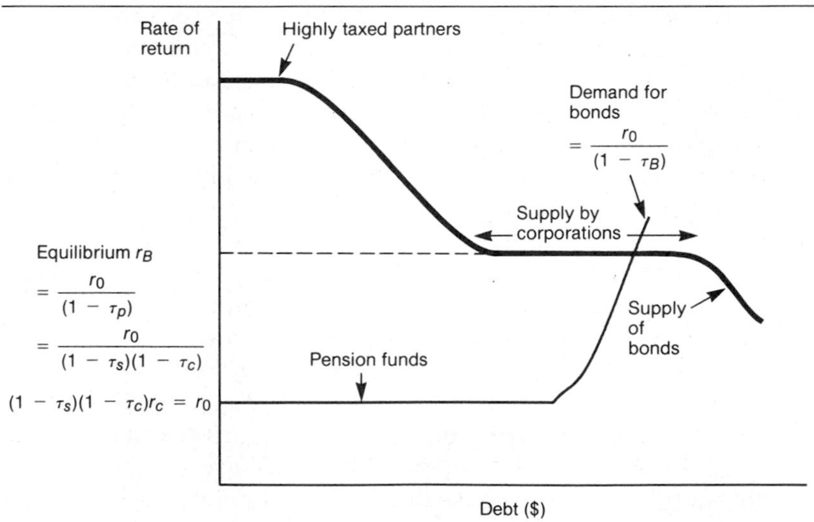

pension or insurance funds). The net effect of these transactions is to eliminate taxes on dividend income at a slight cost in liquidity, while investors earn the before-tax rate of return on total investment.

If investors can use these procedures effectively to reduce all personal taxes on savings at the margin to zero (including personal taxes on partnership income), and for all financial instruments to be held, then the equilibrium relative rates of return would be:

$$r_p = (1 - \tau_c)r_c = r_B = r_0/(1 - \tau_c) \quad (2)$$

Equation (2) implies that both capital structure decisions of partnerships and the dividend decision by all firms are irrelevant. A capital structure equilibrium for corporations, however, requires at least some other market imperfection, such as leverage-related costs which increase with the debt-to-equity ratio (for a noncorner solution of 100 percent debt). Thus, the aggregate supply curve for debt will eventually fall with the issuance of more and more debt. This fall in the supply curve for corporate debt (relative to equity) is due to, presumably, the marginal increase in these other debt-related market imperfection costs as debt is increased in the aggregate across all corporations, as well as for an individual firm. This aggregate debt market is depicted in Figure 4.

These leverage-related costs must be very large and would include all those items previously mentioned in the literature—bankruptcy costs,[4] contracting and monitoring costs,[5] information and signaling

FIGURE 4. Equilibrium in the aggregate taxable debt market in the "before-tax theory"

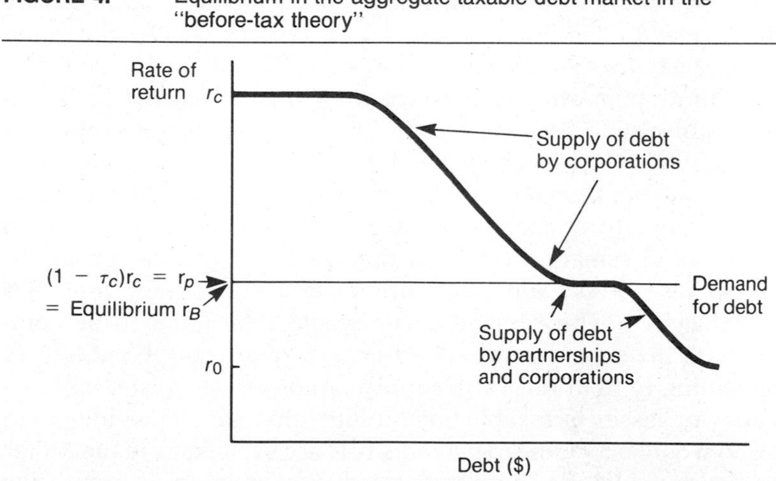

costs,[6] differential flotation costs,[7] incomplete markets,[8] etc., as well as the DeAngelo-Masulis (1980)[9] "wasted" tax deductions such as unused investment tax credits in the aggregate economy.[10]

Two related points from the before-tax equilibrium of Figure 4 can be noted. For the same risk projects, the partner (versus a corporation) would want to have a much lower percentage of debt financing. Since a partnership would be indifferent between debt and equity without these leverage-related costs, it would undoubtedly favor equity once these costs become sizeable. The second point is that municipal bonds, with $r_0 = (1 - \tau_c)r_B$ and as drawn in Figure 4, will be an inframarginal investment by corporations and financial institutions, simply offsetting tax-deductible debt liabilities.[11]

Why two separate tax theories?

It should now be obvious why the after-tax and before-tax theories were presented separately in the previous two subsections. To some extent they are competing equilibrium theories in that reconciliation does not seem very feasible with what most people consider our current real-world institutions and tax laws.

There are two points to be considered in reconciling these two competing theories. First, if the shareholders' personal taxes on dividends can be laundered via the pension fund/life insurance annuity route, it should also be possible for the bondholders to do the same to eliminate their personal taxes on interest received. If this is true, then the demand curve for corporate bonds in Figure 1 will not be upward-sloping, but would remain a horizontal line at r_0. No supply/demand equilibrium would result in that case. As this point was recognized by Miller and Scholes (1978) and subsequently by others, an attempt was made to locate a class of corporate bondholders who would be willing to pay taxes (up to the corporate tax rate). Then this class can be labeled the "marginal" corporate bondholders, and the demand curve for these bonds would have two linear horizontal segments in Figure 1. This demand curve would start at r_0 and remain there until the resources of pension funds, Keogh plans, IRAs, and single-premium life insurance annuities were exhausted. The demand curve would then jump to be coincident with the supply curve, due to these "marginal" bondholders being willing to hold the extra supply of corporate taxable bonds.

The two classes of taxable bondholders that have been identified and who would be willing to play this role are estates, as in the Miller and Scholes model, and corporate taxable financial institutions (like commercial banks). Estates may be willing to pay up to the corporate tax rate on their interest income in that this cost would be less than the present value of the benefits from reduced estate taxes. Corporate taxable financial institutions, being more plentiful, may be a more likely candidate for the marginal taxable bondholder. They certainly hold plenty of taxable bonds in their asset portfolios and make direct taxable loans to corporations and individuals, as well as arbitrage between taxable and tax-exempt bonds.

This leads to a problem, however. Who would be willing to hold corporate equities, including those of the marginal financial institutions? One must remember that to launder all personal income taxes on the return to savings may be possible, but to launder the corporate income tax is another matter of a different dimension.

The second point, then, relates to whether individuals would be willing to hold corporate equities even if the certainty equivalent rate is r_0 and individuals can earn r_B on their own accounts through pension funds/life insurance plans, etc. Obviously, to earn more than r_B requires that investors assume risk through holding equities. Those individuals whose limitations on the amount that can be contributed to their pension plans exceed their desire for holding low-risk bonds earning the lower bond rate, r_B, will hold the remainder in risky equity but at a higher expected return for the increased risk. There would be no advantage to having the pension fund buy bonds in this case, while buying equities on margin on one's own account to achieve an equivalent risky position. The deduction of interest on personal borrowing is limited by the amount of investment income received on one's own account. Both routes of investing in equities achieve equivalent results.[12]

Ultimately, the answer to our question, why two separate tax theories, rests on who is the marginal investor. If the marginal investor, the direct holder of securities, is taxed at a rate equal to τ_c, then, as in Figure 1, the demand curve slopes up to meet the horizontal and higher supply curve for aggregate taxable bonds (the after-tax theory). Alternatively, if the marginal investor driving the equilibrium has a tax rate less than τ_c and, in the extreme, equal to zero, the before-tax theory with complete laundering of personal taxes on interest income, dividend income, and partnership income results in a horizontal demand curve for aggregate corporate bonds as in Figure 4.

SOME MANAGERIAL IMPLICATIONS OF THE TWO MAJOR EQUILIBRIUM TAX THEORIES

These two competing tax equilibrium models often indicate that corporate financial managers take different strategies with regard to corporate policies. We will discuss each of the major financial decisions outlined below in the context of the after-tax equilibrium model first, and then in the context of the before-tax model. We must point out that the final arbitrator of any differences can be forthcoming only from careful empirical tests using data that emanate from the actions of real-world participants. So far empirical tests indicate that neither model has consistently come out the winner.

Debt versus equity financing (the basic capital structure decision)

The after-tax equilibrium model. As noted earlier the driving marginal capital market participant in this model is the aggregate of all corporations when making this debt versus equity financing decision. Therefore, for the corporations paying the top marginal corporate income tax rate, it is clear that they would be indifferent to financing their assets with debt or equity. If they use debt financing, they would have to pay the higher before-tax unit cost of r_B, but would receive the full value of the tax deductibility of interest payments equal to $(\tau_c + \tau_s - \tau_c\tau_s)r_B$. The net, or after-tax, cost of this debt would be identical to the unit cost of equity financing; namely, $(1 - \tau_s)(1 - \tau_c)r_c$ or r_0. It can be demonstrated easily that this equality of unit costs also implies that the market value of the entire firm and the per share stock value are independent of this capital structure decision.

In this equilibrium, if a particular corporation is not liable for taxes at the top marginal corporate income tax rate, it should prefer equity to debt financing. The value of the deductibility of interest payments would be less than for the "marginal" price-setting corporation which is at the top corporate tax rate. These inframarginal corporations would be those that have many other tax deductions or credits (for example, from accelerated depreciation or investment tax credits) or those smaller corporations not yet having taxable profits large enough to be at the top marginal bracket.

The above interpretation is a literal reading of Miller's after-tax equilibrium theory (1977). Maintaining the spirit of Miller's analysis, the supply curve of aggregate taxable bonds in Figure 1 can have a slight dip (going from left to right) if there are some leverage-related costs due to market imperfections or unused tax deductions and credits, so that the equilibrium τ_c may not have to be the top marginal corporate tax rate. It is an empirical issue, in this case, whether the supply/demand equilibrium intersection in Figure 1 occurs prior to, or after, the top marginal corporate tax rate. If the equilibrium occurs at a rate less than the top rate, then all corporations at the top rate should use debt financing (relative to equity) until they have enough tax deductions to drive their marginal tax rate to the lower market equilibrium corporate tax rate and a lower ratio of the return on bonds relative to municipals than would be found if the marginal tax rate on bonds were equal to the strict corporate tax rate. Conversely, corporations with a lower marginal tax rate than that impounded in the pricing of r_B should use equity financing.

The same principle, as discussed previously, applies for partnerships. Partners whose τ_p is greater than $\tau_c + \tau_s - \tau_c\tau_s$ should prefer debt financing as the value of the tax deductibility of interest will be worth more to them than for the "marginal" participant (namely, the corporations), and partners whose τ_p is less than the above critical impounded tax rates should prefer equity financing. Nonprofit institutions should not use debt financing if they have to pay interest at r_B while receiving no tax deduction.

The before-tax equilibrium model. As noted before, corporations should prefer debt to equity financing if no capital market imperfections other than taxes are considered. The full value of the corporate tax deductibility of interest payments would accrue to the shareholder such that the market value of equity and the market value of the entire firm would increase, the larger the amount of debt that is used to finance the assets of the firm. In fact, it can be shown that the increase in the total market value of the firm and of the equity is equal to the firm's corporate tax rate times the market value of its debt. Thus, a firm at the top marginal corporate tax rate of 0.46 is essentially having the federal government pay for one half its financing costs. The key is the asymmetry in the way the federal government defines its corporate tax law: Payments to bondholders are tax-deductible, whereas payments to shareholders are not. Therefore, the after-tax cost of debt would be $(1 - \tau_c)r_B$, which is less than the after-tax cost of equity, $(1 - \tau_c)r_c$; see equation (2).

In fact, only one class of firms should be indifferent to the debt/equity decision. These would be firms not paying any taxes, such as corporations without any corporate tax liability or partnerships which can launder all their personal taxes.

Finally, we should again note that, especially in the context of this before-tax model, there have been innumerable academic papers that lead to "debt capacity" theories for corporations by trading off, at the margin for each corporation, this enormous corporate tax subsidy for debt financing against the many potential market imperfection costs that increase as the proportion of debt increases.

The dividend policy decision

The after-tax equilibrium model. In this equilibrium, personal income taxes of the marginal shareholder, as well as the marginal bondholder, are not necessarily laundered. All that is required is that τ_s is small enough relative to τ_B such that $(1 - \tau_s)(1 - \tau_c) = (1 - \tau_B)$ for the marginal investors. As τ_s is made up of two types of taxes and, if the personal tax rate on a dollar of dividend income is greater than the tax rate on a dollar of capital gain, the shareholder should prefer (with no other market imperfections and given production-investment plans by the corporation) the dollar of capital gain. For this class of shareholders, the corporation would maximize its after-tax wealth by retaining the after-tax profits and investing them in, at worst, a zero net present value venture, such as buying back its own shares (although buying back one's own shares forces some shareholders to realize their capital gains rather than allowing them to accrue).

The dollar of capital gains for most shareholders is effectively taxed at a lower rate than a dollar of dividends in that 60 percent of capital gains are excludable from personal taxes and, more importantly, gains are not taxed at all until realized (so that optimal tax strategies for the shareholders would be to realize capital losses and not always to realize capital gains), and that the tax basis for the capital gain is stepped up at death or when contributing the appreciated stock to charitable institutions (like the University of Chicago or Stanford University).

There are many shareholders whose personal tax rate on dividends and capital gains is the same. These would include the many types of pension plans, the funds of nonprofit institutions, and the fully taxable broker-dealers. To all of these classes of shareholders, there should be no tax impact on the dividend policy decision, so that the perfectly competitive market implication of irrelevance would still hold.

Corporations owning shares in other corporations have a difficult problem. Obviously, corporations holding shares of dividend-paying stocks must balance the cost of excluding only 85 percent of dividend income received (not 100 percent) for a net tax at the top marginal 0.46 corporate tax rate of 6.9 percent, against the possibility that the economy-wide τ_s is not equal to zero. Obviously, if τ_s is greater than 6.9 percent, it would be to the advantage of 0.46 marginal tax rate corporations to hold dividend-paying stocks. If corporations, however, plan to turn over their holdings in stocks and, thereby, incur a capital gains tax in addition to the dividend tax, they could lose the advantages of holding dividend-paying stocks: The sum of these taxes could exceed τ_s. Balanced against the tax disadvantage of the gain is the option to realize capital losses to offset other capital gains as described by Constantinides (1983). As this discussion should indicate, this after-tax model has not fully developed the entire equilibrium requirements; in this case, with respect to identifying the tax status, τ_s, of the "marginal" shareholder for purposes of establishing clear-cut managerial dividend policy implications.

The before-tax equilibrium model. This model explicitly considers the dividend issue and claims that the marginal shareholders will launder their personal tax on a dollar of dividends until it is equal to their personal tax on a dollar of capital gains. Thus, the perfectly competitive market implication of dividend policy irrelevancy is maintained in this equilibrium for the individual shareholder, as well as for pension funds, the funds of nonprofit institutions, and for broker-dealers.

The cost of capital (or capital asset pricing model) implication

The capital asset pricing model (CAPM) is now so popular and frequently used in real-world applications that it has become a standard chapter(s) in all recent textbooks on modern finance. The primary value of the CAPM is to identify explicitly the risk-expected return trade-off, in equilibrium, for individual assets and securities. It provides an explicit and understandable measure of risk (namely, the asset's β) and among its primary applications is its use as a shorthand proxy to establish a minimum expected, or required, rate of return a new project must surpass (considering the risk of the project) to preserve the wealth of the firm's current owners. Of course, this use of the CAPM is the same as determining a project's cost of capital. We won't list the stringent conditions, however, that must be met before the CAPM can be used to determine a cost of capital.

When using the CAPM, the project's cost of capital is given by the following required expected return:

$$E(R_p) = R_F + [E(R_M) - R_F]\beta_p \tag{3}$$

where

$E(R_p)$ = The project's expected rate of return
R_F = The economy's risk-free rate of return
$E(R_M)$ = The expected rate of return on the market portfolio

β_p = The project's systematic risk; the covariance of the project's rate of return with the market portfolio's rate of return, divided by the variance of the market portfolio's rate of return.

The after-tax equilibrium model. In this equilibrium, the appropriate risk-free rate of return is the municipal bond rate. The marginal investors are fully taxable and their holdings in "riskless" corporate and Treasury bonds (or bills) are fully taxable to return the same after-tax return as they would have earned on holding municipal bonds. Also, the rate of return on equity, after abstracting from its risk, is the municipal bond rate. Therefore, the R_F in equation (3) is equal to r_0. Restating equation (3) in the after-tax equilibrium and thereby restating the CAPM and a project's cost of capital:

$$E(R_p) = r_0 + [E(R_M') - r_0]\beta_p \tag{3a}$$

From this relation,[13] we infer the following managerial implications: (*a*) a risk-free project whose $\beta_p = 0$ need only have an expected rate of return after all taxes equal to r_0; (*b*) a risky project having a $\beta_p > 0$ must have an expected rate of return at least equal to that as given in equation (3*a*); (*c*) the certainty-equivalent rate of return on risky stocks or projects is obtained by subtracting from $E(R_p)$ the difference between $E(R_M')$ and r_0 for each unit of β_p, namely, the appropriate slope coefficient as determined by this model; and (*d*) $E(R_M')$ and $E(R_p)$ are after all tax returns.

The before-tax equilibrium model. In this equilibrium, marginal investors are identified as being those who launder all of their personal income taxes: R_F in equation (3) is equal to r_B, the before-tax rate of interest on riskless bonds; see, for example, Hamada (1969, 1972). Thus, in this equilibrium we restate equation (3):

$$E(R_p) = r_B + [E(R_m) - r_B]\beta_p \tag{3b}$$

Comparing equations (3*a*) and (3*b*), we see an obvious difference in the cost of capital between the two equilibriums. This difference is highlighted in Figure 5.

Corporate pension fund policy

As we mentioned in the Introduction, we cannot hope to cover in detail the numerous ways in which taxes can affect the corporation's many types of investment decisions. We will, as a compromise, analyze how the tax-induced equilibrium relative rates of return should impact on a corporation's pension fund policy. This particular example will be employed to serve as a dramatic illustration of the

FIGURE 5 The CAPM or cost of capital for the "after-tax" and "before-tax" theories

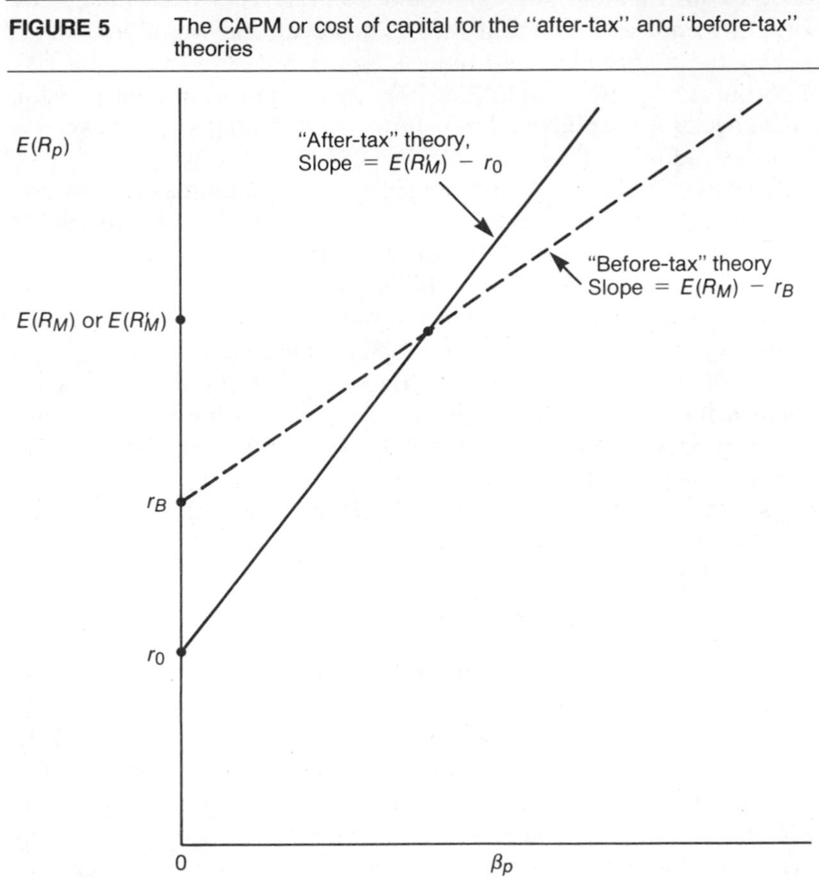

Note: $E(R_M)$ and $E(R'_M)$ need not be the same.

important role the tax equilibrium can play on the manager's investment decision.

The after-tax equilibrium model. In this equilibrium, non-taxable investors such as pension funds are inframarginal. As the corporate tax rate must be paid on equity profits and cannot be avoided even by nontaxable pension funds that hold these shares, the before-tax rate of return on bonds, r_B, will be larger than the rate of return on stocks, $(1 - \tau_c)r_c$, which is identical to r_0 if $\tau_s = 0$. Instead, pension funds should invest in partnership shares as they are not liable for any of the partnership taxes; see equation (1a). Thus, on a certainty-equivalent or risk-adjusted basis, pension funds earning r_B on bonds (or r_p on partnership shares) would be preferred to earning r_0 on corporate equities. As noted before, however, individual investors, seeking the higher expected returns associated with the higher risk of corporate equities, might hold corporate equities in their pension funds, because the allowed limits for pension fund investing exceeds their desired level of saving.

If, on the other hand, the pension fund is administered by the corporation (a defined benefit plan), the corporation can borrow at the after-tax rate r_0 and put the proceeds in the pension fund to earn r_B. This route is not possible for individuals in their own plans. This spread should benefit the owners of the corporation, see Black (1980), Bulow (1982), and Tepper (1981). There would not be such a spread, of course, if the pension fund invested in common shares.

The before-tax equilibrium model. From equation (2), this equilibrium model requires $r_B = (1 - \tau_c)r_c$. As the earnings on assets in corporate pension funds are tax-exempt, corporate pension sponsors should be indifferent to investing in bonds or equities. However, the corporation itself does prefer debt financing relative to equity financing (at least up to the point where the marginal costs related to nontax capital market imperfections equal the tax advantage of debt financing).

Thus, a corporation can borrow on its own account, receive the tax deduction, and use the proceeds to finance its defined benefit pension fund. This pension fund then should invest these proceeds in bonds in that these bonds would act as perfect collateral for the corporation's debt such that the nontax market imperfection costs associated with debt financing by the corporation would not be affected. The corporation can continue to borrow at a net cost of $(1 - \tau_c)r_B$, as interest payments are tax-deductible, and the pension fund would earn at the rate r_B. This spread would accrue to the owners of the corporation as long as the pension fund is a defined benefit plan and as long as the corporation can return the excess assets of the pension plan to the corporate account at some future date; see Bulow and Scholes (1984). If the pension fund invested in equities, presumably the nontax market imperfection costs would be binding on the corporation, whereas it is not, if the corporate pension fund invested in bonds.

Inframarginal individual investors

In the after-tax equilibrium model, Miller explicitly recognized that there may be some possibilities for tax arbitrage profits by inframarginal individual investors. As long as we realize that the individual income tax structure is progressive and that equilibrium in the capital markets requires only one price per security (set by the marginal participant), then we ought also to realize that it may be possible for investors who have individual marginal tax rates different from the marginal price-setting investor, to make risk-free arbitrage profits by taking advantage of the difference in their tax rates versus the tax rate of the marginal investor. Miller called this an investor surplus and thought that the tax authorities would limit them; however, subsequent articles, by Kim, Lewellen, and McConnell (1979), Harris, Roenfeldt, and Cooley (1983), and others, have continued to pursue this point. In one sense, the after-tax equilibrium may not be a stable equilibrium if there exists an infinite risk-free money pump for enough of these potential tax arbitragers at the after-tax set of relative market rates of return. Then, taking advantage of these arbitrage opportunities will result either in the relative rates of return changing, or the tax bracket of all these investors converging to that of the marginal investor.

Examples of such tax arbitrage opportunities would be for low marginal tax individuals to borrow through the corporation to receive the corporate tax deduction for interest payments and lend on their personal accounts so that their interest received would be taxed at less than the corporate tax rate. Other examples can be conceived. Thus, this is an important set of questions to address. In fact, the next section will consider this class of issues in detail.

IMPLICATIONS OF NEW SECURITIES AND OF DIFFERING MARGINAL INVESTORS IN THE MARKET

General background and motivation

In recent years we have seen the growth of many new financial instruments. The most important of these developments has been the growth of exchange-traded options and the growth of the financial futures market. By highlighting these innovations, however, we are not slighting the development of other important new financial innovations, such as zero-coupon bonds, coupon stripping, safe-harbor leasing, industrial development bonds, large limited partnerships, new short-term instruments, international havens, dividend capture programs, and many other innovations, including floating-rate preferred stocks. The development of futures and options markets, however, is of major importance because instruments traded in these markets facilitate the short-selling of securities at low cost. In so doing, they allow investors to eliminate tax differentials with low risk through efficient hedging. Unconstrained short-selling is more likely to cause the after-tax model of asset pricing to be overturned by investors, and for this reason we will highlight the uses of these instruments in this section.

We are not claiming that these instruments were introduced to reduce taxes or in response to changes in tax policy. Although taxes might be one of the reasons, other exogenous events such as increased volatility of interest rates and stock prices must be included in the list of other reasons for the growth of these markets.

From prior finance theory, many would claim that options and futures are redundant assets. We can create options by using stocks and bonds in certain combinations, and we can create forward contracts which are akin to futures by using bonds or combinations of options. Yet these new contracts have prospered and survived even though there are alternative ways to approximate them. The word *approximate* is important because the new innovation might have been to create contracts that better approximate the demands of market participants, and to provide the contracts at lower cost than the alternatives.

Using these markets and forms of financial instruments, investors can circumvent regulations and restrictions, such as short-selling rules, stock issue rules, and margin rules. Let us take the margin rules as an example. Options and futures on stock indices provide an easy way for many individual and institutional investors to circumvent margin rules. If margin restrictions were meaningful prior to the development of these markets, they have lost a good part of their punch after their development.

With the reduction in costs of many of these restrictions, an additional major area of the use of futures and options is taxation. When modeling the effects of new or old taxes on corporate and individual behavior, new forms of financial contracts or financial instruments can change the equilibrium. Investors with surplus can destroy the equilibrium by using these contracts to hedge their risks. The after-tax equilibrium can change dramatically when we introduce different actors with different tax brackets into our models, and a way for these investors to hedge their risks at very low transaction costs.

These new innovations reduce transaction costs and cause the breakdown of old rules and regulations. Transaction costs are important, for without them options and futures markets probably would not exist and many tax rules would be meaningless. To show this, we will summarize the effects of the taxation of financial futures on the equilibrium relative pricing in markets by concentrating on stock and bond futures.[14]

To study these effects we must consider the actions of four groups of participants in the market. Three of these groups have been used in the previous sections of the paper. These three groups are: (1) fully taxable investors; (2) corporations; and (3) tax-exempt organizations, including corporate pension funds. The fourth group that must be introduced explicitly into the analysis is the fully taxable broker-dealer.

When compared to the other groups in the market, broker-dealers, in recent years, have moved closer to becoming the marginal traders. They have the lowest transaction costs. They are taxed as corporations when dealing in securities: They have no restrictions on the deduction of losses on securities trading, and are not worried about distinctions between income and capital gains in seeking profits. With the new markets in options and futures, these dealers can take in "partners" quickly and efficiently by using these markets to hedge their risk at far lower transaction costs than before the existence of these markets. They can borrow securities for short-selling to hedge their trading risks in seeking to profit on disparities caused by the differential taxation of income, including dividends, and capital gains on securities. As we will see, they can respond the same way as tax-exempt institutions to pricing disparities, but at possibly far lower transaction costs and with fewer restrictions.

Effects of the futures market on equilibrium relative rates of return

To understand the effects of futures contracts on the equilibrium pricing of bonds and stocks, we need to develop a simple model of the pricing of futures contracts. A futures contract is a contract to buy an asset at a set price at a future date. Although futures contracts are settled for cash each day, and rewritten at a new futures price, we will assume that they are akin to forward contracts that are settled at maturity of the contract.[15] Since buyers and sellers of financial futures contracts are making commitments to buy and to sell in the future, no cash changes hands at the initiation of the contract. Like insurance contracts, however, there is a contingent liability to buy or to sell the asset and a good faith deposit, called margin, is required: The deposit can be in the form of earning assets. In the analysis to follow, we assume that we escrow the full amount in an account earning at the interest rate r_B.

In addition to the nomenclature we used in the previous sections, we will use the following definitions:

S = Current price of the spot asset, for example, a stock or a bond

F = Futures price of the asset
D^* = Future value of expected cash flows, dividends, or coupons, accumulated to the majority of the contract
S^* = Future value of the asset at maturity of the contract

To price a financial futures contract in a world of no taxes, consider the returns on the following two alternative investments:

	Investment		*Return (or profit)*
Alternative (1):	Asset	S	$S^* - S + D^*$
versus			
Alternative (2):	Futures		$S^* - F$
	plus Bonds	S	Sr_B

Since the uncertainty of the returns on these two alternative investment strategies depends only on the terminal stock price S^*, each investment has the same risk. Since each alternative also requires the same total dollars of investment, the returns must be the same for an equilibrium. Setting the returns equal to each other results in the following relation between the futures price and the spot price of the asset:

$$F = S(1 + r_B) - D^* \tag{4}$$

The futures price is above the spot price in equation (4) by the amount of interest earned on carrying the spot minus the lost cash flow that is paid on the asset, such as coupons and dividends. As seen from the two alternative investment strategies, a futures contract allows investors to separate the two components of owning a risky asset, the bond rate of return, or the sure part of its return, and its risk premium part of its return, into constituent parts. The expected return on the futures contract is equal to the expected risk premium on the underlying asset. Equation (4) is the relation for pricing a futures contract in the before-tax equilibrium.

On introducing taxes into the analysis, the question arises as to what equilibrium rate of interest should be used in equation (4). In an after-tax world it would seem natural to use r_0, the after-tax rate on municipal bonds, as indicated earlier. In this after-tax model, the price of stock futures contracts in equation (4) would be given by the following equation because $r_0 = r_B(1 - \tau_B) = (1 - \tau_s)(1 - \tau_c)r_c$ (see equation (1)):

$$F = [1 + r_B(1 - \tau_B)]\, S - D^* \tag{5}$$

In this relation, D^* is cash dividends and $\tau_B = \tau_c + \tau_s - \tau_c\tau_s$. Hereafter, we assume that the personal tax rate on shares, τ_s, is close to zero, and that the marginal investor in the futures markets is a highly taxed individual investor with a rate equal to τ_c. With after-tax pricing[16] in equation (5), the futures price is below the before-tax price of the future as is given in equation (4).

Implications for equilibrium pricing using bond futures. Although equation (5) would be appropriate for pricing futures on stocks in the after-tax model, this equilibrium requires that marginal investors pay tax on the receipt of coupon income, C^*, on taxable bonds, B. If this were not true, both the marginal tax on shares and on bonds would be zero. This would imply that we return essentially to a before-tax world in that equal personal taxes on all assets throughout the economy result in the same equilibrium as if all effective personal taxes were zero. Assuming then that interest and coupon income are taxed at the same rate, τ_B, the following is the pricing equation for bond futures contracts:

$$F = [1 + r_B(1 - \tau_B)]\, B - C^*\,(1 - \tau_B) \tag{6}$$

The pricing of futures, as is given in equation (6), has important implications for investment strategies of tax-exempt institutions, including corporate pension funds (who are inframarginal in the after-tax equilibrium since their $\tau_B = 0$). If bond futures are priced according to equation (6), then the appropriate strategy for a pension fund depends on whether the "current yield" on bonds, C^*/B, is greater than or less than the interest rate r_B. If $r_B > C^*/B$, pension funds could profit by buying long bond futures and short-term bonds. These transactions would result in the following before-tax dollar return, R:

$$R = B^* + C^* + \tau_B B[r_B - C^*/B] \tag{7}$$

where B^* is the terminal value of the long bonds and C^* is the value of the accrued coupons earned on the bonds at maturity of the futures contract.

As seen from equation (7), this would result in a greater return than holding long bonds in the portfolio of the pension fund. If $r_B < C^*/B$, pension funds could profit by selling long bond futures, and buying long bonds. Pension funds would realize positive excess returns as long as the price of the future remains below the before-tax equilibrium pricing relation, equation (4).

If pension funds could earn excess returns by using futures in investment strategies, brokers and dealers could also earn excess returns even though they pay taxes on income at the marginal federal rate of 46 percent. They are the most efficient fully taxable trader.

Brokers are indifferent to a dollar of profit made by acting as agent on selling and buying securities and a dollar of profit made on arbitrage or on extremely low-risk trading using futures and hedging with other assets for their own account.

If $r_B > C^*/B$, broker-dealers, just like pension funds, would buy long bond futures and short-term bonds. Obviously, the broker-dealer can hedge the risk of the long bond futures position, an uncertain terminal value, B^*, by selling long bonds. The net return would be $\tau_B B[r_B - C^*/B]$. As long as τ_B in the equilibrium pricing of futures is greater than zero, brokers can make hedging profits. Likewise, if C^*/B is greater than r_B, brokers could profit as long as the equilibrium τ_B is greater than zero; that is, the after-tax equilibrium holds. Without transaction costs, the price of the futures contract, in a tax world, must be priced as if there were no taxes, as is shown in equation (4). With transaction costs and efficient traders, it is unlikely that the pricing relations will differ significantly from equation (4).

Futures markets reduce the cost of trading for broker-dealers because these markets provide a liquid market to price and to take positions. If it were possible to measure and detect the differential effects of taxes on high- and low-coupon bonds in the term structure of interest rates prior to futures markets, it is far less likely that these tax-induced differentials exist today. Similarly, any theory stating that the market in bonds is segmented, thereby creating presumed differences in price due to liquidity or habitat theories, would seem to require rethinking when we introduce the possibility of eliminating these pricing differentials at very low risk and cost. The pricing differentials will become insignificant, for without true risk premiums as opposed to term premiums or tax premiums, significant excess returns could be earned by buying or selling these bonds in all combinations of differing maturities, and by taking offsetting positions in the futures market. This converts all the bonds of differing maturities to short-term instruments, with the risk of a price change that is similar to that of Treasury bills. The development of these new markets provides ways to eliminate differences and to reduce transaction costs.

With futures, it is also possible for pension funds and broker-dealers to eliminate any tax-induced pricing differentials in risky corporate bonds. If corporate bonds sell at discounts to induce fully taxable investors to hold these instruments, the procedure would be similar to that described above for noncorporate bonds. It is also possible, with a combination of bond futures and stock futures, to hedge the risky part of corporate bonds and, therefore, to end up earning excess returns. Again this assumes that the tax on shares, τ_s, is close to zero.

Implications for equilibrium pricing using stock index futures. Although we have demonstrated that an equilibrium in the pricing of bond futures contracts requires the before-tax equation (4), we do not have an equilibrium in the pricing of stock index futures. The main difference is that, with bond futures, interest and coupons are treated as interest for tax purposes; however, with stock futures, dividends are not treated as interest for corporate tax payers. As explained previously, 85 percent of the dividends received are excluded from corporate tax if certain minor requirements are satisfied by corporations holding dividend-paying securities.

If stock index futures are priced in the after-tax equilibrium, as in equation (5), pension funds should hold short-term bonds and stock index futures in lieu of holding core portfolios of common stock. Using the pricing relation in equation (5), the dollar return to the pension fund using this strategy, R_p, would be given by the following relation:

$$\begin{aligned} R_p &= S^* - F + Sr_B \\ &= S^* - S + D^* + r_B \tau_B S \end{aligned} \tag{8}$$

Pension funds would earn an excess return of $r_B \tau_B S$ over holding common stocks directly in the fund. Similarly, broker-dealers would earn an excess return by holding stock futures and shorting stock to hedge their risk. For both types of investors, this strategy dominates alternatives for any level of risk. The return bonus is equal to the effective tax rate used in pricing the futures contract times the interest on the assets used in the strategy (the fourth term on the right side of equation (8)). This cannot be an equilibrium: Pension funds and broker-dealers would buy futures until the price of the futures contract approaches the before-tax price, as given in equation (4).

On the other hand, if stock index futures are priced in the before-tax model, as in equation (4), opportunities exist for corporations to capture dividends. In the after-tax model, holding stocks on corporate accounts to capture dividends is an inferior strategy to holding taxable bonds.[17] By holding stocks, corporations earn the risk-adjusted after-tax rate on municipal bonds, r_0, and pay an additional tax of approximately 6.9 percent on the 15 percent of the dividend income they receive that is not excluded from tax. By holding bonds, corporations earn r_0.

By hedging stock positions with stock index futures priced in the before-tax model of equation (4), corporations can earn excess returns over holding taxable bonds on corporate account. The corporation sells its holding of Treasury bills and buys a diversified portfolio of common stocks, simultaneously selling stock index futures to hedge the risk of the common stock holdings. Before tax, the net cash flow from these transactions would be $r_B S$, the same rate of return as holding Treasury bills on a corporate account. After tax, however, the effects differ dramatically. After simplification, the following relation gives the after-tax dollar return, R_c, from this strategy:

$$R_c = r_B S(1 - \tau_c) + 0.85\tau_c D \tag{9}$$

By following this strategy, the corporation makes a sure profit, a rate above the after-tax short-term bond rate in the market. This profit results from the corporate dividend exclusion of 85 percent of the dividends received. The futures price takes out the full dividend as in equation (4); therefore, the corporation ends up keeping the last term in equation (9) as a bonus. This bonus can be quite large. For example, with interest rates of 8.5 percent and dividend yields of 4.5 percent, the bonus is 1.76 percent and, when compared to an after-tax bond return of 3.91 percent, the bonus is 45 percent of the interest rate.

Since broker-dealers make a profit if the futures price is above or below the before-tax pricing relation, equation (4), the rules for the taxation of dividends must be changed or corporations will remain inframarginal and make abnormal gains by capturing dividends, as in equation (9). Futures markets have changed a potential corporate dividend-received penalty into a potential advantage.[18]

It is also interesting to speculate what would happen to the preferred stock equilibrium. Let us assume that, in the after-tax world, corporations would hold the entire stock of preferred issues and corporations could issue preferred stock at a risk-adjusted rate just above the municipal bond rate since corporations holding the preferred issues can exclude only 85 percent of the dividends received from federal taxes. It would make little difference to corporations if they buy taxable bonds, common stocks, or preferred stocks.[19] The after-tax returns would be approximately the same. Dividend payments are not deductible, but are excluded on corporate accounts; interest payments are deductible, but are included on corporate accounts. If corporations are holding the entire stock of preferred issues, broker-dealers cannot arbitrage by selling preferred issues and hedging with futures.

Broker-dealers cannot sell preferred stocks short and pay the low dividend rate. If corporations lend preferreds for short-selling purposes, the supply of preferred issues is not increased. The lending corporation loses the right to exclude dividends, receiving instead taxable income from the broker in lieu of dividends from the issuing corporation. Corporations would not lend preferred stock. Without the ability to borrow preferred stock for short-selling, a broker-dealer cannot arbitrage the rates. Everyone wants to borrow at the sure municipal rate and to lend at the government rate.

With new financial instruments, the tax equilibriums might change. With futures, the balances shift toward the before-tax equilibrium. Future changes in the tax laws might shift the balance to the after-tax equilibrium. By understanding why new contracts are introduced, we gain some clues into understanding what effects their introduction will have on rules and regulations, and, in particular, tax rules.

CONCLUSION

Although we have described the response of four major groups—individuals, corporations, tax-exempt institutions, and broker-dealers—to the tax laws, their responses change as conditions change in the economy. For example, although at high rates of interest individuals might use a particular strategy to reduce tax on investment income, the same strategy could be unprofitable at low rates of interest. Tax authorities also respond to changes in the economy and propose changes in tax laws. For example, at high levels of inflation, rules are changed to liberalize depreciation on capital assets. The tax authorities also respond to tax shelters and to other schemes that seem to convert ordinary income into untaxed or low-taxed capital gains. It is difficult to measure the effects of taxes on relative prices and returns in the market: The tax effects change over time.

There is empirical evidence of tax effects both on the relative pricing of securities and on the behavior of inframarginal investors. Some evidence supports the before-tax and some the after-tax equilibrium model. The difficulties in describing these two models arise not only because tax effects are dynamic, but also because each group has tax laws particular to itself, and income from assets is taxed at differential rates. For individuals, the return from shares is nominally split into a tax on dividends at a higher rate than a tax on capital gains, a rate differential that has been changed many times over the last 20 years. While the current maximum tax on dividend and interest income is 50 percent, the current maximum tax on capital gains is only 20 percent, and only if they are realized.

The empirical evidence must be interpreted with caution because the relative influence on pricing of each of the four groups changes over time. In some time periods, individuals might be the marginal investors and pension funds inframarginal; at other times, broker-dealers or pension funds might be the marginal investors. Tax laws might induce investors to make the shift. Since the early 1950s, there has been a dramatic and continued growth in the assets and relative position of pension funds among investors. Individuals use them, due to their high tax-free returns, to substitute for saving for retirement on their own accounts. On observing changes in the tax laws, it appears as if our objective is to keep taxes low on the returns to capital, possibly for fear that high taxes would be detrimental to savings and to capital formation. Since income on savings is subject to double taxation, once when earned and not consumed, and then again each time consumption is deferred, individuals will substitute current consumption for future consumption. Likewise, corporate income has the same potential for double taxation: once when earned and again through taxes on dividends and capital gains income. The tax laws, however, have been written to provide the opportunity to reduce the tax on income from savings both at the individual level through pension plans, profit-sharing plans, IRAs, etc., and at the corporate level through fast write-offs of investments, leasing arrangements, and other incentives that reduce, and sometimes eliminate, taxes on investing in capital projects.

These opportunities, however, also open the door for others to use tax laws to affect public policy; for example, special-interest groups continue to propose tax exemptions for many pet projects. The different treatments of the tax on assets open up opportunities for investors to game the system at the margin. The IRS has been trying for years to define a debt instrument for purposes of the corporate interest deduction. Although the distinction is obvious in many cases, it is difficult to distinguish for highly leveraged firms, or for claims that have many equity features in addition to the payment of interest. Similar questions arise as to what is a capital asset, subject to capital gains treatment, and what is its close competitor, a bond. As noted in our section on futures and options markets, investors or broker-dealers can buy capital assets and hedge risks; with little remaining risk it is hard to distinguish the risk of the net investment from the risk of investing in bonds. We artifically distinguish investments that are not distinct; investments are substitutes for each other regardless of their names and differences in the tax law.

It would have made our task much easier if the returns to savings were not taxed; it would have made our task much easier if there were no corporate tax. Both individuals and corporations would then be marginal, as would tax-exempt institutions and broker-dealers. Our task would have also been easier if it were not necessary to expand the analysis to include the growth of new markets, such as the options and futures markets, and their use by groups such as broker-dealers. These new complications make it even more difficult to sort out the effects of taxation on equilibrium-relative pricing.

Although we started by considering only existing models of taxation on corporate finance, we added fuel to existing controversy by considering how both the completion of markets by adding new markets such as markets in options and futures and their use in hedging risks by broker-dealers, affects equilibrium pricing. Since broker-dealers are the most efficient traders in most security markets, their role will continue to grow as long as pricing differentials, due to differing tax treatment, continue to exist, or tax laws are not revised.

With differing tax laws, the main empirical predictions of both the before-tax and after-tax models must be internally inconsistent. For corporation finance, the primary inconsistent prediction of the before-tax model is that we should observe that nearly all tax-paying corporations have high debt-to-equity ratios. The evidence does not support this prediction: Corporations have too little debt in their capital structures to square with the presumed advantages of borrowing at the after-tax rate on corporate accounts. Also there is little empirical evidence, other than weak evidence in Masulis (1980, 1983) that those corporations which substitute debt for equity in their capital structures experience large abnormal gains in their share prices on the announcement of the change.

This evidence tends to support the after-tax model. In addition, other evidence, such as corporations issuing and holding preferred stock, tends to support the after-tax model. The preferred stock evidence is not yet complete, for it has been difficult to compare the closeness of the returns on preferred stocks and municipal bonds, due to differences in risk and duration of these instruments. With the recent growth, however, of the floating-rate preferred issues, it is easier to test for differences in returns. As noted previously, taxable estates and trusts do hold a significant amount of taxable corporate and government bonds, as do many corporations. For these corporations, there is no evidence that they realized a decline in the price of their common shares on adding bonds to corporate accounts, even if these bonds were financed partially with equity.

The evidence, however, for pension plans does not seem to support either model. If anything, the evidence is more damaging to the after-tax model if the assets in corporate pension funds are corporate assets. Pension funds hold common stock. In this model, however, corporations should hold only bonds in their pension plans, for bonds in the pension plans earn r_B, while the corporation pays only $r_B(1 - \tau_B)$ to fund the plan. Common stocks in pension funds return a risk-adjusted rate of return of only r_0, which is less than r_B, the before-tax return on bonds. The before-tax model has little to say about funding policy unless holding bonds in the pension fund is an advantage in borrowing on a corporate account.

The evidence on dividends, however, tends to support the proposition that the tax on shares is much lower than the corporate tax rate, τ_c; see Hess (1983). This is somewhat consistent with the after-tax theory. Black and Scholes (1974) and Miller and Scholes (1982) provide evidence that the return on shares that pay dividends differs insignificantly from the returns on shares that do not pay dividends. Most other evidence suggests that the return differences and therefore pricing differences are quite small. If there were large tax effects on the pricing of shares of firms paying dividends, it would be more of a mystery as to why corporations continue to pay out such a large fraction of their earnings in the form of dividends when they could just as easily repurchase shares. With the new markets, corporations could move from being inframarginal to marginal because of their preference for holding dividend-paying stocks and hedging with futures: The before-tax return to dividend-paying shares would be less than the return to nondividend-paying shares. Broker-dealers, however, would have a strong incentive to bring the pricing differential to zero.

The same arguments apply to bonds. If investors could reduce the tax on shares by levering on personal accounts to wash out the receipt of dividend income by interest paid on borrowing, investors also could convert coupon income into untaxed or low-taxed capital gains by a similar strategy. Evidence on these strategies at the margin would support the prediction of the before-tax model.

There has been no direct evidence as to the effect of taxation on the returns to bonds. Once again, obtaining evidence by testing whether there are positive before-tax excess rates of return to holding high-versus low-coupon bonds is difficult because it is difficult to obtain reliable time series of the prices of corporate bonds; it is difficult to control for differences in risks, and it is difficult to control for differences in duration; see, however, Schaefer (1982).

Tests of the capital asset pricing model, however, indicate that the estimates of the risk-adjusted rates, r_0, are significantly above r_B. On its face, this evidence weighs against the after-tax model. However, if the sure rate of interest is only a construct, and an individual cannot borrow and lend without risk, it is possible that measured returns can be above r_B and still be consistent with the after-tax equilibrium.

All of the tests for tax effects are difficult to interpret because we are looking for evidence of small differences in returns with techniques and data that cannot measure the differences with enough precision. This must be coupled with the knowledge that what we are trying to measure might be changing from one time period to the next.

We have discussed only the effects of taxation on corporate financial management at the macro level—big decisions such as corporate capital structure and dividend decisions—and have ignored the myriad of other second-level corporate decisions that are influenced by taxes. In every one of these micro decisions, corporate officers decide whether they are inframarginal or marginal, given market prices to infer whether they can profit by taking into account the effects of taxes and markets in making investment and financing decisions.

Notes

1. By making precise assumptions about the nature of a subset of these other market imperfections, the equilibrium models described in many papers differ from these two polar cases. As a direct cost of these precise assumptions, however, these models lose generality, especially, in considering the role that taxes play: That role is our primary focus in this paper.
2. The horizontal segment of the demand curve in Figure 1 represents corporations holding the taxable bonds of other corporations.
3. This same argument can be applied, in principle, on a dollar of interest received or even on a dollar of partnership income.
4. Direct bankruptcy costs were measured for the regulated railroad industry and were found to be very small in Warner (1977). The theoretical consideration of bankruptcy costs (usually in the context of our before-tax equilibrium), has been the subject of numerous papers; see, for example, Kim (1978), Kraus and Litzenberger (1973), Haugen and Senbet (1978), Scott (1976, 1977). The effect of the possibility of bankruptcy or reorganization on the product sales or labor services of the corporation and thus, on the capital structure decision, is discussed in Titman (1982). Brennan and Schwartz (1977) discuss how the risk of bankruptcy increases with leverage and that this increases the probability of losing the tax benefits from all of the firm's debt (in the before-tax equilibrium) if they cannot be sold, and that this loss must be balanced against the tax benefits of the marginal dollar of new debt.

5. Because contracting and monitoring costs associated with issuing debt exist and presumably increase with more leverage, bond covenants are not written to cover all possible managerial actions over the life of the bond that can redistribute or expropriate wealth from the bondholders to the other claimants of the firm. The effects of this potential for expropriation on the capital structure decision are discussed at great length in many papers, such as: Jensen and Meckling (1976), Myers (1977), Kim, McConnell, and Greenwood (1977), Galai and Masulis (1976), Smith and Warner (1979), and Fama and Miller (1972, Chapter 4).
6. Because it is costly to obtain and verify new information and because insiders may receive it first, managers are apt to signal their new information to the general investment public by their capital structure and dividend decisions. A sample of theoretical papers on this subject are: Leland and Pyle (1977), Ross (1977), and Miller and Rock (1982). Empirical studies on signaling with changes in capital structure include Masulis (1983), Vermaelen (1981), and Asquith and Mullins (1983).
7. Presumably flotation costs associated with obtaining undistributed profits, issuing new debt, and issuing new common shares differ (possibly, ranked in the order mentioned). Many have written on this, the latest being Myers in his presidential address to the AFA (1984).
8. If the number of distinct securities is less than the number of states-of-nature, this could affect relative prices and result in monopoly rents (incomplete markets). Presumably this exists, if it does, because it is costly to create new securities to complete the capital markets. A sampling of the many papers written on the effects of incomplete markets on the capital structure decision would include Modigliani (1982), Baron (1976), Taggart (1980), Senbet and Taggart (1984).
9. DeAngelo and Masulis (1980) indicate that the aggregate supply curve of taxable debt in Miller's debt and taxes equilibrium will not be infinitely horizontal, as in Figure 1, in that corporations may not have any taxable income from which they can deduct interest payments. The investment tax credit, accelerated depreciation expenses, and other tax deductions may leave a given corporation and the aggregate of all corporations with no need for further tax deductions, such as interest payments. Then the before-tax interest rate may not be grossed up fully, relative to r_0.
10. As we indicated in footnote 1, all these capital market imperfection models imply their own specific equilibrium. It is an empirical issue which of these models, or the two equilibrium tax models discussed in this paper, are the closest to depicting reality. Noting again that the focus of this paper is taxes, discussion is purposefully limited on each of these market imperfection models.
11. After adjusting for differences in risk and maturity, the spread between r_0 and r_B has been empirically investigated in many studies, such as Skelton (1983), Buser and Hess (1983), Trzcinka (1982), and Trzcinka and Kamma (1983). One should note, however, that virtu-

ally the same spread is predicted by both the after-tax and before-tax equilibrium models.

12. The conditions required for the risk-expected return equilibrium above r_B are discussed in Hamada (1982).
13. The prime on $E(R_M')$ in equation (3*a*) is to warn that, when changing from a no-tax world to a tax world, the expected rate of return on the market need not remain unchanged; nor is the composition of the market portfolio well defined in this after-tax model.
14. It is possible to expand the same arguments to options on common stocks and bonds since a futures contract can be approximated by a combination of a call option and a put option on the underlying asset. Futures contracts are easier to use as a descriptive tool in the context of describing different tax effects.
15. Black (1976) was the first to point out, then Cox, Ingersoll, and Ross (1981) elaborated on it, that a futures contract and a forward contract differ if the interest rate is not constant. Later empirical work indicated that the differences are extremely small, and we will ignore them for this analysis.
16. If one recalls our previous discussion, Miller's after-tax equilibrium requires τ_s to be much smaller than τ_B. Therefore, we have assumed that the after-tax marginal rate on dividend income is zero. Although somewhat controversial, empirical evidence tends to suggest that dividends are taxed at a rate far less than 0.46, the marginal federal tax rate on corporate income. This assumption, if not literally true, will only modify our results, not change their direction.
17. Earlier, we discussed the effects of the 85 percent dividend exclusion when τ_s was not constrained to be greater than zero.
18. Provisions of the Tax Reform Act of 1984 appears to reduce the effectiveness of these strategies.
19. Although only 85 percent of the dividend is excludable from taxation, implying that issuing common stock might be preferable to issuing preferred stock, the personal tax on shares, τ_s, might be large enough to make issuing preferred an advantageous strategy. Also, firms paying taxes at low corporate tax rates would find it advantageous to issue preferreds rather than bonds.

REFERENCES

Asquith, P. and D. Mullins. "Equity Issues and Stock Price Dilution." Unpublished paper, Harvard Business School, September 1983.

Baron, D. "Default Risk and the Modigliani-Miller Theorem: A Synthesis." *American Economic Review* (June 1976), pp. 204–12.

Black, Fischer "The Pricing of Commodity Contracts." *Journal of Financial Economics* 3, Nos. 1/2 (January/March 1976), pp. 167–79.

Black, Fischer "The Tax Consequences of Long-Run Pension Policy" *Financial Analysts Journal* 36 (July/August 1980), pp. 1–10.

Black, F. and M. Scholes "The Effects of Dividend Yield and Dividend Policy on Common Stock Prices and Returns." *Journal of Financial Economics* 1, No. 1 (May 1974), pp. 1–22.

Brennan, M. J., and E. S. Schwartz. "Corporate Income Taxes, Valuation, and the Problem of Optimal Capital Structure." *Journal of Business* 51, No. 1 (January 1977), pp. 103–14.

Bulow, Jeremy. "Corporate Investment Policy." NBER Working Paper, 1982.

Bulow, J. and M. Scholes. "Who Owns the Assets in a Defined-Benefit Pension Plan." In *Financial Aspects of the U.S. Pension System*. Bodie and Shoven. NBER and University of Chicago Press, 1984.

Buser, S. and P. Hess. "The Marginal Cost of Leverage, the Tax Rate on Equity and the Relation between Taxable and Tax-Exempt Yields." Unpublished paper, Ohio State University, October 1983.

Constantinides, G. "Capital Market Equilibrium with Personal Tax." *Econometrica* (May 1983).

Cox, John, J. Ingersoll, and S. Ross. "The Relation Between Forward Prices and Futures Prices." *Journal of Financial Economics* 9, December 1981, pp. 321–46.

DeAngelo, Harry, and R. W. Masulis. "Optimal Capital Structure Under Corporate and Personal Taxation." *Journal of Financial Economics* 8, No 1 (March 1980), pp. 3–29.

Fama, E. F. and M. Miller. *The Theory of Finance*. New York: Holt, Rinehart & Winston, 1972.

Galai, D. and R. Masulis. "The Option Pricing Model and the Risk Factor of Stock." *Journal of Financial Economics* 4, (January/March 1976).

Hamada, R. "Portfolio Analysis, Market Equilibrium and Corporation Finance." *Journal of Finance* (March 1969).

————. "The Effect of the Firm's Capital Structure on the Systematic Risk of Common Stocks." XXVII. *Journal of Finance* (May 1972), pp. 435–452.

————. "Differential Taxes and the Structure of Equilibrium Rates of Return: Managerial Implications and Remaining Conundrums." Unpublished CRSP Working Paper No. 68, University of Chicago, December 1982.

Harris, J., R. Roenfeldt, and P. Cooley. "Evidence of Financial Leverage Clienteles." *Journal of Finance* 38, No. 4 (September 1983).

Haugen, R. and L. Senbet. "The Insignificance of Bankruptcy Costs to the Theory of Optimal Capital Structure" XXIII, No. 5. *Journal of Finance* (1978), pp. 383–93.

Hess, P. "Tests for Tax Effects in the Pricing of Financial Assets." *Journal of Business* (October 1983).

Jensen, M. And W. Meckling. "Theory of the Firm Managerial Behavior, Agency Costs and Ownership Structure" 3. *Journal of Financial Economics* (October 1976), pp. 305–60.

Kim, E. H. "A Mean-Variance Theory of Optimal Capital Structure and Corporate Debt Capacity" XXXIII. *Journal of Finance* (March 1978), pp. 45–64.

Kim, E. H., J. McConnell, and P. Greenwood. "Capital Structure Rearrangements and Me-First Rules in an Efficient Capital Market" XXXII. *Journal of Finance* (June 1977).

Kim, E. H., W. G. Lewellen, and J. J. McConnell. "Financial Leverage Clienteles: Theory and Evidence." *Journal of Financial Economics* 7, No. 1 (March 1979), pp. 83–109.

Kraus, A. and R. Litzenberger. "A State-Preference Model of Optimal Financial Leverage", XXVII. *Journal of Finance* (September 1973), pp. 911–22.

Leland, H. and D. Pyle. "Information Asymmetries, Financial Structure, and Financial Intermediation", XXXII. *Journal of Finance*, (May 1977).

Masulis, R. W. "The Effects of Capital Structure Change on Security Prices: A Study of Exchange Offers." *Journal of Financial Economics* 8 (June 1980), pp. 139–78.

Masulis, R. W. "The Impact of Capital Structure Change on Firm Value: Some Estimates." *The Journal of Finance* 38, No. 1 (March 1983), pp. 107–26.

Miller, M. "Debt and Taxes." *The Journal of Finance* XXXII, No. 2 (May 1977), pp. 261–75.

Miller, M. and F. Modigliani. "Dividend Policy, Growth, and the Valuation of Shares." *The Journal of Business* XXXIV, No. 4 (October 1961), pp. 411–33.

Miller, M. and K. Rock. "Dividend Policy Under-Asymmetric Information." Unpublished paper, University of Chicago, 1982.

Miller, M. and M. Scholes. "Dividends and Taxes." *Journal of Financial Economics* 6, No. 4 (December 1978), pp. 333–64.

Miller, M. and M. Scholes. "Dividends and Taxes: Some Empirical Evidence." *Journal of Political Economy* 90, No. 6 (December 1982), pp. 1118–41.

Modigliani, F. "Debt, Dividend Policy, Taxes, Inflation, and Market Valuation" 37. *Journal of Finance* (May 1982), pp. 255–74.

Modigliani, F. and M. Miller. "The Cost of Capital, Corporation Finance, and the Theory of Investment." *The American Economic Review* XLVIII, No. 3 (June 1958), pp. 261–97.

Modigliani, F. and M. Miller. "Corporate Income Taxes and the Cost of Capital: A Correction." *The American Economic Review* LIII, No. 3 (June 1963), pp. 433–43.

Myers, S. C. "Determinants of Corporate Borrowing" 5. *Journal of Financial Economics* (November 1977), pp. 147–75.

Myers, S. "A Simple Model of Financing and Investment Decisions." 39. *Journal of Finance* (May 1984).

Ross, S. "The Determination of Financial Structure: The Incentive-Signalling Approach." *Bell Journal of Economics* 8, No. 1 (Spring 1977), pp. 23–40.

Schaefer, S. "Tax-Induced Clientele Effects in the Market for British Government Securities: Placing Bounds on Security Values in an Incomplete Market." *Journal of Financial Economics* (July 1982).

Scott, J. "A Theory of Optimal Capital Structure" 7, No. 1. *Bell Journal of Economics* (Spring 1976), pp. 33–54.

Scott, J. "Bankruptcy, Secured Debt, and Optimal Capital Structure" XXXII. *Journal of Finance* (March 1977), pp. 1–20.

Senbet, L. and R. Taggart. "Capital Structure Equilibrium under Market Imperfections and Incompleteness" 39. *Journal of Finance* (March 1984), pp. 93–104.

Skelton, J. "Banks, Firms and the Relative Pricing of Tax-Exempt and Taxable Bonds" 10. *Journal of Financial Economics* (November 1983).

Smith, C. and J. Warner. "On Financial Contracting: An Analysis of Bond Covenants" 7. *Journal of Financial Economics* (June 1979).

Taggart, R. "Taxes and Corporate Capital Structure in an Incomplete Market." *Journal of Finance* 35 (1980), pp. 654–59.

Tepper, I. "Taxation and Corporate Pension Policy." *Journal of Finance* 36 (March 1981), pp. 1–13.

Titman, S. "The Effect of Capital Structure on a Firm's Liquidation Decision." Unpublished paper, University of California At Los Angeles, February 1982.

Trzcinka, C. "The Pricing of Tax-Exempt Bonds and the Miller Hypothesis." *Journal of Finance* 37 (September 1982), pp. 907–24.

Trzcinka, C. and S. Kamma. "Marginal Taxes, Municipal Bond Risk and the Miller Equilibrium: New Evidence and Some Predictive Tests." Unpublished paper, State University of New York at Buffalo, December 1983.

Vermaelen, T. "Common Stock Repurchases and Market Signalling: An Empirical Study." *Journal of Financial Economics* 9 (June 1981), pp. 139–83.

Warner, J. "Bankruptcy Costs: Some Evidence." *Jornal of Finance* XXXII (December 1977), pp. 337–47.

Warner, J. "Bankruptcy, Absolute Priority, and the Pricing of Risky Debt Claims." *Journal of Financial Economics* 5 (May 1977).

---

* This author would like to thank the London Graduate School of Business Studies for the opportunity of spending a reflective year in which the conditions were ideal for rethinking some of the issues in this paper.

9

The Economic Effects of Dividend Taxation*

James M. Poterba
Massachusetts Institute of Technology and NBER

Lawrence H. Summers
Harvard University and NBER

This paper tests three competing hypotheses about the economic effects of dividend taxation using British data on security returns, dividend payout rates, and corporate investment. Unlike the United States, Britain has experienced several major dividend tax reforms in the last three decades, providing an ideal natural experiment for analyzing dividend taxes. We conclude that the traditional "double-taxation" view is most consistent with the empirical evidence. This view implies that dividend taxes reduce corporate investment and exacerbate distortions in the intersectoral and intertemporal allocation of capital. We reject the new "tax capitalization" view that dividend taxes are nondistortionary lump sum taxes on the owners of corporate capital. We also reject the hypothesis that firms pay dividends because marginal investors are effectively untaxed.

The Economic Effects of Dividend Taxation

INTRODUCTION

The question of how taxes on corporate distributions affect economic behavior is central to evaluating a number of major tax reform options. Shifts toward either consumption taxation or corporate tax integration would result in dramatic reductions in the taxes levied on dividend income. On the other hand, movement toward a comprehensive income tax would raise the effective tax burden on dividends. Although many financial economists have studied the question of why firms pay dividends despite the associated tax penalties imposed on many investors, no consensus has emerged as to the effects of dividend taxation on firms' investment and financial decisions.

This paper summarizes our research program examining the empirical validity of several widely held views about the economic effects of dividend taxation. Empirical analysis of dividend taxation using American data is difficult, because there has been relatively little variation over time in the relevant legislation. We therefore focus on empirical analysis of the British experience since 1950, which has been characterized by four major reforms in the taxation of corporate distributions. These reforms have generated substantial variations in the effective marginal tax rate on dividend income, and provide an ideal natural experiment for studying the economic effects of dividend taxes.

At the outset, it is important to clarify why developing a convincing model of the effects of dividend taxation has been so difficult for economists. Straightforward analysis suggests that since some shareholders are tax-penalized when firms pay dividends instead of retaining earnings, firms should not pay dividends. Dividend taxes should collect no revenue and impose no allocative distortions. Even the most casual empiricism discredits this analysis. The payment of dividends is a common and enduring practice of most large corporations, and it appears to result in substantial tax liabilities for many investors. In modeling the effects of dividend taxes, it is therefore necessary to provide some account of why dividends are paid. Given the simple model's clear no-dividend prediction, any model which rationalizes dividend payout will seem at least partly unsatisfactory. However, some choice is clearly necessary if we are to make any headway toward understanding the economic effects of dividend taxes.

We consider three competing views of how dividend taxes affect decisions by firms and shareholders. They are not mutually exclusive, and each could be relevant to the behavior of some firms. The first view, which we label the "tax irrelevance view," argues that contrary to naive expectations, dividend-paying firms are not penalized in the marketplace.[1] It holds that in the United States, because of various nuances in the tax code, marginal investors do not require extra pretax returns to induce them to hold dividend-paying securities. Some personal investors are effectively untaxed on dividend income. Other investors, who face high transactions costs or are nontaxable but face limitations on expenditures from capital, find dividends more attractive than capital gains for nontax reasons. These investors demand dividend-paying securities. If this view is correct and dividend-paying firms are not penalized, there is no dividend puzzle. Moreover, changes in dividend tax rates or dividend policies should affect neither the total value of any firm nor its investment decisions. Dividend taxes are therefore nondistortionary. The tax irrelevance view implies that reducing dividend taxes would have no effect on share values, corporate investment decisions, or the economy's long-run capital stock.

A second view regarding the dividend payout problem, which also holds that dividend taxes do not have distortionary effects, may be called the "tax capitalization hypothesis."[2] The premise of this view is that the only way for mature firms to pass money through the corporate veil is by paying taxable dividends. The market value of corporate assets is therefore equal to the present value of the after-tax dividends which firms are expected to pay. Moreover, because these future taxes are capitalized into share values, shareholders are indifferent between policies of retaining earnings or paying dividends. On this view, raising dividend taxes would result in an immediate decline in the market value of corporate equity. However, dividend taxes have no impact on a firm's *marginal* incentive to invest. They are essentially lump sum taxes levied on the initial holders of corporate capital, with no distortionary effects on real decisions. The tax capitalization view implies that reducing dividend taxes would confer windfall gains on corporate shareowners, without altering corporate investment incentives.

A third, and more traditional, view of dividend taxes treats them as additional taxes on corporate profits.[3] Despite the heavier tax burden on dividends than on capital gains, firms are rewarded for paying dividends. The explanation for this reward is unclear; managerial signaling could provide one rationale. Therefore, in spite of their shareholders' higher tax liability, firms can be indifferent to marginal changes in their dividend payments. This view suggests that the relevant tax burden for firms considering marginal investments is the *total* tax levied on investment returns at both the corporate and the personal level. Dividend tax reductions both raise share values and provide incentives for capital investment, because they lower the pretax return which firms are required to earn. Dividend tax changes would therefore affect the economy's long-run capital intensity.

Our empirical work is directed at evaluating each of these three views of dividend taxation. The results suggest that the "traditional" view of dividend taxation is most consistent with the British postwar data on security returns, payout ratios, and investment decisions. While there is no necessity for the effects of dividend taxes to be parallel in the United States and the United Kingdom, our results are strongly suggestive for the United States.

The plan of the paper is as follows. The first section lays out the three alternative views of dividend taxation in greater detail, and discusses their implications for the relationship between dividend taxes and corporate investment and dividend decisions. The next section describes the nature and evolution of the British tax system in some detail. The "natural experiments" provided by postwar British tax reforms provide the basis for our subsequent empirical tests. The third section presents evidence on how tax changes affect investors' relative valuation of dividends and capital gains by focusing on "ex-dividend" share price movements in the United Kingdom. Our results show that tax rates do appear to influence the value of dividend income. This analysis is extended by examining share price changes in months when dividend tax reforms were announced, presenting further evidence that tax rates affect security valuation. The fifth section tests the alternative theories' implications for the effects of dividend tax changes on corporate payout policies. We find that dividend tax changes do affect the share of profits which firms choose to distribute. Section six focuses directly on investment decisions, testing which view of dividend taxation best explains the time series pattern of British investment. Finally, we discuss the implications of our results for tax policy and suggest several directions for future research.

THREE VIEWS OF DIVIDEND TAXATION

The irrelevance of dividend policy in a taxless world has been recognized since Miller and Modigliani's (1961) pathbreaking work. If shareholders face differential tax rates on dividends and capital gains, however, the irrelevance result may no longer hold. Dividend policy may affect shareholder wealth, and shareholders may not be simultaneously indifferent to investments financed from retained earnings and investments financed from new equity issues.

To illustrate these propositions, we consider the after-tax return which a shareholder with marginal tax rates of m and z on dividends and capital gains, respectively, receives by holding shares in a particular firm.[4] The shareholder's after-tax return R is

$$R_t = (1 - m)\frac{D_t}{V_t} + (1 - z)\left(\frac{V^0_{t+1} - V_t}{V_t}\right) \tag{1.1}$$

where D_t is the firm's dividend payment, V_t is the total value of the firm in period t, and V^0_{t+1} is the period $t + 1$ value of the shares outstanding in period t. To focus on tax-related aspects of the firm's problem, we shall ignore uncertainty, treating V^0_{t+1} as known at time t.[5] The total value of the firm at $t + 1$ is

$$V_{t+1} = V^0_{t+1} + V^N_t \tag{1.2}$$

where V^N_t equals new shares issued in period t. Equation (1.1) can be rewritten, assuming that in equilibrium the shareholder earns his required return so $R_t = \rho$, as

$$\rho V_t = (1 - m)D_t - (1 - z)V^N_t + (1 - z)(V_{t+1} - V_t) \tag{1.3}$$

Equation (1.3) is a difference equation for the value of the firm, V_t;

$$V_{t+1} = \left(1 + \frac{\rho}{1 - z}\right)V_t + V^N_t - \left(\frac{1 - m}{1 - z}\right)D_t \tag{1.4}$$

It may be solved forward, subject to the transversality condition

$$\lim_{T\to\infty} \left(1 + \frac{\rho}{1 - z}\right)^{-T} V_T = 0 \tag{1.5}$$

to obtain an expression for the value of the firm:

$$V_t = \sum_{j=0}^{\infty} \left(1 + \frac{\rho}{1 - z}\right)^{-j}\left[\left(\frac{1 - m}{1 - z}\right)D_{t+j} - V^N_{t+j}\right] \tag{1.6}$$

The total value of the firm is the present discounted value of after-tax dividends, less the present value of new share issues which current shareholders would be required to purchase in order to maintain their claims on a constant fraction of the firm's total dividends and profits.

Before considering the different views of dividend taxation, we shall sketch the firm's optimization problem. The firm's objective is to maximize its market value, subject to several constraints. The first is its cash flow identity:

$$(1 - \tau)\Pi_t + V_t^N = D_t + I_t \tag{1.7}$$

where Π_t is pretax profitability, I_t is gross investment expenditures, and τ is the corporate tax rate. $\Pi_t = \Pi_t(K_t)$, where K_t is the capital stock at the beginning of period t.[6] Next, there is an equation describing the evolution of the firms' capital stock:

$$K_t = K_{t-1} + I_t \tag{1.8}$$

We assume that there is no depreciation, and ignore adjustment costs or the possible irreversibility of investment. Finally, there are restrictions on the firms' financial policies: dividends cannot be negative, and new share issues must be greater than some minimal level $\overline{V}^N$,[7] reflecting restrictions on the firm's ability to repurchase shares or to engage in transactions with equivalent tax consequences. These two constraints can be written

$$D_t \geq 0 \tag{1.9}$$

and

$$V_t^N \geq \overline{V}^N \tag{1.10}$$

where $\overline{V}^N \leq 0$.

Before formally solving for the firm's investment and financial plan, we observe one important feature of any solution to this problem. The firm would never simultaneously issue new equity and pay dividends. If a firm sets both $D_t > 0$ and $V_t^N > \overline{V}^N$ in any period, there would exist a feasible perturbation in financial policy which would not affect investment or profits in any period but would raise share values. This perturbation involves a reduction in dividends, compensated for by a reduction in new share issues. To vary dividends and new share issues without affecting Π_t or I_t, we require

$$dV_t^N = dD_t \tag{1.11}$$

From equation (1.6), the change in share value caused by a dividend change in period $t + j$ which satisfied equation (1.11) is

$$\begin{aligned} dV_t &= \left\{\frac{(1-m)}{(1-z)}dD_{t+j} - dV^N_{t+j}\right\}\left(1+\frac{\rho}{1-z}\right)^{-j} \\ &= -\frac{(m-z)}{(1-z)}dD_{t+j}\left(1+\frac{\rho}{1-z}\right)^{-j} \end{aligned} \tag{1.12}$$

If m exceeds z, reducing dividends whenever feasible will raise V_t.

Since this perturbation argument applies at any positive level of dividends, it establishes that firms with sufficient profits to cover investment needs should reduce new share issues and repurchase shares to the extent possible. For some firms, I_t may exceed $(1-\tau)\Pi_t$, and there will be new share issues. Even if $m > z$, therefore, some new equity may be issued. Similarly, some firms may have too few investments to fully utilize their current profits. If feasible, these firms should repurchase their shares. Only after exhausting tax-free distribution channels should these firms pay dividends. No firm, however, should ever operate on *both* the dividend and share issue margins simultaneously. The "dividend puzzle" consists of the observation that some firms pay dividends while also having unused opportunities to repurchase shares or engage in equivalent transactions which would effectively transmit tax-free income to shareholders. Edwards (1984) reports that, in a sample of large British firms, over 25 percent paid dividends and issued new equity in the same year, while 17 percent not only paid dividends but *raised* their dividends during years when they issued new shares.

The conclusions described above apply when there is only one shareholder and his tax rates satisfy $m > z$. However, the actual economy is characterized by many different shareholders, often with widely different tax rates. While m may exceed z for some shareholders, there are many investors for whom $m = z$ and still others facing higher tax rates on capital gains than on dividends.[8] If there were no short-selling constraints, then as Brennan (1970) and Gordon and Bradford (1980) show, there would be a unique market-wide preference for dividends in terms of capital gains. It would equal a weighted average of different investors' tax rates, with higher weights on wealthier, and less risk-averse, investors. If there are constraints, however, then different firms may face different investor clienteles, possibly characterized by different tax rates. If some traders face low transactions costs (Miller and Scholes (1982), Kalay (1982)) or are nearly risk-neutral, they may effectively determine the market's relative valuation of dividends and capital gains and become the marginal investors.

The firm chooses I_t, V^N_t, K_t, and D_t to maximize V_t subject to equations (1.7), (1.8), (1.9), and (1.10). The firm's problem may be rewritten as

$$\begin{aligned} \text{Max} \sum_{t=0}^{\infty} \left(1 + \frac{\rho}{1 - z}\right)^{-t} \Bigg\{ & \left[\left(\frac{1 - m}{1 - z}\right) D_t - V_t^N\right] \\ & - \lambda_t[K_t - K_{t-1} - I_t] \\ & - \mu_t[(1 - \tau)\Pi(K_t) + V_t^N - D_t - I_t] \\ & - \eta_t(V_t^N - \overline{V}^N) - \xi_t D_t \Bigg\} \end{aligned} \tag{1.13}$$

where λ_t, μ_t, η_t, and ξ_t are the Lagrange multipliers associated with the constraints. The first-order necessary conditions for an optimal program are:

$$I_t: \quad \lambda_t + \mu_t = 0 \tag{1.14}$$

$$K_t: \quad -\lambda_t + \left(1 + \frac{\rho}{1 - z}\right)^{-1} \lambda_{t+1} - \mu_t(1 - \tau)\,\Pi'(K_t) = 0 \tag{1.15}$$

$$V_t^N: -1 - \mu_t - \eta_t = 0 \qquad \eta_t(V_t^N - \overline{V}^N) \leq 0 \tag{1.16}$$

$$D_t: \quad \left(\frac{1 - m}{1 - z}\right) + \mu_t - \xi_t = 0 \qquad \xi_t D_t \leq 0 \tag{1.17}$$

By interpreting these conditions under the different views of dividend taxation, we can isolate the implications of each for the effects of dividend taxation on the cost of capital, investment, payout policy, and security returns.

The tax irrelevance view

The first view of dividend taxation which we consider assumes that share prices are set by investors for whom $m = z$. We label this the "tax irrelevance" view; it was advanced by Miller and Scholes (1978, 1982). Miller and Scholes argue that the marginal investor in corporate equities is effectively *untaxed* on both dividends and capital gains income.[9] Hamada and Scholes (1984), who call this view the "before-tax theory," note that it essentially assumes "that all personal income taxes—to bondholders, stockholders, and partners of businesses—can be effectively laundered."

Several scenarios could lead to marginal investors being untaxed on capital income. The marginal investor may be an institutional investor for whom $m = z = 0$. Alternatively, in the United States, the marginal investor may be an individual investor for whom dividend income relaxes the deduction limit for interest expenses, making m effectively zero. This investor might, as a result of tax-minimizing transactions such as holding shares with gains and selling shares with losses, also face a zero tax rate on capital gains.

The interpretation of first-order conditions (1.14)–(1.17) in the $m = z = 0$ case is straightforward. The last two constraint conditions simplify substantially. As long as the firm is either paying dividends or issuing shares, one of η_t or ξ_t, the shadow values of the D_t and V_t^N constraints, will equal zero. Using either equation (1.16) or equation (1.17), and $m = z = 0$, this implies that $\mu_t = -1$. The value of \$1 of additional profits is just \$1. The shadow value of capital, λ_t, can be determined from equation (1.14). Since $-\mu_t = \lambda_t$, $\lambda_t = 1$. The shadow value of one more unit of capital in place, λ_t, corresponds to "marginal q" in the investment literature. Firms invest until the incremental increase in their market value from a \$1 investment is exactly \$1, regardless of the source of their marginal investment funds.

The knowledge that $\lambda_t = \lambda_{t+1} = 1$ enables us to solve equation (1.15) for the equilibrium marginal product of capital:

$$(1 - \tau)\Pi'(K_t) = \frac{\rho}{(1 + \rho)} \tag{1.18}$$

The Taylor expansion of $\rho/(1 + \rho)$ around $\rho = 0$ allows us to approximate the right side of this expression by ρ, yielding the standard result that $(1 - \tau)\Pi'(K_t) = \rho$. We define the cost of capital as the value of $\Pi'(K)$ which just satisfies equation (1.18), and using the approximation find

$$c = \frac{\rho}{(1 - \tau)} \tag{1.19}$$

The firm's cost of capital is independent of its payout policy. Changes in the corporate tax rate will affect investment decisions. However, investment policy will be independent of both the firm's dividend payout choices and the prevailing nominal dividend tax rate, since it is always effectively reduced to zero by tax-wise investors. Assuming that $m = z = 0$ for the marginal investor leads immediately to Miller and Modigliani's (1961) irrelevance result for a taxless world.

The tax irrelevance view also implies that the risk-adjusted required return on all equity securities is equal, regardless of their dividend yield. Assuming that all returns are certain, the basic capital market equilibrium condition is[10]

$$\rho = d_i + g_i \qquad \text{all } i \tag{1.20}$$

where d_i is the dividend yield and g_i the expected capital gain on security i. There should be no detectable differences in the returns on different shares as a result of firm dividend policies.

The assumption that $m = z = 0$ for marginal investors is ultimately verifiable only from empirical study. Some evidence, such as the somewhat controversial finding that on ex-dividend days share prices decline by less than the value of their dividends, suggests that the marginal investor may not face identical tax rates on dividends and capital gains. The tax irrelevance view also has difficulty explaining the substantial amount of dividend tax revenue collected by both the Internal Revenue Service and (in the United Kingdom) the Board of Inland Revenue. If most personal investors were effectively untaxed on dividend receipts, relatively little tax revenue should be raised.

The second and third views of dividend taxation assume that shares are valued as if the marginal investor faced a higher effective tax rate on dividends than on capital gains. They attempt to explain why, in spite of this tax disadvantage, dividends are still observed. We label the next two views the "tax capitalization" and the "traditional" views. Each yields different predictions about how the cost of capital, investment, and dividend policy are affected by dividend taxation.

The tax capitalization view

The "tax capitalization view" of dividend taxes was developed by Auerbach (1979), Bradford (1981), and King (1977). It applies to mature firms which have after-tax profits in excess of their desired investment expenditures. Retained earnings are therefore the marginal source of investment funds for these firms. This view assumes that firms cannot find tax-free channels for transferring income to shareholders so that the $V^N = \overline{V}^N$ constraint binds. Therefore, the firm pays a taxable dividend equal to the excess of profits over investment:

$$D_t = (1 - \tau)\Pi_t - I_t + \overline{V}^N \tag{1.21}$$

Dividends are determined as a residual.

The first-order conditions (1.14)–(1.17) can be reinterpreted for a firm in this situation. We showed above that a firm which was paying dividends would repurchase shares to the maximum extent possible, so $V_t^N = V^N$. Formally, the knowledge that $D_t > 0$ allows us to set $\xi_t = 0$ in equation (1.17), implying that $\mu_t = -[(1 - m)/(1 - z)]$.

The marginal value of a unit of capital, from equation (1.14), is therefore

$$\lambda_t = [(1 - m)/(1 - z)] < 1 \tag{1.22}$$

Marginal q is less than one in equilibrium. Firms invest until investors are indifferent at the margin between receiving additional dividend payments and reinvesting money within the firm. When the firm pays a \$1 dividend, the shareholder receives $(1 - m)$ after tax. If the firm retains the dollar and purchases capital, its share value will appreciate by q and the shareholder will receive $(1 - z)q$ in after-tax income. If the shareholder is indifferent between these two actions, the equilibrium value of marginal q must equal $[(1 - m)/(1 - z)]$.

The cost of capital under the tax capitalization view can be derived from equation (1.15). It will depend on both the *current* marginal source of investment finance, and on the source which is *expected* to be available in period $t + 1$.[11] This is because λ_{t+1}, which depends upon whether retentions or new share issues are next period's marginal source of funds, affects the cost of capital in period t. The assumption in the tax capitalization view is that mature firms will never again issue new shares and always set $V_t^N = \overline{V}^N$, so that the marginal source of funds in this and all future periods is retained earnings. We can therefore set $\lambda_t = \lambda_{t+1} = [(1 - m)/(1 - z)]$, and find that

$$(1 - \tau)\Pi'(K_t) = \frac{\rho/(1 - z)}{1 + \rho/(1 - z)} \tag{1.23}$$

Again using a Taylor approximation to the right side, the cost of capital can be written

$$c = \frac{\rho}{(1 - \tau)(1 - z)} \tag{1.24}$$

The dividend tax rate has no effect on the cost of capital, and permanent changes in dividend taxes, unless accompanied by changes in the capital gains tax, will have no effect on investment activity.

This view implies that the dividend tax is a lump sum levy on wealth in the corporate sector at the time of its imposition. The total value of corporate equity, using equation (1.6) and defining D'_{t+j} as the dividends paid to period t shareholders in period $t + j$,

$$V_t = \left(\frac{1 - m}{1 - z}\right) \sum_{j=o}^{\infty} \left(1 + \frac{\rho}{1 - z}\right)^{-j} D'_{t+j} \tag{1.25}$$

Changes in the dividend tax rate therefore have direct effects on the total *value* of outstanding equity,[12] even though they do not affect the rate of return earned on these shares. The tax capitalization view treats current equity as "trapped" within the corporate sector, and therefore as bearing the full burden of the dividend tax.

Permanent changes in the dividend tax rate will have no effect on the firm's dividend policy. The cost of capital, hence the firm's investment and capital stock, are unaffected by dividend taxes. Dividend payments, the difference between $(1 - \tau)\Pi(K_t) + \overline{V}_t^N$ and investment expenditures, are therefore unaffected as well. Temporary tax changes, however, do have real effects. For example, consider a temporary dividend tax which is announced in period $t - 1$. It will set the dividend tax rate to m in period t, but zero in all previous and subsequent periods. We set $z = 0$ in all periods for convenience. Since $\lambda_t = 1 - m$ but $\lambda_{t+j} = 1$ for all $j \neq 0$, we can use equation (1.15) to determine the period-by-period cost of capital around the tax change:

Period	$t - 2$	$t - 1$	t	$t + 1$
Cost of capital	$\frac{\rho}{1-\tau}$	$\frac{\rho + m}{1-\tau}$	$\frac{\rho - m}{1-\tau}$	$\frac{\rho}{1-\tau}$

The general formula for the cost of capital is

$$c = (1 - \tau)^{-1}\left[1 - \left(1 + \frac{\rho}{1 - z}\right)^{-1}(\lambda_{t+1}/\lambda_t)\right] \tag{1.26}$$

The cost of capital depends in part on the *change* in the shadow value of capital which is expected to take place between one period and the next. Since λ_t is low because of the dividend tax, the cost of capital is *high* in the period immediately prior to the imposition of the tax, and *low* during the taxed period. Since changes in the cost of capital have real effects, temporary tax changes may alter investment and therefore dividend payout. This result may be seen intuitively. Firms will go to great lengths to avoid paying dividends during a temporary dividend tax period. As a consequence, they will invest even in very low productivity investments.

Finally, since the capitalization view assumes that dividends face higher tax rates than capital gains, it predicts that shares which pay dividends will earn a higher pretax return to compensate shareholders for their tax liability. The after-tax capital market line corresponding to equation (1.20) is

$$\rho = (1 - m)d_i + (1 - z)g_i \tag{1.27}$$

which can be rewritten as

$$R_i = \frac{\rho}{1 - z} + \frac{m - z}{1 - z}d_i \tag{1.28}$$

where $R_i = d_i + g_i$. There should be detectable differential returns on securities with different dividend yields.

There are two principal difficulties with the capitalization view of dividend taxation. First, if marginal q is less than one and marginal and average q are not very different, then firms should always prefer acquiring capital by takeovers instead of direct purchases. This is because the purchase price of a new capital good is unity, but the market value of capital goods held by other corporations is only $(1 - m)/(1 - z)$.

Second, this view's premise is that dividends are the only way to transfer money out of the corporate sector. Firms are constrained in that they cannot further reduce new equity issues or increase share repurchases. In the United States, at least, there are many methods potentially available to firms which wish to convert earnings into capital gains. These include both share repurchases and takeovers, as well as the purchase of equity holdings or debt in other firms and various other transactions. The proposition that all marginal distributions must flow through the dividend channel may be untenable. The tax capitalization view therefore does not *explain* dividend payout in any real sense. Rather it *assumes* that dividends must be paid and that firms are not issuing new shares and then analyses the effect of changes in dividend tax rates.

A further difficulty is this view's assumption that dividend payments are a residual in the corporate accounts and therefore subject to substantial variation. The arrival of "good news," which raises desired investment, should lead dividends to fall sharply. Most empirical evidence[13] suggests that dividend payments are substantially less volatile than investment expenditures and that managers raise dividends when favorable information about the firm's future becomes available.

The traditional view

The third view of dividend taxation, which we label the "traditional" view, takes a more direct approach to resolving the dividend puzzle. It argues that, for a variety of reasons, shareholders derive benefits from the payment of dividends. Firms derive some advantage from the use of cash dividends as a distribution channel, and this is reflected in their market value. While the force which makes dividends valuable remains unclear, leading explanations include the "signaling" hypothesis, discussed for example by Ross (1977), Bhattacharya (1979), and Miller and Rock (1984), the need to restrict managerial discretion as outlined in Jensen and Meckling (1976), and the "self-control" theory of Shefrin and Statman (1984).

To model the effect of the payout ratio on a shareholder's valuation of the firm, we must generalize our earlier analysis. A convenient device for allowing for "intrinsic dividend value" is to assume that the discount rate applied to the firm's income stream depends on the payout ratio: $\rho = \rho(D/(1-\tau)\Pi)$, $\rho' < 0$. Firms which distribute a higher fraction of their profits are rewarded with a lower required rate of return. This changes the fundamental expression for the value of the firm, equation (1.6), to

$$V_t = \sum_{j=0}^{\infty} \beta(t,j) \left[\left(\frac{1-m}{1-z} \right) D_{t+j} - V_{t+j}^N \right] \tag{1.29}$$

where

$$\beta(t,j) = \prod_{k=-1}^{j-1} \left[1 + \rho\left(\frac{D_{t+k}}{(1-\tau)\Pi_{t+k}} \right) / (1-z) \right]^{-1} \tag{1.30}$$

Although dividend taxes make dividend payments unattractive, the reduction in discount rates which results from a higher payout ratio may induce firms to pay dividends.

The first-order conditions characterizing the firm's optimal program are slightly different in this case than under the previous two views, because the choice of dividend policy now affects the discount rate. The new first-order conditions are shown below:

$$I_t: \quad \lambda_t + \mu_t = 0 \tag{1.14a}$$

$$K_t: \quad -\lambda_t + \left(1 + \frac{\rho_{t+1}}{1-z}\right)^{-1} \lambda_{t+1} - \mu_t(1-\tau)\Pi'(K_t) \tag{1.15a}$$

$$+ \frac{\rho'\left(\frac{D_t}{(1-\tau)\Pi_t}\right) \frac{D_t}{(1-\tau)\Pi_t} \cdot \frac{\Pi_t'}{\Pi_t}}{(1-z)(1+\rho_{t+1}/(1-z))} \cdot V_t = 0$$

$$V_t^N: -1 - \mu_t - \eta_t = 0 \qquad \eta_t(V_t^N - \bar{V}^N) \leq 0 \tag{1.16a}$$

$$D_t: \quad \left(\frac{1-m}{1-z}\right) + \mu_t - \xi_t - \frac{\rho'\left(\frac{D_t}{(1-\tau)\Pi_t}\right) \cdot \frac{V_t}{\Pi_t(1-\tau)}}{(1-z)(1+\rho_{t+1}/(1-z))} = 0 \qquad \cdot \xi_t D_t \leq 0 \tag{1.17a}$$

For convenience, we define $\rho_{t+1} = \rho(D_t/(1-\tau)\Pi_t)$.

To solve these equations for marginal q and the cost of capital, we *assume* that the returns from paying dividends are sufficient to make $D_t > 0$.[14] If this were not the case, this view would reduce to the tax capitalization model where dividends are just a residual. Positive dividends require $\xi_t = 0$, so $\mu_t = -1$ from equation (1.16*a*) and $\lambda_t = 1$ from equation (1.14*a*). Therefore, the equilibrium value of marginal q is unity. This follows, because at the margin investors are trading \$1 of after-tax income for \$1 of corporate capital. For values of q less than unity, these transactions would cease.

The cost of capital can also be derived from these conditions. Since $\mu_t = -1$, equation (1.17a) may be rewritten as

$$\frac{z-m}{1-z} = \frac{\rho'\left(\frac{D_t}{(1-\tau)\Pi_t}\right)}{(1-z)\left(1+\frac{\rho_{t+1}}{1-z}\right)} \cdot \frac{V_t}{\Pi_t(1-\tau)} \tag{1.31}$$

This expression may be used to simplify equation (1.15a):

$$\begin{aligned} &\lambda_t + \left(1+\frac{\rho_{t+1}}{1-z}\right)^{-1}\lambda_{t+1} + (1-\tau)\Pi'(K_t) \\ &+ \left(\frac{z-m}{1-z}\right)\cdot\frac{D_t}{(1-\tau)\Pi_t}\cdot(1-\tau)\Pi'(K_t) = 0 \end{aligned} \tag{1.32}$$

Assuming $\lambda_t = \lambda_{t+1} = 1$, and again approximating $[\rho_{t+1}/(1-z)]/[1+\rho_{t+1}/(1-z)] \doteq \frac{\rho_{t+1}}{1-z}$, we find

$$-\frac{\rho_{t+1}}{1-z} + (1-\tau)\Pi_t'(K_t)\left[1+\left(\frac{z-m}{1-z}\right)\frac{D_t}{(1-\tau)\Pi_t}\right] = 0 \tag{1.33}$$

which can be written

$$(1-\tau)\Pi'(K_t) = \frac{\rho(\alpha_t)}{(1-m)\alpha_t + (1-z)(1-\alpha_t)} \tag{1.34}$$

where $\alpha_t = D_t/(1-\tau)\Pi_t$, the dividend payout ratio. The steady-state cost of capital is therefore

$$c = \frac{\rho(\alpha)}{(1-\tau)[(1-m)\alpha + (1-z)(1-\alpha)]} \tag{1.35}$$

It involves a weighted average of the tax rates on dividends and capital gains, with weights equal to the dividend payout ratio.

The cost of capital will also be affected by a dividend tax change. The precise effect may be found by differentiating equation (1.35):

$$\begin{aligned} \frac{dc}{d(1-m)} &= \frac{-\alpha c}{[(1-m)\alpha + (1-z)(1-\alpha)]} \\ &+ \frac{\partial c}{\partial \alpha}\frac{d\alpha}{d(1-m)} \end{aligned} \tag{1.36}$$

The foregoing conditions for choice of D_t imply $\sqrt{\frac{\partial c}{\partial \alpha}} = 0$ at the optimal dividend payout, so we can write

$$\frac{dc}{d(1-m)} \cdot \frac{(1-m)}{c} = \frac{-(1-m)\alpha}{(1-m)\alpha + (1-z)(1-a)} < 0 \quad (1.37)$$

A reduction in the dividend tax rate will therefore lower the cost of capital, increasing current investment spending.

The traditional view also implies that, when the dividend tax rate falls, equilibrium capital intensity and the required return ρ may rise. Under the extreme assumption that capital is supplied inelastically, the only effect of a dividend tax cut is an increase in the equilibrium rate of return, ρ. If capital were supplied with some positive elasticity, a reduction in the dividend tax rate would raise both capital intensity and the rate of return.[15] Dividend tax changes can have substantial allocative effects.

The traditional view also suggests that, as dividend taxes fall, the dividend payout ratio should rise. The firm equates the marginal benefit from dividend payments with the marginal tax cost of those payments. Dividend tax reductions, whether temporary or permanent, will lower the marginal cost of obtaining signaling or other benefits, and the optimal payout ratio should therefore rise.

Finally, we should note the implications of this view for the relative pretax returns on different securities. The pricing relation is a generalization of equation (1.28):

$$R_i = \frac{\rho(\alpha_i)}{1-z} + \left(\frac{m-z}{1-z}\right)d_i \quad (1.38)$$

This implies two effects for dividend yield. First, in periods when firm i actually pays dividends ($d_i > 0$), the measured pretax return will rise to compensate investors for their resulting tax liability. However, even in periods when *no dividend* is paid, the required return on higher-yield stocks may be lower than on low-yield stocks as a result of the signaling or other value which payout provides.

While it may provide an explanation of the dividend puzzle, the traditional view depends critically on a clear reason for investors to value high dividend payout, but as yet provides only weak motivation for the $\rho(\alpha)$ function.[16] It is particularly difficult to understand why firms use cash dividends as opposed to less heavily taxed means of communicating information to their shareholders. An additional difficulty with this view is that firms rarely issue new equity. It is possible that even though firms issue shares infrequently, however, new equity is still the marginal source of funds. For example, some firms might use short-term borrowing to finance projects in years when they do not issue equity, and then redeem the debt when they finally issue new shares. Moreover, the wide variety of financial activities described above, which are equivalent to share repurchase, may allow firms to operate on the equity-issue margin without ever selling shares.

Summary

In this section, we have described three distinct views of the economic effects of dividend taxation. While we have treated them as opposing alternatives, they may each be partially correct. Different firms may be on different financing margins, and the tax rates on marginal investors may also differ across firms. We allow for both these possibilities in interpreting the empirical results reported below.

Table 1 summarizes the cost of capital and equilibrium "q" under each of the alternatives. We also report each view's prediction for the responsiveness of investment, and the payout ratio, to a permanent increase in the dividend tax rate. The prediction for the pretax return premium earned by dividend-paying shares is also recorded. In subsequent sections, we test each of these different predictions using British data on security returns, dividend payout, and corporate investment expenditures.

TABLE 1 The alternative views of dividend taxation

	Traditional View	*Tax Capitalization View*	*Tax Irrelevance View*
Cost of Capital	$\frac{\rho(\alpha)}{[(1-m)\alpha+(1-z)(1-\alpha)](1-\tau)}$	$\frac{\rho}{(1-z)(1-\tau)}$	$\frac{\rho}{1-\tau}$
$\frac{dI}{dm}$	<0	0	0
$\frac{d\alpha}{dm}$	<0	0	0
Equilibrium marginal "q"	1	$\frac{1-m}{1-z}$	1
Dividend premium in pre-tax returns	$\frac{m-z}{1-z}$	$\frac{m-z}{1-z}$	0

Note: These results are derived in the text and are recorded here for later reference. The level of investment is I, and α is the dividend payout ratio. All of the tax changes are assumed to be permanent.

THE TAXATION OF DIVIDENDS IN GREAT BRITAIN: 1950–1983

The previous section's stylized discussion of taxes focused on the U.S. tax environment. Our empirical tests rely on the major changes in British tax policy that have occurred over the last three decades. These changes are described in this section. Subsequent sections present our empirical results.

In the United States, discriminatory taxation of dividends and retained earnings occurs at the shareholder level, where dividends and capital gains are treated differently. In Britain, however, there have been some periods when *corporations* also faced differential tax rates on their retained and distributed income. During other periods, the personal and corporate tax systems were "integrated" to allow shareholders to receive credit for taxes which had been paid at the corporate level. Between 1965 and 1973, Britain experimented with a tax system identical in outline to that of the postwar United States. Five systems of dividend taxation have been tried in Britain during the last three decades. In this section, we describe these tax systems in some detail. This will provide the setting for the empirical work in subsequent sections.

Two summary parameters are needed to describe the effects of the various tax regimes on dividends. The first, which measures the amount of the tax discrimination at the shareholder level, is the *investor tax preference ratio* (δ). It is defined as the after-tax income which a shareholder receives when a firm distributes a £1 dividend, divided by his after-tax receipts when the firm's share price rises by one pound.[17] In the United States, $\delta = (1 - m)/(1 - z)$. The investor tax preference ratio is central to analyzing share price movements around ex-dividend days, since if m and z are the tax rates reflected in market prices, a firm paying a dividend of d should experience a price drop of $(1 - m)/(1 - z)d$ or δd.

The second parameter which may affect investment and payout decisions is the *total tax preference ratio* (θ). It is defined as the amount of after-tax income which shareholders receive when a firm uses £1 of after-tax profits to increase its dividend payout. This return must be measured relative to the amount of after-tax income which shareholders would receive if the firm retained this pound. This variable determines firm payout policy under the traditional view of dividend taxation and equilibrium q under the tax capitalization hypothesis. In the American tax system, where corporate tax payments are unaffected by payout policy, $\theta = \delta = (1 - m)/(1 - z)$. In Britain, the relationship is more complex, depending on the change in corporate tax payments which results from a £1 reduction in gross dividends.

The different tax regimes

To characterize the changes in δ and θ which provide the basis for our empirical tests, we consider each British tax regime in turn. We follow King (1977) and express the total tax burden on corporate income as a function of the prevailing tax code parameters, and then derive δ and θ. More detailed discussions of British dividend taxation may be found in King (1977), House of Commons (1971), the Corporation Tax Green Paper (1982), and Tiley (1978).

1950–1951: Differential profits tax regime I. Prior to the 1952 budget, firms faced a two-tier tax system with different tax rates on distributed and undistributed income. The tax code was described by s, the standard rate of income tax, τ_u, the tax rate on undistributed profits, and τ_d, the tax rate on distributed profits. There was no capital gains tax, so $z = 0$. Corporations were subject to *both* income taxes and profits taxes, although profits taxes could be deducted from a company's income in calculating income tax liability. Income tax was paid at rate s. The corporate tax liability of a corporation with pretax profits II and gross dividend payments D was[18]

$$\begin{aligned} T^c &= [s + (1 - s)\tau_u](\Pi - D) + (1 - s)\tau_d D \\ &= [(1 - s)\tau_u + s]\Pi + [(1 - s)(\tau_d - \tau_u) - s]D \end{aligned} \tag{2.1}$$

In addition, shareholders were liable for

$$T^p = mD \tag{2.2}$$

In practice, part of this tax was collected by the corporation when it paid dividends; it withheld sD as prepayment of part of the shareholders' taxes. Shareholders therefore received $(1 - s)D$ immediately after a gross dividend D was paid. A taxpayer whose marginal rate was greater than s would subsequently be liable for taxes of $(m - s)D$; one with $m < s$ would receive a refund.

The investor tax preference ratio for this system is easy to derive. The shareholders' after-tax income associated with a £1 dividend equals $(1 - m)$, where m is the marginal dividend tax rate. Since there are no taxes on capital gains, the shareholder tax preference ratio is $\delta = (1 - m)$.

We can also compute θ for this tax regime. To raise gross dividends by £1, the firm must forego $[1 + (dT^c/dD)]$ pounds of after-tax retentions. The second term is the marginal change in tax liability which results from raising D by £1. The parameter $\hat{\theta}$, which is the change in gross dividends per pound of foregone retentions, is defined as

$$\theta = \frac{1}{1 + \dfrac{dT^c}{dD}} = \frac{1}{(1 - s)(1 + \tau_d - \tau_u)} \tag{2.3}$$

from equation (2.2). The total tax preference ratio is defined by

$$\theta = \delta\hat{\theta} = \frac{(1 - m)}{(1 - s)(1 + \tau_d - \tau_u)} \tag{2.4}$$

For most investors who paid taxes at rates above the standard rate of income tax, the tax system discriminated against dividend payout. In addition, τ_d exceeded τ_u, sometimes by as much as 40 percentage points.

1952–1958: Differential profits tax regime II. The tax law was changed in 1952 to eliminate the deduction of profit taxes from income subject to income tax. The analysis of this tax regime closely parallels that above. This system required the firm to pay

$$\begin{aligned} T^c &= [s + \tau_u](\Pi - D) + \tau_d D \\ &= (s + \tau_u)\Pi + (\tau_d - \tau_u - s)D \end{aligned} \tag{2.5}$$

while for shareholders equation (2.2) continued to hold. The payment of a £1 gross dividend would again provide the shareholder with $(1 - m)$ pounds of after-tax income, so $\delta = (1 - m)$. Following the earlier expression for θ we find $dT^c/dD = \tau_d - \tau_u - s$, so

$$\hat{\theta} = \frac{1}{1 - s + \tau_d - \tau_u} \tag{2.6}$$

and

$$\theta = \frac{1 - m}{1 - s + \tau_d - \tau_u} \tag{2.7}$$

This tax system was less favorable to the payment of dividends than the previous regime had been, since by eliminating deductability of profits tax it increased the burden induced by differential corporate profits tax rates.

1958–1964: Single-rate profits tax. In 1958, Chancellor Barber Amory announced a major reform in corporate taxation. The differential profits tax was replaced by a single-rate profits tax. All profits were taxed at the rate τ_p, *regardless* of a firm's dividend policy. In addition, the firm was liable for income tax at rate s on its undistributed earnings, while it withheld sG for shareholders' income tax liability on the dividends it distributed. Shareholders were still taxed at rate m on gross dividends, but since firms were *not* subject to income tax on distributed profits, there were *offsetting* burdens at the two levels. The total tax burden on corporate source income was

$$T^c = (s + \tau_p)\Pi - sD \tag{2.8}$$

while $T^p = mD$. This implies $\delta = (1 - m)$, but $\hat{\theta} = \dfrac{1}{(1 - s)}$, so

$$\theta = (1 - m)/(1 - s) \tag{2.9}$$

For values of the marginal tax rate near the standard rate of income tax, this tax system is *neutral* with respect to distribution policy. For higher marginal rates, it discriminates against dividends. However, it was generally a much more favorable tax system for dividends than either of the previous regimes.

1965–1973: Classical corporation tax. The Labour Party victory in 1964 marked the beginning of harsher taxation of corporate income. The 1965 Finance Bill introduced a new system of corporate taxation parallel to that in the United States. Profits were taxed at a corporate tax rate, τ_c, and there was no distinction between retained and distributed earnings. This implies $T^c = \tau_c\Pi$, and since $dT^c/dD = 0$, $\hat{\theta} = 1$. Shareholders continued to pay dividend taxes at rate m. However, the shareholder preference ratio was altered by the introduction in early 1965 of a capital gains tax at a flat rate of 30 percent on all realized gains. As a taxable basis, each asset was ascribed its value on April 6, 1965. We use z to represent the *effective* marginal capital gains tax rate, taking account of the reductions afforded by deferred realization.[19] The investor tax preference ratio for this tax system is $\delta = (1 - m)/(1 - z)$. Since $\hat{\theta} = 1, \theta = (1 - m)/(1 - z)$. Unlike the previous tax regime, the classical system made no attempt to avoid the double taxation of dividends. As a result, it imposed a substantially heavier tax burden on dividends.

1973–Present: The imputation system. The Conservative return to power in 1970 set in motion a further set of tax reforms, directed at reducing the discriminatory taxation of dividend income. The current tax system resembles the system which was used between 1958 and 1964, with several differences. All corporate profits are taxed at the corporation tax rate, τ_c. When firms pay dividends, they are required to pay an advance corporation tax (ACT) at a rate of τ_a per pound of gross dividends. However, whereas in the 1958–64 regime this tax on dividends was treated as a withholding of *investor* income taxes, under the current regime it is a prepayment of *cor-*

porate tax. At the end of its fiscal year, the firm pays $\tau_c \Pi - \tau_a D$ in corporate taxes, taking full credit for its earlier ACT payments.[20] Since total corporate tax payments equal $\tau_c \Pi$, $\hat{\theta} = 1$ under this tax system.

Shareholders receive a credit for the firm's ACT payment. A shareholder calculates his tax by first inflating his dividend receipts by $1/(1 - \tau_a)$ and then applying a tax rate of m. However, he is credited with tax payments of $\tau_a/(1 - \tau_a)$, so his effective marginal tax rate is $(m - \tau_a)/(1 - \tau_a)$. If his marginal income tax rate is above τ_a, the imputation rate, then he is liable for additional dividend taxes. Shareholders with marginal tax rates below τ_a are eligible for tax refunds.

The shareholder tax preference ratio under the imputation system is given by

$$\delta = \frac{1 - [(m - \tau_a)/(1 - \tau_a)]}{1 - z} \tag{2.10}$$

Since $\hat{\theta} = 1$, we know $\theta = \delta$ and can rewrite this as

$$\theta = \frac{1 - m}{(1 - \tau_a)(1 - z)} \tag{2.11}$$

The imputation rate has typically been set equal to the standard rate of income tax, the rate paid by most taxpayers (but not most dividend recipients). For standard rate taxpayers, the imputation system provides an *incentive* for paying dividends; retentions yield taxable capital gains, but there is essentially no tax on dividends at the shareholder level. For individuals facing marginal dividend tax rates above the standard rate, there may be an incentive for retention, provided $m > z + \tau_a(1 - z)$. Pension funds and other untaxed investors have a clear incentive to *prefer* dividend payments. For these investors, $m = z = 0$ and the tax system provides a subsidy, since £1 of dividend income is effectively worth $1/(1 - \tau_a)$ pounds. Finally, brokers and dealers in securities have a less powerful incentive to encourage firms to pay dividends. They are allowed to reclaim ACT paid by corporations in which they hold shares only up to the amount of ACT paid by the brokerage firm in regard to *its* dividend distribution. Thus, for many brokers, marginal dividend receipts cannot be inflated by the $1/(1 - \tau_a)$ factor.

Summary statistics

Table 2 summarizes the tax parameters for each different tax regime. Estimates of the two summary statistics, δ and θ, using weighted-average marginal tax rates are reported in Table 3 for the last 30 years. The values of m and z which we used to compute these statitics are weighted averages of the marginal tax rates faced by different classes of investors, with weights proportional to the value of their shareholdings. These weighted average tax rates were first calculated by King (1977) and have been updated in King, Naldrett, and Poterba (1984). These tax rates are indicative of the major changes in tax policy which have occurred over time. If one class of investor is in fact "the marginal investor," then the weighted averages are substantially misleading as indicators of the tax rates guiding market prices. Even if this is the case, however, there is still some information in our time series since the tax burden for most types of investors moved in the same direction in each tax reform. We present empirical evidence below suggesting the relevance of weighted average marginal tax rates.

TABLE 2 Tax code parameters and dividend taxation

Tax Regime	*Years*	*Investor Tax Preference Ratio (δ)*	*Total Tax Preference Ratio (θ)*
Differential profits tax I	1950–52	$1 - m$	$\frac{1 - m}{(1 - s)(1 + \tau_D - \tau_u)}$
Differential profits tax II	1952–58	$1 - m$	$\frac{1 - m}{1 - s + \tau_D - \tau_u}$
Single rate profits tax	1958–65	$1 - m$	$\frac{1 - m}{1 - s}$
Classical corporation tax	1966–73	$\frac{1 - m}{1 - z}$	$\frac{1 - m}{1 - z}$
Imputation system	1973–	$\frac{1 - m}{(1 - \tau_a)(1 - z)}$	$\frac{1 - m}{(1 - \tau_a)(1 - z)}$

Note: See text for further details and parameter definitions.

The time series movements in δ and θ deserve some comment. The dividend tax burden was heaviest in the 1950–58 and 1965–73 periods, and lightest in recent years. The most dramatic changes in δ occur in 1965 (capital gains tax) and 1973 (imputation). For θ, there are additional changes in 1958 and 1966. These substantial changes raise the prospect of detecting the effects of dividend taxation on the behavior of individuals and firms. Similar descriptive statistics for the U.S. tax system would display far fewer movements in the postwar period, and *no* dramatic jumps.

TABLE 3 The British tax system, 1950–1981

Year	*Dividend Tax Rate (m^*)*	*Capital Gains Tax Rate (z)*	*Shareholder Tax Preference Ratio $(1 - m^*)/(1 - z)$*	*Total Tax Preference Ratio (θ)*
1950	0.568	0.000	0.432	0.674
1951	0.575	0.000	0.425	0.619
1952	0.560	0.000	0.440	0.598
1953	0.545	0.000	0.455	0.612
1954	0.530	0.000	0.470	0.621
1955	0.518	0.000	0.482	0.624
1956	0.517	0.000	0.483	0.596
1957	0.515	0.000	0.485	0.575
1958	0.502	0.000	0.498	0.673
1959	0.488	0.000	0.512	0.807
1960	0.485	0.000	0.515	0.840
1961	0.485	0.000	0.515	0.841
1962	0.484	0.000	0.516	0.843
1963	0.483	0.000	0.517	0.844
1964	0.509	0.000	0.491	0.801
1965	0.529	0.138	0.550	0.936
1966	0.500	0.174	0.608	0.706
1967	0.488	0.173	0.619	0.619
1968	0.483	0.169	0.622	0.622
1969	0.472	0.157	0.627	0.627
1970	0.456	0.152	0.641	0.641
1971	0.444	0.150	0.654	0.654
1972	0.425	0.148	0.674	0.674
1973	0.214	0.143	0.916	0.916
1974	0.105	0.133	1.032	0.978
1975	0.048	0.130	1.094	0.970
1976	−0.004	0.131	1.156	1.019
1977	−0.031	0.134	1.190	1.055
1978	−0.040	0.135	1.202	1.070
1979	−0.043	0.136	1.207	1.041
1980	−0.101	0.134	1.271	1.047
1981	−0.120	0.133	1.292	1.064

Notes: Column 1 is the weighted average marginal tax rate on all shareholders, reported by M. King, Public Policy and the Corporation (London: Chapman and Hall, 1977), p. 218, and updated by M. King, M. Naldrett, and J. Poterba, "The U.K. Tax System," in The Taxation of Income from Capital: A Comparative Study of the U.S., U.K., Sweden, and West Germany ed. M. King and D. Fullerton (Chicago: University of Chicago Press, 1984). This is the time series for $m^* = (m - \tau_a)/(1 - \tau_a)$ as reported in the text. Column 2, the effective capital gains tax rate, is also drawn from King (1977). Columns 3 and 4 were computed by the authors as described in the text. They may not correspond exactly to calculations based on Columns 1 and 2 since they are averages of quarterly ratios.

The use of legal changes to identify economic relationships is always problematic since such changes may themselves be endogenous responses to economic conditions. The history of British corporate tax reform provides little reason to think that this is an important problem for our empirical work. Major reforms typically followed elections which brought about changes in the governing party. For example, the 1965 reforms closely followed the Labour Party's victory in the 1964 election, and the 1973 reforms were consequences of the Conservative victory in the 1970 elections. A reading of the press reports suggests that corporate tax reform was not an issue in either election.

The remainder of the paper is devoted to various tests of how the tax changes described in this section have influenced (i) the market's relative valuation of dividends and capital gains, (ii) the decisions made by firms with respect to their dividend payout, and (iii) the investment decisions of British firms.

DIVIDEND TAXES AND DIVIDEND VALUATION

The changes in investor tax rates on dividend income and capital gains provide opportunities for testing the "tax irrelevance" view by examining share price movements around ex-dividend days. If marginal investors value dividend income as much as they value capital gains, then when shares experience ex-days their price should decline by the full amount of the dividend payment. If the marginal investors are taxed more heavily on dividends than on capital gains, however, then share prices will fall by *less* than the dividend payment. Moreover, if marginal investors are untaxed, then changes in dividend tax rules should not affect the marginal valuation of dividends and capital gains.

Numerous authors, including Elton and Gruber (1970), Black and Scholes (1973), Green (1980), Kalay (1982), Eades, Hess and Kim (1984), Auerbach (1983a), Hess (1982), and others have used daily data to analyze relative share price movements in the United States. Although their results are controversial, these studies suggest that share prices decline on ex-days, but by less than the amount of the dividend. These results have been interpreted as confirming the hypothesis that marginal investors are taxed.

British data provide an opportunity for studying the general issue of whether taxes affect dividend valuation, as well as the role of short-term trading in determining the ex-dividend day behavior of share prices. As noted in the last section, there have been substantial changes in the shareholder tax preference ratio during the last 25 years. The principal changes occurred in 1965 and 1973.

There have also been important changes in the tax rates affecting securities traders involved in tax arbitrage around ex-dividend days. The most significant changes affecting short-term traders were introduced in the 1970 Finance Act.[21] Prior to 1970, "dividend stripping" by trading around ex-days was apparently widespread. Since, then, however, the Inland Revenue has been empowered to levy penalties on investors engaged in securities transactions which are principally motivated by tax considerations. For an individual investor, if trading around ex-days (i.e., selling shares before the ex-day and repurchasing them later) reduces his tax liability by more than 10 percent in any year, the tax savings from these transactions may be voided by the Inland Revenue.

After 1970, trading by institutions around ex-days could be declared void if they bought and then sold the same share within one month of its ex-dividend day. If its transactions are disallowed, the institution could be required to pay taxes, in spite of its tax-exempt status. Since 1970, a dealer who trades in a security around its ex-day and holds his shares for less than a month will not be able to deduct his full capital loss from taxable income.[22] A fraction of his capital loss, varying inversely with the holding period, is disallowed for tax purposes. As the holding period declines to only the ex-day, the fraction disallowed rises to nearly 100 percent.

The interactions among these tax provisions are difficult to describe, and the extent to which the Board of Inland Revenue exercises its authority remains unclear. However, one cannot doubt that the opportunities for avoiding taxes by trading around ex-days were substantially reduced in 1970. To the extent that trading around ex-days is important in determining ex-dividend price movements, we would expect to observe noticeable changes in dividend valuation, if at all, only around 1970. This should be contrasted with the traditional and tax capitalization views, which predict major changes in the relative value of dividends and capital gains when the tax reforms affecting ordinary investors occurred but none when rules affecting dividend stripping took palce.

Data and methods[23]

To estimate the share price response to dividends, we obtained daily data on the share prices and dividends of 16 large U.K. firms. A listing of the firms in our data set and further background data may be found in Poterba and Summers (1984a). We obtained a listing of ex-dividend dates from the London Business School Share Price Data Base, and then consulted microfilm copies of the London *Financial Times*. The closing share prices on the trading day before the ex-date and the ex-date itself were recorded for each firm.[24] For each firm in the sample, we included all ex-dates between 1955 and 1981 corresponding to cash dividend payments which were taxable as ordinary income and not accompanied by any dividend rights, stock options, or other special features. Our data set contained 633 ex-days, distributed evenly among the years 1955–81. We also obtained data on the value of the *Financial Times* Industrial Ordinary Share Index, and used this index to construct a market return series.

We estimated the follow model for R_{it}, the total pretax return on security i:

$$R_{it} = \beta_{0i} + \beta_{1i} \cdot R_{mt} + \sum_{j=1955}^{1981} \alpha_j I_{jit} d_{it} + \nu_{it} \tag{3.1}$$

where R_{mt} is the market return, β_{0i} is a firm-specific intercept term, and β_{1i} is a company-specific coefficient which should resemble the security's beta. The dividend yield on each day is d_{it}. The variable I_{jit} is equal to 1 if the dividend falls in year j and 0 otherwise. We also estimate equation (3.1) constraining β_{0i} to be constant across firms. Both equations were estimated by a generalized least squares procedure which allowed for heteroscedasticity across different firms. Since there were few instances in which two firms had coincident ex-days, we did not need to correct for residual correlation across firms.

When two tax regimes occur within one year, we allow for two α_j's in that year. The α_j coefficients reflect the *excess* pretax return on ex-dividend days, and therefore correspond to $1 - \delta$ for each year. If the "tax irrelevance" view is correct, the parameter α_j should not depend upon the relative tax rates on dividends and capital gains.[25] Under the other views we would expect α_j to vary over time, especially when the imputation system was introduced in 1973, but also as the composition of shareholders varies over time.[26]

Results

The results of estimating equation (3.1) are shown in Table 4. The α coefficients are clearly subject to substantial variability over time, even when the tax system does not vary. However, there is a pronounced drop in the estimated coefficients beginning in the second half of 1973. There is even a clear difference in the estimates for the first and second halves of 1973. This suggests the importance of the 1973 imputation reform in altering the relative valuation of dividends and capital gains. The difference in the average value of $\hat{\alpha}$ between the 1965–73 and 1973+ tax regimes is 0.51, which corresponds very closely to the value of 0.54 computed from the weighted average marginal tax rates in Table 3.

The estimated coefficients did not change substantially, however, when the capital gains tax was introduced in 1965. This may indicate that effective marginal capital gains tax rates were actually negligible. Constantinides (1983) and Stiglitz (1983) have shown that optimal portfolio strategies can substantially reduce effective capital gains tax rates, so the naive assumptions of constant turnover probabilities used in constructing z in Table 3 may be substantially incorrect.[27]

There is also little change in the estimated coefficients before and after 1970, when the ex-day trading restrictions were introduced. This is evidence *against* the importance of short-term trading in determining the behavior of share prices around their ex-days and, when coupled with the changes in valuation around 1973, suggests that views which hold that a weighted average marginal tax rate affects security market equilibrium are more accurate descriptions of reality than those which assume that marginal investors are broker-dealers.

While the annual ex-day coefficients in Table 4 are informative about how taxes may affect security values, they are not "tests" in any usual sense. To test the proposition that the estimates of α reflected tax rates, we compare our estimate of α for *each year* with $(1 - \delta)$ in Table 3. The hypothesis that $\hat{\alpha}_t = (1 - \delta_t)$, *all t*, was rejected at standard significance levels. However, tests of the hypothesis $\hat{\alpha} = (m - \tau_a)/(1 - \tau_a)$, imposing $z_t = 0$, did not reject the null. This again suggests that although our measures of capital gains tax rates may be very imprecise indicators of actual tax rates, underlying variation in dividend tax rates as measured by our crude weighted averages is reflected in share price movements.

The results reported here suggest the potentially substantial influence of dividend taxation on the stock market's relative valuation of dividends and capital gains. However, while daily share price movements are likely to yield the most precise evidence on dividend valuation, they may be contaminated by unusual return patterns around ex-days or other subtle factors.[28] If taxes play an important role in the valuation of dividend income, it should also be possible to detect this phenomenon in a sample of monthly security returns. Miller and Scholes (1982) have argued that previous monthly studies using American data, for example, Litzenberger and Ramaswamy (1979, 1982), were contaminated by information effects and that their discovery of a tax effect was therefore spurious. Monthly data are of course subject to other biases, and they are noisier than the daily series. However, in Poterba and Summers (1984a), we used monthly British data for the period 1955–81 and again found evidence that tax changes induced movements in dividend valuation.[29]

The results in this section cast doubt on the value of the tax irrelevance hypothesis in explaining why British firms pay divi-

TABLE 4 The stock market's relative valuation of dividends and capital gains: 1955–1981

Year	*Model Without Fixed Effects*		*Model With Fixed Effects*		*Average Tax Rate Value*
1955	0.637	(0.194)	0.694	(0.198)	0.518
1956	0.149	(0.177)	0.208	(0.181)	0.517
1957	0.439	(0.165)	0.501	(0.171)	0.515
1958	0.393	(0.151)	0.451	(0.155)	0.502
1959	0.537	(0.182)	0.610	(0.187)	0.488
1960	0.361	(0.201)	0.441	(0.207)	0.485
1961	−0.142	(0.207)	−0.056	(0.213)	0.485
1962	0.378	(0.194)	0.457	(0.199)	0.484
1963	0.276	(0.205)	0.360	(0.210)	0.483
1964	0.050	(0.174)	0.105	(0.180)	0.509
1965	0.304(0.186)/0.546(0.240)		0.351(0.188)/0.589(0.242)		0.533/0.427
1966	0.272	(0.150)	0.300	(0.155)	0.392
1967	0.259	(0.148)	0.301	(0.152)	0.381
1968	0.254	(0.190)	0.308	(0.195)	0.378
1969	0.460	(0.180)	0.499	(0.187)	0.373
1970	0.459	(0.151)	0.518	(0.155)	0.359
1971	0.298	(0.145)	0.339	(0.150)	0.346
1972	0.455	(0.180)	0.519	(0.189)	0.326

1973	0.365(0.305)/−0.044(0.297)		0.368(0.290)/−0.014(0.333)		0.302/−0.109
1974	−0.146	(0.160)	−0.088	(0.166)	−0.032
1975	−0.600	(0.185)	−0.551	(0.192)	−0.094
1976	−0.031	(0.164)	−0.005	(0.171)	−0.156
1977	−0.109	(0.174)	−0.072	(0.180)	−0.190
1978	−0.115	(0.168)	−0.036	(0.174)	−0.202
1979	−0.056	(0.137)	−0.019	(0.143)	−0.207
1980	−0.093	(0.139)	−0.029	(0.143)	−0.271
1981	−0.064	(0.145)	−0.023	(0.149)	−0.292
Average Values:					
Regime I (1955–65)	0.308		0.376		0.499
Regime II (1965–73)	0.369		0.415		0.368
Regime III (1973–81)	−0.143		−0.095		−0.174

Notes: The coefficients in columns 1 and 3 were estimated from the equation:

$$R_{it} = \beta_{0i} + \beta_{1i} \cdot R_{mt} + \sum_{j=1956}^{1981} \alpha_j I_{jit} d_{it} + \nu_{it}$$

The results in column 1 impose the restriction $\beta_{0i} = \beta_0$, all i, while those in column 3 do not impose this restriction. The data in the last column are the dividend return premia, $[(m - \tau_a)/(1 - \tau_a) - z]/(1 - z) = 1 - \delta$, calculated from the weighted average tax rates reported in Table 2. See J. Poterba and L. Summers, "New Evidence that Taxes Affect the Valuation of Dividends," *Journal of Finance* 39 (December 1984), for further description.

dends. Although it is of course possible that British and American institutions differ in ways that preclude generalizing from the British experience, this seems unlikely. Miller and Scholes (1978), in their analysis of the taxation of dividends in the United States, suggested that the interaction between various tax provisions can cause dramatic reductions in the effective marginal tax rate on capital income. They focused on several devices in the tax code which might reduce the effective dividend tax rate: (i) the potential for dividend income to raise the limitation on interest income deductibility; (ii) the availability of life insurance policies and single-premium annuities as essentially tax-free accumulation vehicles; and (iii) the use of pension funds to allow assets to earn the before-tax interest rate.[30]

While some of the relevant tax features appear in the British tax code, others do not. Interest payments are not deductible from taxable income in the United Kingdom, except in special circumstances involving home mortgages and several other minor cases. Moreover, there are strict (and quite low) limits on the amount deductible. The first Miller-Scholes device is therefore inaccessible to British investors. The life insurance mechanism, however, may be more powerful as a tax avoidance device in Britain than in the United States. Tax subsidies are provided for the payment of insurance premiums, and the proceeds of the policies are generally exempt from capital gains.[31] Tiley (1978) observes that

> in recent years, these [insurance tax subsidies] have been used to promote tax avoidance schemes . . . taxpayers took advantage of the rules concerning relief from premiums to buy shares or unit trusts with, in effect, the aid of an exchequer subsidy, or higher rate taxpayers put their assets into funds where income could accumulate virtually free of tax thanks to [tax] concessions for insurance companies. (p. 717)

Finally, with regard to pension funds, the British and American systems are similar. Corporate contributions are deductible for corporate tax purposes, and individual pension contributions are not treated as taxable income. Pension funds are untaxed, and the earnings of pension funds are tax-exempt. When pension income is received during retirement it is subject to ordinary income taxation. As in the United States, the issue of whether marginal investors are accumulating through these channels is unclear. There may be other devices for sheltering income, available in the United Kingdom but not in the United States, which we have failed to mention. These would only strengthen our case showing that the potential for tax-free accumulation is clearly present in Britain.

Before presenting additional evidence to distinguish between the tax capitalization hypothesis and traditional view of dividend taxes, we turn in the next section to an alternative methodology for studying the impact of tax changes on the market valuation of dividends. This will provide further information on whether the stock market exhibits a preference for dividends or capital gains.

ASSET PRICE CHANGES AND TAX ANNOUNCEMENTS

Ex-day evidence is only one way of trying to measure the effect of tax changes. Another involves the "event study" methodology which is often used to investigate the effects of regulatory reforms, mergers, or other financial news on corporate valuation. By looking for changes in share prices when major tax reforms were announced or when expectations were otherwise altered, we can derive further tests for the influence of taxes on asset valuation.

Using previous results, note that the value of a share, V_0', can be written as the present value of the after-tax dividends its shareholders expect to receive:

$$V_0' = \sum_{j=0}^{\infty} \left[\prod_{k=0}^{j} \left(1 + \frac{\rho_k}{1 - z_k}\right)^{-1} \right] [\delta_j D_j'] \qquad (4.1)$$

where ρ_k is the after-tax return required by the marginal investor in period k and D'_j is the dividend in period j paid to the owners of all currently outstanding shares. It follows immediately from equation (4.1) that ignoring future equity issues, a permanent change in the dividend tax rate, through its effect on δ_j, will cause an equal proportional reduction in the value of all firms. This holds regardless of the time path of their expected future dividends. However equation (4.1) makes it clear that a *temporary* change in dividend taxes will impact different firms differently. Temporary changes in dividend taxes will have their greatest impact on firms which are expected to distribute a large amount of dividend income in the immediate future. In the extreme case of a firm that was not expected to pay any dividends for the duration of a tax change, the change would have no effect on market value.

In practice, the fluidity of tax policy leaves some ambiguity as to whether a particular policy is (i) temporary and likely to be reversed, or (ii) the first step in a program of escalating reform. These two possibilities have distinctly different implications for the impact of a tax increase on the share values of different firms. If higher dividend taxes are expected to be short-lived, then low-yielding firms which are valuable primarily because of dividends projected to be paid in the distant future will experience smaller share price declines than high-yielding firms which derive most of their value from a high level of current dividends. Alternatively, if the increase in dividend taxes is viewed as the harbinger of still higher tax rates in the future, then low-yielding firms will decline by *more* than those with high yields, as the market expects heavy taxes now, but *even heavier* taxes when these firms finally distribute their profits.

Most of the tax changes during our sample period were clearly temporary. In 1958, when the split-rate corporate profits tax was abolished and replaced by a single rate tax which was much more favorable toward dividend payout, support for the measure came from the Conservative Party. Labour was opposed, and the possibility that the tax change would be reversed when the opposition gained control of Parliament was recognized clearly. Indeed, that was what happened. In 1964, Labour won a narrow victory and promptly announced a new plan to raise taxes on capital income by adopting a corporation income tax system which would effectively "double-tax" dividend payments. Support for this policy again was split clearly along party lines. When the Conservative Party regained power in 1970, it was not long before plans were announced (in the 1971 budget) for a return to an integrated tax system which would substantially reduce the tax burden on dividends.

If dividend tax reforms are perceived as temporary and the stock market equates the value of each share with the present value of its after-tax dividend stream, then increases in the dividend tax rate should reduce the value of high-payout shares by a larger amount than low-payout shares. This may be tested by relating the excess return on different firms during budget announcement months to each firm's typical dividend yield. Evidence that dividend tax increases reduce the value of high-yield shares by more than they reduce low-yield share prices would constitute strong evidence against the "tax irrelevance" hypothesis.

Data and methods

Our study focuses on three events which substantially affected the outlook for British dividend taxation. They are described below:

April 1958 budget speech. Chancellor Heathcoat Amory announced reforms in the profits tax, abolishing the differential 30 percent tax on distributed profits and the 3 percent tax on undistributed earnings. Effective April 1, 1958 (retroactively), he introduced a single-rate profits tax of 10 percent. This reform was not fully anticipated; *The Economist* (April 19, 1958) indicated that Mr. Amory had shown "political courage" in adopting it. During April 1958, the excess return on the market, calculated as the total return on the *Financial Times*–Actuaries Share Index, minus the Treasury bill rate, was 1.7 percent. Over the longer February to April period, when expectations may have been changing, the excess market return was 7.3 percent.

November 1964 mini-budget. After Labour's electoral victory in October 1964, Chancellor James Callaghan announced sweeping plans for fiscal reform. They included the switch to a classical system of corporate income taxation beginning in 1966 and the imposition of a capital gains tax beginning in April 1965. The two proposals should have had opposite effects on dividend-paying firms. Introducing a capital gains tax should have raised the value of dividend income, helping high-payout firms. The switch to a corporation tax system, however, and the repeal of the integrated tax system which had prevailed between 1958 and 1964, imposed a heavier tax burden on high-dividend firms than on high-retentions companies. This was reflected in the large change in $\hat{\theta}$ calculated earlier. The general move toward heavier taxation was recognized as one cause of the stock market's −4.7 percent excess return during the month of November 1964.

March 1971 budget speech. This was the first budget speech after the Conservative victory of 1970. Chancellor Barber announced plans to end "the substantial discrimination in favour of retained as opposed to distributed profits" by adopting a new system of corporation tax which would impute corporate tax payments to shareholders. The budget also promised substantial reductions in the marginal tax rates applicable to investment income received by personal investors, and should therefore have proved highly attractive for firms with currently high dividend payout. The excess return on the overall market during March 1971 was 6.5 percent.

To test for the effects of tax changes on different firms, we generalized the monthly after-tax CAPM used by Gordon and Bradford (1980) and Poterba and Summers (1984a) to include terms which would capture the effects of budget announcements. The equation estimated was:

$$R_{it} - \beta_i R_{mt} - (1 - \beta_i)R_{ft} = \alpha_0 + \alpha_k I_{kit} d_{it} + (\eta_{1s} + \eta_{2s} d_{it}^*) I_{sit}^* + \epsilon_{it} \quad (4.2)$$

where d^* is the average dividend yield on a security during the previous 24 months and I_{kit} is an indicator variable which is set equal to one if the *it*th observation corresponds to a month in the first, second, or third "tax regime." Tax Regime I is defined to include observations prior to the introduction of a capital gains tax in 1965. Tax Regime 2 extends from 1965 to 1973, when the imputation system took effect, and Tax Regime 3 is the period after April 1973. This equation is a modified CAPM which takes account of possibly differential valuation of dividends and capital gains, allowing for changes when major tax reforms occur. Poterba and Summers (1984a) estimate several models of this type and provide a fuller justification for the specification.

The critical variables for our present study are the last terms in equation (4.2). I^*_{sit} is an indicator variable for the months involving major tax reform announcements, where s = 4/58, 11/64, or 3/71. The coefficients η_{1s} and η_{2s} capture the effects of tax announcements on security returns, with η_{2s} reflecting differences which can be attributed to average dividend yield. If a tax reform, say that in 1958, raised the value of high-yield shares, then we would predict that $\eta_{2,1958}$ would be positive. The corresponding coefficient for 1971 should also be positive, and it is difficult to predict the sign of the 1964 announcements because they involved changes in both dividend and capital gains taxes.

The data set we used for our study is a sample of over 40,000 company-months of security returns, drawn from the London Business School Share Price Data Base. A more complete description of this data set may be found in Poterba and Summers (1984a).

Results

The results of estimating equation (4.2) on this monthly data set are reported in Table 5. We show both the η_1 and η_2 coefficients in the table, and show results from several different definitions of the "event period" during which information was revealed. For example, the first row of the table corresponds to a one-month event period. That is, I^*_{sit} is equal to 1 only during *the month* of the tax policy announcement. Since expectations were probably evolving throughout the period immediately prior to the actual policy announcement, in particular in election months as in 1964, we also consider somewhat longer event periods. Two- and four-month event period specifications are also reported in Table 5. In all cases, we define the event period as ending in the announcement month. Many previous studies of "events" and their effects on share prices have suggested that the market quickly adjusts to new information, so allowing for adjustment in the months after the budget speeches seemed unnecessary.[32]

TABLE 5 Tax changes and share recapitalization

Duration of Event Period	*Variable*	*1958 Change in Profits Tax*	*1964 Announcement of Capital Gains/ Corporation Tax*	*1971 Announcement of Imputation System*
1 month	Constant	−0.024 (0.028)	0.001 (0.010)	−0.017 (0.007)
	Dividend yield	4.304 (5.352)	0.030 (3.384)	1.466 (2.002)
2 months	Constant	−0.019 (0.016)	−0.006 (0.001)	−0.0170 (0.0074)
	Dividend yield	4.981 (3.815)	1.860 (1.841)	1.464 (2.003)
4 months	Constant	−0.019 (0.016)	−0.002 (0.005)	−0.008 (0.005)
	Dividend yield	4.982 (3.816)	0.188 (1.193)	1.042 (1.384)
Predicted dividend yield effect		+	?	+

Notes: Coefficients are estimated from the equation:

$$R_{it} - R_{ft} - \beta_i (R_{mt} - R_{ft}) = \alpha_0 + \alpha_K I_{Kit} d_{it} + (\eta_{1s} + \eta_{2s} d_{it}^*) I_{sit}^* + \epsilon_{it}$$

using a data set of monthly share returns compiled from the London Business School Share Price Data Base. See J. Poterba and L. Summers, "New Evidence that Taxes Affect the Valuation of Dividends," *Journal of Finance* 34 (December 1984), for a more detailed description of this data set and the text for further details on the variable definitions. Standard errors are reported in parentheses.

The results in Table 5 provide some support for the view that anticipated taxes are reflected in security prices. In 1958, firms with high dividend yields experienced substantially greater returns during the period around the budget speech than their low-yield counterparts. A one percentage point increase in a firm's dividend yield would have induced a 4 percent higher return during the month of April 1958. Similarly, in 1971, the estimated dividend yield coefficients are positive in all estimated equations. They suggest that, when comparing two firms, one with a dividend yield one point higher than the other, the high-yield firm would have earned a return about one and one half percentage points greater than that of the low-yield firm. Unfortunately, none of the estimated coefficients is significantly different from zero at the 95 percent confidence level.

This may in part reflect the difficulties of identifying the times when new information was revealed, as well as the inherent imprecision associated with the use of monthly data.

The 1964 budget speech had much weaker effects on the differential returns between high- and low-payout firms. The one- and four-month event variables have tiny coefficients, and the somewhat larger 2-month variable, which includes both the event month for the budget speech and the previous month, when the election took place, has a larger coefficient but a t-statistic only slightly greater than one. This event, as we noted above, had effects on the tax treatment of both high- and low-payout shares. Under the assumption that capital gains taxes were paid at very low effective rates, however, the reform should have reduced the value of high-yield firms. It remains somewhat surprising that this effect does not leave a stronger trace in the data.

One of the major difficulties in any event study is identifying the times when information was actually revealed to market participants. To the extent that, conditional upon electoral outcomes, budget proposals were easy to anticipate, the elections of 1964 and 1970 may have been the important "events" for the revaluation of different securities. We experimented with these events, as well as the actual budget speeches, in our empirical work and again found small revaluation effects, generally in the predicted directions, around election periods.

The weak evidence in this section confirms the conclusion of the preceding section that changes in the tax rules facing typical investors have important effects on the market valuation of dividends. As discussed at the end of the last section, this conclusion is probably applicable to the United States as well as Britain. We therefore are led to reject the tax irrelevance view as a model for analyzing the role of dividend taxes. In the next two sections, we examine the two remaining views of the effects of dividend taxation.

DIVIDEND TAXES AND CORPORATE DIVIDEND POLICY

The evidence presented in the last two sections suggests that dividend tax changes alter the stock market's relative valuation of dividends and capital gains. It constitutes a partial refutation of the "tax irrelevance" view, which argues that tax avoidance by individuals, coupled with ex-day trading by brokers and institutions, should eliminate any tax-induced valuation effects. However, the finding that taxes influence security returns does not enable us to distinguish between the "tax capitalization" and the "traditional" views of dividend taxation. Both assume that dividend taxes are capitalized into share prices and reflected in market returns. These two views differ in their predictions about how dividend tax changes will affect corporate financial and investment decisions. The tax capitalization view suggests that neither financial nor real choices will be influenced by a reduction in dividend taxes, while the traditional view predicts that both the payout ratio and the level of corporate investment will respond to a tax reform. In this section and the next, we examine the direct effects of postwar British dividend tax changes on corporate dividend payout and on real investment decisions.

The tax capitalization view derived corporate dividend payments as a residual, the difference between current profits and the firm's investment demands. Assuming that all investment could be financed from retained earnings, we showed in the first section that a permanent dividend tax reduction would not affect the firm's investment decisions. Funds for investment are already inside the firm and therefore subject to eventual dividend taxation. While a permanent reduction in dividend taxes raises the value of these claims on resources within the corporate sector, it does not alter the rules for investing these resources so as to maximize the firm's value. Since dividend taxation affects neither investment, the capital stock, nor current profitability, it cannot have any effect on $D = (1 - \tau)\Pi - I + \overline{V}^N$.

The traditional view, by comparison, predicts that any permanent change in the effective marginal dividend tax rate will affect corporate payout decisions. Dividend policy is chosen by balancing the marginal reduction in the firm's value due to higher investor tax liabilities against the marginal increase in value due to changes in the return, $\rho(D/(1 - \tau)\Pi)$, required by investors. A dividend tax reduction will lower the cost of obtaining further reductions in the required return and therefore should increase the firm's payout ratio.

The tax irrelevance view suggests that changes in the investor tax preference ratio should have no effect on corporate payout decisions. Discriminatory corporate taxes, however, could alter the level of dividend payments, since they cannot be laundered by tax-conscious investors.

The effects of a temporary reduction in the dividend tax are somewhat different. First, we consider the tax capitalization view. The cost of capital depends on the expected change in the equilibrium value of marginal q. During times just before an increase in the dividend tax, firms will anticipate capital losses from holding corporate capital, and will reduce their investment activity. By reducing

I_t but leaving $\Pi(K_t)$ unchanged, such a change in investment activity would *raise* the observed dividend payout ratio of the corporate sector. Similarly, immediately prior to a dividend tax reduction, firms would expect to gain substantially from the upward revaluation of marginal q, and would therefore invest. This would lead to a reduction in dividend payments prior to a dividend tax cut.

The traditional view also predicts changes in payout ratios as a result of temporary dividend tax reductions. However, temporary and permanent changes would cause the same proportionate reduction in dividend payout, since the first-order condition for optimal dividend choice, equation (1.17*a*), depends only on current values of the tax parameters. This conclusion depends critically upon the assumption that capital market participants use only the *current period's dividend yield* in choosing the appropriate discount rate for the firm's earnings.

If instead investors chose ρ on the basis of the average dividend yield for a few adjacent periods, the firm would be able to raise its value by altering the timing of its dividend payments. For example, if the discount rate is determined by the value of $(\Sigma\, D)/(\Sigma(1 - \tau)\Pi)$ during a several-quarter period, the firm could raise its dividend payments during the less heavily taxed period, compensating with a reduction in dividend payout during high-tax periods, and could raise its total value. This would induce swings in dividend policy around the introduction of temporary dividend tax changes, as well as when permanent but anticipated dividend taxes were introduced. The tax irrelevance view yields predictions for re-timing in dividends when the corporate tax rules change, but predicts no effect of personal tax reforms.

Data and methods

To test the different payout predictions of the different views, we examined the aggregate payout behavior of Britain's Industrial and Commercial Companies. The tests reported in this section employ seasonally unadjusted data on gross dividend payments and corporate profits. We draw heavily on Poterba (1984a), where the data are described in greater detail. In the United States, the dividend payout ratio is defined as the ratio of dividend payments, before personal tax, to corporate profits after corporate tax. In Britain, this definition is misleading because corporate taxes, hence after-tax profits, depend upon the firm's payout policy when a nonclassical corporate tax system is in effect. The dividend payout concept which we employ is the ratio of gross dividends paid to the *maximum feasible gross dividends* of the firm.[33] This definition ensures that movements in the payout ratio measure changes in the fraction of their dividend-paying capacity which firms are using, and not changes in the corporate tax treatment of dividends. Under a tax system like that in the United States, it is equivalent to the standard measure of the payout ratio.

Explicit dividend controls were in force for much of the 1970s, and they substantially reduced the gross dividends paid by the industrial and commercial companies.[34] The presence of dividend controls can contaminate any investigation of the relationship between dividends, profits, and the tax code. To avoid these difficulties, we report regression results for two time periods. The first, 1955–72, is prior to the introduction of dividend controls. The second sample period includes the precontrol period as well as data for 1980–83, the period after the dividend controls had been lifted. In using data for 1980–83 we allow for the possibility of structural change in the payout relation by adding a dummy variable for the post-1980 period.

The equation that we estimate is:

$$\begin{aligned}\log D_t = {} & \beta_0 + \beta_1 \log D_{t-1} + \beta_2 \log D_{t-4} \\ & + \beta_3 \log Y_t + \beta_4 \log(Y_{t-1}/Y_t) \\ & + \beta_5 \log(Y_{t-4}/Y_t) + \beta_5 \log\theta_t + \beta_6 \Delta log\,\theta_{t+1} \\ & + \beta_7 \Delta log\,\theta_t + \beta_8 S_1 + \beta_9 S_2 + \beta_{10} S_3 + u_t\end{aligned} \tag{5.1}$$

where D denotes gross dividends, Y equals maximum feasible dividends, and (S_1, S_2, S_3) are seasonal dummy variables. The total tax preference ratio, θ, is included to capture the effect of tax reforms. Lagged dividend and profit terms are included to allow for flexible adjustment dynamics toward the new steady state. The equation was estimated both by OLS and with a maximum likelihood correction for second-order serial correlation. The results were not particularly sensitive to the specification of the disturbance term.

Results

Estimates of equation (5.1) are reported in Table 6. They clearly demonstrate the importance of dividend taxes in determining the extent to which firms utilize their dividend-paying capacity. Equations estimated without any allowance for short-run adjustments in dividend policy around tax changes suggest long-run dividend payment elasticities with respect to the total tax preference ratio of between 2.6 and 1.8, depending on the specification and time period chosen. There is also evidence that tax policy *changes* induce short-run adjustments in dividend payout. An anticipated 10 percent in-

TABLE 6 Dividend payments and tax reforms, British evidence

Equation	Time Period	Constant	$log(DIV_{-1})$	$log(DIV_{-4})$	$log(\theta)$	$\Delta log(\theta_{+1})$	$\Delta log(\theta)$	$log(PROFIT)$	Post–1980	ρ_1	ρ_2	R^2
1.	1955–72	0.398	0.414	0.396	0.196	−0.833	0.689	0.122				0.91
		(0.687)	(0.107)	(0.080)	(0.104)	(0.420)	(0.352)	(0.070)				
2.	1955–72	0.170	0.608	0.289	0.120	−0.792	0.956	0.083		−0.39	−0.37	0.92
		(0.612)	(0.113)	(0.098)	(0.096)	(0.405)	(0.205)	(0.071)		(0.15)	(0.15)	
3.	1955–72	0.811	0.309	0.482	0.390		0.092					0.88
		(0.734)	(0.149)	(0.104)	(0.146)			(0.069)				
4.	1955–72	0.561	0.484	0.390	0.265		0.055			−0.31	−0.36	0.89
		(0.547)	(0.113)	(0.109)	(0.118)			(0.073)		(0.16)	(0.15)	
5.	1955–83*	1.877	0.349	0.449	0.407	−0.847	0.459	−0.040	−0.150			0.86
		(0.729)	(0.988)	(0.084)	(0.148)	(0.281)	(0.313)	(0.082)	(0.066)			
6.	1955–83*	0.645	0.609	0.280	0.177	−0.730	0.844	0.036	−0.084	−0.26	−0.54	0.91
		(0.558)	(0.095)	(0.083)	(0.098)	(0.243)	(0.270)	(0.066)	(0.038)	(0.10)	(0.11)	
7.	1955–83*	1.963	0.302	0.489	0.540			−0.042	−0.195			0.84
		(0.750)	(0.096)	(0.087)	(0.148)			(0.087)	(0.068)			
8.	1955–83*	1.056	0.501	0.372	0.321			0.001	−0.125	−0.24	−0.47	0.89
		(0.589)	(0.095)	(0.086)	(0.102)			(0.072)	(0.041)	(0.11)	(0.11)	

Notes: All equations are estimated using quarterly, seasonally unadjusted data on the dividend payments and maximum possible gross dividends of the Industrial and Commercial Companies. Equations 1–4 were estimated for the period 1956:1–1972:3, while those in rows 5–8 also include the post-dividend control period, 1980:1 to 1983:2. The profit variable is maximum feasible gross dividends, described in the text.

crease in the tax preference ratio, corresponding to roughly a 4 percent reduction in the shareholder tax rate on dividends, causes dividends to fall by 8 percent of their planned value in the quarter immediately prior to the tax reform. Moreover, there is a somewhat smaller transitory increase in the level of dividend payments immediately after a tax change is instituted. Controlling for short-term adjustments in payout policy alters the estimated steady-state effects of a dividend tax change. The long-run elasticity of dividend payout with respect to the tax preference ratio declines to between 1.03 and 2.05 in the dividend equations which incorporate changes in the tax rates.

The dividend equations estimated for the early sample period, 1955–72, yield plausible models of the elasticity of dividends with respect to profits. They indicate a long-run elasticity of gross dividends with respect to maximum feasible dividends of between 0.5 and 0.8, and the hypothesis that this elasticity is unity can never be rejected. Less plausible results emerge from the regression models which include post-1980 data. Estimates of the long-run maximum dividend elasticity are substantially lower than those for the earlier sample, and negative estimates are obtained in two of the four reported equations. The hypothesis that this elasticity is unity still cannot be rejected, however, in either of the equations which were estimated with an AR2 error structure. Poterba (1984a) suggests that the low maximum dividend elasticities are probably due to divergences between accounting profits and real profits at the end of the sample period.

The evidence on dividend payout and tax policy reported above did not distinguish between changes in the investor tax preference ratio and the effect of varying corporate tax rates on retained and distributed earnings. The tax capitalization and traditional view predict that changes in either of these tax parameters should affect dividend payout, while the "tax irrelevance" view suggests that only corporate tax changes should affect dividends. Poterba (1984a) tests the hypothesis that investor tax preference changes affect dividend payout. Although the effect of corporate tax changes can be estimated more precisely than investor tax effects, both types of tax reforms influence corporate dividend decisions. This provides further evidence against the tax irrelevance hypothesis, as well as the capitalization view, and buttresses the traditional view of dividend taxation.

The British time-series data are not the only source of variation in dividend tax rates.[35] American dividend taxes were substantially lower before World War II, and particularly before 1936, than in subsequent years. Brittain (1966) and Poterba and Summers (1984b) document that changes in weighted average marginal tax rates on dividends in the United States have had a significant impact on corporate dividend policies. Brittain (1966) concluded that "rising individual tax rates [between 1920 and 1960] were found to depress dividends. Most estimates showed [they] were sufficient to account for the pronounced downward trend in payout, that which occurred between the late 1920s and the early postwar period." [p. 196]. These effects cannot all be attributed to retiming of dividend payments. This finding provides further evidence in favor of the traditional view of dividend taxes. In Poterba and Summers (1984b), we argue that the failure of dividend payout ratios to rise over the past 15 years is strong evidence against Miller and Scholes' (1978, 1982) claim that the U.S. income tax has evolved toward a consumption tax.

INVESTMENT BEHAVIOR AND DIVIDEND TAXES

The evidence in the last section focused on the direct linkages between tax rates and dividend payout. One of the principal motivations for our interest in dividend taxes, however, was their possible impact on corporate investment decisions. In this section we summarize the results of Poterba and Summers (1983) on the relationship between "Tobin's q" and the investment behavior of British firms. This allows us to obtain further evidence on the difference between the traditional and the tax capitalization views.

These two views predict different steady-state values of the ratio of the market value of corporate equity divided by its replacement cost. Because the level of investment activity can be shown to depend upon the difference between the current value of q and its steady-state level, the two views yield different specifications for the investment function.

Earlier, we derived the value of marginal q predicted by the tax capitalization view. Under a classical corporate tax regime similar to that prevailing in the United States, $q = (1 - m)/(1 - z)$. Managers ask "will this project raise share values by as much as it reduces the after-tax dividend income of shareholders?" and they undertake some investment projects which do not raise the firm's value by the project's full cost. In equilibrium, therefore, the market value of the firm will equal $(1 - m)/(1 - z)$ times the replacement value of the firm's assets. In contrast, under the traditional view, the equilibrium value of marginal q is always unity. If marginal and average q are equal,[36] the total value of the firm will therefore equal the full replacement cost of its capital in place.

Data and methods

As argued by Keynes (1936) and Tobin (1969), and justified formally in the context of an adjustment cost model by Hayashi (1982) and Summers (1981), the level of investment will depend on the deviation of Tobin's q from its equilibrium value, q^e. Thus, it is natural to postulate that:

$$I = I[(V/pK) - q^e] \tag{6.1}$$

where V/pK is the ratio of the market value of a firm to its replacement cost, or Tobin's q. Since alternative views about dividend taxes have differing implications for the level of q^e, by comparing alternative specifications of q^e in equation (6.1) we can, in principle, distinguish these views.

Before turning to the empirical estimates, one additional complication remains. Our discussion so far has ignored debt finance and corporate taxes. In Poterba and Summers (1983) we show how these considerations influence q^e under the alternative models of investment. In particular, we show that the appropriate investment functions under the two views are:

$$\frac{I}{K} = f(Q_{TRAD}) = f\left[(\frac{V - B}{pK} + u + b - 1)/(1 - \tau)\right] \tag{6.2}$$

and

$$\frac{I}{K} = f(Q_{TC}) = f\left[(\frac{1}{\theta}\frac{(V - B)}{pK} + u + b - 1)/(1 - \tau)\right] \tag{6.3}$$

where V represents the market value of equity, pK, the replacement cost of capital, u is the present value of all depreciation allowances and investment incentives on a £1 investment, τ is the corporate tax rate on retained earnings, b is the fraction of investment financed with debt, and B is the present value of remaining depreciation allowances on existing capital. The only difference between the two equations is that the tax capitalization hypothesis implies the presence of a term $1/\theta$ multiplying the market value of equity, correcting for the effects of tax capitalization in affecting the firm's investment decisions.

The investment models which we estimate take the simple form

$$\left(\frac{I}{K}\right)_t = \beta_0 Q_{TC,t} + \beta_2 Q_{TC,t-1} + \epsilon_t \tag{6.4}$$

and

$$\left(\frac{I}{K}\right)_t = \beta_0 + \beta_1 Q_{TRAD,t} + \beta_2 Q_{TRAD,t-1} + \epsilon_t \tag{6.5}$$

These specifications are derived and explained in greater detail in Poterba and Summers (1983), where the ϵ_t is interpreted as a random shock to the cost-of-adjustment function. The appeal of the "q" investment approach is that, whereas other approaches to estimating the investment impact of personal taxes require us to specify the firm's cost of capital, the "q" formulation does not. Since the investor's discount rate ρ enters the cost of capital and is unobservable, efforts to define the cost of capital are prone to error.

Our first tests of the two views are based on comparisons of the fit of equations (6.4) and (6.5). Because all firms may not be on the same margin, the aggregate investment function might be a weighted average of the "capitalization" and the "double tax" investment functions. To allow for this possibility, we also specified an investment equation with a weight of σ on equation (6.5) and $(1 - \sigma)$ on equation (6.4). This weighted average investment equation takes the form

$$\frac{I}{K} = \beta_0 + (\beta_1 + \beta_2 L)\left(\frac{\{\sigma + (1 - \sigma)\frac{1}{\theta}\}\frac{V - B}{pK} + b + u - 1}{(1 - \tau)}\right) + \epsilon \tag{6.6}$$

where L is the lag operator. The traditional view of the dividend tax is supported by estimates of $\hat{\sigma}$ near unity. If, however, $\hat{\sigma}$ is close to zero, then tax capitalization would appear to be the more appropriate model for investment decisions.

To estimate these models, we used annual data on the Industrial and Commercial Companies in Great Britain for the period 1950–80. Our investment variable, I/K, is the gross investment rate for these companies. The values of Q_{TRAD} and Q_{TC} were constructed using financial market data provided by the Bank of England. Tax rates were measured using the "weighted average" marginal tax rates which were described earlier.

Results

The results of estimating investment models with both sets of Q variables are shown in Table 7. They are based on slightly revised data and therefore differ (trivially) from earlier findings in Poterba and Summers (1983). The findings demonstrate the superiority of the Q specification based on the "traditional view" of dividend taxation. In each regression pair, the Q_{TRAD} equation fits better than the Q_{TC} specification. In addition, the Q_{TRAD} models suggest a larger effect of Q on investment activity. These results favoring the traditional

TABLE 7 Investment equations under the competing dividend tax views

Equation	Estimation Method	Dividend Tax View	β_0	$\beta_1(\times 10^{-2})$	$\beta_2(\times 10^{-2})$	ρ_1	ρ_2	SSR $(\times 10^{-4})$	D.W.	R^2
(1*a*)	OLS	Capitalization	6.51 (0.23)	1.04 (0.38)	0.66 (0.38)			2167	0.37	0.49
(1*b*)	OLS	Traditional	6.61 (0.17)	1.28 (0.38)	0.96 (0.37)			1470	0.46	0.65
(2*a*)	AR2	Capitalization	6.89 (0.41)	0.61 (0.18)	0.37 (0.18)	1.25 (0.18)	−0.45 (0.18)	477	1.69	0.88
(2*b*)	AR2	Traditional	6.90 (0.31)	0.90 (0.19)	0.51 (0.19)	1.28 (0.17)	−0.50 (0.17)	361	1.70	0.91
(3*a*)	IV	Capitalization	6.20 (0.24)	1.63 (0.74)	0.62 (0.64)			2476	0.54	—
(3*b*)	IV	Traditional	6.46 (0.20)	1.41 (0.68)	1.20 (0.63)			1558	0.63	—
(4*a*)	AR2–IV	Capitalization	6.58 (0.42)	0.97 (0.25)	0.98 (0.29)	1.15 (0.20)	−0.43 (0.20)	575	2.00	—
(4*b*)	AR2–IV	Traditional	6.80 (0.30)	1.16 (0.24)	1.04 (0.27)	1.06 (0.20)	−0.37 (0.20)	398	1.83	—

Notes: The estimated equations correspond to the model

$$(I/K)_t = \beta_0 + \beta_1 Q_{j,t} + \beta_2 Q_{j,t-1} + \epsilon_t \qquad j = TRAD,\ TC$$

where ϵ_t is allowed to follow a second-order AR process. All equations are estimated for the period 1950–80, and standard errors are shown in parentheses. See J. Poterba and L. Summers, "Dividend Taxes, Corporate Investment, and Q," *Journal of Public Economics* 22, pp. 135–67.

model are buttressed by other specifications reported in Poterba and Summers (1983).

The most direct test of the two models comes from estimating the weighting parameter in equation (6.6). The point estimates for this equation are shown below:

$$\frac{I}{K} = \underset{(0.21)}{6.74} + \left(\underset{(0.42)}{11.28} + \underset{(0.42)}{1.16}L\right) \left[\frac{\{\underset{(0.27)}{1.10} - 0.10\frac{1}{\theta}\} \cdot \frac{V - B}{pK} + u + b - 1}{(1 - \tau)}\right] + \epsilon_t \qquad (6.7)$$

$$SSR = 440 \qquad R^2 = 0.68$$

The hypothesis that $\sigma = 1$ cannot be rejected at standard significance levels, suggesting that we cannot reject the "traditional" view of the investment equation. However, the point hypothesis that $\sigma = 0$, corresponding to tax capitalization view, is decisively rejected by the investment data. It appears that at least the bulk of investment decisions are made by corporations who act as if marginal investment is financed through new share issues.

This finding confirms the analysis in the preceding section suggesting that the traditional view of dividend taxes is most consistent with the British experience. It does not appear that firms lower their investment thresholds when they can finance investment out of retained earnings, as suggested by the tax capitalization hypothesis.

CONCLUSION

Our empirical tests using data on security returns, payout behavior, and investment decisions all point to a common conclusion. The traditional model of dividend taxes which regards them as additional corporate tax burdens provides the best approximation to their effects. We are led to reject models of the economic effects of dividend taxes which suggest that dividend payments have no adverse tax consequences, as well as those which argue that firms pay dividends because money is "trapped" within the corporate sector. Although these conclusions are based on British data, our comparison of the tax laws in Britain and the United States suggests that they are likely to be applicable in the American context as well.[37]

Our results have important implications for tax policy as well as dividend policy and valuation. They imply that the total tax burden

on corporate income includes both corporate taxes *and* dividend and capital gains taxes levied on corporate shareholders. In an economically meaningful sense, dividends are double-taxed. A reduction in dividend tax rates would increase dividend payout and corporate investment, and lower firms' cost of capital.[38]

A further implication of these results is that estimates of the total tax burden on corporate capital income which assume that dividend taxes do not have a marginal impact on retentions-financed investment, such as the calculations in Auerbach (1983c) and King and Fullerton (1984), significantly understate the tax burden on corporate income. Estimates such as those reported by Jorgenson and Sullivan (1981), which ignore dividend taxation entirely, are similarly flawed. The empirical question of which dividend tax rate to use in calculating effective corporate tax rates is difficult to answer with any precision. However, our findings suggest that the weighted average approach used by King (1977), Feldstein and Summers (1979), and Feldstein, Dicks-Mireaux, and Poterba (1983) may be satisfactory. Taking this approach renders invalid the frequently quoted conclusion that the United States no longer taxes corporate investment income.

Our results also suggest that measures directed at providing dividend tax relief would reduce the inefficiencies associated with the double taxation of corporate capital income. These inefficiencies include distortions in the allocation of capital between corporate and noncorporate uses, distortions in the choice between present and future consumption, distortions in corporate financial policy,[39] and distortions in the allocation of risk bearing. In considering the merits of dividend tax relief, however, it is necessary to weigh these efficiency gains against the equity effects and the efficiency costs of alternative revenue sources.

Miller and Scholes (1978) argue that the failure of the business community to strongly support Carter administration proposals calling for dividend tax relief constitutes evidence that dividend taxes are not burdensome. We would suggest the alternative hypothesis that this failure is attributable to the same agency problems which lead shareholders to require dividend payments in the first instance. Dividend payments are the shareholders' way of monitoring managers. When dividend taxes are reduced, shareholders find monitoring cheaper and do more of it. Corporate managers' failure to lobby for dividend relief reflects their decision to lobby for their own rather than their shareholders' interests. An alternative possibility is that managers saw dividend relief as an alternative to even more attractive forms of corporate tax reduction.

Our analysis has abstracted from two important aspects of reality, clientele effects and firms' use of debt finance. Neither of these abstractions accounts for our qualitative conclusions. Evidence presented by Blume, Crockett, and Friend (1974) and Lewellen et al. (1978) suggests that clientele effects are not large. Clienteles might attenuate the burden of dividend taxes, but would not eliminate it unless taxpaying investors held only zero dividend stocks. The data clearly reject this possibility. With respect to debt finance, it would be straightforward to append to our formulation of the firm's decision problem either a "Miller model," as in Miller (1977), or a debt-capacity model (as in Gordon and Malkiel (1981)) in which bankruptcy risk limited debt-equity ratios. Neither approach would alter our conclusions. Nonetheless, it would be valuable to analyze the effects of dividend taxation in a richer model than the one we have presented here.

Our findings suggest the importance of providing both a theoretical motivation for, and empirical measures of, the dividend preference function of investors. Theoretical explanations might be further developed along the lines of the incentive signaling approach to corporate finance. While models explaining why dividends are paid have been suggested, this work has not yet reached the point of generating empirically falsifiable predictions about the effects of varying dividend yields, either across time or across firms on required returns. The most promising direction for empirical research appears to involve examining the effects of dividend yield on the required return of dividend-paying firms during periods when dividends are not paid.[40] The extent to which it is appropriate to control for risk in such a calculation is unclear, since higher yields may reduce required returns precisely because they reduce risk. We are currently pursuing research along these lines.

Notes

1. Miller and Scholes (1978, 1982) are the principal exponents of this view.
2. Although this view is linked with the long-standing notion of "trapped" equity in the corporate sector, it has been formalized by Auerbach (1979), Bradford (1981), and King (1977).
3. This is the implicit view of many proponents of tax integration; see, for example, McClure (1977).
4. The tax rate z is the marginal *effective* tax rate on capital gains, as defined by King (1977). Since gains are taxed on realization, not accrual, z is the expected value of the tax liability which is induced by a capital gain accruing today.

5. A closely related model which incorporates uncertainty and investment adjustment costs is solved in Poterba and Summers (1983).
6. We consider the firm's problem in discrete time to avoid the difficulties of infinite investment over infinitely short time intervals which would result in a continuous-time model without adjustment costs.
7. Share repurchases are possible to some extent in the United States. However, regular repurchasing can lead to IRS actions treating the repurchase as a dividend. In Britain, where share repurchase is explicitly banned, these questions do not arise. The situation is more complex when transactions essentially equivalent to share repurchase, such as direct portfolio investments, are considered.
8. The principal class of American investors for whom m is less than z is corporate holders of common stock, who may exclude 85 percent of their dividend income from their taxable income, thereby facing a dividend tax rate of $0.15 \times 0.46 = 0.069$, while being taxed at a 28 percent rate on their realized capital gains.
9. Another case in which the market would exhibit an indifference between dividends and capitals is when the marginal investor is a broker or dealer in securities, facing equal (but nonzero) tax rates on both dividends and short term capital gains.
10. The extension to the CAPM framework which incorporates risk is straightforward and involves replacing ρ with $r_f + \beta_i(r_m - r_f)$ where r_f is the post-tax risk-free return, β_i is firm i's beta, and r_m is the expected post-tax return on the market.
11. More complete discussions of the importance of the marginal source of funds over time may be found in King (1974), Auerbach (1983b, pp. 924–25), and Edwards and Keen (1984).
12. If the desired wealth-to-income ratio is fixed, raising dividend tax rates may actually *raise* equilibrium capital intensity by reducing the portfolio value of each unit of physical capital. The discussion in the text precludes this possibility by assuming that ρ is fixed.
13. The survey evidence reported by Lintner (1956) and the regression evidence in Fama and Babiak (1968) suggest that managers adjust dividend payments slowly in response to new information.
14. If, despite the fact that $\rho_t' < 0$ firms continued to set $D_t = 0$ at the optimum, the analysis would be similar to the tax capitalization model where $\rho = \rho(0)$.
15. In the partial equilibrium model described here, the supply of capital is perfectly elastic at a rate of return $\rho(\alpha)$. Therefore, the whole adjustment to the new equilibrium would involve changes in capital intensity.
16. Black (1976), Stiglitz (1980), and Edwards (1984) discuss many of the proposed explanations for "intrinsic dividend value" and find them unsatisfactory in some dimension.
17. For consistency, in our section on ex-dividend price changes it will prive helpful to focus on the dividend *announced* by the firm. Prior to March 1973, that was the gross dividend in the notation of King (1977). After 1973, it was the *net* dividend. We define δ relative to the

announced dividend. King (1977) follows a different procedure for the post-1973 regime but, aside from semantic differences, the results with respect to θ are identical.

18. The term *gross dividends* refers to dividends received by shareholders prior to paying shareholder taxes, but after the payment of all corporate taxes. Note that King (1977) uses G to represent gross dividends, and D for net dividends. We use D for gross dividends.
19. Deferred realization is one of the techniques which enables American investors to lower their capital gains tax liability. Trading so as to generate short-term losses and long-term gains, taking advantage of the differential taxes on the two, is another technique; it is unavailable to British investors, since the tax rate on all gains is equal. Step-up of asset basis at death is another feature of the U.S. tax code which lowers effective capital gains rates still further. Prior to 1971, estates in the United Kingdom were subject to both estate duty *and* capital gains tax on assets in the estate. Since 1971, however, capital gains liability has been forgiven at death and heirs become liable for capital gains tax only on the difference between the price which they receive when they dispose of the asset, and its value at the time of inheritance.
20. If $\tau_a G > \tau_c \Pi$, the firm is unable to recover its ACT payments. The "unrelieved ACT" may be carried forward indefinitely and backward for a period of not more than two years. A substantial fraction of British firms are currently unable to recover their full ACT payments and therefore face corporate tax discrimination between retentions and distributions. See Mayer (1982) and King (1983) for further details on the workings of ACT.
21. The anti-dividend-stripping provisions in the 1970 Act are described in Tiley (1978), pp. 761–64, and Kaplanis (1983).
22. Miller and Scholes (1982) suggest brokers and dealers as the ex-day price setters.
23. The data used in this section are described, and further results are reported, in Poterba and Summers (1984a).
24. The prices used are the average of closing bid and asked prices.
25. The tax changes in 1973 altered the value of dividend income to nonprofit institutions and personal investors engaged in tax-free accumulation, as well as to naive personal investors paying high marginal dividend taxes. For securities dealers and brokers, however, who were unable to fully reclaim the advance corporation tax on the dividend they received, the tax change should have had a smaller effect.
26. Approximately 6 percent of British equity was held by untaxed institutions in 1957; by 1980, the fraction had risen to 26 percent.
27. The capital gains tax rate series computed by King (1977), which we report, assumed that shareholders followed a policy of liquidating 10 percent of their equity holdings each year, regardless of their trading gains or losses. This assumption clearly overstates the liability which would follow from an optimal trading strategy.
28. Some evidence of unusual return patterns around American ex-days

is reported in Black and Scholes (1973) and Eades, Hess, and Kim (1984). Mas (1984) presents corroborative evidence for the United Kingdom.

29. Countries besides the United Kingdom in which dividend tax changes have taken place provide a valuable source of information on the dividend question. Lakonishok and Vermaelen (1983) provide some evidence that the Canadian tax reform of 1971 affected ex-day price behavior in a manner consistent with the short-term trading hypothesis. Amoaku-Adu (1983) and Khoury and Smith (1977) provide opposing evidence, however, showing that share values and dividend policies responded as predicted by the "weighted average investor tax rate" model. Further work remains to be done on this question.
30. Although in principle all of these devices could generate substantial tax savings for personal investors, the extent to which they are actually used in the United States remains controversial. Feenberg (1981), for example, showed that investors for whom the interest deductability limitation was binding received only 2.5 percent of total dividend payments in 1977.
31. A much more complete account of life insurance taxation is provided in Tiley (1978), Chapter 34. A related discussion of pension accumulation is found in Chapter 36.
32. The long tradition of evidence for rapid market adjustment dates to Fama, Fisher, Jensen, and Roll (1969).
33. This is one of the dividend payout concepts suggested by Feldstein (1970).
34. Evidence in Poterba (1984a) suggests as much as a 50 percent reduction in desired dividends.
35. A number of studies have demonstrated that British tax reforms have influenced payout policy. These include Feldstein (1970), King (1971, 1977), and Fane (1975).
36. Hayashi (1982) presents the formal conditions for equality between the average and marginal values of q.
37. Our analysis is corroborated by the work of Long (1978) and Poterba (1984b) on the valuation of securities issued by the Citizens Utilities Company. Due to a quirk in the tax law this company was allowed to issue both shares with taxable and nontaxable dividends. Long (1978) shows that the taxable securities sell for more than the nontaxable securities. Poterba (1984b) shows using ex-day evidence that marginal investors in taxable shares appear to be taxed. These facts can be reconciled only in terms of a dividend preference model, implicitly the traditional view.
38. This suggests an important difficulty with many previous studies of investment behavior. Most of the econometric studies proceeding within the flexible accelerator framework pioneered by Jorgenson (1963) and Hall and Jorgenson (1967) have ignored the role of personal tax variables. While this omission may not be too important for the United States, where tax rates on shareholders have evolved slowly over time, it is potentially critical for modeling investment in Britain or other nations in which radical tax changes have taken place.

39. Estimates of the intersectoral distortions due to capital income taxation are found in Harberger (1962) and Fullerton, et al. (1981). For evidence on distortions in intertemporal choices, see Feldstein (1978) and Summers (1981).
40. Elton, Gruber, and Rentzler (1983) report some investigations along these lines.

REFERENCES

Amoaku-Adu, Ben. "The Canadian Tax Reform and Its Effects on Stock Prices." *Journal of Finance* 38 (1983), pp. 1669–76.

Auerbach, Alan. "Wealth Maximization and the Cost of Capital." *Quarterly Journal of Economics* 93 (1979), pp. 433–46.

Auerbach, Alan. "Stockholder Tax Rates and Firm Attributes." *Journal of Public Economics* 21 (1983a), pp. 107–27.

Auerbach, Alan. "Taxation, Corporate Financial Policy, and the Cost of Capital." *Journal of Economic Literature* 21 (1983b), pp. 905–40.

Auerbach, Alan. "Corporate Taxation in the U.S." *Brookings Papers on Economic Activity*, 1983:2 (1983c).

Bhattacharya, Sudipto. "Imperfect Information, Dividend Policy, and the Bird in the Hand Fallacy." *Bell Journal of Economics* 10 (1979), pp. 259–70.

Black, Fischer. "The Dividend Puzzle." *Journal of Portfolio Management*. Winter (1976), pp. 72–77.

Black, Fischer and Myron Scholes. "The Behavior of Security Returns Around Ex-dividend Days." Unpublished manuscript, University of Chicago, 1973.

Black, Fischer and Myron Scholes. "The Effects of Dividend Policy and Dividend Yield on Common Stock Prices and Returns." *Journal of Financial Economics* 1 (1974), pp. 1–22.

Blume, Marshall, Jean Crockett, and Irwin Friend. "Stockownership in the United States: Characteristics and Trends." *Survey of Current Business* 54 (1974), pp. 16–40.

Bradford, David. "The Incidence and Allocation Effects of a Tax On Corporate Distributions." *Journal of Public Economics* 15 (1981), pp. 1–22.

Brennan, Michael. "Taxes, Market Valuation, and Corporate Financial Policy." *National Tax Journal* 23 (1970), pp. 417–27.

Brittain, John. *Corporate Dividend Policy*. Washington: The Brookings Institution, 1966.

Central Statistical Office. *Economic Trends: Annual Supplement*, 1983. London: HMSO, 1983.

Constantinides, George. "Capital Market Equilibrium with Personal Tax." *Econometrica* 51 (1983), pp. 611–36.

Corporation Tax Green Paper. Command Paper No. 8456, London: HMSO, 1982.

Eades, Kenneth, Patrick Hess, and Han Kim. "On Interpreting Security Returns During the Ex-dividend Period." *Journal of Financial Economics* 13 (1984), pp. 3–34.

Edwards, Jeremy. "Does Dividend Policy Matter?" *Fiscal Studies* 5 (1984), pp. 1–17.

Edwards, Jeremy and Michael Keen. "Wealth Maximization and the Cost of Capital." *Quarterly Journal of Economics* XCIX (1984), pp. 211–14.

Elton, Edwin and Martin Gruber. "Marginal Stockholder Tax Rates and the Clientele Effect." *Review of Economics and Statistics* 52 (1970), pp. 68–74.

Elton, Edwin, Martin Gruber, and Joel Rentzler. "A Simple Examination of the Empirical Relationship Between Dividend Yields and Deviations from the CAPM." *Journal of Banking and Finance* 7 (1983), pp. 135–46.

Fama, Eugene and H. Babiak. "Dividend Policy: An Empirical Analysis." *Journal of the American Statistical Association* 63 (1968), pp. 1132–61.

Fama, Eugene, Lawrence Fisher, Michael Jensen, and Richard Roll. "The Adjustment of Stock Prices to New Information." *International Economic Review* 10 (1969), pp. 1–21.

Fane, George. "The Determination of Quarterly Dividend Payments in the U.K." *In Modelling the Economy*. ed. G. A. Renton. London: Heinemann, 1975; pp. 537–51.

Feenberg, Daniel. "Does the Investment Interest Limitation Explain the Existence of Dividends?" *Journal of Financial Economics* 9 (1981), pp. 265–69.

Feldstein, Martin. "Corporate Taxation and Dividend Behavior." *Review of Economic Studies* 37 (1970), pp. 57–72.

Feldstein, Martin. "The Welfare Cost of Capital Income Taxation." *Journal of Political Economy* 86 (1978), pp. 529–51.

Feldstein, Martin and Lawrence Summers. "Inflation and the Taxation of Capital Income in the Corporate Sector." *National Tax Journal* 32 (1979), pp. 445–70.

Feldstein, Martin, Louis Dicks-Mireaux, and James Poterba. "The Effective Tax Rate and the Pretax Rate of Return." *Journal of Public Economics* 21 (1983), pp. 129–58.

Fullerton, Don, A. Thomas King, John Shoven, and John Whalley. "Corporate Tax Integration in the United States: A General Equilibrium Approach." *American Economic Review* 71 (1981), pp. 677–91.

Gordon, Roger and David Bradford. "Taxation and the Stock Market Valuation of Capital Gains and Dividends: Theory and Empirical Results." *Journal of Public Economics* 14 (1980), pp. 109–36.

Gordon, Roger and Burton Malkiel. "Corporation Finance." In Henry J. Aaron and Joesph A. Pechman ed. *How Taxes Affect Economic Behavior*. Washington: The Brookings Institution, 1981.

Green, Jerry. "Taxation and the Ex-dividend Day Behavior of Common Stock Prices." NBER Working Paper No. 496, Cambridge, Mass., 1980.

Hall, Robert and Dale Jorgenson "Tax Policy and Investment Behavior." *American Economic Review* 53 (1967), pp. 247–59.

Hamada, Robert and Myron Scholes. "Taxes and Corporate Financial Management." In Edward Altman and Marti Subrahmanyam. *Recent Advances in Corporate Finance*. Homewood, Ill: Dow-Jones Irwin, 1984.

Harberger, Arnold C. "The Incidence of the Corporate Income Tax." *Journal of Political Economy* 70 (1962), pp. 215–40.

Hayashi, Fumio. "Tobin's Marginal q and Average q: A Neoclassical Interpretation." *Econometrica* 50 (1982), pp. 213–24.

Hess, Patrick. "The Ex-dividend Day Behavior of Stock Returns: Further Evidence on Tax Effects." *Journal of Finance* 37 (1982), pp. 445–56.

House of Commons. *Report of the Select Committee on Corporation Tax*, House of Commons Paper, 622. London: HMSO, 1971.

Jensen, Michael and William Meckling. "Theory of the Firm: Managerial Behavior, Agency Costs, and Ownership Structure." *Journal of Financial Economics* 3. (1976), pp. 305–60.

Jorgensen, Dale. "Capital Theory and Investment Behavior." *American Economic Review* 53 (1963), pp. 247–59.

Jorgenson, Dale and Martin Sullivan. "Inflation and Corporate Capital Recovery." In *Depreciation, Inflation, and the Taxation of Income from Capital*. ed. Charles Hulten. Washington: Urban Institute Press, 1981.

Kalay, Avner "The Ex-dividend Day Behavior of Stock Prices: A Reexamination of the Clientele Effect." *Journal of Finance* 37 (1982), pp. 1059–70.

Kaplanis, Costas. "Ex-dividend Day Equilibrium and Taxes." Unpublished manuscript, London Business School, 1983.

Keynes, John Maynard. *The General Theory of Employment, Interest, and Money*. London: Macmillan, 1936.

Khoury, Nabil and Keith Smith. "Dividend Policy and the Capital Gains Tax in Canada." *Journal of Business Administration* 8 (1977), pp. 19–32.

King, Mervyn. "Corporate Taxation and Dividend Behavior—A Comment." *Review of Economic Studies* 38 (1971), pp. 377–80.

King, Mervyn. "Taxation and the Cost of Capital." *Review of Economic Studies* 41 (1974), pp. 21–35.

King, Mervyn. *Public Policy and the Corporation*. London: Chapman and Hall, 1977.

King, Mervyn. "Advance Corporation Tax and Incentives: A Note." Unpublished manuscript, London School of Economics, 1983.

King, Mervyn and Don Fullerton. *The Taxation of Income from Capital: A Compartive Study of the U.S., U.K., Sweden, and West Germany*. Chicago: University of Chicago Press, 1984.

King, Mervyn, Michael Naldrett, and James Poterba. "The U.K. Tax System." In *The Taxation of Income from Capital: A Comparative Study of the U.S., U.K., Sweden and West Germay*. ed. Mervyn King and Don Fullerton. Chicago: University of Chicago Press, 1984.

Lakonishok, Josef and Theo Vermaelen. "Tax Reform and Ex-dividend Day Behavior." *Journal of Finance* 38 (1983), pp. 1157–79.

Lewellen, Wilbur, Kenneth Stanley, Ronald Lease, and Gary Schlarbaum "Some Direct Evidence on the Dividend Clientele Phenomenon." *Journal of Finance* 33 (1978), pp. 1385–99.

Lintner, John. "Distribution of Incomes of Corporations Among Dividends, Retained Earnings, and Taxes." *American Economic Review* 46 (1956), pp. 97–113.

Litzenberger, Robert and Krishna Ramaswamy. "The Effect of Personal Taxes and Dividends on Capital Asset Prices: Theory and Empirical Evidence." *Journal of Financial Economics* 7 (1979), pp. 163–95.

Litzenberger, Robert and Krishna Ramaswamy. "Dividends, Short Selling Restrictions, Tax-induced Investor Clienteles, and Market Equilibrium." *Journal of Finance* 35 (1980), pp. 469–82.

Litzenberger, Robert and Krishna Ramaswamy. "The Effects of Dividends on Common Stock Prices: Tax Effects or Information Effects?" *Journal of Finance* 37 (1982), pp. 429–43.

Long, John B. Jr. "The Market Valuation of Cash Dividends: A Case to Consider." *Journal of Financial Economics* 6 (1978), pp. 235–64.

Mas, Ignacio. "Anomalous Share Price Movements Around Ex-Dividend Days: The British Evidence." Unpublished S.B. Thesis, Massachusetts Institute of Technology, Cambridge, Mass., 1984.

Mayer, Colin. "The Structure of the Corporation Tax in the U.K." *Fiscal Studies* 3 (1982), pp. 121–42.

McClure, Charles. *Must Corporate Income Be Taxed Twice*? Washington: Brookings Institution, 1977.

Miller, Merton. "Debt and Taxes." *Journal of Finance* 32 (1977), pp. 261–75.

Miller, Merton and Franco Modigliani. "Dividend Policy, Growth, and the Valuation of Shares." *Journal of Business* 34 (1961), pp. 411–33.

Miller, Merton and Kevin Rock. "Dividend Policy Under Asymmetric Information." Unpublished manuscript, University of Chicago, 1984 (revised).

Miller, Merton and Myron Scholes. "Dividends and Taxes." *Journal of Financial Economics* 6 (1978), pp. 333–64.

Miller, Merton and Myron Scholes. "Dividends and Taxes: Some Empirical Evidence." *Journal of Political Economy* 90 (1982), pp. 1182–42.

Poterba, James. "Public Policy and Corporate Dividend Behavior: The Postwar British Experience." MIT Working Paper, Cambridge, Mass., 1984a.

Poterba, James. "The Citizens Utilities Case: A Further Dividend Puzzle." MIT Working Paper No. 339, Cambridge, Mass., 1984b.

Poterba, James and Lawrence Summers. "Dividend Taxes, Corporate Investment, and Q." *Journal of Public Economics* 22 (1983), pp. 135–67.

Poterba, James and Lawrence Summers. "New Evidence that Taxes Affect the Valuation of Dividends." *Journal of Finance* 39 (1984).

Poterba, James and Lawrence Summers. "Testing Alternative Models of Dividend Taxation: Time Series Evidence." Work in progress, Cambridge, Mass., 1984b.

Ross, Stephen. "The Determination of Financial Structure: An Incentive-Signalling Approach." *Bell Journal of Economics* 8 (1977), pp. 23–40.

Shefrin, Harold and Meir Statman. "Explaining Investor Preference for Cash Dividends." *Journal of Financial Economics* 13 (1984), pp. 253–282.

Stiglitz, Joseph. "The Inefficiency of Stock Market Equilibrium." Unpublished manuscript, Princeton University, 1980.

Stiglitz, Joseph. "Some Aspects of the Taxation of Capital Gains." *Journal of Public Economics*, 21 (1983), pp. 257–94.

Summers, Lawrence. "Taxation and Capital Accumulation in a Life Cycle Growth Model." *American Economic Review* 71 (1981), pp. 533–44.

Tiley, John. *Revenue Law*. London: Butterworths, 1978.

Tobin, James. "A General Equilibrium Approach to Monetary Theory." *Journal of Money, Credit, and Banking* 1 (1969), pp. 15–29.

---

* We wish to thank Ignacio Mas for research assistance and Fischer Black, Peter Diamond, Mervyn King, Andrei Shleifer, and Myron Scholes for helpful discussions. This research is part of the NBER Research Programs in Taxation and Financial Markets. Views expressed are those of the authors and not the NBER.

10

Taxes and Corporate Financial Management: Comments

Jean-Paul Valles
Vice President-Finance
Pfizer, Inc.

Taxes and Corporate Financial Management: Comments

INTRODUCTION

It has been said that there are only two certainties in life: death and taxes. Also, as we all know, there are a million different ways to die or be taxed. Furthermore, we are also aware that in both cases we all try to avoid as many of the ways as possible and postpone the unavoidable outcome. Being vice president of finance of one of the largest pharmaceutical companies in the world does not qualify me to discuss longevity or quality of life even though Pfizer is working at it. However, it will hopefully be helpful in discussing the assigned broad topic of "Taxes and Corporate Financial Management." Only the autopsy will tell!

Taxes and corporate financial management are truly inseparable. As a matter of fact, in more and more cases, corporate tax reports to the vice president of finance. It may be helpful to review the interrelationship between tax and corporate finance in the various areas where it manifests itself. In the process some of the recent tax developments will be highlighted, along with their implications for corporate financial practice.

MANUFACTURING

Good financial analysis of investment proposals is one of the keys to success. Maximizing return on fixed assets is of critical importance to industrial companies. Tax legislation has many purposes besides raising revenues. Quite often its aim is to influence the decision-making process in a way which will help achieve other social objectives. For example, many years ago the U.S. government started "Operation Bootstrap in Puerto Rico" in order to promote the industrialization of the island via the tax code. Special corporations were created, e.g., the "Possessions Corporations," also known since 1976 as the "936" corporations.

In a nutshell, these "possessions" corporations are exempt from U.S. federal income tax.Later, the U.S. government sweetened the incentive by allowing the tax-free repatriation of funds to the United States without U.S. income tax on a current basis instead of having to wait until the liquidation of the "936" corporation, which occurred usually at the end of the tax-exemption period. When the new U.S. tax law on dividend was passed, the Purerto Rican government passed a "tollgate" tax on these dividends which could be lowered by keeping some part of the funds in Puerto Rico for a specified period of time—the so-called "2J Investment".

This incentive for U.S. companies to invest in Puerto Rico was extremely successful. It is particularly attractive to high-technology companies, since the U.S. tax exemption applies to the portion of the system profit deemed to be earned in Puerto Rico. By transferring the manufacturing capabilities, the know-how, the trademark, the patents, and the other intangibles in Puerto Rico, the Puerto Rican company should deserve the bulk of the profit. Of course, the split of the system profit between Puerto Rico and the United States became a major bone of contention between the companies with Puerto Rican operations and the IRS. As these uncertainties regarding taxes grew, the attractiveness of Puerto Rico declined. Congress decided under TEFRA (Tax Equity and Fiscal Responsibility Act of 1982) to eliminate this uncertainty for the future only. It allowed use of one of two methods. The first one is a "cost-sharing" alternative (R&D of the product area on a three-digit SIC Code basis is shared on the basis of percentage of sales). This still leaves the same relative uncertainty with respect to the pricing issue under Section 482 of the code. The second alternative is a 50-50 profit split between Puerto Rico and the United States, after allocating certain expenses to Puerto Rico (R&D, interest, G&A). This alternative should remove most of the uncertainties on audit, especially after the regulations as to how to allocate are issued.

It is interesting to note that, in September 1983, Pfizer Inc. settled the Puerto Rican pricing issue with the IRS for the years 1972–82.

It is worth highlighting the fact that the "passive" income earned by the possession company on qualified investments made in Puerto Rico is earned tax-free. This leads to interesting financial management decisions with respect to interest arbitrage and timing of dividend repatriation. (We should mention that TEFRA tightened this area by decreasing the amount of "passive income" a "possessions" corporation can earn and still qualify for the tax exemption. From 50 percent of total income in 1982, it gradually drops to 35 percent of total in 1985.)

A similar type of incentive was given by the Irish government to companies which are willing to invest in Ireland. Profit on products manufactured in Ireland are not subject to any Irish tax for many years. However, an interesting aspect of this tax exemption from a U.S. point of view is that any dividend repatriated to the United States does not carry with it foreign tax credits from Ireland of any significance because no foreign taxes are incurred on the Irish income. Therefore, some repatriations are subject to a 46 percent U.S. federal tax. Utilizing these funds in U.S. property or in a manner which would be construed by the IRS as a constructive dividend would also carry a 46 percent tax rate. This situation led to a significant amount of funds being invested in the Euro-dollar market. The relatively recent creation of the "international banking facility" (IBF) allows these funds to earn Euro-dollar rates but be in the United States and therefore avoid the "sovereign" risk. Yet, these funds are not considered as having been repatriated.

It is obvious that the tax considerations are crucial to the economics of investments and the cash flow they will provide.

In 1982, the U.S. statutory tax rate of 46 percent was reduced for Pfizer Inc. by 16.3 percentage points as a result of tax-exempt operations in Puerto Rico and Ireland. Furthermore, most of the $782 million in cash (including time deposit), short-term investments (at cost which approximate market value), and long-term marketable securities (at cost) which Pfizer Inc. showed on its December 31, 1982 balance sheet were related to the tax-exempt manufacturing locations.

Puerto Rico and Ireland are two of many examples of tax incentives in the area of manufacturing with great implications to corporate financial management. However, one should always remember that a tax exemption can be changed by one stroke of the pen. Pfizer opened a plant in Puerto Rico in June 1982 under the tax exemption then in effect. Under TEFRA, it is a new ball game (not as favorable) starting January 1, 1983!

FINANCING OF PROJECTS

Leasing of plant and equipment is probably an area where tax and corporate financial management interplay a lot.

Long-term leasing is always an alternative way to finance a project as opposed to ownership. This area has been in a state of great flux during the last few years. For example, in 1981 the so-called *safe harbor leasing* was allowed. It permits the sale for cash of the tax benefit (depreciation and investment tax credit) to a third party. Pfizer Inc. availed itself of this tool. It is worth noting that this was not a financing of a specific investment in the true sense of the term but a way to raise some cash which could be used to finance any project. TEFRA for all practical purposes made safe harbor leasing a thing of the past starting in 1984, when it introduced "finance leasing." The "lessor" must finance the specific investment but can have less of a real economic interest in the property and the property does not have to be returned to him at the end of the lease. The lessee can buy it back for 10 percent of the original cost. The trade-off for the lessee is that the lease payments will be higher than under a straight lease since the lessor has to spread the investment tax credit equally over five years. There are many other technicalities regarding finance leasing which are beyond the scope of this discussion. However, it should be clear how important tax matters are in the financing of investment.

Another key area where tax and investment financing meet is what is referred to as IDBs or industrial development Bonds—IDBs issued by local governmental authorities with the guarantee of the user of the funds to pay both the interest and principal. As a result, the user can borrow at a low interest rate which results from the income tax exemption granted to these bonds. Certain investments can qualify. For example, in December 1982 Pfizer borrowed $14.7 million of floating-rate monthly demand pollution control refinancing bonds—the effective interest so far this year has been just around 5 percent.

RESEARCH AND DEVELOPMENT

The United States was the only country in the world which did not allow for tax purposes the full benefit of spending money in the United States on R&D. This is the so-called 861 *regulation*. From a corporate financial management point of view, in many cases, it is an incentive to do research abroad and has a vital impact on the utilization of foreign tax credit. In simple terms, Section 861 allocates a part of the U.S. R&D expenses to foreign source income. As a result, the rules adopted by the IRS will result in less foreign tax credit utilization through its Section 861 regulations. If there is excess foreign tax credit which cannot be used, the profit and loss statement will be impacted and the cash flow will be affected. The impact is even more significant than for excess investment tax credit, because the current-year foreign tax credit has to be used before using the oldest one which expires—five years old. In corporate financial planning this may require drastic measures to increase foreign source income, i.e., large repatriation of dividends from abroad which have a low foreign tax credit.

It is interesting that the research and development allocation required under Section 861 is now suspended because of a two-year moratorium ending at year-end 1983. It is hoped that this moratorium will be extended as a minimum or made permanent. In my opinion, this is critical to keep the United States the leader in research. Whatever is decided will greatly affect the financial management of research-intensive multinational companies.

In the same spirit of keeping the United States at the state of the art in technology, R&D ventures have recently been formed. In summary, venture capital is put in at the start by investors. The money is used for contract research by the partner company, who has the know-how. If the R&D yields fruit, the company has the right to use the new technology and the investors receive a share of the profit in various possible forms, such as royalties. At the start, the investors have large losses at ordinary income rates (tax shelter aspect) with cash flow in later years at capital gain rates. For the company, it finances R&D and has no impact on their profit and loss statement if properly set up. This mode of financing has been used mainly by small high-technology companies. It will likely become more popular even with large R&D-intensive companies in the future.

Here again taxes are quite important in the decisions of how to finance R&D and where to do the R&D.

FOREIGN EXCHANGE RISK

Starting with 1983, multinational companies have to adopt Financial Accounting Standard Statement No. 52. This is probably one of, if not the most complicated topic in accounting. How one finances its foreign operations—e.g., capital, intercompany accounts, etc.—will have a major impact on the exposure to foreign exchange fluctuations. This will be complicated by which functional currency is selected—(e.g., the local currency or the U.S. dollar—and which currency of billing is used for export from various countries. If one decides to hedge the profit and loss statement against exchange-rate fluctuations, one has to take into account the after-tax impact of the hedge. For example, it is clear that the gains/losses in a tax-exempt country (e.g., Ireland) will be the same pre- and post-tax, while they will be halved post-tax in countries with a 50 percent tax rate. Taxes again greatly impact corporate financial management.

DIVIDEND POLICY WITH RESPECT TO FOREIGN SUBSIDIARIES

As a general rule, foreign source income is taxed in the United States when the income is repatriated in the form of dividends to the U.S.

parent. When a dividend is declared by a foreign subsidiary and paid to the parent, it usually carries with it some foreign tax credit which is based on the amount of taxes paid abroad on the income from which the dividend is paid and other foreign tax withheld on the dividend. One key exception to this general rule of taxation on foreign income only when repatriated is the so-called sub-part F income. For example, in the case of a tax-exempt Irish operation, if the nonmanufacturing income (mostly interest income on investment portfolio) is greater than 10 percent of the total income, this income is taxed at the 46 percent U.S. tax rate by the United States regardless of whether it is repatriated or not. Therefore, from the financial planning point of view there are *no* additional taxes to repatriate these funds.

Analyzing the amount of foreign tax credit which can be generated by various dividend repatriation scenarios, the amount of foreign tax credit which can be used and the cash flow needed is an area where tax and corporate financial planning are truly one and the same.

Related to this topic is the matter of which legal structure is to be selected for the foreign subsidiaries. For example, if a company in the United Kingdom is a subsidiary of the parent in the United States, the U.K. withholding tax on dividends is reduced because of a tax treaty between the United States and the United Kingdom. A significantly higher U.K. withholding tax would be imposed if the U.K. company were a subsidiary of a company located in a nontreaty country (e.g., Panama) even though it is itself a subsidiary of a U.S. parent. Again, tax and corporate financial planning go together since the question of dividend repatriation is critical.

CAPITAL STRUCTURE

How much you want to finance via equity or debt is a very difficult topic to decide. Among the many considerations, one of vital importance is the fact that interest payments on debt are tax-deductible to the company, whereas dividends are not. The convertible debenture is a hybrid. Again, tax and financial management are interrelated.

One interesting recent development is the debt for stock "swaps." If properly structured, this technique allows one to buy back debt which is selling at discount with stock (hopefully well valued by the market). A tax-free profit of the difference between the face value and the market price of the bond will result. This benefit is in addition to the strengthening of the equity-to-debt ratio.

TAXES AND FINANCING ACQUISITION

A "pooling of interests" acquisition which requires a payment in stock usually has no tax for the seller, if he does not sell the shares given to him. His tax basis remains his original basis, which is often quite low if the company acquired was a small company which has grown rapidly. A purchase of assets with cash is a taxable transaction to the seller. Therefore, the tax consequences of the mode of financing are often quite important in determining the price of the acquisition.

An interesting recent development has been the divestiture of a part of the business via a so-called "ESOP leveraged buyout" (employee stock ownership plan). This very complex topic is, in simple terms, a technique whereby employees borrow money from the bank and lend it to the company which buys itself from its parent. The contribution made to the ESOP by the company to reimburse the loan is made with pretax dollars—hence the advantage.

INVENTORY CONTROL

Depending on the type of business one is in and the expectation with respect to cost, an analysis should be made to make sure that the cash flow to the corporation cannot be significantly improved if a LIFO (Last In First Out) method of accounting is used for tax purposes instead of FIFO (First In First Out). Pfizer was one of the first pharmaceutical companies to go on LIFO in the mid-1970s. The improvement in cash flow has been material.

EXPORTS

For companies which have significant exports from the United States, it may be worthwhile from a profitability and cash flow point of view to form a DISC (domestic international sales corporation). TEFRA has somewhat changed the rules, but basically the principle remains that a DISC provides a tax incentive for export.

INSURANCE

Another complex area where tax and finance interface is insurance. The tax situation with respect to so-called "captive" insurance companies is not clear at this time. Among the key issues which may determine the tax benefit, if any, of having a "captive" insurance company are: (1) whether or not only foreign risks are insured, (2) whether or not the amount of original capital was sufficient, and (3) whether or not it insured unrelated third-party risks. The pure captive for insuring U.S. risk has no tax benefit according to recent court decision. What tax benefits other types of captive will have is not known. By the way, regardless of the tax benefit, it still may be worthwhile to form a captive insurance from a cash flow point of view.

SALARY REDUCTION PLAN OR 401K

Congress has allowed the creation of the 401K plan. It is basically a savings plan for employees in which they can invest pretax dollars in the plan and have the return on this investment reinvested pretax. The tax is deferred until withdrawals are made. In many respects it is similar to (and can be in addition to) an individual retirement account (IRA). If properly sold to the employees, a high participation rate will occur (in excess of 90 percent at Pfizer). A significant portion of the pretax salary saved by the employees is used by the fund to buy newly issued company shares. Over time, such a program is a significant source of funds via selling new equity.

CONCLUSION

It is hoped that, by structuring this paper in various sections, it has been demonstrated beyond a reasonable doubt that taxes permeate every area of corporate financial management. One could have gone on with more examples and/or broadened the type of industries (e.g., utilities, banking, oil and gas) and continue to show the relationship between taxes and finance. It is also hoped that it has been shown how changes in tax laws and regulations are critical to corporate financial management. It was stated at the beginning that two certainties existed in life—death and taxes. It should now be clear that in corporate financial management taxes have to be analyzed to death!

11

Debt, Retained Earnings, and Taxes: An International Perspective

Michel Levasseur
Professeur a l'Universite Paris-Dauphine

In this paper, we compare the after-tax cost of both retained earnings and debt in the United States and six European countries. Taking into account corporate and personal taxes, we suggest that in all of these countries the same result occurs. At equilibrium, the marginal personal income tax rate borders on the corporate tax rate. In general, the tax advantage of debt is counterbalanced by the tax on retained earnings. Despite the fact that tax laws are quite different in each of the seven countries, we cannot reject the hypothesis that both financings have the same after-tax cost for each domestic firm. In conclusion, differences in local tax laws do not appear crucial for the choice of a financing policy by a corporation.

Debt, Retained Earnings, and Taxes: An International Perspective

INTRODUCTION

The different means of financing have costs that can be influenced by prevailing tax laws. On the theoretical level, there has been an ongoing argument in this area (see Hamada and Scholes' paper appearing in this book). The effects of tax laws are diverse and often opposed. The integration of corporate and personal taxes often shows contradictory results. The purpose of this article is to demonstrate, through a specific theoretical model, the effects of different legislation. The main characteristics of this paper's development are, first, an account of the financing needs of a growing company and then, second, a simplification of the problem to that of domestic finance. We shall not discuss the particularities of international tax policy. Neither will we study the presence of tax havens nor the privileges of the multinationals. Rather, we will be considering how a British firm and its stockholders are treated within the United Kingdom and the six other countries studied here.

The first part will give a simple theoretical model measuring tax effects on the cost of two financing means, debt and retained earnings. The second part will present a comparative analysis of several different types of legislation.

THE IMPLICATIONS OF TAX LAWS ON FINANCING COSTS

It is difficult to separate the decision to pay dividends from that of company financing. Generally, the firm has the acknowledged choice either to distribute its results and increase its equities or resort to self-financing. This approach has the merit of separating decisions related to debt and investment from those of dividend policy. Nevertheless, it hardly explains why companies distribute their earnings, since dividends are more heavily taxed than capital gains and a new issue is costly. It is therefore necessary to include a preference for liquidities, agency costs, and signaling decisions.

Increasing dividends and debts

On one hand, increasing debt has the direct consequence of the tax saving an amount of money paid to the state. This result is well known and solely dependent on the deductibility of interest paid. Consider for \$1 of additional debt a saving of:

$$r\tau_c \tag{1}$$

where r represents the interest rate and τ_c the rate of corporate tax. As this saving reverts ultimately to the stockholders in the form of revenue increase, it necessarily enters into personal taxation:

$$-r\tau_c\tau_s \tag{2}$$

where τ_s represents the marginal tax rate of a stockholder's income.

On the other hand, the additional dollar of issue debt generates an income for the lender equaling r dollars; the latter is also quite obviously subject to personal taxation.

There is therefore a cash outflow worth:

$$-r\tau_B \tag{3}$$

where τ_B is the marginal rate of tax on the lender's income.

Moreover, this additional dollar of debt deters the company from using \$1 more as equity. In this last case, the paid return (risk adjusted and thereby as much as the debt interest rate) would have been taxed to the marginal rate of the marginal stockholder. Therefore, it is necessary to count among the tax savings the personal tax on this equity return:

$$+r\tau_s \tag{4}$$

To summarize, the issue of an additional dollar in debt may generate a tax advantage or disadvantage appearing as:

$$r[(\tau_c - \tau_c\tau_s) + (-\tau_B + \tau_s)] \tag{5}$$

The tax advantage connected with debt in the United States

The preceding result easily gives us some propositions found in financial literature. In the first place, suppose that, because of the numerous deductions allowed stock, incomes are not taxed on the personal level. The rates τ_B and τ_s are null, and debt would generate a systematic and annual advantage of 46 percent of the deducted interest. In the second position, if we, like Miller in 1977, consider that equities income, unlike that of bonds, is not taxed, then the rate τ_s equals 0. The tax advantage of debt is reduced to $r\{\tau_c - \tau_s\}$. At equilibrium, the marginal bond investor has a marginal tax rate of his income equaling τ_c. There is no more encouragement for debt through a tax advantage. The saving in taxes realized at the corporate level is equal to the increase to the bondholders.

Finally, we shall consider in the following section that equity income (1) is uniformly taxed at the marginal rate of personal income; τ_p. The annual tax effect of the debt growth is therefore equal to:

$$r[0.46(1 - \tau_p)]$$

or in capitalized present value: $0.46\ (1 - \tau_p)$

FIGURE 1 Increase in debt

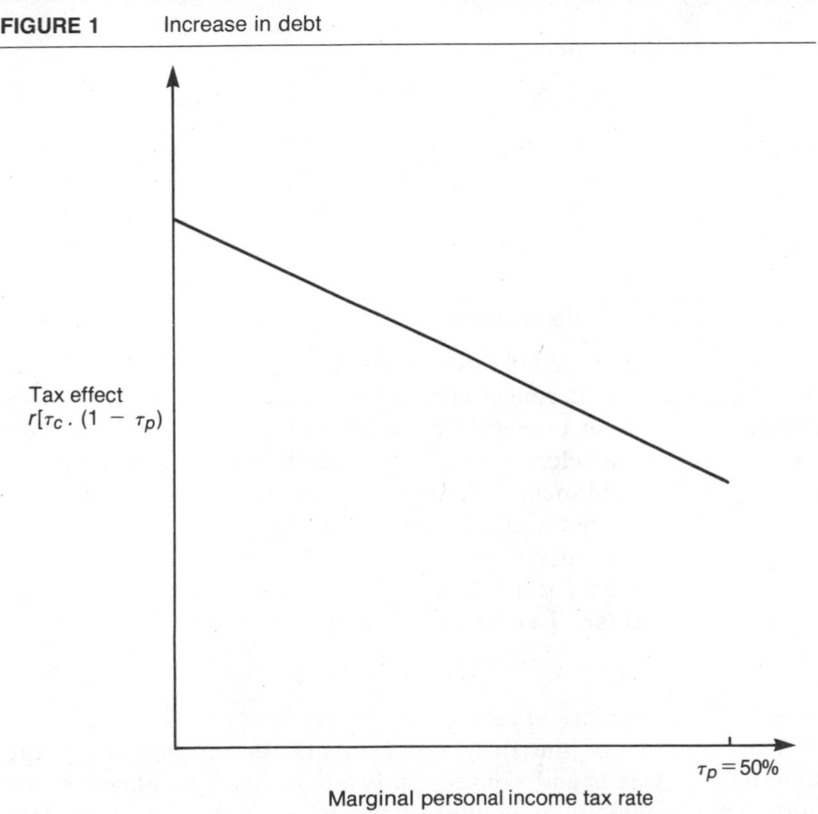

It is therefore decreasing. The more companies go into debt, the more bonds they must sell to heavily taxed investors.

The tax advantage for retaining earnings

If a company is partly financed by retained earnings, each dollar of equity thereby benefits from a tax advantage. In fact, the risk-adjusted return of this dollar can only be equal to r. But a portion g of that payment will occur under the form of capital gains. The rate g (assumed certain) is also the growth rate for the stock price and the whole company. Only 40 percent of that portion g of the income of the dollar invested is taxed on the personal level. We may therefore consider that the retaining of $1 provides an annual advantage equivalent to the difference between a tax on capital gains at the personal income tax rate and the reduced tax. Thus:

$$g\tau_s - g \cdot 0.4\tau_s$$

Capitalizing this annual stream, we get:

$$(g/r)\tau_s(1 - 0.4) \quad (6)$$

Considering that the marginal rate of taxation of dividends for marginal investors is that of the marginal tax on their income, it is easy to notice that, in Figure 2, the tax advantage originating from retained earnings grows with τ_p.

Tax advantages and the imputation system

The measurements of tax effects that have been discussed in the preceding paragraphs concern the United States. The purpose of this article is to provide a comparison with several other countries. We must therefore develop a more comprehensive analytical formulation which would include the presence of fixed-rate capital gains taxes, disparities between dividend and bond income taxes, and finally the imputation system.

The most general formulation of the tax advantage of debt would be the following (see Levasseur and Olivaux, 1983):

$$(1 - \tau_c)(1 + a)(1 - \tau_s) - (1 - \tau_B) \quad (7)$$

where a is the tax credit rate.

The taxation of the distributed results is influenced by the imputation system and consequently so is the advantage of the additional profitability obtained through the deductibility of debt interest.

FIGURE 2 Increase in dividends or decrease in retained earnings with g growth rate

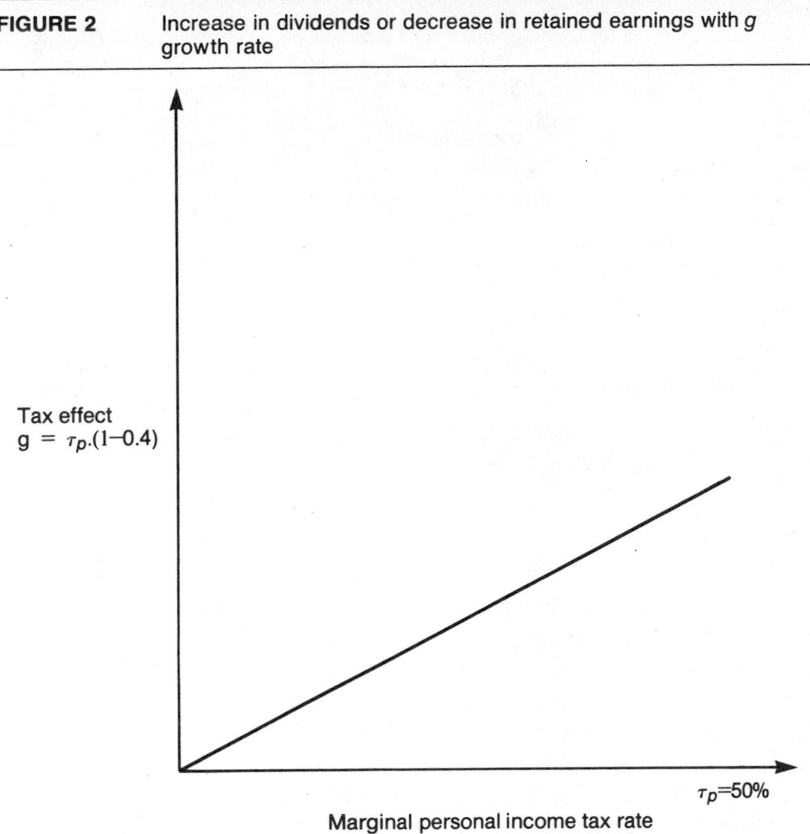

The analysis of the tax advantage linked to retained earnings leads to the following quantity:

$$\frac{g}{r}\left[(1 + a)(1 - \tau_s) - (1 - \tau_g)\right] \tag{8}$$

where τ_g is the personal tax rate of capital gains.

The introduction of the imputation system contributes to the lightening of the tax load on dividends and therefore has a negative effect on the advantage acquired by retaining earnings.

Financing policies and market equilibrium

The example of company X Y Z (see Table 1) illustrates the case of a firm having an expected return before taxes of 14.8 percent and a

TABLE 1

Balance Sheet X Y Z

Total Value of the Firm	*Liabilities*	
10,000	6,000	Debt
	4,000	Equities

Income Statement X Y Z

E.B.I.T.	1,480
Interest (10%)	600
Earning before taxes	880
Corporate taxes (46%)	405
Net result	475
Dividends	101
Retained earnings	374

Uses			Sources
Net investment	936	374	Retained earnings
		562	New debt

10 percent risk-adjusted profitability rate. The total value of its assets is 10,000 and its annual growth rate is 9.36 percent. This company chose to pay out dividends worth 2.53 percent of its share market value and to finance 40 percent of its needs with equity and 60 percent with debt. In this instance, it can balance its uses and sources statement without hurting its financial structure.

An investor having $400 can choose between purchasing bonds yielding 10 percent before taxes or X Y Z shares. He may therefore collect a dividend of $30.1 and a capital gain of $37.4. His choice will depend exclusively on the marginal rate of income tax. As Table 2 shows, Investor A, who is lightly taxed, will opt for bonds and collect a net return of 8 percent instead of 5.44 percent with shares. On the other hand, Investor B, who is heavily taxed, will buy shares which will earn him a profit rate of 5.51 percent instead of 5 percent. Only investor C, whose marginal rate of income tax is in this case 45 percent, will remain indifferent.

On the whole, companies would be well advised to issue stock to satisfy the demand from investors having a marginal income tax rate higher than the indifference rate and offer bonds to those who don't. Globally, an equilibrium which would equalize the costs of both sources of financing after taxes is a conceivable idea. At each firm's level, as Miller suggested in 1977, but for slightly different reasons, there is indifference over the means of financing.

TABLE 2

Investor A		$\tau_p = 20\%$ *Equities = \$400*
Dividends	\$10.10	
Taxes	2.02	
		\$ 8.08
Capital gains	\$37.40	
	2.99	
		34.41
Total		\$42.49

Net return 10.62%
Risk premium before taxes 4.8%
Risk premium after taxes 2.07%
Risk premium after taxes and leverage 5.18%
Net adjusted return for equities 5.44%
Net return for bonds 8%

Investor B		$\tau_p = 50\%$ *Equities = \$400*
Dividends	\$10.10	
Taxes	5.05	
		\$ 5.05
Capital gains	\$37.40	
Taxes	7.48	
		29.92
Total		\$34.97

Net return 8.74%
Risk premium 3.23%
Net adjusted return for equities 5.51%
Net return for bonds 5%

Investor C		$\tau_p = 45\%$ *Equities = \$400*
Dividends	\$10.10	
Taxes	4.55	
		\$ 5.55
Capital gains	\$37.40	
Taxes	6.70	
		30.70
Total		\$36.25

Net return 9.05%
Risk premium 3.55%
Net adjusted for equities 5.5%
Net return for bonds 5.5%

Let us note that the equilibrium point corresponds to the point of intersection of the two straight lines in Figure 2. For τ_p = 45 percent when g = 9.36 percent, the fiscal advantage of the debt just equals the retaining advantage.

$$\{0.46\ [1 - 0.45]\} = 0.0936\ \ \{0.45\ \ [1 - 0.4]\}$$

THE EFFECTS OF DIFFERENT TAX LEGISLATION

This section discusses the present tax systems of six member nations of the European Economic Community (Federal Republic of Germany, Belgium, France, Italy, United Kingdom, and the Netherlands) and contrasts them with the American system, which is the most widely studied. As expected, the laws governing taxes vary from nation to nation; however, it is interesting to note that, despite differences, a certain group of nations including the United States of America, the United Kingdom, the Netherlands, and to a certain extent Belgium have similar results. If we limit our study to these countries, we may immediately confirm the effectiveness of the theoretical model. Unfortunately, and for the same reason, two other countries, France and Italy, require a more thorough analysis. And, finally, the case of Germany is somewhat different.

The Anglo-Saxon countries and Benelux[2]

In 1977, Miller proposed that tax savings achieved through interest deductions within a corporation be entirely passed on to bond owners. It is easy to object that Miller's analysis contains one unrealistic hypothesis. Dividends and capital gains are, in the United States, taxable. Certainly, in a more recent article, Miller and Scholes (1978) emphasize different financial mechanisms that reduce effective taxation on those incomes. Frenberg's 1981 study did nothing to support this hypothesis. The first part of the following study will demonstrate that Miller's result can be retained even in the instance of taxation on common stock revenues.

The United States It is necessary first to recall certain essential points of the American tax system. The maximum rate of taxation of corporate incomes is 46 percent. Since January 1982, the date that President Reagan's reform went into effect, individuals have been taxed at a maximum rate of 50 percent. The dividends are taxed at the marginal rate applicable to an investor's income and do not benefit from a tax credit. The same is true for the interest on bonds issued by companies. Long-term capital gains are taxed to a lesser extent. Only 40 percent of them are added to the taxable income.

Quantity B emphasizes the advantage (or disadvantage) of financing by debt in preference to withholding earnings,

In the case of the United States, it appears:

$$B = 0.46\ (1 - \tau_p) - \frac{g}{r}\,[\tau_p - 0.4\,\tau_p]$$

where τ_p is the marginal tax rate on the investor's income
g is the growth rate for the stock price
r is the interest rate

The first term, 0.46 $(1 - \tau_p)$, measures the tax advantage of the debt, the second one, that of retaining earnings. By way of illustration, if we take a value of 0.9 for the ratio g/r (it is not reasonable in such an economy to consider a ratio too far from 1), Figure 3 appears as:

FIGURE 3

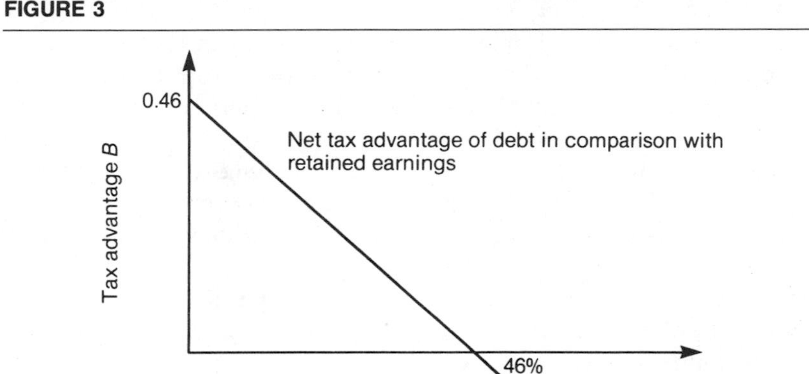

This result is interesting because it is identical to Miller's. Moreover, it would be wise for those investors whose marginal tax rate is less than 46 percent to own bonds while those who are taxed over 46 percent should keep common stocks. And, furthermore, there is irrelevance at equilibrium for each company about its financing. But this result is achieved differently. At the rate of 46 percent, there is an obvious tax advantage for the debt of 0.46 (1 − 0.46) = 0.2484. But it just meets the one for the retained earnings: 0.9 (0.46 − 0.4 × 0.46) = 0.2484. Equilibrium exists in such a way and not because the advantage has been entirely passed on to bondholders.

FIGURE 4

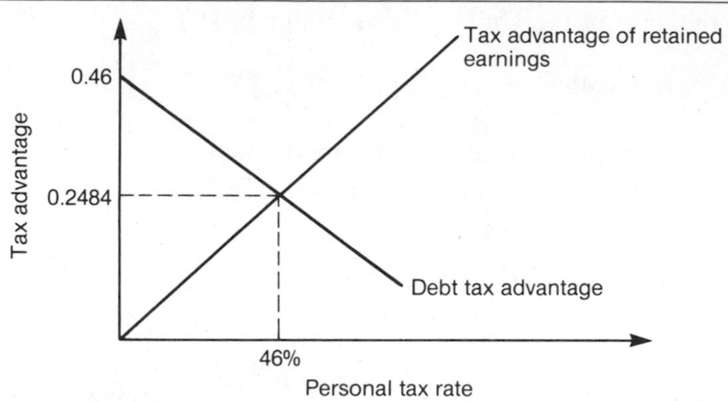

Obviously, this result may appear deceptive in so far as it is based on the value of 0.9. Taken by the ratio g/r, the result does not seem to be strongly affected by the values of g/r. τ_p amounts to 50 percent for g/r of 76 percent and 43.4 percent for g/r of 100 percent.

The United Kingdom. The British tax system exhibits the following characteristics. The maximum corporate tax rate amounts to 52 percent. The maximum tax income rate for individuals is normally 60 percent. However, investment income surpassing 6,250 £ for a year are burdened with an enhanced rate of 15 percent. Therefore, a maximum rate of 75 percent is applied to dividends and interest on bonds. Dividends enjoy a tax credit of 3/7. On the other hand, the interest paid by a bond is taxed at the marginal personal rate. Finally, capital gains are normally taxed at the rate of 30 percent. Nevertheless, investors may be exonerated if the total annual capital gains do not exceed 5,500£.

Proceeding as we did for the United States, we can estimate the B quantity using equations (7) and (8). The following appears,

$$B = 0.52[1 - \{\tau_p \cdot \frac{10}{7} - \frac{3}{7}\}] - [\tau_p - \{\tau_p \cdot \frac{10}{7} - \frac{3}{7}\}] - \frac{g}{r}[\{\frac{10}{7}\tau_p - \frac{3}{7}\} - \tau_g]$$

Taking $g/r = 0.9$, we get

$$B = 1.6\tau_p + 0.7 + 0.9\tau_g$$

FIGURE 5

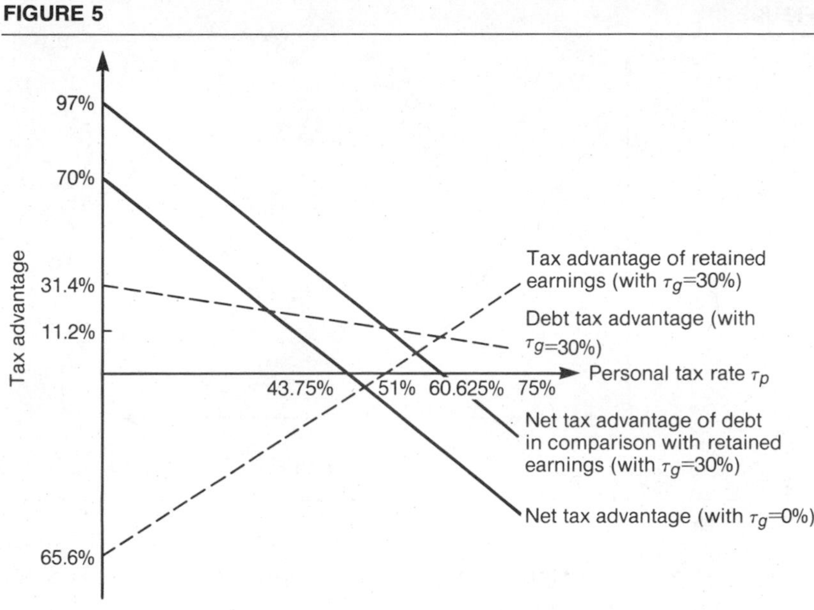

The most striking feature about the British system is that, despite great differences with its American counterpart, there is a great structural similarity of result. The United Kingdom has a tax credit unknown in the United States, a taxation on capital gains that has nothing to do with the marginal rate of personal income tax. Nevertheless, it is possible to posit the point of equilibrium between the debt tax advantage and that of retained earnings for the marginal personal rates ranging from 43.75 percent to 60.25 percent. It is true that this result is not obtained in the same way. The attractiveness of borrowing is not so strong for the undertaxed British shareholders (31.4 percent as opposed to 46 percent), but the retained earning alternative is far more expensive due precisely to the tax credit (65.6 percent as against 0 percent). Finally we should note that the introduction of a fixed-rate tax system on capital gains does not have a determining role.

The Netherlands. The Dutch tax system may be briefly described in the following terms. The maximum corporate tax rate on profits is 48 percent; individuals are taxed at the maximum rate of 72 percent. Dividends enjoy no tax credit. To be eligible for taxation, capital

FIGURE 6

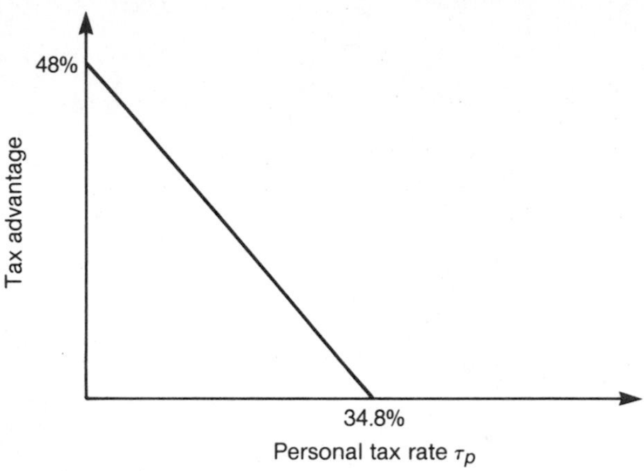

gains must be proved speculative in nature or ultralucrative. We shall consider them nontaxable.

In this case, the quantity B is equal to $0.48(1 - \tau_p) - g/r(\tau_p)$ or, with $g/r = 0.9$ $B = -1.38\tau_p + 0.18$.

The result is very similar to that found in the United States. Equilibrium appear for a smaller marginal income tax rate. The absence of a capital gains tax readily encourages the tax advantage linked to retained earnings.

In conclusion, the model seems to work well for these three countries although their laws are different. The presence of a tax credit in the United Kingdom and the different modalities of taxes on capital gains are not sufficient to induce excessive disparities at the level of the results.

The Latin Countries

Two countries of this group, France and Italy, present different results. And, to a certain extent, Belgium appears related to this group.

France. In France, corporate and personal taxes work in the following manner. Corporate taxes hover at the 50 percent level, whereas individuals assume a maximum rate of 60 percent. Stockholders enjoy a tax credit (called "avoir fiscal") amounting to 50 percent of paid dividends. Bond income can be treated as ordinary income, but, the bondholders have the option of bearing a unique and fixed tax of 25 percent. Capital gains are taxed at the rate of 15 percent for major sales. In other instances, they are exonerated from tax.

This quantity B is equal to

$$B = 0.5(1 - \{1.5\tau_p - 0.5\}) - (t_B - 1.5\tau_p + 0.5) - \frac{g}{r}(1.5\tau_p - 0.5 - 0.15)$$

with $g/r = 0.9$, $B = 0.6\tau_p - \tau_B + 0.835$. We have two equations: for $0 < \tau_p < 0.25$, $B = -1.6\tau_p + 0.835$ and for $0.25 < \tau_p$, $B = -0.6\tau_p + 0.585$.

Figure 7 shows that, in regard to the structure of effective taxation for rates τ_p ranging from 0 to 25 percent, the results for France and the United Kingdom are similar. If the bond income were taxed in the same way as the other income, an equilibrium point for $\tau_p = 52.2$ percent would be reached. However, the figure is greatly transformed if the movement of τ_p to beyond 25 percent is taken into consideration.

The tax advantage of retained earnings continues to increase with t. But, at this point, the debt tax advantage changes dramatically by beginning to increase instead of decrease. The explanation is simply that the fixed rate of 25 percent on bond income is even more favorable to the heavily taxed holder. From what has just been stated, should we conclude that, for France, debt financing is definitely preferable? The answer is not so obvious.

FIGURE 7

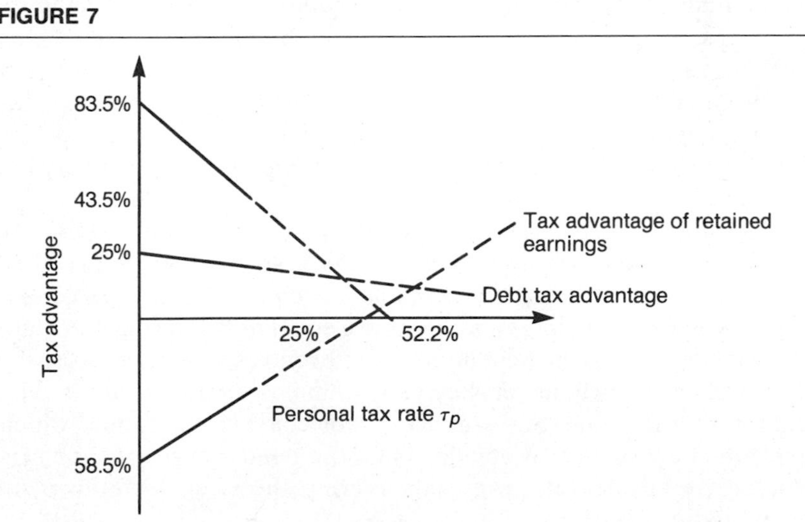

FIGURE 8

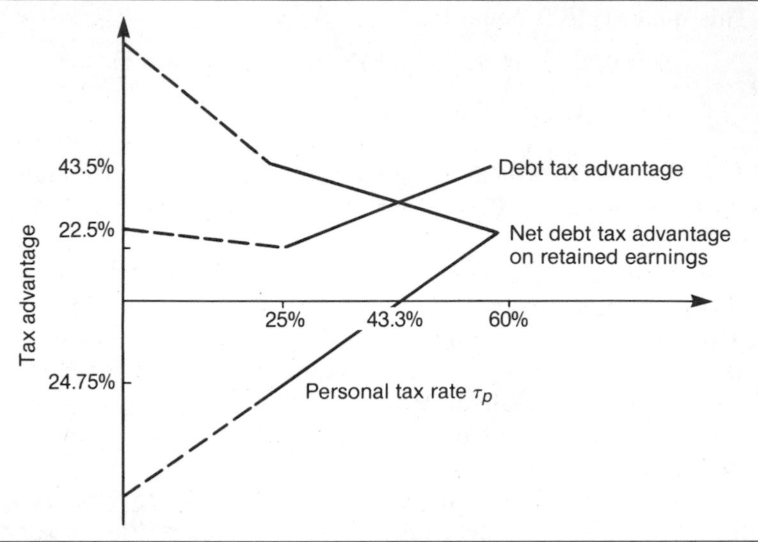

In reality, the greatest part of debt remains untouched by this advantage. The banks are taxed to the rate of 50 percent on their financial revenues. In this case, the equilibrium point of figure 8 practically reappears. In spite of this result, a crucial factor must be the investors' demand for the bonds, a demand which is effectively stimulated. The state, through public organizations and local administrations, issues the greatest number of bonds in France, which explains this particular type of taxation. Furthermore, as the issue of bonds is tightly controlled, private companies may not overuse this tax privilege. The bond market is kept under the auspices of the Treasury Department which has the final say on who may or may not take part.

Therefore, in our opinion, this model continues to be particularly relevant for France; as long as companies resort to bank loans when needed, an equilibrium point is reached showing that the tax advantages of retained earnings and debts are equal or bordering on equality. It is however in the best interests of French companies to turn to the bond market whenever they can. Common shares, ill-treated by the Internal Revenue Service, are "poor cousins" to bonds, which explains the growth and popularity of the bond market at the Paris Bourse (stock market), even considering the effects of the most recent nationalizations.

Italy. The Italian tax system is extremely complex. There are local and national corporate taxes, both calculated on the same basis and both having significantly high rates. The Italian companies in 1982 paid 27 percent of earnings to the central government and 16.2 percent to the local authorities. After deducting local corporate tax from the tax basis of the national tax, rates are set at 39.15 percent. Personal taxes cannot exceed the rate of 72 percent. Dividends and interest on bonds are exempt from local taxes and taxed on the national basis. Nevertheless, dividends enjoy a tax credit of one third the paid dividends, and the interest of bonds can be added to the other incomes or taxed at a fixed rate of 21.6 percent. Capital gains are taxable only if proved speculative in nature.

In this case, B is equal to

$$0.3915(1 - \{\tau_p\frac{4}{3} - \frac{1}{3}\}) - (\tau_B - \{\tau_p\frac{4}{3} - \frac{1}{3}\}) - \frac{g}{r}(\frac{4}{3}\tau_p - \frac{1}{3})$$

or, with $g/r = 0.9$, $B = -0.389t - t_B + 0.489$.

We show in Figure 9 for $0 < \tau_p \leq 21.6$ percent, and in Figure 10 for $\tau_p > 21.6$ percent, the tax advantage in Italy.

Although the rate levels are different and the average tax rate is lower than in France, the same sort of result appears. Supposing bank loans form the bulk of all debt, then an equilibrium point would be reached for an approximate 35.2 percent rate of marginal tax on income. However, banks assume a rate of 39.15 percent.

The results are thus similar to those for France. Despite certain distinguishing features, such as the rate of tax credit equaling one third, the corporate tax rate of 39.15 percent, and the absence of a

FIGURE 9

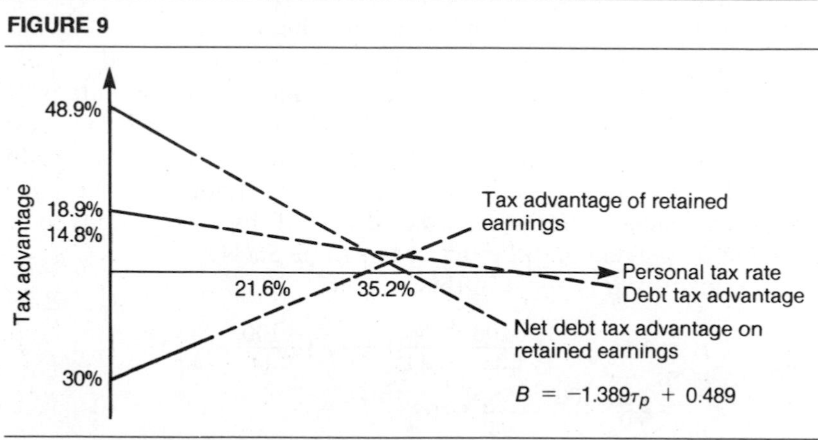

FIGURE 10

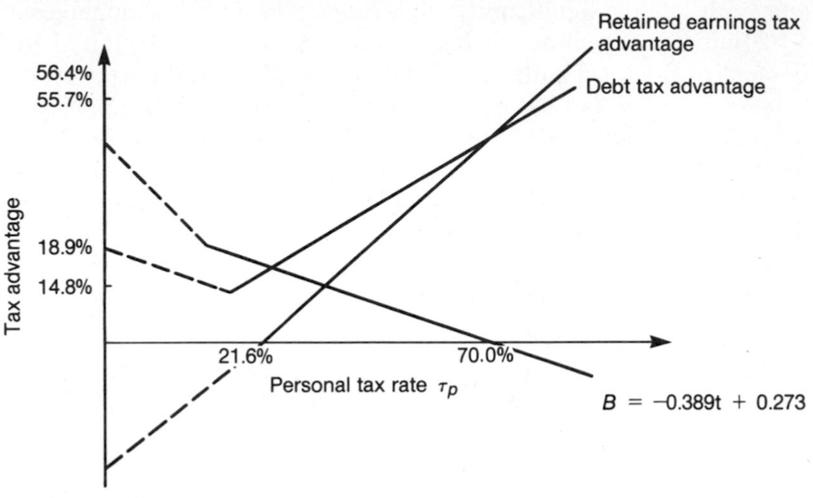

capital gains tax, the same phenomenon can be noted. The fixed rate of 21.6 percent stimulates the demand for bonds. However, unlike France, the tax advantage in Italy of retaining earnings can exceed, for t superior to 70 percent, the advantage of issuing bonds. But this fact must not hide what is even more important: Because admission to the stock market is difficult, the *choice* between borrowing from the banks or retaining earnings can be irrelevant for Italian firms.

Germany

The German system stands out from the others as being the only one to offer a tax credit of 100 percent! Corporate profits, if retained, are taxed at 56 percent. If they are paid as dividends, the tax rate is 36 percent. The maximum personal tax rate is 56 percent. Bond interest is taxed at the marginal income rate. The dividends have a tax credit of 36/64 of distributed profits. On the whole, it amounts to the same thing to consider the income paid as dividends by corporations to be taxed at 56 percent and the tax credit to be 56/44.

The quantity B is equal in this case to:

$$B = 0.56\left(1 - \left\{\tau_p \frac{100}{44} - \frac{56}{44}\right\}\right) - \left(\tau_p\left\{\tau_p \frac{100}{44} - \frac{56}{44}\right\}\right) - \frac{g}{r}\left(\left\{\tau_p \frac{100}{44} - \frac{56}{44}\right\} - 0\right)$$

or

$$B = -\frac{g}{r}(t - 0.56) \cdot \frac{100}{44}$$

In the German Federal Republic, there can be no tax advantage achieved through debt due to the tax credit that entirely retrocedes the corporate tax on paid dividends. On the other hand, retaining earnings is costly except for the investor who is taxed at the maximum rate (56 percent), see Figure 11.

FIGURE 11

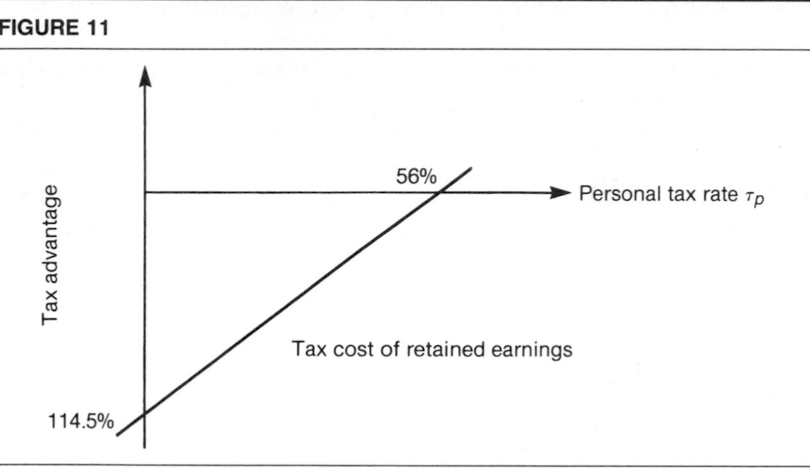

Germany is seemingly in a category by itself, as this result would have us believe. True, there is no tax advantage achieved through debt. True, only the maximum personal tax rate is an equilibrium one. But in the final analysis, Germany's result bears similarities to the others. In the United States, the equilibrium point in our example is set at 46 percent although the marginal rate of maximum taxation on personal income is 50 percent following President Reagan's fiscal reform. In the United Kingdom, it ranges from 40 to 60 percent for a maximum rate of 75 percent. In France, it hovers at 52 percent for a maximum rate of 60 percent (65 percent in 1983).

CONCLUDING REMARKS

A recurring factor appears throughout this paper. The equilibrium personal tax rate borders quite often on the corporate tax rate. We find a 46 percent rate for both personal and corporate in the United

States, a 44–60 percent personal rate as opposed to a 52 percent corporate rate in the United Kingdom, 52 percent to 60 percent in France, 39.7 percent to 45 percent in Belgium, and 56 percent for both in Germany. Only Holland registers a greatly lower equilibrium personal rate, 35 percent, as opposed to 48 percent for corporate tax. In general, Miller's results published in 1977 are consistent, although a quick first reading of his propositions may cloud the full extent of their accuracy. The tax debt advantage is never on the 50 percent level, which is the most important point, regardless of the diversity in legislation. This tax advantage must always be counterbalanced by the tax on retained earnings. In conclusion, we may report that, in all these countries, the dividing line between shareholders and lenders is found at the level of those incomes that are taxed at the same rate as corporations.

APPENDIX: THE BELGIUM CASE

A study of the Belgian tax system would definitely place this country among the members of the first group discussed. However, effective practices place it with France and Italy.

The maximum rate for corporate taxes is 45 percent and that of personal taxes, 67.5 percent. Paid dividends are entitled to a tax credit of 51 percent on the amount paid after a withholding tax of 20 percent. Therefore, the effective tax credit is 40.8 percent. Bond revenues and dividends are theoretically taxed with the other incomes. The personal taxes are reduced by the amount of the 20 percent withholding tax. However, the conditions surrounding the application of the tax law are such that the major part of dividends and bond interest bears only the 20 percent tax, which is withheld by companies. Finally, only capital gains on speculative sales are subject to taxation.

The quantity B is equal to:

$$0.45(1 - \{\tau_p 1.408 - 0.408\}) - (\tau_p - \{\tau_p 1.408 - 0.408\}) \\ - \frac{g}{r}(\tau_p 1.408 - 0.408)$$

or with $g/r = 0.9$, $B = -1.4928\tau_p + 0.5928$.

For a number of years, the Belgian authorities have been notably tolerant of this "legal form of cheating." And if their leniency was meant to alleviate the tax burden on bonds, their motives must have been similar to those of the French. Nevertheless, their tight control over the local market has ensured that this "loophole" would serve only their interests and those of corporate firms.

FIGURE 12

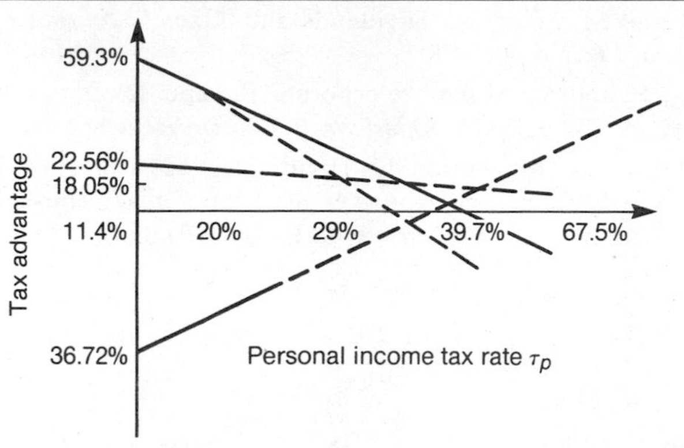

Notes

1. In the model below, the ratio capital gains/market value of equity has been given and appears as the growth rate of the firm; therefore any increase in the stockholders' income is realized through an increase in the dividend payments.
2. Note: We are discussing those tax laws in application as of July 1982. This paper includes only basic rules and guidelines and chooses to ignore particular exemptions and deductions connected with dividends and interests. The only discussion of local tax policy can be found under the heading of "Italy" where there is a correlation between local and national tax policy.

REFERENCES

Brennan, M. "Taxes, Market Valuation and Corporate Financial Policy." *National Tax Journal* 23 (December 1970).

Frenberg, D. "Does the Investment Interest Limitation Explain the Existence of Dividends?" *Journal of Financial Economics* 9, No. 3 (1981).

International Bureau of Fiscal Documentation, Guides to European Taxation, Amsterdam, June 1982.

Levasseur, M. and J. L. Olivaux. "Théorie du Financement des Entreprises et Evolution de la Fiscalité Française." *Revue Economique* 32, No. 3 (1981).

Levasseur, M. and J. L. Olivaux. "Endettement, Politique de dividende et impôts: le cas européen et le cas américain." *Cahier de Recherche, CEREG*, No. 8302 (1983).

Miller, M. and F. Modigliani. "Dividend Policy, Growth and the Valuation of Shares." *Journal of Business* 34, No. 4 (1961).

Miller, M. and M. Scholes. "Dividends and Taxes." *Journal of Financial Economics* 6, No. 4 (1978).

Modigliani, F. and M. Miller. "Corporate Income Taxes and the Cost of Capital: A Correction." *American Economic Review* 53, No. 3 (1963).

Olivaux, J. L. "La Distribution des Dividendes: ses Domaines Financiers, Fiscaux et Juridiques en France et aux Etats-Unis." Thèse de Doctorat d'Etat, C.E.R.E.G., Université de Paris IX Dauphine. Juin 1983.

12

Business Taxation Under Rapid Inflation: The Israeli Tax Reform

Saul Bronfeld
Bank of Israel

Itzhak Swary*
The Hebrew University of Jerusalem
Visiting Associate Professor, New York University

This paper examines the effects of inflation upon business taxation under a tax system based on nominal income. There are two principal effects, first an allocative effect, the discouragement of investment in most productive assets and, second, a distributive effect, the determination of the real tax burden of firms by the rate of inflation and the specific combination of investments and capital structure.

In recent years, galloping inflation has caused serious distortions in the Israeli economy. Therefore, in 1982 the Israeli government introduced a comprehensive, articulated tax system based on real income designed to be neutral to inflation. Herein, we discuss the various distortions of a nominally based tax system and present the principles of the 1982 Israeli business tax reform. Although based on the Israeli experience, the discussion is of general interest. A nominal-income based tax system in any inflationary environment involves shortcomings and distortions. The magnitude of the distortions involved is a function of the rate of inflation, the tax code, and the structure of the domestic capital market.

Business Taxation Under Rapid Inflation: The Israeli Tax Reform

INTRODUCTION

This paper examines the effects of inflation on business taxation under a tax system based on nominal income. Although the analysis presented herein is based mainly on the Israeli experience, the paper discusses the general shortcomings of a nominal-income based tax system under inflation. The implications of such a system are relevant to almost all countries, and depend on the rate of inflation, the specific features of the business tax code, and the structure of capital markets.[1]

Israel has experienced a steep rise in the annual inflation rate from about 10 percent in 1972 to 40 percent in the years 1974–78 and over 100 percent since 1979. As a response to increased inflation, various partial or complete indexation mechanisms, embracing wages, personal taxes, and financial assets (issued by the government or the banks) were developed.

Until 1982, the tax system in Israel, as elsewhere, was based on nominal income and was not adjusted to the effects of inflation. The tax system was not neutral to inflation; while the tax burden on some firms increased, on others it decreased substantially over time. This discriminatory effect was primarily a function of the structure of assets and liabilities. The Israeli experience indicates that, although firms learned how to protect themselves against the adverse effects of inflation, misallocation of resources and an adverse effect on income distribution in the economy as a whole was unavoidable.[2] This situation led to the adoption of the so-called Israeli inflation tax code in August 1982.

The second section of this paper examines the effect of inflation on business taxation under the nominal-income based tax system with reference to the Israeli case. The rationale for and the basic elements of the 1982 business tax reform are presented. The combined effects of inflation and tax reform on capital structure and investment policy are discussed. Finally, the cost-benefit of implementing a tax system based on real income is summarized.

MAJOR EFFECTS OF INFLATION ON BUSINESS TAXATION UNDER A NOMINAL-INCOME BASED TAX SYSTEM: THE ISRAELI EXPERIENCE

The nominal-income based tax system which existed in Israel until 1982 was not sufficiently responsive to changes in the price level for several reasons: The difference between the sale price of current assets (e.g., inventories, foreign currency holdings) and their historical cost was fully taxed, although part of this difference represented inflationary gains. Depreciation was calculated on the basis of historical cost. In some cases accelerated depreciation was allowed. However, at the prevailing rate of inflation, it did not provide an adequate capital consumption allowance. Nominal interest payments on business loans were tax-deductible. Realized inflationary capital gains were taxed at 10 percent, whereas the tax rate on ordinary income was (and still is) 61 percent.

To analyze the effect of inflation on business taxation, it is assumed that no change in the relative prices of different assets and real interest rate takes place as a result of inflation (the effects of changes in relative prices are discussed later). The effect of inflation on the tax burden imposed on firms depends on the interaction between investments and capital structure. Two categories of assets are considered: assets whose inflationary gains were tax-exempt or taxed at a very low rate, and whose expected market value kept pace with the general rate of inflation[3] (e.g., land, buildings, index-linked bonds, and other traded securities), and assets on which the inflationary gains were fully taxed (e.g., inventories, machinery, and equipment), or whose economic value was eroded by inflation, which was not tax-deductible (e.g., cash and noninterest-bearing customer credit).

There are two sources of finance equity, and debt, that is, liabilities on which the interest (including the inflationary component) was tax-deductible.[4]

There are four possible interactions between investments and capital structure—they include investment in taxable assets financed by equity, investment in tax-exempt assets financed by debt, investment in taxable assets financed by debt, and investment in tax-exempt assets financed by equity.[5] These alternatives are illustrated in Figure 1.

In the first situation, investment in taxable assets is financed by equity, the inflationary profits from the investment are taxable, and

FIGURE 1 Possible interaction between investments and capital structure under inflation

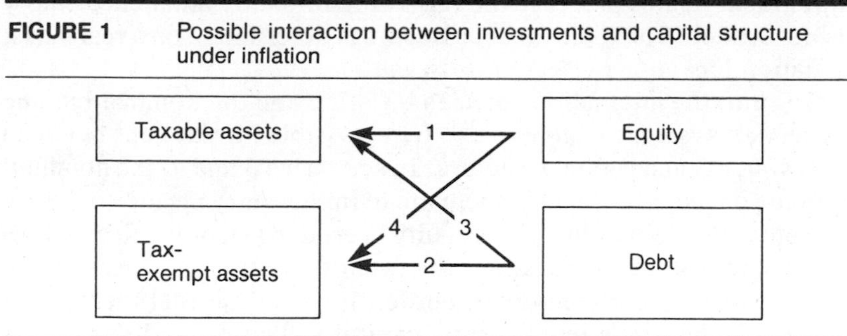

there is no tax allowance for the inflationary erosion (opportunity cost) of equity: Tax is paid on the inflationary gain which essentially preserves the real value of equity and the firm's equity is therefore eroded. The effective tax rate increases as inflation increases. In practice, the taxable inflationary profits are created by depreciation, by the FIFO method for inventory valuation, and by taxation of the return on interest-bearing liquid assets.

When investment in tax-exempt assets is financed by debt, as in the second case, most of the inflationary profits from the investment are tax-exempt, and the interest expense on the debt financing of the investment is fully deductible. Therefore, the higher the rate of inflation, the greater the amount of tax shield produced. Financing tax-exempt assets by borrowing not only defers tax payments but also produces a tax shield for the firm (i.e., interest expenses are deductible against other income). The firm's tax shield depends on the rate of inflation and on the difference between the ordinary tax rate and the reduced rate paid on tax-exempt assets.[6] Deductibility of nominal interest payments, which includes the repayment of principle of debt, is, of course, a necessary condition for creating this tax shield.

In the third case, investment in taxable assets is financed by debt and the entire nominal profit (including the inflationary component) from the investment is taxed; the interest expenses (including the inflationary component) however, are tax-deductible. Therefore, the effects of inflation on the gross income offset the deductible expenses. Hence, the taxable income of such investment is hardly affected by inflation.

Finally, when investment in tax-exempt assets is financed by equity, the entire income from such investment is tax-exempt and there is no tax allowance for the opportunity cost of capital. The inflationary gains preserve the real value of equity and hence equity is not eroded. Thus, the taxable income is determined on a real basis; inflation has no tax effect in this case.

In sum, the interaction between inflation and the nominal-income based tax system can give rise to four possible interactions between investments and capital structure. In scenarios 3 and 4, the nominal-income based tax system is adequate in inflationary periods, while in the other two, either the firm's equity is eroded (1), or the firm enjoys a tax shield which increases as the rate of inflation increases (2). In other words, the effective tax burden imposed on real income depends on the firm's investments, capital structure, and the rate of inflation.

To relate this analysis with recent corporate finance literature, the optimal capital structure and investment decision under such taxation and inflation will be discussed.

Miller's theorem and optimal capital structure

In Israel, savings are encouraged by exempting the returns on several financial assets from personal taxes. The returns on indexed bonds issued by the government and some financial claims issued by the banking system such as savings schemes and foreign currency deposits are either exempt from personal taxes or taxed at low rates. Only the real interest on government bonds and foreign currency deposits is subject to a 35 percent tax rate. The government believes that this exemption is essential to encourage savings under rapid inflation because taxation of nominal interest earned on savings is equivalent to taxation of the principal (in real terms) and would involve a negative real return of a large magnitude.[7]

Capital gains on securities traded on the stock exchange are tax-exempt (dividends are subject to a 35 percent tax rate). The capital gains on other assets (including nontraded securities) have been divided into inflationary gains subject to a 10 percent tax rate and real gains. Firms need government approval for issuing bonds if they desire the interest paid to bondholders to be tax-exempt; this is rarely requested and corporations usually borrow indirectly from the public through financial intermediaries. Thus, for practical purposes the inflationary component of the return on financial assets is exempt from personal taxes. Therefore, we ignore the personal income tax effect (Miller (1977)) and concentrate on the corporate tax effect. Following the (corrected) original Modigliani and Miller (1963) analysis, the value of the firm can be increased by the use of debt since interest expenses can be deducted from taxable corporate income.

This result yields the unrealistic conclusion that, in the presence of corporate taxes, a firm should issue only debt. A noncorner optimal capital structure may be obtained if the tax gains of debt financing are offset by leverage-related costs such as (an increasing) expected bankruptcy cost incurred by shareholders, by agency costs, and by signaling behavior.[8]

One important question is how the optimal capital structure changes as the inflation rate increases. It is reasonable to assume that, when inflation accelerates, the (real) tax gain of debt financing increases more than the expected cost of the offsetting factors, because the principal of debt repayment is also tax-deductible (see Cohn and Modigliani (1983)). Thus, debt financing becomes more attractive and the debt-equity ratio is increased to obtain an optimal capital structure.[9]

In recent years, many firms in Israel have exploited the opportunity to produce tax shields under inflation. In Israel, it is mainly investments in real estate and traded securities financed by debt which produce such a tax shield. The fact that the returns on personal savings are tax-exempt, whereas interest expenses by the business sector are tax-deductible, enables the business sector and financial intermediaries to generate an infinite number of tax shields.[10]

Investment decision

Assuming that relative prices do not change in an inflationary environment, firms will increase their investment in tax-exempt assets.[11] It should be noted, however, that debt financing of investments in tax-exempt assets produces a tax shield (interest expenses) that may be fully utilized only if there is sufficient taxable income.

As we have shown, the effect of inflation on firms' business taxation depends on the interaction between financing and investment decisions. Furthermore, as implied by our analysis concepts, frequently used rates such as the corporate income tax rate (see Hochman and Palmon (1983)), or the marginal corporate income tax rate (see Hamada and Scholes (1983)) have no useful meaning. There is a specific marginal tax rate for each capital budgeting decision which is the effective tax rate given the interaction between the financing and investment decision of the firm. It is the determination of the relevant effective tax rate which prevents us separating investment and financing decisions both with and without inflation.

The distortions in the Israeli economy caused by the nominal-income based tax system, given the high rate of inflation in recent years, affected economic growth and efficiency and relative prices.

Because inventory, machinery and equipment, and R&D were classified as taxable assets, the nominal-income based tax system discouraged investment in most productive assets and, hence, reduced the incentive to improve productivity. In particular, since depreciation is valued at historical rather than replacement cost, the higher the inflation rate, the lower the (real) value of depreciation allowances. In other words, most investments in the productive assets were discouraged because the return (including the inflationary component) on such investments was taxable.[12] (This effect could have been eliminated to the extent that firms were able to construct inflationary tax shields as described above.)

Moreover, despite previous assumptions, anticipated inflation rates and taxes clearly have an effect on relative prices. Constructing inflationary tax shields by corporations obviously affects relative prices. The increased demand for tax-exempt assets and debt financing drives up both interest rates and the prices of these assets (e.g., real estate, traded shares, and government index-linked bonds in Israel (see Feldstein (1980a), (1980b)).

The relative price changes in Israel were: the supply of government index bonds—infinitely elastic and, because their prices are exogenously determined by the government, their prices are not sensitive to tax shelter considerations. The returns on both common stock and real estate have not significantly exceeded the inflation rate in recent years. As for the real interest rate: Irving Fisher's well-accepted analysis of the effect of changes in anticipated inflation (assuming no income tax) on the rate of interest states that a 1 percent increase in the expected rate of inflation leads to a 1 percent increase in the nominal rate of interest. Feldstein (1976) has arrived at the conclusion that, in a world with taxes, an increase in inflationary expectations should result in the Fisher equations after taxes, i.e., savers receive the same after-tax real rate of return. Gandolfi (1982) has demonstrated that the response of nominal interest rates should lie between the Fisher and Feldstein effects. Gandolfi's results depend mainly on the existence of lower tax rates on capital gains.

Inflation also affects investors' demands for debt and stock via the effect of inflation on the personal marginal tax rate. Since the inflationary returns from most financial assets are exempt from personal taxes in our analysis, savers should consider the Fisher effect in their saving function. However, the increased supply of firms for debt drives the interest rate above the one implied by the Fisher effect. In practice, it seems that interest rates in Israel were slightly above the rate implied by the Fisher effect during the late 1970s.

In sum, the effect of inflation on firms' investment policy and optimal capital structure depends on both the tax effect of inflation on business taxation and its impact on marked prices.

Finally, there is a locked-in effect: Under most tax codes, taxes (ordinary or capital gains tax) on long-term assets are due at the time of realization, whereas interest expenses are tax-deductible on an accrual basis. Therefore, the effective tax rate is reduced as the asset-holding period increases. This phenomenon, known as the locked-in effect, is used to defer tax payments.[13] The magnitude of the locked-in effect depends on the income tax rate, and the cost of capital. For example, gains on land held by contractors and gains on securities held by financial intermediaries are taxed as ordinary income. Therefore, under the nominal-income based tax system, the higher the tax rate the longer the holding period is likely to be. Thus, contractors, for example, have an incentive not to build on sites which they have held for a long period. As a result, the locked-in effect causes inefficiencies in production (e.g., in the timing of new construction in this case). The magnitude of this inefficiency depends on the nature of the investment opportunities available (see Protopapadakis (1983)). Obviously, under a nominal-income based tax system, rapid inflation substantially increases the incentive for deferring taxes, which in turn causes distortions due to the locked-in-effect.

THE PRINCIPLES AND MAIN ELEMENTS OF THE ISRAELI 1982 TAX REFORM

The intent underlying the Israeli 1982 tax reform is to neutralize the effects of inflation on the firm's taxable income and create a tax system in which the magnitude and direction of any distortions are independent of the inflation rate. This is achieved by making the inflationary components of the firm's profits tax-exempt and by allowing the decline in the real value of assets (such as cash) to be tax-deductible. On the other hand, the inflationary component of interest expenses (including linkage differentials) which represents the repayment of the principal in real terms, is not tax-deductible as it does not represent a real expense. Such treatment is symmetrical inasmuch as real interest is subject only to personal taxes, and is tax-deductible for the business sector. In addition, only real capital gains are taxed at the ordinary corporate tax rate. Finally, depreciation is indexed to represent the real value of the asset consumed.

Although these principles are quite simple, their implementation raises several conceptual and practical problems. In theory, asset value can be protected from erosion by exempting the inflationary component of the realized profit (i.e., taxing only real income). Al-

TABLE 1 Alternative calculations of deductible expenses for different assets as classified under the reform

			Unprotected Assets Total Amount Deductible			*Protected Assets Reevaluation of Depreciation*		
Year i	*Historical Depreciation* (1)	*Capital Preservation Allowance*[a] (2)	*Current Prices* (1) + (2) = 3	*Constant Prices*[b] (4)	*Present Value at 5 Percent* (5)	*Current Prices*[c] (6)	*Constant Prices*[b] (7)	*Present Value at 5 Percent*
1	200	500	700	466.7	444.5	300	200	190.5
2	200	400	600	266.7	241.9	450	200	181.4
3	200	300	500	148.1	129.1	675	200	172.8
4	200	200	400	79.0	65.0	1,012.50	200	164.5
5	200	100	300	39.5	30.9	1,518.75	200	156.7
Total	1,000	1,500	2,500	1,000	911.4	3,956.25	1,000	865.9

[a] Computed as [1000 − 200 (i − 1)](0.5) of the depreciated value of the asset at historical cost.
[b] At year 0 prices.
[c] Indexed depreciation = 200×1.5^{i}.

Note: This table is based on data provided in the appendix. (Please combine the data and the Table) ternatively, this protection can be achieved by allowing nominal interest expenses to be tax-deductible or by granting a capital preservation allowance to equity, and taxing nominal income when realized.

The real-income approach obtains more accurate results since it matches, for tax purposes, the timing of income and related costs. However, this approach makes it necessary to identify the inflationary component of every transaction and related interest expenses. For example, when merchandise is sold, the inflationary component of the sale price must first be calculated by comparing it with the inflation-adjusted (historical) cost of goods sold and imposing tax only on the real profit. When turnover is slow, as with buildings, this approach can be readily applied since it is quite easy to identify the inflationary component on each transaction. Obviously, this is much more difficult where there are many transactions and rapid turnover (such as inventory). Similarly, a real-income based tax system requires that only real-interest expenses be tax-deductible. However, separating nominal and real-interest expenses is not easy. First, the CPI is calculated only once a month and, second, in many transactions the interest expenses are included in the cost of the transaction (e.g., leasing, cost of product, etc.). Therefore, it is easier to use the nominal-income approach of granting a capital preservation allowance or nominal expenses and taxing nominal income when realized. This procedure is less accurate than the real-income approach, but it is easier to implement since the accounting system is in nominal terms. With this approach, the timing of taxing profits and providing inflationary exemptions do not necessarily match; however, if this method is applied only to assets with rapid turnover this does not cause serious problems. The Israeli tax reform applies a dual system which uses each approach for different groups of assets. The reform distinguishes between two asset categories: protected assets and unprotected assets.

Protected assets (PA) are characterized by total or almost total tax exemption on nominal income. Hence, they are considered inflation-protected assets. These assets are mainly held for relatively long periods, e.g., real estate, nontraded securities, and investment in subsidiaries. The tax treatment includes indexation adjustment of historical depreciation for tax purposes in order to reflect the assets' real value of services during the year. In addition, capital gains on protected assets are divided into nominal and real gains or losses. The tax rate on the nominal capital gains on such assets is 10 percent, whereas real capital gains or losses are treated at the ordinary corporate tax rate.

Unprotected assets (UA) are those which are not defined as protected assets.[14] They are taxed according to the nominal-income based tax system, i.e., depreciation is deductible on a historical-nominal basis, and all income and capital gains are treated at the ordinary corporate tax rate. The reform treats inventory, equipment and machinery, cash, and most traded securities as unprotected assets.

On the financing side, the reform distinguishes between owners' equity and debt. For tax purposes, neutralization of inflation is achieved either by taxing only real income and recognizing only the real component of interest expenses (a real-income based tax system), or by taxing nominal-income based income and recognizing nominal expenses.

The reform's treatment of protected assets applies the use of the real-based approach to the income derived from such assets and related expenses. Accordingly, protected assets up to the amount of owners' equity does not entitle the company to any capital preservation allowance (CPA) and, for any remaining portion financed by debt, the inflationary interest expenses are not tax-deductible. This treatment leads to determination of gross income and deductions on a real basis. On the other hand, for income derived from unprotected assets and corresponding expenses, the reform applies the nominal-income based tax system. Accordingly, any owners' equity that exceeds the magnitude of protected assets, entitles the owner to CPA. Thus, income is determined on a nominal basis, and deductions are also recognized on a nominal basis.

The main elements of the reform are the capital preservation allowance, the changes during the year, the added income (equity), and indexing depreciation and capital gains on protected assets. When equity is greater than the sum of protected assets, at the beginning of the year, the difference (henceforth, the net erosible equity) is multiplied by the annual rate of inflation. The outcome is part of the capital preservation allowance which is deducted from the firm's taxable income. The following simple example illustrates the calculations associated with the capital preservation allowance.

Beginning of the year balance sheet

		I.S.		*I.S.*
(PA)	Land	2,500	Equity	4,000
(UA)	Inventory	7,500	Bank Credit	6,000
		10,000		10,000

I.S. = Israeli Shekel

Given that the annual inflation rate is 120% and taxable income preceding the reform I.S. 8,000:

Equity *PA*

The net erosible equity (4,000 − 2,500) = 1,500

CPA: 1,500 × 120% = 1.800

Taxable income preceding the reform = 8,000 I.S.

CPA = (1,800)

Taxable Income = 6,200 I.S.

Under rapid inflation, changes in net erosible equity occurring during the year are also considered. Any changes in owner equity (except for profits occurring during the year), and any changes in the magnitude of investment in protected assets (purchased or realized) are also multiplied by the rate of inflation occurring from the date of the change to the end of the year.

When the owners' equity is less than the sum of protected assets, taxable income is below real income by the net erosible equity multiplied by the annual rate of inflation. For the part of protected assets which exceeds the owners' equity and is thus financed by debt, the income derived from the protected assets is taxed on a real basis, whereas expenses are deducted on a nominal basis. Therefore, any such negative results are offset by the interest expenses and increase the taxable income. It should be noted that the nominal component of interest expenses is calculated indirectly; the deductible interest rate is reduced by the inflation rate times the debt which finances protected assets. To illustrate the added income concept we use the previous example with bank credit changed to 8,500 I.S., equity changed to 1,500 I.S., and the taxable income preceding the reform is 5,500 I.S.

Equity *PA*

The net errosible equity: (1,500 − 2,500) = −1,000

Added income = 1,000 × 120% = 1,200

Taxable income preceding the reform (interest expenses − 6,000 I.S.)	=	5,500
Added income	=	1,200
Taxable income		6,700 I.S.

The added income reflects the nominal interest on the part of the debt which is a finance-protected asset (i.e., only real interest is tax-deductible).

IMPLICATIONS OF THE TAX REFORM

The main purpose of the tax reform is to create a tax system based on real income in which any distortions are independent of the inflation rate and are essentially similar to those in a world with no inflation. In this section we examine the implications of the tax reform for optimal capital structure, investment decisions, and the locked-in effect.

Optimal capital structure

As discussed earlier, under a nominal-income based tax system the after-tax cost of debt financing falls when inflation increases. Increasing inflation therefore generally implies a higher optimal debt-equity ratio. This result derives from the fact that the real principal repayment to the lender, compensating him for the decline in the purchasing power of his claim, is deductible by the corporation.[15] The reform provides two important changes: (1) The real principal of debt repayment is tax-deductible only when unprotected assets are financed by debt. In such cases, the deductibility of the principal repayment is offset by taxing the nominal income derived from the unprotected asset, hence no inflationary tax shield is provided. (2) When investment in unprotected assets is financed by equity, the reform entitles the company to a CPA, which is equivalent to the deduction of principal of debt repayment. Thus, as far as the inflation effect is concerned, debt and equity are treated equally.

Therefore, the tax reform eliminates both the opportunity to produce an inflationary tax shield by debt financing, and the incentive to increase the firm's leverage position as a result of inflation. It should be noted, however, that the effect of the deductibility of real interest expenses on the optimal capital structure is not eliminated (see Miller (1977), Hamada (1982)). It is the additional effect of inflation which is eliminated.

Investment decision

As discussed earlier the return (NPV) on investment in protected assets is independent of the inflation rate under the tax reform. On the other hand, the effect of inflation on investment in uprotected assets is not entirely eliminated even after the tax reform. This stems from potential timing differences, i.e., taxing of inflationary profits and allowances for inflationary expenses (CPA or interest expenses) do not necessarily match. Expenses are recognized for tax purposes earlier and hence defer tax payment on a zero real rate. This tax deferment provides an advantage for investment in an unprotected asset over a similar investment classified as a protected asset. This advantage can be measured as the ratio between the net present value of a given investment, classified as a protected asset compared to the equivalent investment classified as an unprotected asset. Such relative advantage is a function of the cost of capital, the inflation rate, and the investment horizon.

For example (see appendix), consider a 5-year asset, 5 percent real interest rate, and 50 percent annual inflation rate. The NPV of the expenses related to such investment treated as an unprotected asset is about 5.2 percent larger than the NPV of the expenses of a similar investment classified as a protected asset (NPV of 911.4 and 865.9, respectively). Assuming zero cost of capital, there is no difference in the respective NPV. In a simulation of these variables, Kroll (1983) reveals that the most significant factor is the length of the project's life. In the previous example, an increase of the project's life to 10 years increases the difference in the net present values to about 15.5 percent.

In sum, the return on unprotected assets under the reform are sensitive to the inflation rate and the length of the project's life despite the intentions of the reform. This undesired result is the outcome of both the practical need to simplify the implementation of the reform, and the desire to encourage investment in productive investment. However, it should be noted that most of the assets classified as unprotected assets are intrinsically short-lived.

The locked-in effect

The reform eliminates the impact of inflation on the locked-in incentive related to protected assets. As discussed in the investment decision, there still exists an inflationary locked-in incentive to hold unprotected assets for long periods, for tax-deferral purposes. However, most unprotected assets by their nature (e.g., inventory) have a short life span and it is costly to extend their holding period; thus, the inflationary locked-in incentive is not significant. One exception is traded securities classified as unprotected assets. Traded securities do not bear significant costs associated with the length of holding. Therefore, the reform treats traded securities classified as unprotected assets in a special way; any realized as well as the *unrealized* profits (determined by their year-end market price) are taxable each year.[16] This treatment of traded securities eliminates the potential advantage of tax deferral and hence the related locked-in incentive.

SUMMARY AND CONCLUSIONS

This paper examined the effect of inflation on business taxation. One of the major costs of inflation to the economy is in its effect on business taxation. As the rate of inflation increases, the allocative and distributive effects of inflation become more severe in a nominal-income based tax system. With inflation at a rate of 130 percent in 1982, Israel adopted an inflation business tax reform. This reform is a mixture of a real-based approach and a nominal-based approach in which only real income is taxed and almost any distortion is independent of the inflation rate. It should be noted, however, that the implementation of a comprehensive and an articulated tax system which is neutral to inflation also involves high costs, especially because (unlike the nominal-income based tax system) it is based on an accounting system which is not adjusted to either inflation or the tax treatment of income, expenses, and asset valuation. Thus, the implementation of such a system may be justified costwise as inflation becomes a more serious and permanent phenomenon.[17]

APPENDIX: THE TAX EFFECT OF THE CLASSIFICATION OF DEPRECIABLE ASSETS

To illustrate the implications of classifying machinery and equipment as unprotected or protected assets, consider the following example:

Data

1.	Historical cost of asset	I.S. 1,000
2.	Lifespan	5 years
3.	Scrap value	0
4.	Annual rate of inflation	50 percent

The nominal cash flow alternatives are:

Asset defined as:

1. *Unprotected.* The deductible expense is equal to depreciation at historical cost plus the CPA.
2. *Protected.* The deductible expense is indexed depreciation.

Notes

1. Economists have recently devoted a great deal of effort and interest to the effect of inflation on the tax system. See, among others, Feldstein, Green, and Sheshinski (1979), Feldstein and Summers (1979), Bailey (1980), Stiglitz (1980), and Hasbrouck (1983).

2. The effect of fully anticipated inflation on the level of investment is discussed in Feldstein and Summers (1979). As inflation increases, firms tend to use production processes which are more labor-intensive. However, firms could mitigate adverse effects of inflation on capital formation by changing the durability of assets, as discussed in Nelson (1976) and Auerbach (1979). These papers suggest that the higher the rate of inflation the more likely it is that replacement will be deferred. Bar-Yosef and Swary (1981) include accelerated depreciation and capital gains tax in their model and show that, for alternative sets of parameters, firms could use early replacement and sale-and-lease-back strategies to offset the effect of a relatively low inflation rate (below 25 percent). However, it was found that such strategies are ineffective at higher rates of inflation.
3. The income derived from an asset includes both the flow of income and/or realized capital gains. Furthermore, the effective tax rate is considered as the present value of tax payments. This point is particularly important for deferred capital gains (see also the discussion of the locked-in effect).
4. Transaction in linked credits (to the price level on foreign exchange rate) are common in Israel. For tax purposes, linkage differentials are treated the same way as interest expenses.
5. The financing and investment decisions would not necessarily be taken simultaneously. The interrelation presented is merely for convenience of illustration.
6. Gandolfi's (1982) analysis implicitly suggests such opportunities through long holding of capital asset. Furthermore, Protopapadakis's (1983) estimates show that the effective marginal tax rates on capital gains in the United States fluctuated between 3.4 percent and 6.6 percent between 1960 and 1978.
7. For example, under 130 percent inflation rate, an 8 percent real interest rate before tax is equivalent to 31 percent negative real return (assuming a 60 percent marginal tax rate).
8. See, among others, Kim (1982), DeAnglo and Masulis (1980).
9. The empirical evidence of the U.S. aggregate firm leverage behavior (Zwick (1977), and Gordon and Malkiel (1980)) shows that the debt to firm's total value ratio rises as the inflation rate increases. Recall that in the United States the personal tax on interest should be considered as well (Miller and Scholes, 1982).
10. This situation is not necessarily a feature of other tax systems. In the United States, for example, the extent to which the business sector is permitted to deduct nominal (rather than real) interest income depends on the relative magnitudes of the marginal tax rates facing corporate borrowers on one hand, and the rate facing those who lend to corporations, on the other hand (see, for example, Feldstein and Summers, 1979; Hamada 1982; Hamada and Scholes, 1983; and Park and Williams 1983).
11. Firms in different industries differ in the ability to pursue such operations. For example, financial intermediaries are pressed by the authorities to increase their equity capital; on the other hand, their

branching activities (almost the only exempt asset in banking) are subject to regulatory licensing.

12. Feldstein (1982) presents evidence on this effect in the United States in the period 1953 through 1978. The interaction of inflation and the nominal income based system in the United States contributed substantially to the decline of business investment since the 1960s.
13. For an extensive discussion of the issue of locked-in effects, see Holt and Shelton (1962), Green and Sheshinski (1978) and Stiglitz (1980). Constantinides (1983) analyzes both the locked-in effect and the short-term versus long-term capital gains and losses to establish optimal trading rules.
14. The terms *protected* and *unprotected* assets used by the reform code are to some extent misleading, because the effect of inflation is neutralized for both assets categories and the difference is merely in the technique used to achieve this neutralization, i.e., nominal- or real-based tax approach (see appendix).
15. The investors' demand for debt and equity can also be affected by inflation, mainly through changes in marginal tax rates of investors.
16. Taxing unrealized income derived from traded securities is not common in other countries (e.g., United States) even though the locked-in incentive exists for any interest rate. Constantinides (1983) formally derived the optimal trading policy to utilize the timing option on the realization of capital gains and losses on stocks.
17. Mendenhall (1980) indicates an 8 percent rate of inflation as a rate which should lead to implementation of an inflation-neutral tax system. In our opinion, considering the Israelis' difficulties in implementing such a system, the threshold rate should be much higher.

REFERENCES

Auerbach, Alan J. "Inflation and the Choice of Asset Life." *Journal of Political Economy* 87 (1979), pp. 621–38.

Bailey, Martin J. "Inflation and Tax-Induced Resource Misallocation." *National Tax Journal* 33 (1980), pp. 275–78.

Bar-Yosef, Sasson and Itzhak Swary. "Investment Decisions and Corporate Taxes Under Inflation." Unpublished manuscript, Hebrew University, 1981.

Cohn, Richard A. and Franco Modigliani, "Inflation and Corporate Financial Management." Paper presented at the Conference on Recent Advances in Corporate Finance, November 9–10, 1983, at New York University, Graduate School of Business Administration.

Constantinides, George M. "Optimal Stock Trading with Personal Taxes: Implications for Prices and the Abnormal January Returns," Working Paper No. 75, Center for Research in Security Prices, Graduate School of Business, University of Chicago, 1983.

DeAngelo, Harry and Ronald W. Masulis. "Optimal Capital Structure Under Corporate and Personal Taxation." *Journal of Financial Economics* 8 (1980), pp. 3–29.

Feldstein, Martin S. "Inflation, Income Taxes and the Rate of Interest: A Theoretical Analysis." *American Economic Review* 66 (1976), pp. 809–20.

———. "Inflation, Tax Rules and the Stock Market." *Journal of Monetary Economics* 6 (1980a), pp. 309–31.

———. "Inflation, Tax Rules and the Price of Land and Gold." *Journal of Public Economics* 14 (1980b), pp. 309–18.

———. "Inflation, Tax Rules and Investment: Some Econometric Evidence." *Econometrica* 50 (1982), pp. 825–62.

———, Jerry R. Green, and Eytan Sheshinski. "Corporate Financial Policy and Taxation in a Growing Economy." *Quarterly Journal of Economics* 93 (1979), pp. 411–32.

———, and Lawrence Summers. "Inflation and the Taxation of Capital Income in the Corporate Sector." *National Tax Journal* 32 (1979), pp. 445–570.

Gandolfi, Arthur E. "Inflation, Taxation and Interest Rates." *Journal of Finance* 37 (1982), pp. 797–807.

Gordon, Robert H. and Burton G. Malkiel. "Taxation and Corporate Finance." Princeton University Financial Research Center, Memorandum No. 31, 1980.

Green, Jerry R. and Eytan Sheshinski. "Optimal Capital-Gains Taxation Under Limited Information." *Journal of Political Economy* 86 (1978), pp. 1143–58.

Hamada, Robert S. "Differential Taxes and the Structure of Equilibrium Rates of Return: Managerial Implications and Remaining Conondrums." Working Paper No. 68, Center for Research in Security Prices, Graduate School of Business, University of Chicago, 1982

Hamada, Robert S. and Myron S. Scholes. "Taxes and Corporate Financial Management." Paper prepared for the Conference on Recent Advances in Corporate Finance, November 9–10, 1983 at New York University, Graduate School of Business Administration.

Hasbrouck, Joel. "The Impact of Inflation Upon Corporate Taxation." *National Tax Journal* 36 (1983), pp. 65–82.

Hochman, Shalom and Oded Palmon. "The Irrelevance of Capital Structure for the Impact of Inflation on Investment." *The Journal of Finance* 38 (1983), pp. 785–94.

Holt, C. C. and J. P. Shelton. "The Lock-In Effect of the Capital Gains Tax." *National Tax Journal* 15 (1962), pp. 337–51.

Kim, E. H. "Miller's Equilibrium, Shareholder Leverage Clienteles, and Optimal Capital Structure." *Journal of Finance* 38 (1982), pp. 301–19.

Kroll, Yoram. "Analytical Examination of a Business Tax Reform Under

Rapid Inflation: The Israeli Case." Unpublished manuscript, Hebrew University, 1983.

Mendenhall, John R. "Tax Indexation for Business." *National Tax Journal*, 33 (1980), pp. 257–64.

Miller, Merton H. "Debt and Taxes." *Journal of Finance* 32 (1977), pp. 261–75.

Miller, Merton H. and Myron S. Scholes. "Dividend and Taxes: Some Empirical Evidence." *Journal of Political Economy* 90 (1982), pp. 1118–40.

Modigliani, Franco and Merton H. Miller. "Corporation Income Taxes and the Cost of Capital: A Correction." *American Economic Review* 53 (1963), pp. 433–43.

Nelson, Charles R. "Inflation and Capital Budgeting." *Journal of Finance* 31 (1976), pp. 923–31.

Park, Sang and Joseph Williams. "Taxes, Capital Structure and Bondholders Clientele." Unpublished manuscript, New York University, 1983.

Protopapadakis, Aris. "Some Indirect Evidence on Effective Capital Gains Tax Rates." *Journal of Business* 56 (1983), pp. 127–38.

Stiglitz, Joesph E. "On the Almost Neutrality of Inflation: Notes on Taxation and the Welfare Costs of Inflation," NBER Working Paper Series, No. 499, 1980.

Zwick, B. "The Market for Corporate Bonds." Federal Reserve Bank of New York *Quarterly Review* 2 (1977), pp. 27–36.

---

* Also served as the Israeli Income Tax Deputy Commissioner from September 1981 through August 1983.

We wish to thank Joseph Ahrony, Yoram Peles, Henny Sender, Anthony Saunders, and Ramon Rabinovitch and the participants of the accounting workshop at Rice University for their helpful comments.

Part IV

Inflation and Corporate Financial Management: Introduction

Inflation, which refers to increases in the general price level in the economy, has been a persistent worldwide phenomenon in the last decade or so, since the oil shock of 1973. It has had a major impact both directly and indirectly through its effect on interest rates, foreign exchange rates, and on economic decision making at the macro as well as the firm level.

Since inflation influences finanacial management at the level of the firm due to several reasons, it is useful to distinguish between them at a conceptual level. A major reason why inflation has an impact on corporate financial decisions is due to its interaction with taxation, since most countries compute taxes on a money or nominal basis. It is, therefore, useful to separate the influence on the decision-making process due to inflation even when there are no tax effects. In a world without taxes, the nominal interest rate should reflect the real interest rate as well as compensation for inflation. If the rate of inflation is known with certainty, the real interest rate compounded by this rate will yield the nominal interest rate. If the inflation rate and/or the real interest rate are uncertain, a risk premium must be taken into account in the relationship. An important point to emphasize in an inflationary context is that the valuation of assets, whether financial or real, can be undertaken by using either nominal or real variables. If the real cash flows are used, they should be discounted at the real rate of interest. On the other hand, nominal or money cash flows, computed by compounding the real cash flows at the rate of inflation, can be used along with the nominal interest rate, similarly compounded. It is generally true that the "real-real" and "nominal-nominal" methods yield identical results. However, the relationship is most obvious when there are no taxes or uncertainty which complicate the relationship of inflation and interest rates.

Even when there are no taxes, the usual accounting notion of net income has to be modified for several reasons in order to properly reflect economic income. First, depreciation provisions based on historical capital costs may be inadequate to reflect the amortization required to replace the equipment. This would, therefore, lead to an upward bias in the net income calculations. However, without tax effects, there is no effect on the cash flow since depreciation is added back to net income to compute cash flow. Second, the method of inventory valuation employed affects the computation of net income. If the first-in-first-out (FIFO) method is used, net income is overtaxed since it includes book gains from inventories and does not reflect true opportunity costs. The third effect is somewhat more subtle and works through the nominal interest rate. The nominal interest payments reflect two factors: one, a payment of interest in real terms and the other, a payment that preserves the real value of the principal which is eroded by inflation. The former is a cost in economic terms, while the latter is implicitly a use of the economic profits which reduces the real value of the debt owed. Hence, the inflationary component of interest should be added back to determine economic income. Thus, several adjustments are required to be made before the accounting statements reflect the true profitability of a firm.

In the presence of taxes, the real-real and nominal-nominal approaches should, in principle, yield identical results. However, the actual computations have to be modified for several reasons, rendering the real-real approach difficult to implement in practice. The main source of this problem is that tax shields, such as depreciation, are often fixed in nominal items and therefore have to be discounted in nominal terms. Hence, it is often necessary to use the nominal-nominal method to value at least some of the cash flows. Apart from the impact of inflation and taxes through cash flows, there is an effect also through the discount rate. This is due to the fact that nominal interest rates are tax-deductible and hence the after-tax real cost of debt falls due to inflation. Of course, it may be argued that the nominal interest rate may itself be higher, due to inflation, since lenders would have to be compensated for the higher tax they pay on the inflated interest income.

An aspect of inflation that is often important is the uncertainty surrounding it. If inflation can be perfectly anticipated, lenders and borrowers can build the rate of inflation and any related tax effects into the nominal interest rate. Hence, *ex-post*, neither lenders nor borrowers benefit from inflation. If there is an unexpected component of inflation, one of the two parties will benefit ex-post. Of course, the nominal interest rate should include a premium for the risk of inflation. In terms of recent experience, high rates of inflation have been associated with high levels of inflation uncertainty, which are often difficult to disentangle from each other empirically.

What is the joint impact of inflation and taxation on value? The fact that depreciation tax shields are computed in nominal terms means that their real value declines with inflation. The deductibility of nominal interest, on the other hand, provides a "bonus" in terms of tax shields that rise with inflation. Finally, the valuation of inventory and the taxation of nominal capital gains have a direct effect on cash flows and hence on value.

An issue which has become more important in recent years is the impact of inflation on the payments due to debtholders. Since inflation increases the nominal interest payments by requiring a compensation for the erosion on the real value of the principal, borrowers are forced to make larger payments in the earlier years and correspondingly less later on. This change in the pattern of payments may have a severe impact on borrowers, particularly if the cash flows from the projects financed by the debt do not grow correspondingly with inflation. This is one of the major problems facing both firms and national governments, and is one of the important dimensions of the third-world debt burden today.

Richard Cohn and Franco Modigliani analyze these and other issues relating to inflation in their survey paper. They point out that the real-real and nominal-nominal methods of valuation, properly applied, yield identical results. However, one may be forced to use the nominal-nominal method in practice since the real value of future cash flows may depend on inflation. They analyze the effect of inflation and taxes on both the cash flows and the cost of capital, before turning to the impact on value. They survey the theoretical arguments regarding the effects of inflation on value and the empirical evidence on stock market values in an inflationary period. They conclude, on the basis of the data, that due to irrationality on the part of investors who do not see through the veil of inflation, *E/P* ratios have been systematically higher since the early 1970s, thus raising the real cost of capital. They also discuss how the pension plan liabilities of a firm, an important obligation in economic terms, should be accounted for. Since pensions paid to employees are tied to their final wages, which are expected to keep up with inflation, Cohn and Modigliani suggest taking the real cash flow, i.e., based on current wages, and discounting it at the real rate or using the nominal counterpart of this procedure. They examine an opposing viewpoint which suggests that the current obligations, i.e., the real cash flows, should be discounted at the nominal rate due to the option that the employer has to terminate the employee's contract or discharge him at the current time. According to this argument, if the employer chooses to retain the worker, this would lead to an increase in the obligation in the following period. Cohn and Modigliani argue that the employment contract is a multiperiod one and cannot be viewed on a year-to-year basis. They argue that, although the possibility of separation of employees reduces the value of the liabilities somewhat, the consistent valuation using the real-real or nominal-nominal approaches yields a better approximation of the correct value than the real-nominal approach suggested by those who emphasize the employer's option to terminate.

Richard Goeltz responds to the Cohn-Modigliani hypothesis-survey by citing a very different set of concerns from corporate management. He cites a checklist of areas that his own firm uses in adjusting its policies to inflation and inflation expectations. These include (1) a pricing policy reflecting real return objectives; (2) a rational executive compensation program which considers inflation; (3, 4) careful controls over working capital positions and discounts; (5) careful control of subsidiaries, especially those exposed to inflation risk; (6) a firm-specific approach to debt management; and (7) a rational insurance program. It is quite clear from Mr. Goeltz' comments that he is acutely aware of the inflation-risk questions and one can only wonder if his experience is typical of most firms.

The last paper in this section is a description of the Brazilian method of accounting for inflation by Luiz Manoel Ribeiro Dias. In view of the long experience with inflation in Brazil, this is highly relevant to other countries. He analyzes the accounting and tax treatment of inflationary profit and shows how distortions can creep in due to the combined effect of inflation and taxes.

13

Inflation and Corporate Financial Management

Richard A. Cohn
University of Illinois at Chicago

Franco Modigliani
Massachusetts Institute of Technology
Cambridge, Massachusetts

In discounting cash flows for capital budgeting purposes, one can, in principle, use either anticipated nominal flows and the appropriate nominal discount rate or the corresponding real flows and rate. But inflation has real effects, especially as a result of taxes, that need to be considered in implementing proper investment and financing decisions. Furthermore, a divergence between the firm's own forecast of inflation and the financial market's can have important implications.

Some recent studies of the effects of inflation on stock valuation suggest that the level of E/P *ratios is, surprisingly, directly related to the rate of inflation. If this seemingly irrational relationship is transitory (and there is reason to believe that it is), inflation provides corporate financial managers with intriguing investment and financing opportunities.*

Another important aspect of inflation is its implications for final-average pension plans. Because such plans' liabilities are basically real, they should be valued as such for accounting and planning purposes.

Inflation and Corporate Financial Management

INTRODUCTION

In this paper we discuss the principal implications of inflation for corporate financial management. We seek to acquaint practitioners of corporate finance with the lessons of the large though disparate body of academic literature dealing with the interactions between inflation, valuation, and corporate finance.

Our initial concern is: How does inflation change standard financial decisions? We concentrate on the principal corporate financial decisions: investment and financing. We also investigate the implications of inflation for corporate pension plans, an area of some controversy. To limit the scope of the paper to manageable proportions, issues involving inflation and working capital management, including inventory management, and the specialized problems of regulated firms are not addressed. Also, we will gloss over issues which are by now broadly agreed, to focus on those which are less well understood or controversial.

Tools developed in a world of stable prices can provide poor service when applied in a world of inflation if they are not properly reinterpreted and adapted. Inflation raises important questions of proper measurement. Inflation appears to be a potential source of mismeasurement by management and even by the securities markets, a potential mismeasurement which has, in turn, important feedbacks for corporate decisions.

The second section examines issues of investment and financing in a world of rational financial managers and markets. The following section investigates the possibility that inflation has produced distortions in market valuation and considers the implications of distortions for corporate financial decisions. Then, the nexus between inflation and corporate pension plans is addressed and, finally, the paper is summarized.

INFLATION AND CORPORATE INVESTMENT AND FINANCING

Although finance textbooks are often not explicit as to how inflation considerations should be incorporated in capital budgeting decisions, the academic literature is in general agreement with respect to the principal modifications that, due to inflation, must be made in investment analyses. There is reason to believe, however, that corporate financial managers have frequently failed to take inflation considerations properly into account. In a master's thesis at MIT, Naugle (1980) conducted a questionnaire survey of the top 100 companies in the Fortune 500, aimed at ascertaining whether their capital budgeting procedures were rational in the face of increasing inflation. Thirty one, or 47 percent, of the 66 firms from which he obtained valid responses appeared to fail to pass the test of rationality. A thorough discussion of the lessons of the academic literature in this area would therefore seem warranted.

Textbooks almost invariably argue that potential investments should be selected on the basis of net present value (*NPV*). The interesting question, however, is how inflation affects the net present value calculation.

Any present value reflects a future value and a discount rate or set of discount rates. The net present value of an investment opportunity represents the aggregate present value of all the relevant cash inflows and outflows, discounted at a rate usually referred to as the cost of capital.

In the presence of inflation, one must keep clearly in mind the distinction between nominal future net returns (or cash flows) and nominal discount rates (or cost of capital) on the one hand and real flows and discount rates on the other. Nominal future flows are, of course, simply the realized future cash flows. Real cash flows are returns expressed in terms of constant prices, or equivalently, deflated by a "general price index" (that is, by the price index of an appropriately defined broad basket of commodities). Similarly, the one-period *nominal* discount factor (one plus the discount rate) measures the number of *dollars* the investors require next period for giving up $1 this period, while the *real* discount factor measures the number of dollars *of current purchasing power* that investors demand next period per dollar invested now; put differently, it is the number of commodity baskets next period that investors require per initial commodity basket. The relation between the (short-term) nominal rate, say R, and the real rate, say r, is given by the well-known formula $(1 + R) = (1 + r)(1 + p)$, where p is the rate of inflation over the period of the loan. This relation is commonly simplified to $R = r + p$ by dropping the term rp which, for limited inflation, is very small compared to $r + p$.

A basic proposition about capital budgeting, and, more generally, about valuation, in the presence of anticipated inflation is that there are two alternative warranted ways of proceeding. One way is to discount future *nominal flows* at the *nominal discount rate* (the nominal-nominal approach); the other is to discount future *real flows* at the *real discount rate* (the real-real method). (See, e.g., Brealey and Myers (1981), pp. 86–88). It can be readily verified that these two procedures will give the same answer if applied consistently—that is, provided the inflation rate implied by the relation between the nominal and real forecasted future flows is the same as the inflation rate implied by the relation between the nominal and the real rate.[1] The net present values thus obtained will be the same because, while the expected nominal flows (the "numerators") are raised in the nominal calculation, as a result of rising prices, this increase is precisely undone in the present value calculation when the inflation is reflected in the nominal discount rate (the denominator).

Inconsistencies in the estimate of inflation, explicitly or implicitly built into the numerator and denominator, on the other hand, will, generally, lead to wrong decisions. In particular, deflating nominal flows by real discount factors will overstate the true net *PV* (if inflation is positive), while discounting real flows by nominal discount factors will lead to the opposite bias.

The fact that the two approaches consistently applied will give the same answer does not necessarily imply that one should be indifferent between the two methods. On the contrary, given the extreme unreliability of long-term inflation forecasts, strikingly confirmed by recent experience, there is much to be said in favor of approaches that can dispense from, or depend less critically on, forecasts of forthcoming inflation. We suggest that, because generally effective planning requires, in any event, the development of forecasts of outputs, inputs, and earnings in constant prices, one can make a good prima facie case for the real-real approach as the basic procedure. At the same time, in some instances the nominal-nominal approach may prove more effective. These propositions can be illustrated by some examples.

The case of pure equity financing

Consider the case where a firm is entirely equity-financed. In the absence of inflation (and assuming further that the firm has no significant true growth opportunity), it is well known that the required rate of (equity) return, say ρ, can be inferred from the earnings-price ratio (E/P). The appropriate measure of earnings for this purpose is sustainable, cyclically "noise-free" earnings, not simply the latest 12 months' earnings per share.[2]

The same conclusion continues to hold under inflation except that E/P must now be recognized as the required *real* rate of return. This rate must be distinguished from the nominal rate of return from holding the security, say ρ_n, which includes, in addition to the earnings, also any capital appreciation. Since earnings may be expected to rise at the rate of inflation (at least when inflation is neutral—see below), as long as E/P is constant, the price must also rise at the rate of inflation, producing a capital gain per dollar equal to the rate of inflation, p. Thus, the nominal equity rate is $\rho_n = \rho + p$.

Suppose, first, that after-tax profits can be taken as inflation-neutral, that is, (roughly) proportional to the price level. (Note that this neutrality requires the absence of assets depreciable for tax purposes.) In this case, it should be apparent that the NPV can be conveniently computed through the real-real approach by combining the forecast of the real cash flows, presumably already needed for other purposes, with the estimate of the required real rate of return, inferred from E/P. This approach eliminates altogether the need for a forecast of future inflation. Not only does this save costs, but it also avoids the danger, inherent in the nominal-nominal calculation, that different, and hence inconsistent, forecasts of inflation may be embedded in the estimation of flows and in that of the nominal required rate. This danger is particularly serious when those responsible for cash flow estimates differ from those responsible for choosing the required rate of return.

Consider next the case where inflation is not neutral in that future real flows depend on the future price level (or on the rate of inflation). Even in this case, it may be possible, through a variant of the real-real approach, to eliminate the need for an explicit forecast of inflation, notably where the nonneutrality derives from some component of the net nominal flow being fixed in nominal terms. An important illustration of this problem is provided by the depreciation tax shield, arising when net corporate income is taxed after deducting depreciation. In this case, since tax depreciation is based on historical acquisition cost, the depreciation deduction is fixed in nominal terms once the depreciable asset is acquired and placed in service. Accordingly, to compute the contribution to NPV from the present value of the depreciation tax shield, one should discount these flows at the *nominal rate*. (Note that this implies that inflation, by raising the nominal rate, reduces the value of the tax shield.) This would suggest the need for a forecast of inflation in order to estimate the p term of the nominal discount factor, $\rho_n = E/P + p$. In reality, a good case has been made in the finance literature that the depreciation flow should be discounted at the nominal "riskless" interest rate rather than at the equity rate, which generally includes a risk premium. This conclusion rests on the consideration of the relatively low level of uncertainty surrounding the realization of the depreciation tax shields, compared with other operating cash flows, especially given the opportunity to carry losses back three years for tax purposes. Opportunities to carry losses forward and to enter into sale and leaseback arrangements also serve to mitigate uncertainty associated with the eventual realization of these tax shields.

Now, an estimate of the nominal rate, and in fact of the whole term structure of nominal rates, can be conveniently derived from the yields in the markets for short-term nominal instruments and for bonds of various maturities. They reflect the market consensus about the future of nominal rates, and hence they can be used directly to discount fixed nominal flows like the depreciation tax shield. Thus, even when some flows, such as the depreciation deduction, are fixed in nominal terms, the NPV calculation can be carried out without relying on an explicit forecast of inflation. To this end, one would discount at the equity rate the (inflation-neutral) real cash flow before interest and taxes (*EBIT*), adjusted for taxes (by multiplying by one minus the tax rate), and then add on the depreciation tax shield discounted at the market interest rate.

To be sure, an internal forecast of future prices might reveal an apparent inconsistency with the implicit market forecast of the real rate and of inflation implicit in R. It is important to remember that even in this case rational behavior calls for basing calculations on the market rate, rather than on that implied by the internal forecast. In other words, even if there is sufficient confidence in the internal forecast to conclude that the market will prove wrong, this information is most effectively used not for calculating NPV but, if anything, to "speculate" against the market. Thus, if the market appears to understate future inflation and future rates, the firm could capitalize on this information by borrowing long and lending short.

Nonneutral inflation and debt financing

Of course, the real value of future flows may depend on the rate of inflation (or, equivalently, the nominal value of future flows may not be proportional to the price level) for reasons other than the nominal fixity of the flows. Similarly, the required rate of return may be systematically related to the rate of inflation. This dependence may spring from many causes, such as regulation, features of tax laws, long-term contracts, "fixity" of exchange rates, etc. In such cases, it will generally not be possible to avoid a forecast of inflation, whether one uses the real-real or the nominal-nominal approach.

This same conclusion holds, in principle, when a firm is financed by a combination of equity and debt capital because the real cost of debt capital to a firm depends not only on the market nominal rate but also directly on the rate of inflation. Specifically, in the presence of corporate income taxes of the U.S. description, the real cost per dollar of debt, r_c, can be expressed as:

$$r_c = (1 - \tau)R - p = (1 - \tau)r - \tau p \tag{1}$$

where τ is the corporate income tax rate.

It will be seen from equation (1) that inflation should tend to reduce the cost of debt but for reasons entirely different from the traditional—and largely erroneous—view that it redistributes wealth from creditors to debtors. That redistributional gain can occur only when inflation is, at least partially, unanticipated. But when the inflation is fully anticipated, the nominal rate will tend to rise enough to compensate for the loss of real value of the principal, leaving the real rate unchanged (or possibly even raising it to maintain the real rate after personal taxes). But equation (1) shows that, in the presence of corporate income taxes, inflation reduces r_c even if the real rate is unchanged, the reason being that the income tax allows the deduction of all interest, including that part which compensates the creditor for inflation and is therefore in the nature of a repayment of principal.

Of course, what is relevant for capital budgeting is not the cost of debt funds but the overall real cost of capital, defined as the required tax-adjusted *EBIT* per dollar of capital. The relation between r_c and the overall real cost, say ρ, is conventionally expressed in terms of the so-called weighted average cost of capital:

$$\rho = i\frac{S}{V} + r_c\frac{D}{V} \tag{2}$$

Here, i represents the required rate of return on equity capital;

$$i = \frac{(EBIT - RD)(1 - \tau) + pD}{S} = \frac{(EBIT)(1 - \tau) - r_c D}{S} \tag{3}$$

while the "weights" S/V and D/V represent the shares of equity and debt, respectively, in the overall capital structure. These weights,

S/V and D/V, should be interpreted as representing the target shares for the firm as a whole rather than the share existing at the moment, or contemplated for the particular investment.

It is readily apparent from the above formulas that, with a levered capital structure, consistent capital budgeting will unavoidably require a forecast of inflation. Indeed, in the real-real approach, one needs an estimate of the real required return given by equation (2). Although an estimate of the equity component i given by equation (3) might, in principle, be derived directly from current and historical market data, measuring the real cost of debt capital involves not only the observable long-term rate R but also an explicit forecast of inflation. Nor can this requirement be avoided by relying on the nominal-nominal approach. Indeed, in this case, one needs to measure the nominal required rate of return, which is obtained from equation (2) by adding the rate of inflation, p, to both sides. Using equation (1), this yields:

$$\begin{aligned} \rho_n &= \rho + p = i\frac{S}{V} + [(1-\tau)R - p]\frac{D}{V} + p \\ &= (i+p)\frac{S}{V} + (1-\tau)R\frac{D}{V} \end{aligned} \tag{4}$$

In equation (4) the nominal cost of debt component, R, can be read from the market, but the (nominal) cost of equity requires a forecast of p. Furthermore, as already pointed out, that forecast should be the very same one that underlies the estimate of nominal flows.

However, the conclusion derived from equations (1) and (2), that even the real cost of capital depends on inflation, needs to be properly qualified in that it assumes that r_c can change independently of i. But this independence cannot be taken for granted. Indeed, according to the so-called Modigliani-Miller (1958) proposition, at least under certain conditions (absence of taxes and rational investor behavior), the relation between i and $r_c D/V$ will be such that the overall cost of capital will be independent of leverage, and need not vary when r_c varies.

Recently, Miller, in a well-known contribution (1977) argued that this conclusion is valid, even allowing for taxes. Furthermore, his model would seem to imply that the conclusion would hold as well in the presence of inflation (see Hochman and Palmon (1983)). If he were right, the overall cost of capital would be unaffected by leverage or by the rate of inflation, and could be inferred from the relation between market value and *EBIT* cash flow.

This conclusion, however, has been widely criticized. In particular, Modigliani (1982), (1983), taking into account the role of portfolio diversification neglected by Miller, has confirmed that, in the presence of taxes, (1) some leverage is valuable, tending to reduce the cost of capital, and that, (2) for given leverage, the cost of capital is further reduced by inflation.[3] This result is consistent with the conclusion based on equations (1) and (2), although it should be recognized that the market expectation of inflation also has some indirect effects on the cost of capital through i, depending on the extent to which inflation affects the real rate.

How, then, should one arrive at a forecast of (average) inflation over the life of the project? If one accepts the market long-term rate, R, as the best available estimate of the future of nominal interest rates, the problem is that of decomposing R into the expected real rate and expected inflation implicit in it. Under normal circumstances, a practical way to do that is that of estimating the real rate component. Such an estimate might be derived, without an explicit forecast of inflation, from the history of realized short-term real interest rates. While these rates have not remained constant, they have tended to fluctuate within a fairly narrow spread, resulting in a relatively stable moving average—at least until the last two or three years. One may therefore be able to put together an estimate of the prospective average real rate over the life of the project from past data, with proper adjustment for unusual developments, like the persistent large government deficits currently in prospect.

The estimate of the short real rate so derived might have to be further adjusted for term premium, i.e., systematic differences in yields between short and long maturities. (These premiums, which can be, in principle, of either sign, would again have to be inferred from historical behavior and other considerations.) Subtracting the resulting estimate of the real long rate from the nominal rate yields the implied market forecast of average inflation. Of course, the validity of this method now depends closely on the method followed by the market in projecting real rates resembling that described above. In any event, the resulting price forecast would have to be examined for reasonableness and consistency with explicit inflation forecasts spread through the financial press.

Alternatively, the firm may be in a position to elaborate its own independent forecast from other methods and sources. If available, such a forecast can be used to advantage to improve investment decisions both in terms of measuring the cost of capital or hurdle rate, and in terms of choosing the financing package. The choices in this respect go from financing at a fixed long-term rate with no or minimal call provisions to financing through a sequence of short-term loans, or more realistically, through a longer-term loan, but with interest floating with a short-term rate.

Once we recognize that inflation over the life of the project is uncertain, it appears that the real cost of debt funds is itself uncertain and dependent on the form of financing chosen, as well as on the realization of inflation. We can illustrate this proposition in terms of the real cost of the two limiting types of borrowing mentioned earlier, long-term noncallable L, and floating short-rate loans S. From equation (1) we deduce:

$$\tilde{L} = (1 - \tau)RL - \tilde{p} \qquad (5a)$$

$$\tilde{S} = (1 - \tau)\tilde{R}S - \tilde{p} = (1 - \tau)\tilde{r} - \tau\tilde{p} \qquad (5b)$$

where the tilde denotes a stochastic (uncertain) variable. Capital budgeting must rely on a measure of expected cost. It is apparent from equations (5*a*) and (5*b*) that that measure depends both on the financial package adopted and on what forecast of inflation one is prepared to rely, the market's (implicit) expectations or the firm's own forecast.

We can throw light on the considerations relevant to a choice by considering alternative circumstances. Suppose, first, that the internal forecast is lower than the implicit market forecast (and the difference is not compensated by a higher forecast of the real rate). Then, the internal forecast implies that, over the relevant period, the average value of the short-term rate, RS, will be lower than the current long-term rate (adjusted for term premium). In this case, a very good case can be made, insofar as a project is to be financed, for choosing a short-term type of instrument. One can readily establish that this choice will reduce the expected real interest cost, r_c, by $(1 - \tau)(p_m - p_f)$, where p_m is the implicit market forecast, and p_f the firm's forecast. Furthermore, if the uncertainty of future inflation is substantially larger than that of the real rate, as experience suggests, that choice will also reduce the uncertainty of the r_c outcome. Note, however, that because inflation reduces the cost of capital, the lower inflation expectation will also imply a larger value of r_c than implied by the market expectation, by an amount $\tau(p_m - p_f)$. The cost of capital should be based on this higher cost rather than on the lower implicit market estimate.

Suppose, on the other hand, that the firm's forecast of inflation exceeds the market's. In this case, the minimization of expected r_c will call for long-term financing, especially if it can be made more flexible through call protection (although, as long as the difference in expectations is not large, a case can still be made for short-term financing in order to minimize risk). Supposing long-term financing is adopted, then the firm's higher expectation of inflation will imply a value of r_c lower than that corresponding to the market forecast. In this case, however, it is advisable to maintain the cut-off at the higher level of r_c implied by the market expectation. In other words, any project not having positive net present value for r_c based on market expectations should be rejected even if it has positive *NPV* at the lower r_c implied by the firm's expectation. The reason is that any funds borrowed could be expected to produce a higher return through financial speculation, i.e., investing them in short loans than by investing them in the project.

To summarize, we have shown that capital budgeting can be based indifferently on the real-real or nominal-nominal approach as long as they are applied consistently. We have suggested that, in view of the great difficulties in arriving at reliable projections of long-run inflation, one should give preference to approaches that do not require forecasts of inflation or do not lean heavily on such a forecast. We have illustrated a number of cases where some variant of the real-real approach appears to offer that advantage, though admittedly these are cases of limited practical relevance. We have further shown that the fact that inflation is typically more uncertain than real rates makes a good prima facie case for preferring short- to long-term financing, although the choice should be influenced by the internal expectation of inflation relative to the market's as well as by the availability and cost of call clause and related arrangements.

The discussion of this section has been concerned with identifying rational managerial behavior in a world of rational investors and financial institutions. However, before one finds fault with firms that appear to behave irrationally with respect to inflation, such as those identified by Naugle, one must consider the possibility that the world is not one of rational investors and institutions. We examine the evidence on this question and its implications for corporate decisions in the following section. There are strong reasons to suppose that inflation may produce serious distortions in the value of the market as a basis for the calculation of required returns.

INFLATION-INDUCED DISTORTIONS IN MARKET VALUATION AND IMPLICATIONS FOR INVESTMENT

Inflation and the valuation of common stock

The economics of corporate finance has long been grounded in the normative view that the goal of firms' management should be the maximization of the firm's stock price. In this section we investigate the relationship between inflation and the value of corporate equity.

Common stocks have traditionally been thought of as a sound asset to hold in the presence of inflation, in contrast to assets fixed in nominal terms whose real value is eroded by inflation. This assessment rests on the consideration that stocks of nonfinancial corporations represent levered claims against real assets. If real assets' values tend to keep up with the price level under inflationary conditions, and creditors lose as a result of unanticipated inflation, then stockholders should gain in real terms to the extent that creditors lose. Actually, this popular view needs to be greatly qualified since, as indicated earlier, its validity is limited to the case when inflation is totally, or at least partially, unexpected. When it is fully anticipated, one may expect the nominal interest rate to rise in step with the inflation, leaving no special advantage for the borrower to reap. However, as was also indicated, despite Miller's contrary conclusion, there is reason to believe that inflation should benefit levered corporate enterprises, because of the corporate income tax which allows the deduction of all interest, including the inflation premium component (see Modigliani (1982), (1983)).[4]

The traditional, as well as the tax angle view that inflation is good for corporate stock, has all but been shattered by the experience of the last three decades, particularly the last decade and a half. Numerous researchers have documented a negative relationship between stock prices, or rates of return, and inflation (Lintner (1973), Bodie (1976), Jaffe and Mandelker (1976), Nelson (1976), Modigliani and Cohn (1979)).

The clearest way to view the association between stock prices and inflation is to examine the relationship between earnings-price (E/P) ratios and inflation. Because earnings are inherently a real variable, as was argued above, the E/P ratio is in principle a real rate. But Figure 1 shows an unmistakable positive correlation between the E/P ratio of the Standard & Poor's 500 stock index, based on reported earnings, and the inflation rate. Since the relationship between E/P ratios and inflation is a direct one, the relationship between the price-earnings (P/E) ratio and inflation is inverse.

Of course the question of earnings measurement must be raised in any discussion of the nexus between inflation and E/P ratios. Many are wary, and properly so, of errors induced by inflation in reported earnings as measures of true economic earnings in a period of inflation. There are three types.

Two of these measurement errors are well known, while one of them continues to be poorly understood. The two that are generally

FIGURE 1

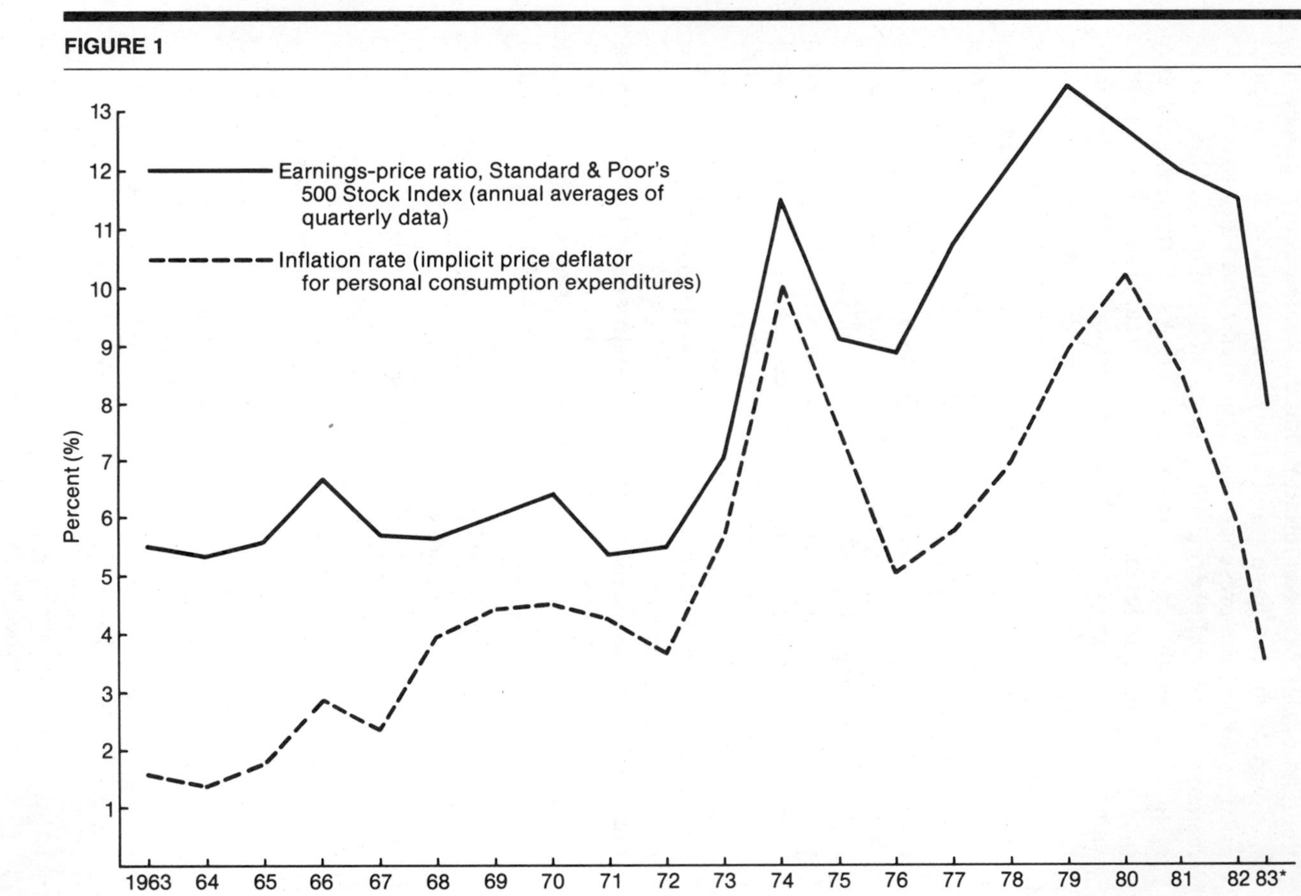
Earnings-price ratio, Standard & Poor's 500 Stock Index (annual averages of quarterly data)
Inflation rate (implicit price deflator for personal consumption expenditures)
Percent (%)
13
12
11
10
9
8
7
6
5
4
3
2
1
1963
64
65
66
67
68
69
70
71
72
73
74
75
76
77
78
79
80
81
82
83*

understood have to do with measuring the cost of goods sold for nonfinancial firms. First, firms that employ FIFO accounting for inventories tend, in a period of inflation, to expense a cost of goods sold that reflects less than the economically relevant replacement cost of inventories, which is essentially what would be reflected in the use of LIFO accounting. Another way of putting it is that the reported income of FIFO firms includes "paper" gains on inventories. Second, since depreciation is based on the historical acquisition cost of assets, reported depreciation tends to understate depreciation appropriately calculated on a replacement cost basis when there has been a significant increase in the general price level since a substantial fraction of the firm's depreciable assets was acquired. The effect of both these errors is to cause reported income to exceed income adjusted for both biases, to which we will refer hereafter as adjusted income.

The third measurement error, the one that seems not to be generally understood, is important because it works in the opposite direction. Reported income per period is net of *nominal* interest; however, during the period inflation reduces the real value of the principal by pD, where p is the inflation rate. The pD component of interest, as implied previously, is, in real terms, a repayment of principal. True income should therefore be measured net of real interest, not nominal interest. Consequently, in fully adjusting reported income for the effects of inflation so as to produce a true figure, pD must be added back to adjusted income.

Interestingly, Modigliani and Cohn, hereafter referred to as M-C, and Pearce (1982) find that, in recent years, for the nonfinancial corporate sector taken as a whole, year by year, the overestimate of true income due to the first two reasons tends to offset the underestimate due to interest, so that reported income approximates true income fairly closely. While this result applies to the typical firm or to the firms in the stock market as a whole, and thus validates the E/P ratios presented in Figure 1, it need not obtain for any particular firm.

Another way in which to observe the real stock market debacle that has occurred since the onset of inflation in the mid-1960s is to examine what has happened to the ratio of the market value of net corporate debt and equity to the replacement cost of the underlying real assets. This ratio is usually referred to as Tobin's q. The q ratio has fallen from a level somewhat above one in 1964–65 to a level substantially below one, at least until the recent drastic reduction in inflation.

One question raised by the increased E/P ratio in recent years is why corporate investment has not been depressed as a result of the corresponding rise in the cost of equity capital. One possibility is that corporate managers, in implementing the nominal-nominal approach discussed earlier, employ a downward-biased estimate of the weighted-average nominal cost of capital, one based on nominal interest rates on debt but E/P ratios for equity, rather than the correct nominal cost of equity. Naugle (1980) finds some support for this notion.

Why has the E/P ratio risen?

The academic literature contains a number of potential explanations for the observed increase in E/P ratios. One such explanation is taxes. This culprit is cited by Feldstein and Summers (1979) and Feldstein (1980). They point out that FIFO accounting produces paper gains for tax as well as financial reporting purposes. They also point out that tax-deductible depreciation understates true depreciation. As a result of both the inventory and the depreciation effects, the effective tax burden on corporate income rises as a result of inflation,[5] causing a fall in the market value of stock relative to true before-tax earnings, even if the true capitalization rate is unchanged.

This argument could also explain why E/P ratios seem to have risen as a result of inflation. For, at the same time as inflation lowers the value of stock, it also raises reported, relative to true, earnings, through the inclusion of paper profits on inventories and underdepreciation of capital assets, thus raising E/P.

There seems to be little empirical support for this argument. The reason is that the adverse tax effects of FIFO and underdepreciation are virtually completely undone by the offsetting effect of nontaxation of the pD component of earnings, which is deductible for tax purposes in computing corporate income. M-C, Gonedes (1981), R. Gordon (1981), Pearce (1982), and M. Gordon (1983) all find little evidence to support the hypothesis that tax effects account for the real decline in the market value of stock.

Some argue theoretically (see, for example, Carr and Halpern (1981)) that there should be no offsetting tax gain from debt. The reason they give is that interest rates should rise in response to increases in expectations of inflation so as to preserve after-tax real costs of borrowing. They argue that with a corporate tax rate t, the pretax nominal interest rate, R, should be equal to $(r' + p)/(1 - t)$, where r' is the after-tax real interest rate. Thus an increase of one percentage point in p would imply an increase in R of $1/(1 - t)$ percentage points. But Summers (1983) provides ample evidence that interest rates have risen, at most, point for point with inflation, at least until recently.

Feldstein offers another tax-related reason to explain the observed direct relationship between *E/P* and inflation. He correctly points out that investors are taxed at the personal level on paper capital gains stemming from inflation. He then argues that investors in stock demand higher *E/P* ratios under inflationary conditions so as to preserve their after-tax real rates of return. However, if this effect on *E/P* ratios exists, it is likely to be of an inconsequential magnitude. The reason is that the effective tax rate on capital gains at the personal level is extremely modest because of the ability of investors to defer this tax, to determine the timing of the realization of gains, and to escape the tax at death.

Another argument explaining the observed relationship between *E/P* ratios and inflation is the risk-premium hypothesis of Malkiel (1979); see also his article in Boeckh and Coghlan (1982) and Friend and Hasbrouck (1982). They argue that the risk premium required by investors has been directly related to the rate of inflation, and therefore the equilibrium *E/P* ratio has also been related to inflation. Risk and inflation may go together because they are both related to such real shocks as the various oil crises. Historically, high and variable inflation may also give rise to uncertainty, though such nonneutrality is not necessarily rational. Of course, if inflation and risk go together, they are impossible to distinguish.

Both Fama (1981) and Geske and Roll (1983) explain the observed negative relationship between inflation and stock rates of return on the basis of real shocks and their effects on corporate profitability. But neither approach serves to explain the rise in *E/P* ratios.

While Fama does not really explain the link between shocks and inflation, his results can be interpreted in one of two ways. Perhaps diminished rates of return have resulted from decreased profitability, measuring assets at replacement cost with the *q* ratio unchanged. But then the *E/P* ratio would have fallen, not risen, and the real value of stock would not have fallen. Or perhaps shocks have reduced profits while the *E/P* ratio has remained unchanged. But this interpretation is not consistent with a rise in the *E/P* ratio either.

Geske and Roll tell a rather unconvincing story in an attempt to explain the linkage between shocks and inflation. They see real shocks leading to a fall in government revenue and therefore a rise in the deficit, which is in turn monetized, thus producing inflation. A particularly weak link in this story is that dealing with the monetization of the deficit. In recent years Federal Reserve purchases of

Treasury debt have fluctuated little around a rising trend. While the deficit has increased over this period from a negligible to a modest fraction of GNP, Federal Reserve purchases as a fraction of Treasury new issues have fallen from as much as 50 percent in 1964, for example, when the new issues were small, to 4–9 percent in the last few years (Sinai and Rathjens (1983)). While Geske and Roll might have an explanation for a decline in real profits, the empirical evidence does not support such a claim when profits are measured properly, and their argument does not explain a rise in the *E*/*P* ratio.

Another argument explaining the observed rise in the *E*/*P* ratio is inherently untestable. This argument suggests that, because of real shocks, *E* is transitorily high and the true *E*/*P* ratio has not actually increased.

On the basis of a set of time-series tests, M-C concluded that inflation illusion largely accounted for the observed relationship between *E*/*P* ratios and inflation. They found that investors make two errors in valuing corporate stock as a result of inflation causing nominal interest rates to exceed real rates. First, investors capitalize earnings at a rate that follows the nominal rate rather than the appropriate real rate. Second, investors capitalize adjusted earnings rather than true earnings. This second error applies, of course, only to levered firms. Both errors have the effect of driving stock prices below their rationally warranted level.

The M-C hypothesis implies that *E*/*P* ratios are positively related to nominal interest rates even though changes in nominal rates are largely explained by changes in the expected rate of inflation over the period M-C studied, 1953–77. The graph in Figure 2 pictures the relationship between *E*/*P* ratios and nominal interest rates since 1963.

The aggregate stock market experience since 1977 would seem to accord quite well with the M-C hypothesis that nominal interest rates move the market. In particular, the rise in *P*/*E* ratios that began in August 1982 with the onset of the current bull market and which continued through the first half of 1983 would seem largely related to the concurrent fall in nominal interest rates. There is no prima facie evidence that real interest rates fell during this period. The decline in the rate of inflation over the period was approximately the same as the decline in nominal interest rates. In fact, while nominal interest rates were fairly stable during the first half of 1983, inflation continued to fall.

M-C (1982) performed an extensive set of cross-sectional tests of Malkiel's and Friend and Hasbrouck's risk-premium hypothesis. M-C reasoned that, if the decline in the stock market as a whole

FIGURE 2

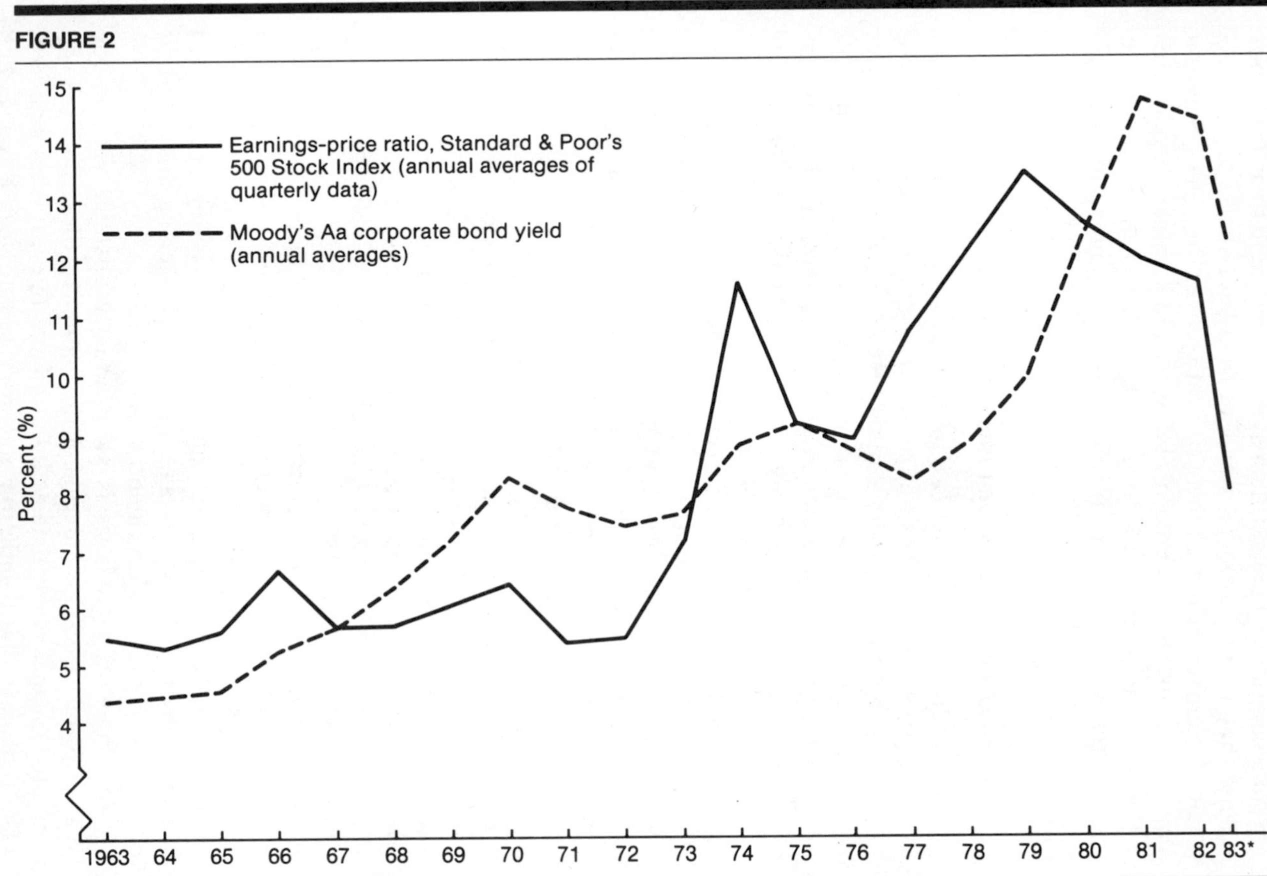

Sources: *Economic Report of the President*, 1983; *Economic Indicators*, September 1983.

resulted from a rise in the average required risk premium, then stocks with above-average risk premiums (as captured by beta) would experience a greater than average decline in their *P/E* ratios. What they found, however, was that high-beta stocks experienced below-average declines in their *P/E* ratios over the 1968–78 period, one characterized by increasing inflation and nominal interest rates. This result is inconsistent with the hypothesis of rising risk premiums for stocks unless the increases in risk premiums are unrelated to beta.

Implications for investment and financing

If one accepts the view that *E/P* ratios are only transitorily high and that the true *E/P* ratio has not risen, then inflation has had no real effect on the cost of equity capital. However, if one accepts the strong evidence for a substantial increase in the *E/P* ratio, then the real cost of equity capital has increased substantially. Investments that do not meet this new high criterion should, on the basis of traditional considerations, not be undertaken.

If the M-C hypothesis is correct, the effect of inflation is to raise the real cost of debt as well as equity. The reason is that the valuation of levered firms is penalized as a result of investors capitalizing adjusted earnings. M-C found direct evidence for this penalty in their cross-sectional study (1982). While Summers (1981) finds empirically that levered firms benefit from inflation, his results conflict not only with those of M-C but also with the difficulties researchers in recent years have experienced in trying to support the "debtor-creditor" or "nominal contracting" hypothesis, the argument that net-debtor firms benefit from unanticipated inflation and unanticipated changes in expected inflation as a result of losses inflicted on creditors of firms (see Bloom et al. (1980) and French, Ruback, and Schwert (1983)).

If inflation causes the valuation of levered firms to suffer as a result of the inflation illusion cited by M-C, then corporate financial managers face a dilemma insofar as retained earnings are not sufficient: They can finance externally only by issuing undervalued equity or by increasing leverage, thereby threatening to make their equity even more undervalued.

But the M-C hypothesis is an inherently unstable view of the valuation process. The undervaluation implied by the hypothesis will tend to disappear over time as inflation and interest rates stabilize. The reason is that if inflation and interest rates cease rising, *E/P* ratios will stop falling. If then earnings continue to keep up with the price level, which, history indicates, is a reasonable expectation, then investors will find themselves earning an unexpectedly high nominal rate of return equal to the *E/P* ratio (in the case of the "no true growth" firm) plus the rate of inflation. This return is in excess of expectations as, according to the hypothesis, shares were priced to yield an expected nominal rate of return equal to the *E/P* ratio. The excess return in turn should make the undervaluation apparent and cause it to disappear. If inflation and interest rates actually fall, this process will be speeded up, for the *E/P* ratios will also fall.

This scenario of eventual revision implies that firms may wish to consider investments based on their values in the event of such a revision. If the M-C hypothesis is correct, real asset values as reflected in the values of claims in the financial markets are irrationally depressed as a result of investors capitalizing income at nominal rates. Managers can then make real investments which will eventually be vindicated when the undervaluation comes to an end.[6] The capital gains will accrue to the firm's shareholders over the period during which the undervaluation diminishes.

To be sure, this argument favors firms obtaining financing for new investment from their internal cash flow rather than new equity issues. New issues would dilute eventual per share gains. For the same reason, debt financing is to be preferred to new equity financing.

One way to raise the amount of cash flow available internally would be to decide not to increase dividends over time as earnings per share, properly measured, increase. Shareholders should further gain from a reduction in the target payout ratio owing to the adverse tax implications of dividends (Modigliani (1982)).

If a firm perceives that it does not have worthwhile real investment opportunities, even based on an elimination of undervaluation, it may wish to consider purchasing shares of other firms. It may also want to consider a repurchase of its own stock.

INFLATION AND CORPORATE PENSIONS

Inflation has profound but widely misunderstood implications for corporate pension plans. Today the typical corporate pension plan is a single-employer, trusteed, noncontributory, final-average defined benefit plan. Munnell (1982, pp. 173–74) cites a Bankers Trust Company study showing that 76 percent of conventional defined benefit plans, those that base benefit promises on compensation as well as length of service, determined benefits solely on the basis of final-average pay during the period 1975–79. By 1979, 83 percent of these plans calculated average pay on the basis of the last five years of employment.

Participants in such plans probably view their claims as at least partially hedged against inflation. Workers presumably anticipate that the compensation on which their pensions will be based will tend to keep up with the general price level.

If employees' expectations are rational, then one would anticipate that at least part of the pension plan assets would be invested so as to produce a stable real rate of return over time. One would anticipate that the managers of pension plans would seek inflation hedges as investments, at least to the extent such investments could be deemed prudent.

It is probably the failure of stocks and bonds to serve as inflation hedges in recent years that has caused corporate pension plans to become increasingly interested in real estate equities as investments. But this route is not the only one that should be considered.

Values of short-term debt securities are affected adversely by unanticipated increases in expected inflation, but not very much. If a one percentage point increase in the expected rate of inflation causes the nominal rate to rise, say from 10 percent to 11 percent, the fall in the value of a 3-month security would be approximately one quarter of 1 percent. The corresponding fall in the value of a 20-year 10 percent bond whose yield to maturity rose to 11 percent would be approximately 8 percent. Short-term debt instruments by their very nature provide much more stable (inflation-invariant) real rates of return, even under conditions of variable inflation, than long-term bonds.

The market for short-term debt instruments may be such, however, that lenders are willing to pay a premium for liquidity and for inflation hedging, resulting in somewhat lower interest rates (although in the recent inflation the premium has actually been negative). Most pension plans today probably have little need for liquidity. Not only do they enjoy highly predictable short-term cash flows, but many of them also anticipate that they will experience net cash inflows for several years to come. On this account, they may find short-term instruments unattractive.

These considerations suggest that long-term but variable- or floating-rate debt instruments should prove to be an appealing investment for pension plans. Such a demand would probably elicit a corresponding supply.

One can fairly easily imagine a good bit of the demand for mortgage credit being met by pension plans using floating-rate instruments. What would seem to be needed for this purpose, however, is not the standard variable-rate mortage, which has proved to be fairly unpopular among borrowers, but a mortgage which provides a more attractive stream of payments for the borrower.[7]

A particularly appealing candidate for this purpose is what has come to be known as the MIT flexible graduated payment mortgage. This instrument provides the lender with a rate of interest tied to a short-term reference market interest rate, but offers the borrower a relatively low monthly payment at the start. The reason is that the payment is determined on the basis of a fixed annuity factor, based on the real short-term interest rate, applied to the remaining balance. For a fuller discussion of this type of mortgage instrument, see Modigliani and Lessard (1975). Such an instrument, when properly understood, is likely to be appealing to both lenders and borrowers.

Another issue we propose to review is the controversial one about the appropriate way of computing pension plan liabilities in the presence of inflation. Accounting disclosure for corporate pension plans in the United States is governed by the Financial Accounting Standards Board's Statements of Financial Accounting Standards Nos. 35 and 36. These statements require disclosure of the present value of accrued benefits together with the assumed rate of return on investment. It is this rate which is used as the discount rate in determining the present value of accrued benefits. The interesting issue is whether accrued liabilities should be discounted to the present using basically a nominal or a real rate. Economic common sense suggests that the second answer is the broadly correct one. The reason is that under a final-average pay plan, the pension actually paid will depend on terminal wages, and it seems reasonable, for both accounting and planning purposes, to expect wages and salaries to tend to keep up with the price level. The effect of such an assumption on projected pension benefits is profound. If, for example, inflation is no more than 5 percent per year, then, even if real wages are merely constant, the pension actually paid to someone retiring 30 years from now would exceed the current liability to him by something like four and one half times. In essence, the pension fund liability is a real liability that keeps up with the price level. Accordingly, to compute the present value of the liability, one should either take the *future nominal* value and discount it at the *nominal rate*, or take the future *real* liability (i. e., in today's prices) and discount it at the *real rate*; but the future real liability is simply today's accrued liability. The only course that would seem patently wrong is to discount today's accrued liability at the nominal rate; the result would be a serious underestimation of the reserves needed to fund liabilities already incurred.

This seemingly obvious conclusion has, in fact, been challenged recently, notably by Bulow (1981). He argues that final-average plan liabilities are, at any point in time, strictly nominal in nature because the employer can discharge the employee or terminate the pension plan at any time and that such liabilities should therefore be discounted at the nominal rate. He points out that the employer pension liability to any employee participating in a final-average plan at the end of any period is, in effect, a pension based on his past final-average salary. Therefore, the present value of what is owed at retirement is the present value of what is owed currently upon retirement. It follows that to measure reserves needed against liabilities incurred by a fund, the currently accrued liabilities should be discounted at the nominal rate. His view has obtained a good bit of support among financial economists; see, for example, Bodie and Shoven (1983).

Bulow is aware that the promised pension will rise if the employee's final-average salary increases in nominal terms as a result of continued employment. Because pensions in a final-average scheme are based on years of service as well as final-average pay, inflation induces an increase from year to year in the pension promised at retirement that is larger than the inflation rate. Specifically, the linkage to final-average pay causes continued employment to raise the real value of employees' benefits, by preventing inflation from downgrading it. The linkage, in effect, revalues past compensation to the most recent average level.

This analysis seems to imply that, in the presence of inflation, under the typical pension contract, the real compensation provided to the worker in the form of an increment in matured real pension rights increases with the number of years of service. Bulow focuses on this particular and peculiar aspect of the impact of inflation on pension arrangements. He suggests that, if the employer does not fire the worker in order to save himself the growing cost of updating the pension, associated with longer tenure, then one must conclude that that cost should be regarded as incurred in future years as the employee is retained. Therefore, it should not be included in the currently outstanding liabilities, a conclusion justifying the discounting of accrued liabilities at the nominal rather than at the real rate.

But Bulow's approach fails to recognize the multiperiod nature of implicit labor contracts. Employees expect to be rewarded for loyal continuing service, and employers expect to reward them for their loyalty. One of the often-stated and widely recognized goals of pension plans is to reward and encourage employee loyalty. Employees presumably do consider the cost in terms of the ultimate pension reduction before they voluntarily resign to seek employment elsewhere.

But once the employment relationship is viewed in terms of implicit contracts, it is not the case that older workers generally cost the employer more, as Bulow's view would suggest. We suggest, therefore, that Bulow's view is legalistic and swayed by the form rather than the substance of pension arrangements. What matters for the issue at hand is not whether employers have the power to fire workers and thereby freeze their nominal obligation, but whether inflation leads them to significantly greater use of this power. This conclusion is supported by the following considerations. Assume, first, a world without inflation: Then all would presumably agree that a firm's obligation should be measured by discounting currently accrued liabilities at the nominal rate, which, of course, is the same as the real rate. Next, suppose there is steady (neutral) inflation but that the pension rules are such that all pensions are fully indexed: to wages for those who remain employed and to the general price level for those who quit or are fired before retirement. It is apparent that, under these conditions, the liability of the fund must be basically the same as in the absence of inflation. But this clearly means that currently accrued liabilities must be discounted at the same rate as before, namely the real rate.

Next, suppose that the pensions of those who are fired or separated for other reasons are not indexed, but suppose, at the same time, that, in fact, nobody is separated. In this case the cash flows confronting the pension fund are identical to those of the previous two cases. It would, therefore, seem appropriate again to discount the accrued liabilities at the real rate and to reject Bulow's prescription of discounting them at the nominal rate, with a drastic decline in the assessed liabilities of the fund. Of course, in reality there will be some separations. However, in the absence of evidence that inflation has brought about a radical increase in the dismissal of older workers or in the relation between wage rate and age, the best way to handle the problem is to apply nominal discounting only to the liabilities accrued for those who have left. But for those who are working, accrued liabilities would be discounted at the same real rate as without inflation, although some allowance should also be made for the prospective rate of attrition. In addition, of course, allowance should also be made for the fact that the pension, once it begins, tends to remain fixed in nominal terms. Note that because of the two "nonneutralities" just mentioned, inflation does tend somewhat to reduce pension liabilities resulting from a given contract, but nowhere as severely as implied by Bulow's recommended approach.

To conclude, although Bulow's argument is ingenious and stimulating, his conclusion that pensions, based on past service, should be discounted at the nominal rate must be rejected on factual and practical grounds. To a first approximation, and abstracting from changes in real wages, the nominal liabilities at any point in time of a final-average plan are in the nature of real liabilities and therefore should be discounted at the real rate.

SUMMARY

In a world of rational investors and financial institutions, corporate managers should analyze investment opportunities either by discounting the relevant nominal flows at an appropriate nominal rate or by discounting the corresponding real flows at the corresponding real rate. Capital budgeting analyses are complicated by inflation because of the following sources of real effects: taxes, debt, and other long-term contracts. An estimate of the securities markets' expectation of inflation is usually needed in order to implement either the real-real or the nominal-nominal approach. A comparison of the manager's expectation of inflation with the markets' can provide important implications for investment and the desired maturity structure of debt financing.

An examination of the effects of inflation on earnings-price (E/P) ratios provides impressive evidence that the world is not one of rational investors. Inflation appears, through its effects on nominal interest rates, to increase irrationally E/P ratios, with the resulting effect of raising the real cost of equity capital, as well as perhaps the real cost of debt. There is reason to suspect, however, that these effects will prove to be transitory, and managers may want to consider investment and financing decisions that would benefit their shareholders in the event of a decline in E/P ratios.

Inflation has important implications for final-average pension plans. To a first approximation, the liabilities of such plans are real in nature, rather than nominal. They should be valued as such, and managers of assets of such plans should, accordingly, consider investing, to some extent, in an inflation-hedged fashion.

Notes

1. Let $\$x$ be the nominal and x the real forecasted flow for next period: then, consistency requires $x = \$x/(1 + p)$. Using the nominal-nominal approach, the PV is:

$$\frac{\$x}{1+R} = \frac{\$x}{(1+r)(1+p)} = \frac{x}{1+r}$$

and the last expression corresponds to the real-real calculation.

2. Earnings should be measured on a fully inflation-adjusted basis, a concept discussed at length in the next section.
3. Specifically, it is shown in Modigliani (1982), (1983) that, abstracting from the effect of dividend policy and assuming that the present value of the capital gain tax is not appreciably different from zero, the cost of capital to a levered firm can be expressed as:

$$\rho = \rho^* \left(1 - l\frac{D}{V}\right),\ l = \frac{R}{\rho^*}(\tau_c - \tau_p)$$

Here, ρ^* measures the required return for an unlevered firm with the same risk characteristics, and τ_p is the average "marginal" personal tax rate, which may be taken as appreciably smaller than τ_c.

4. The tax advantage would exist even if the real rate rose with inflation enough to maintain unchanged the after-personal-tax real rate.
5. Why many corporations, in effect, voluntarily pay taxes on inventory profits must be accounted a great mystery. The usual argument is that corporate managers are reluctant to report lower profits using LIFO than would be shown using FIFO or average cost. But strong evidence exists that investors are not fooled by this reported earnings effect (Sunder (1975)).
6. Much recent merger activity involving acquisitions financed by cash has been based on the idea that the stock market has been undervaluing assets.
7. Black (1980) discusses tax reasons favoring pension plan investments in debt rather than equity securities.

REFERENCES

Bierman, H. Jr. *Financial Management and Inflation*. New York: The Free Press, 1981.

Black, F. "The Tax Consequences of Long-Run Pension Policy." *Financial Analysts Journal* (July-August 1980), pp. 21–28.

Bloom, R., P. T. Elgers, J. R. Haltiner, and W. H. Hawthorne. "Inflation Gains and Losses on Monetary Items: An Empirical Test." *Journal of Business Finance and Accounting* (Winter 1980), pp. 603–18.

Bodie, Z. "Common Stocks as a Hedge Against Inflation." *Journal of Finance* (May 1976), pp. 459–70.

——— and J. B. Shoven. "Introduction to Financial Aspects of the U.S. Pension System." In *Financial Aspects of the United States Pension System*. ed. Z. Bodie and J. B. Shoven. Chicago: University of Chicago Press, 1983.

Boeckh, J. A. and R. T. Coghlan, eds. *The Stock Market and Inflation*. Homewood, Ill.: Dow Jones-Irwin, 1982.

Brealey, R. and S. Myers. *Principles of Corporate Finance*. New York: McGraw-Hill, 1981.

Bulow, J. "The Effect of Inflation on the Private Pension System." National Bureau of Economic Research Working Paper No. C103, March 1981.

Carr, J. L. and P. J. Halpern. "Interest Rate Deductibility and Effective Tax Rates." *Financial Analysts Journal* (May-June 1981), pp. 71–72.

Chen, A. "Uncertain Inflation and Optimal Corporate Investment Decisions." In *Handbook of Financial Economics*. ed. J. L. Bicksler. Amsterdam: North-Holland Publishing Company, 1979, pp. 243–56.

——— and J. A. Boness. "Effects of Uncertain Inflation on the Investment and Financing Decisions of a Firm." *Journal of Finance* (May 1975), pp. 469–83.

Cooley, P. L., R. L. Roenfeldt, and It-K. Chew. "Capital Budgeting Procedures Under Inflation." *Financial Management* (Winter 1975), pp. 18–27.

Fama, E. F. "Stock Returns, Real Activity, Inflation, and Money." *American Economic Review* (September 1981), pp. 545–65.

Feldstein, M. "Inflation and the Stock Market." *American Economic Review* (December 1980), pp. 839–47.

——— and L. H. Summers. "Inflation and the Taxation of Capital Income in the Corporate Sector." *National Tax Journal* (December 1979), pp. 445–70.

French, K. R., R. S. Ruback, and G. W. Schwert. "Effects of Nominal Contracting on Stock Returns." *Journal of Political Economy* (February 1983), pp. 70–96.

Friedman, B. M. "Price Inflation, Portfolio Choice, and Nominal Interest Rates." *American Economic Review* (March 1980), pp. 32–48.

Friend, I. and J. Hasbrouck. "The Effect of Inflation of the Profitability and Valuation of U.S. Corporations." In *Saving, Investment, and Capital Markets in an Inflationary Economy*. ed. M. Sarnat and G. P. Szego. Cambridge, Mass.: Ballinger, 1982, pp. 37–119.

Geske, R. and R. Roll. "The Fiscal and Monetary Linkage Between Stock Returns and Inflation." *Journal of Finance* (March 1983), pp. 1–33.

Gonedes, N. J. "Evidence on the 'Tax Effects' of Inflation under Historical Cost Accounting Methods." *Journal of Business* (April 1981), pp. 227–70.

Gordon, M. J. "The Impact of Real Factors and Inflation on the Performance of the U.S. Stock Market From 1960 to 1980." *Journal of Finance* (May 1983), pp. 553–69.

Gordon, R. H. "Inflation, Taxation and Corporate Behavior." Paper presented at National Bureau of Economic Research Conference on Inflation and Financial Markets, May 1981.

Hochman, S. and O. Palmon. "The Irrelevance of Capital Structure for the Impact of Inflation on Investment." *Journal of Finance* (June 1983), pp. 785–94.

Jaffe, J. F. and G. Mandelker. "The 'Fisher Effect' for Risky Assets: An Empirical Investigation." *Journal of Finance* (May 1976), pp. 447–58.

Lintner, J. "Inflation and Common Stock Prices in a Cyclical Context." *Annual Report*, National Bureau of Economic Research, 1973, pp. 23–36.

Malkiel, B. G. "The Capital Formation Problem in the United States." *Journal of Finance* (May 1979), pp. 291–306.

Miller, M. H. "Debt and Taxes." *Journal of Finance* (May 1977), pp. 261–75.

Modigliani, F. "Debt, Dividend Policy, Taxes, Inflation and Market Valuation." *Journal of Finance* (May 1982), pp. 255–73.

________. "Debt, Dividend Policy, Taxes, Inflation, and Market Valuation: Erratum." *Journal of Finance* (June 1983), pp. 1041–42.

________ and R. A. Cohn. "Inflation, Rational Valuation and the Market." *Financial Analysts Journal* (March-April 1979), pp. 24–44.

________. "Inflation and the Stock Market." In *The Stock Market and Inflation*. ed. J. A. Boeckh and R. T. Coghlan. Homewood, Ill.: Dow Jones-Irwin, 1982, pp. 97–117.

________ and D. R. Lessard, eds. *New Mortgage Designs for Stable Housing in an Inflationary Environment*. Conference Series No. 14, Federal Reserve Bank of Boston, 1975.

________ and M. Miller. "The Cost of Capital, Corporation Finance and the Theory of Investment." *American Economic Review* (June 1958), pp. 261–97.

Munnell, A. H. *The Economics of Private Pensions*. Washington, D.C.: The Brookings Institution, 1982.

Myers, S. C. and N. S. Majluf. "Stock Issues and Investment Policy When Firms Have Information That Investors Do Not Have." Alfred P. Sloan School of Management Working Paper No. 1258–82, Massachusetts Institute of Technology, July 1982.

Naugle, D. G. "Accounting for Inflation in Capital Decisions." Unpublished S.M. thesis, Massachusetts Institute of Technology, 1980.

Nelson, C. R. "Inflation and Rates of Return on Common Stocks." *Journal of Finance* (May 1976), pp. 471–83.

Nichols, W. D. and M. H. Morris. "The Rate of Return Assumption: Insights from the New FASB Statement No. 36 Disclosures." *Financial Analysts Journal* (September-October 1982), pp. 10–15.

Pearce, D. K. "The Impact of Inflation on Stock Prices." *Economic Review* Federal Reserve Bank of Kansas City, March 1982, pp. 3–18.

Rappaport, A. and R. A. Taggart, Jr. "Evaluation of Capital Expenditure Proposals Under Inflation." *Financial Management* (Spring 1982), pp. 5–13.

Sinai, A. and P. Rathjens. "Deficits, Interest Rates, and the Economy." Data Resources Economic Studies Series, No. 113, June 1983.

Summers, L. H. "Inflation and the Valuation of Corporate Equities." National Bureau of Economic Research Working Paper No. 824, December 1981.

———. "The Nonadjustment of Nominal Interest Rates: A Study of the Fisher Effect." In *Macroeconomics, Prices, and Quantities: Essays in Memory of Arthur M. Okun*. ed. J. Tobin. Washington, D.C.: The Brookings Institution, 1983.

Sunder, S. "Accounting Changes in Inventory Valuation." *Accounting Review* (April 1975), pp. 305–15.

von Furstenberg, G. M. "Corporate Investment: Does Market Valuation Matter in the Aggregate?" *Brookings Papers on Economic Activity* No. 2 (1977), pp. 347–97.

Weston, J. F. and M. B. Goudzwaard. "Financial Policies in an Inflationary Environment." In *Treasurer's Handbook*. ed. J. F. Weston and M. B. Goudzwaard. Homewood, Ill.: Dow Jones-Irwin, 1976, pp. 20–42.

14

Comments on the Modigliani and Cohn Paper and Inflation and Corporate Financial Management

Richard Karl Goeltz*
Vice President Finance
Joseph E. Seagram & Sons, Inc.

Comments on the Modigliani and Cohn Paper and Inflation and Corporate Financial Management

COMMENTS ON THE MODIGLIANI AND COHN PAPER

The most provocative aspect of the Modigliani and Cohn (M-C) presentation is the section "Inflation and the Valuation of Common Stocks," wherein they repeat their 1979 argument[1] that equities have not provided a hedge against inflation because investors make "Two errors in valuing corporate stock as a result of inflation causing nominal interest rates to exceed real rates. First, investors capitalize earnings at a rate that follows the nominal rate rather than the appropriate real one. Second, investors capitalize adjusted earnings rather than true earnings."[2] These assertions are startling, given the central position accorded efficient markets in modern financial thought.

Sherlock Holmes in *The Sign of Four* said "When you have eliminated the impossible, whatever remains, however improbable, must be the truth." That statement underlies the M-C thesis. They believe that, over the past 20-odd years, American executives succcessfully preserved true corporate earnings, i.e., reported income, adjusted to reflect underdepreciation, incorrect specification of cost of goods sold, and the benefits from a net debtor position. True profits were maintained, moreover, without any increased risk. Therefore, if share prices have not kept pace with inflation, the market must have been irrational in its comprehension and valuation of real earnings. I wonder, though, if M-C have eliminated the "impossible" as Mr. Holmes did. Alternative explanations seem more persuasive than reliance on a conclusion of persistent, pervasive irrationality by investors.

The skill of M-C and the respect with which they are held in the academic community are demonstrated amply by the many comments their proposition elicited. Any paper which creates so much controversy must be a valuable contribution to the literature of the field. I shall not review all the criticisms and rebuttals, many of which are cited in their own presentation. (See, however, items in footnote 3, *inter alia.*) Rather, I shall emphasize a few issues which are particularly troublesome to me.

My comments are of three types: selective irrationality on the part of investors, prospective real profits, and increased risk with a concomitant effect on the capitalization rate for earnings. These should be viewed within the context of Figure 1 of M-C's paper.[4] By visual inspection, it is apparent that although the earnings-price ratio and inflation rate tracked well beginning in 1972, prior to that time the relationship was not close. From 1963 to 1971, the earnings-price ratio meandered about a flat line of roughly 5.7%, while inflation intensified throughout the period. Rapidly rising prices historically have been deleterious for common stock performance, at least over the short run, but additional factors seem to have depressed returns further during the 1970s.

Selective irrationality

Inflation artificially enhances reported corporate profits because both depreciation and the cost of goods are understated in an economic sense. Investors recognize this distortion and adjust a company's expenses to compensate when valuing its shares. M-C argue that this analysis is incomplete, however. They state that corporations as a group benefit from a net debtor position. The economic gain from the erosion by inflation of monetary liabilities must be added when calculating true profits, an observation made by several researchers in the United States[5] and United Kingdom[6] over the past few years. This point, by the way, has not been buried in academic journals with limited distribution among the investing and general public. The subject was discussed widely in the United Kingdom in 1976 during the debate on inflation accounting.[7] How could the investment community have assiduously ignored the evidence of these studies?

This apparent disregard by investors of total economic income is particularly perplexing in light of the numerous studies of the effect of accounting principles on share prices. Most of these investigations conclude that investors pierce the veil of bookkeeping and focus on true profits. "The evidence is consistent that the market does not respond to earnings increases caused by cosmetic changes in accounting policies."[8]

For example, one paper demonstrated that share prices rose for firms which switched from FIFO inventory accounting to LIFO. The market rewarded a rational economic decision which lowered taxes and consequently improved cash flow, even though reported profits declined.[9] A subsequent, more detailed investigation by Ricks[10] using a matched pair design and a larger sample found that the security returns for firms which adopted LIFO did decline initially compared with those which did not change. However, this penalty was eliminated within 12 months. If rational decisions are not recompensed, at least they are not punished.

Examinations of other types of accounting changes, e.g., switching from deferral to the flow-through method for the investment tax credit and from full-cost to successful efforts by oil exploration companies, also led to the conclusion that the market is not misled by legerdemain. In fact, attempts to bolster earnings by resorting to more liberal accounting principles tend to reduce share prices. Investors may believe, probably correctly, that an artificial enhancement was deemed necessary by management to mask a serious, fundamental deterioration in a company's prospects.

Finally, the effects of the implementation of FAS 8 have been scrutinized. Large and often unanticipated swings in earnings occurred because of this accounting standard, but researchers have not detected a depressing effect on the share prices of multinational firms as a result of the reported increased volatility.[11]

If investors are sophisticated enough (i) to deflate reported income to compensate for underdepreciation and inventory holding gains, and (ii) to disregard accounting changes which affect the level and stability of reported profits but not real cash flows, can we accept M-C's assertion that the benefit from a net liability position is persistently ignored and total true profits capitalized at an incorrect rate? This failure by investors is especially puzzling inasmuch as FAS 33 requires disclosure of the gain or loss on net monetary items. Why would market participants be rational in some aspects of their decisions about equity investments and uniformly myopic or blind in other respects? This purported asymmetry of investor perception is disturbing.

Prospective real profits

Under traditional financial theory, equities constitute a hedge against inflation if, and only if, corporations themselves are able to preserve actual and anticipated real income and profitability without accepting a higher degree of risk. Assume temporarily that corporations were not subject to greater uncertainty in the 1970s although, for reasons enumerated in the next section, I believe they were with a concomitant adjustment in the earnings-price ratio to reflect this exposure. Then, the decline in inflation-adjusted share prices may be attributable to forces which depressed current and, more important, expected real corporate earnings. Equity investments would have performed poorly because a constant multiplier was applied to lower anticipated profits.

A number of developments during the past decade contributed to investors' pessimism about corporate prospects. First, the past 10 to 15 years hardly have been propitious for business in the United States. The litany of shocks is extensive: two sharp increases in the price of fuel; huge capital expenditures to comply with EPA requirements; the influx into the labor force of a massive number of new entrants, many of whom had little training; productivity gains well below the historical norm; and social unrest. Is it reasonable to believe that in such an adverse environment business could, did, and was forecast to function as profitably as before?

Second, until recently, the role of government has been expanding regularly in the United States and other developed nations. Using OECD data, general government expenditure as a percentage of GNP rose in this country from 29 percent in 1965 to 35 percent by the mid-1970s.[12] If labor had accepted a reduced share of national output, profits or the return to capital would not necessarily have been dampened by greater government involvement. However, evidence exists that for the United States and many other countries, employees were able in the late 1960s to secure for themselves a larger portion of GNP.[13] Total compensation of workers as a percentage of GNP in the United States increased from approximately 58 percent in the early 1960s to 60 to 61 percent throughout the 1970s.[14] A two percentage point change may seem small but, when applied to total output, the number is large absolutely and relative to corporate profits. It is true that real per capita income declined occasionally during the 1970s in the United States, but the real income of the family or economic unit did not fall. In many cases, the earnings of one were supplemented by those of a second individual. (Of course, to the extent that households are net creditors, the loss as a result of inflation should be subtracted from their reported wage income. The adjustment for the monetary erosion, if any, could negate the apparent expansion of labor's share of real national income.)

With both government and labor accounting for more of GNP, is it not a logical inference that the amount available to capital must have declined? Some statistical series may indicate that, under certain definitions, real corporate profits have been maintained, but how can these data be reconciled with enlarged roles for government and labor?

Third, the depth and breadth of social welfare coverage have grown materially during the past generation. Entitlement programs have expanded more rapidly than the economy. The unfunded pension liability of the U.S. government for its civilian and military employees is enormous. All benefits must be funded with taxes, today or tomorrow. Business will be forced eventually to contribute to financing them. Perhaps the stock market is recognizing the future claims which society will impose on corporations to the detriment of profits.

A fourth point is related closely to the previous one. Just as nations have provided more comprehensive social programs, corporations have done so on the microeconomic level by substantially increasing medical and pension and other postretirement benefits. The ratio of pretax profits per dollar of pension contribution has deteriorated substantially over the past 10 years. Throughout the past decade, vested benefits consistently exceeded pension assets.[15]

It is not sufficient to consider only the data in published financial statements because, in many cases, the ultimate costs of corporate obligations for pensions and other postretirement benefits have not been recognized fully. Greenwich Research Associates reported that, in 1980, the total unfunded pension liability for the nation's top 1,000 corporations was $76 billion.[16] This constitutes a real future expense for companies which, like that of national social programs, will be incurred. If these costs had been treated by American industry in an actuarially correct manner and recorded, both reported profits and the "true income" defined by M-C would have been sharply reduced. M-C allude to this point by criticizing conventional accounting treatment which assumes no progression in compensation but uses a nominal discount rate to compute accrued benefits for disclosure under FAS 35 and 36.[17]

The acerbic, agitated, and frightened response by some companies to the FASB's preliminary views on employers' accounting for pensions and other postretirement benefits is perhaps more telling support of my position than any quantification of American corporations' pension costs and unfunded pension liabilities. A survey in July 1983 by the National Association of Accountants showed that officers of a significant number of large firms believe, "The new standard would require renegotiation of loan agreements to prevent a technical default. . . . Such a standard would adversely affect their credit ratings. . . . Would make them less attractive to investors."[18]

I suggest that the stock market has been discounting future profits for the burden that generous pension and postretirement benefits represent.

One study tested this hypothesis: "The recognition of these (unfunded vested) liabilities has lowered the average share value by about seven percent."[19] This reduction seems rather minor. If total unfunded liabilities, instead of only those related to vested benefits, had been used, surely the effect would have been more pronounced.

Before leaving the topic of pensions, three final observations are in order. All refer to factors which will harm future corporate profits.

1. Although the liabilities are monetary ones, the benefit to the obligor corporation will not be of the same magnitude as the gain arising from fixed-rate long-term debt. The pension right is established in nominal terms upon retirement and does decline in real terms thereafter as a result of inflation. However, for defined benefit plans based on final wages, which have become more prevalent, the pension obligation for the firm rises more or less in tandem with wages which, in turn, can be expected to move pari passu with inflation. One must postulate a going concern, which implies that pension costs will grow and all promises of pension rights, fully vested or not, must be met. As M-C acknowledge, an assumption of wages and salaries tending to keep pace with the price level has a profound effect on projected pension benefits. I agree with their statement, "The pension fund liability is a real liability."[20]
2. Important legal distinctions do exist between vested and unvested benefits, and management could void unvested benefits by terminating the plan. This technical right, is not, however, a basis for disregarding total unfunded pension liabilities when valuing the shares of ongoing corporations. M-C make just this point in their criticism of Bulow's argument.
3. If corporations gain from net debtor positions, then their creditors suffer losses. To the extent that private pension plans own substantial amounts of long-term debt, the real value of the corpus of assets is diminished by inflation and must be replenished, a step that implies greater corporate contributions, i.e., expenses, in the future. To give perspective to the magnitude of the exposure to erosion, at the end of 1982 private pension financial assets were some $340 billion. Bonds

represented approximately $123 billion or 36 percent of these investments.[21]

Fifth, M-C cite a study by Naugle,[22] who concluded that roughly one half of major corporations fail to treat inflation rationally when making capital budgeting decisions. It seems remarkable that, even though investments were based on invalid criteria and evaluated incorrectly, the results of these expenditures were somehow rewarding economically for corporations as they must have been if the assumption of maintenance of true profits is valid.

A sixth factor also tends to depress the real worth of the firm. With inflation, net working capital must expand with nominal sales. The cash drain attributable to the incremental investment in working capital must be subtracted from the net present value of operating cash flows to obtain the real worth of the firm. As Lintner wrote, "Even if all the impairments of real returns in times of inflation were completely eliminated by the use of replacement cost depreciation and LIFO accounting for inventory, and even if real profit margins and rates of growth in unit sales are always maintained, a company's relative dependence on outside financing will *necessarily be higher* the higher the rate of inflation, whether expected or unanticipated. Moreover, this greater relative dependence on outside financing required by an *increase* in realized inflation during any period will necessarily *reduce* the value of outstanding equity, and consequently will reduce the real rate of return realized in equities."[23] (Emphasis in the original)

M-C argue that this incremental borrowing to finance working capital is not detrimental to the firm; indeed, without it, there would not be economic gains from a net liability position. However, one may legitimately inquire whether the "greater relative dependence on outsiders" is an unmitigated benefit. Heightened uncertainty is entailed, the subject of the next section.

Increased risk

Let us accept the premise that industrial corporations as a group have net monetary liabilities which enable them to maintain real profits. With inflation, one component of interest represents a repayment of principal and liquidation of debt must be recognized when measuring corporate income.

The M-C case for greater corporate leverage would seem to be even strengthened if the actual behavior of the cost of money is considered. A recent study[24] demonstrated that real interest rates, particularly those on long-term instruments, tend to lag inflation and, in fact, often were negative. The higher the rate at which prices increase, the more likely this is to occur. Purchasers of bonds historically have not fully anticipated inflation; nominal rates of interest were accepted that have not always provided an ex-post real rate of return, even on a pretax basis. This research appears to favor strongly a policy of borrowing as much as possible. As a corporate executive explained, "The use of debt always improves the return on equity as long as the nominal return on investment exceeds the nominal interest rate. But the desirability of using debt increases as inflation increases."[25]

It should be noted that, although issuers of bonds may have benefited historically from inflation, short-term, or more generally floating rate, debt has become a larger component of companies' liability structures. The ratio of bank loans, commerical paper, etc. to corporate bonds climbed from 0.72 in 1971 to 1.30 in 1982.[26] It is questionable whether floating-rate borrowing provides any benefit to the borrower during a period of inflation. Although somewhat dated now, a study concluded, "The substantial variation in nominal bill rates during the 1953–71 period seems to be due entirely to variations in expected inflation; in other words, the expected real returns on bills seem to be constant during the period."[27] M-C agree that real rates on short-term instruments do not vary materially with inflation. Moving from history to the future, the deregulation of the financial services industry will virtually guarantee that a full inflation premium is incorporated in the cost of short-term money. Thus, can holding gains on short-term debt be realized consistently?

The question of valuation cannot be restricted to the level of corporate earnings; it must embrace their quality and certainty. During the last decade, business has had to deal with unprecedented volatility in commodity prices and interest and foreign exchange rates. Making capital spending decisions and establishing labor contracts, leases, and long-term purchase or supply agreements became much more difficult and fraught with uncertainty. I am not suggesting that inflation is the cause of wide fluctuations, but it certainly is associated with them. M-C recognize this salient point and remark, "Risk and inflation may go together because they are both related to real shocks . . . if inflation and risk go together, they are impossible to distinguish."[28] Yet, while acknowledging the existence of increased uncertainty and its probable depressing effects on share prices, they seem unwilling to ascribe the poor performance of the stock market to heightened risk.

Just as some macroeconomic developments have created a less

congenial general environment for business, within individual firms greater risk exists now than years ago. A growing nominal debt level may yield benefits to corporations and may even be requisite if true profits are to be preserved with inflation. It also implies, however, increased exposure for the corporation to bankruptcy, to forced abridgment of operations, to foregoing attractive investments, and to potential discomfort in general. These problems must be recognized and have been quantified, to some extent.[29]

The danger of excessive debt always exists but becomes more acute when prices are rising rapidly. As noted before, an element of interest expense is amortization of debt; it constitutes a mandatory sinking fund payment which reduces financial flexibility and reserves. The firm's continued existence at management's desired level of operation becomes dependent upon external sources of funds. Cash flow strains can easily occur.

I would emphasize the obvious here. The gains from being a net debtor must actually be realized in some manner if liquidity is to be obtained. Additional debt must be issued or assets sold with, parenthetically, a cash tax on the gain. Either step may be difficult or impossible to consummate. This uncertainty surely represents another element of risk. I would argue that, because of it, one cannot legitimately add the unrealized gains from a net liability position to reported corporate income on a dollar for dollar basis. If I am correct, then the true profits used by M-C and others may be seriously overstated.

Three analogies may be instructive. Many exploration and oil field service companies and their bankers incorrectly believed that the price of hydrocarbons would rise inexorably and provide the cash flow to amortize loans. Similarly, the commodity boom of the mid-1970s led many farmers to borrow heavily to acquire land and equipment. Overproduction and recession dampened both demand for and prices of agricultural output. During the late 1970s, many homeowners refinanced their dwellings, assuming substantial mortgages to maintain or enhance their standard of living; the proliferation of defaults has been reported widely. The unfortunate experiences of many demonstrate that actual or anticipated purchasing power, whether of oil reserves, agricultural land, or holding gains from being a net debtor, must be converted into spendable cash if it is to have any real worth and be able to support ongoing operations.

Leverage does offer benefits, but a limit clearly exists for both the corporation as a whole and its constituents. Material risks are assumed by the borrower as debt expands in relation to the equity base and interest expense grows compared with earnings before financial charges and taxes. Uncertainty rises, even if the debt-equity ratio remains unchanged in real terms.

Granted, a strong bias toward secular inflation exists worldwide for many reasons. Nevertheless, there are recurrent times for every economy when the rate of price increase slows dramatically compared with immediately preceding periods, e.g., 1983–84. Then the burden of debt, particularly fixed-rate obligations, can become crushing. High nominal/low (or negative) real rates of interest become high nominal/high real rates. Of course, variable-rate debt can mitigate the problem, but recent experience demonstrates that the amelioration is not always full or prompt.

Disinflation tends to be associated with reduced economic activity.[30] Unit volume suffers, compounding the difficulty for companies which are constrained in their ability to raise prices. For American industry, the problem has been exacerbated over the past few years. A strong dollar, attributable *inter alia* to high real interest rates, has led to heightened competition from imports, which limit both volume gains and freedom in pricing. Greater leverage raises the company's breakeven point and, consequently, the exposure to slack demand for its products.

In theory, the attractiveness of borrowing becomes greater with inflation, but a heavier debt burden carries a cost due to the possibilities of:

1. Downgrading by rating agencies with both a resultant increase in the interest rate and a decrease in the certainty of availability of funds;
2. Violations of loan covenants and subjection to upward rate adjustments by lenders when relief is sought from technical default;
3. Unwillingness on the part of bankers and commercial paper buyers to roll over maturing loans and to extend new ones;
4. Bankruptcy.

These potential negative consequences cannot be disregarded.

A somewhat less obvious exposure is also entailed. Under accepted financial theory, in equilibrium, "The tax advantage to using debt is just offset at the margin by the additional agency and possible bankruptcy costs as a result of the extra debt."[31] One of the few immutable rules of business is that a company must preserve its financial flexibility. In a world of steady, fully anticipated inflation, perhaps this dictum would not be more important than in an environment of stable prices. However, inflation tends to accelerate or decelerate and cannot be fully anticipated. The rewards for maintaining freedom of maneuver are likely to be great when there are rapid changes in rates of interest and price increases. A company which has maximized borrowing to protect itself against inflation will have consumed most or all of the desirable reservoir of financial flexibility.

Risk, whether attributable to exogenous factors such as greater volatility in credit, commodities, and foreign exchange markets or to higher leverage for firms that sought to benefit from a larger net liability position, demonstrably became greater during the 1970s. The earnings-price ratio must have risen in response. I am not at all persuaded that tests comparing the relative performance of high- and low-beta stocks address the issue correctly. M-C also admit that these studies may not be a valid measure of increased uncertainty for business.

Concluding comments on "inflation and the valuation of common stocks"

My overall assessment of the M-C hypothesis concerning share valuation is that it contains an element of truth. Inefficiency probably does exist in the stock market, but not to the degree they suggest. The piecemeal, or selective, irrationality of investors is disturbing and sufficient in itself to call the thesis into question. The real factors tending to depress anticipated corporate profits and the increased macro- and microeconomic risks endured by the firm during the past 15 years must have contributed significantly to the failure of share prices to provide insulation against inflation. To their credit, M-C do acknowledge the negative implications of these items but do not seem to give full weight to their importance. The forces may be difficult or impossible to test statistically, but our inability should not lead to a conclusion that they are not germane.

Obiter dicta

There is one aspect of the academic debate on the M-C work cited in their paper which especially merits comment. They say, "The effect of inflation is to raise the real cost of debt as well as equity."[32] This is purported to occur because investors capitalize only part of the firm's true earnings. Are the costs of equity and debt distorted to the same extent? If they are not, then the effect of inflation should vary as a function of leverage. Moreover, evidence exists that nominal long-term rates of interest tend to lag overall price increases, depressing the real cost of borrowing and sometimes causing it to be negative. Thus, a leveraged firm should fare better when inflation accelerates than when prices are changing at a constant rate.

Summers,[33] whose work M-C reject, finds empirical evidence that leveraged firms benefit from inflation, just as theory would lead us to expect. Simlarly, Brainard, Shoven, and Weiss conclude, "Contrary to the M-C hypothesis, firms with interest-intensive cash flows and high debt-equity ratios do not appear to have been especially undervalued in the market in the 1970s."[34] Earlier investigations of both U.S. and U.K. firms also support the proposition that net debtor corporations gain.[35] The evidence regarding the advantages of being a borrower is so mixed that a definitive conclusion cannot be reached now.

Moving from the section on stock valuation, I have a final comment on the M-C paper. They suggest that "Long-term but variable—or floating—rate debt instruments should prove to be an appealing investment for pension funds."[36] I cannot reconcile this proposal with either their work cited here or the historical record of investment returns. In the section, "Implications for Investment and Financing," they state, "The undervaluation implied by the (M-C) hypothesis will tend to disappear over time."[37] As inflation and interest rates stabilize, or even better, actually fall, investors in common stocks should earn an "unexpectedly high nominal rate of return."

Viewing the historical experience, the studies of the United States with which I am familiar, such as Fisher's and Lorie's in 1964 and 1968[38] and Ibbotson's and Sinquefield's in 1977,[39] demonstrated that, on balance and over time, common stocks offer returns superior to those achieved by short-term instruments and bonds. Inasmuch as the time horizon of a pension fund is long-term, equities, not floating-rate debt, should be the preferred investment. The greater ex-ante and ex-post period-to-period variability in the rate of return on equities can easily be tolerated by a pension fund and should be accepted to obtain superior performance.

THE CORPORATE RESPONSE TO INFLATION

Turning from the M-C paper, I shall not enumerate comprehensively the tactics employed by companies for coping with inflation. Those lists are available in myriad articles and books published over the past 10 years by academicians, executives, and consultants.[40] Seagram prepared in 1974 its own check list of the problems entailed by rapidly rising prices and responses to them.

Rather, I shall cite, somewhat eclectically, seven topics or facets of them that do not seem to have been discussed completely in the literature. These are: pricing, compensation for executives, working capital management, prompt payment discounts, management control systems, debt, and insurance. To the extent that they concern the balance sheet, the emphasis generally is on the asset side; M-C and most other academic investigators focus almost entirely on liabilities. Surely, the effect of inflation on the productivity of a firm's working capital and plant, the ability to pass on cost increases, and the cash requirements of maintaining an ongoing business must be germane. Some of my comments apply to the corporation overall, whereas others are more relevant to foreign affiliates of multinational companies.

First, it is axiomatic that *pricing policies* must be established to ensure that the firm's economic value is preserved. Sir John Hicks wrote, "Income . . . may be defined as the maximum which the individual can spend this week and still expect to be able to spend the same amount in *real terms* in each ensuing week."[41] Applying this proposition, *mutadis mutandis,* to the firm, how can the corporation price its products to avoid consuming itself? How can one escape the problem of a Brazilian retailing executive who said, "We have difficulty now when you (sic) sell the product, the money you (sic) get is sometimes not enough to buy more of the product next month. We are subject to mistakes because prices change so often, so quickly that we make a lot of mistakes pricing (our) products."[42]

Seagram holds large stocks of maturing inventory that must age for up to 21 years before sale. For us, setting prices with reference to historical costs would be suicidal. The proper specification of cost of goods sold to ensure ongoing operations is not simply an appealing refinement in the financial reporting system; it is a necessity.

Seagram adopted LIFO in the United States in 1941 and has done so in all jurisdictions where permitted. As inflationary pressures intensified during the past decade, it became evident that simply using replacement value was insufficient. In 1974, the management accounting system was changed for all affiliates. The cost of goods was redefined as the current replacement cost of inventory plus a capital charge which is a function of the optimum age in years of the maturing inventory multiplied by the rate of interest. All values are, of course, in dollar terms, not local currency. Thus, the general manager of an affiliate is able to understand readily the selling price which must be charged to provide funds sufficient to restore the depleted unit to inventory.

There is a serious limitation on the usefulness of our procedure. We may recognize the effect of inflation, but many of our competitors do not. In too many cases, they seem to disregard inflation and to price their products with reference to historical inventory costs. Such a policy implies liquidation over time as insufficient cash is generated on an after-tax basis to fund the continuing operations of the business.

Even when competitive pressures limit our ability to charge an economic amount, the replacement cost plus capital charge inventory accounting system serves valuable purposes. It dispels money illusion; prevents the fallacious recognition of inventory gains; and indicates how well an affiliate, a manger, and an individual brand are performing in real terms. Senior officers are alerted to those products being sold at inadequate prices and, thereby, eroding corporate assets. More detailed, comprehensive studies can be made to determine whether the substandard performance can be rectified and options are available to achieve a real economic return.

Seagram's inventory position is atypical. However, our approach, which emphasizes the need to price products in light of the cash needs of an ongoing enterprise, has general applicability.

On the topic of prices, a program of regular, small increments is preferable to one of large, infrequent adjustments. The psychological shock for consumers is reduced; less resistance is likely to be encountered. Production scheduling is greatly facilitated, permitting longer and smoother runs; savings should be obtained.

Perhaps more important, when the price increases are large and infrequent, customers always seem to have advance knowledge and accelerate purchases at the old price, depriving the seller of the new, higher price. Moreover, stockpiles of excessive inventory are created for the buyer. If the buyer subsequently encounters serious financial difficulty, these surplus goods may be dumped at distress prices, thereby disrupting the market, harming the image of the product, and causing problems for the company's other distributors who are trying to maintain prices.

Second, the role of a *rational executive compensation program* in protecting the firm against inflationary depredation is often overlooked. The professor in my first course in economics said, "There is only one law in economics and that is the law of supply and demand. Everything else is metaphysics." Surely, though, that is a bit too restrictive. Even a cursory view of business allows the existence of a second law: Personal pecuniary rewards motivate the vast majority of businessmen and women. Exhortation alone may be effective in the short term but generally counts for little over the long run. It is then clear that, if the corporation's objective is to realize profits and rates of return measured in real, not nominal, terms, the compensation system must have criteria which emphasize real, not nominal, results. Lamentably, such standards are rarely employed.

Performance of senior executives is customarily judged on the basis of reported earnings, those measured in current dollars.[43] Indeed, some disturbing evidence exists that compensation may not even be a function of nominal returns, much less real ones.[44] To be sure, a few bonus programs, which include such objectives as unit sales and market share, are at least partially responsive to the need to measure achievement in real terms. Even these are seriously vitiated to the extent that real profits are disregarded. Unit volume can usually be increased by cutting prices and raising marketing support.

As long as a company defines standards for salaries, raises, and bonus awards in nominal terms, the maintenance of real income and profitability will be only of secondary interest to executives. As one respected authority said, "Companies may be chasing the wrong bottom line . . . executive compensation systems based on accounting criteria . . . do not accurately reflect changes in a company's economic value."[45]

The need for a remuneration program that rewards real results seems obvious and basic. Yet, this fundamental principle of behavorial science rarely merits comment in articles on managing a firm in an inflationary environment. Corporate seminars on coping with rapidly rising prices will have minimal permanent value unless the education is supported and reinforced by a reward system that focuses on performance measured with inflation expunged.

There is another problem pertaining to compensation which often arises in highly inflationary countries. A well-managed firm will raise its prices continually. This step will cause the commissions paid to sales personnel to grow regularly; their income is tied automatically to inflation. Administrative and production staffs customarily are subject to time-consuming salary review and approval procedures. A gap between the incomes of sales and other employees will emerge and widen. Unless this tendency is recognized and corrected, inequity will be introduced and morale weakened.

Third, working capital control is critically important when inflation exists. The warnings to minimize cash and accounts receivable and to maximize accounts payable are often repeated. *Inventory management* receives less attention. In a stable economy, no rational executive would consider holding surplus stocks and incurring additional financing, warehousing, insurance, handling, and security costs, but such an investment may be fully justified for a company confronting an inflationary spiral. It is one method of responding to rapidly escalating raw material and labor expenses. The costs and benefits of anticipatory purchases of raw materials and of keeping excessive inventory should be analyzed. The tactic should not be rejected summarily. As a colleague in a highly inflationary country states, "I'm not saying holding inventory is a good business practice, but it's a way to stay in business in unfavorable conditions."

I offer three examples of inventory management from Latin America. A very successful Brazilian businessman is fond of giving this explanation for his prosperity: "I am not wealthy enough to sell all of the time." His meaning is self-evident. When, due to price controls, dislocations, or competitive pressure, he is unable to realize an adequate price for his merchandise, it will be withheld from the market. A real asset, inventory, will be retained instead of converting it into a monetary one. The price of the former can be raised subsequently. An account receivable is fixed in nominal terms; its worth will diminish with inflation. The tactic is not restricted to Brazil. It is not uncommon for companies in highly inflationary economies to suspend sales temporarily, waiting until the unit selling price can be raised to cover replacement cost plus a profit margin.

A second illustration, also from Brazil, is extreme. Some of Seagram's largest customers in that country would resell goods at cruzeiro prices equal to the ones at which the items were purchased from us. However, they were selling for cash and paying us in 120 days. The float was invested. The interest income paid for all operating expenses and provided a reasonable profit. With accounts payable to suppliers exceeding the inventory for these large customers who had no accounts receivable themselves, their net investment was negative and return on capital infinite. After some difficulty, we were able to stop this practice.

As a final example of inventory management, one of our Argentine affiliates has developed an effective method of combating competitive pressure while simultaneously preserving the value of working capital. Champagne sales are concentrated during the Christmas season. Orders are taken in July; wine is produced and delivered in October. The customers pay in February but at the then-prevailing price. The affiliate makes sales, places goods in the customers' warehouses, and ensures that the account receivable will be protected from inflation. In essence, the hard asset of inventory is preserved, even though the sale has been consummated.

Fourth, *prompt payment discounts* offered to or by the corporation are an integral component of working capital management. As such, their financial implications for managing accounts receivable and payable must be assessed carefully during inflationary periods. There is, however, another aspect which is often ignored. The foreign subsidiary of a multinational firm often has access to cheaper funds than its suppliers and customers do. When credit is scarce and expensive, the affiliate should consider sharing the benefits of its preferred access to financing by adjusting its use of prompt-payment discounts. Payments to local suppliers could be accelerated, thereby reducing their dependence on higher-cost borrowing. As a quid pro quo, the affiliate can secure the timely delivery of raw materials, a point likely to be particularly important when price controls disrupt the free functioning of the goods markets. Similarly, in dealing with its customers, the affiliate of a multinational may be able to exchange a portion of its borrowing capacity and strength by adjusting credit terms to encourage greater sales efforts from its distributors.

Minimizing accounts receivable and maximizing accounts payable are not categorically the optimum corporate actions, even in a high inflation/high devaluation country. By using prompt payment discounts, the tool of credit can be efficaciously employed. If the corporation can borrow on better terms than others, this resource should not be disregarded. In addition to yielding short-term economic benefits through more secure sources of supply and greater sales, a long-term advantage may be derived from goodwill with suppliers and customers.

Fifth, many U.S. corporations pride themselves on *control*, imposing extensive planning and reporting requirements on the management of subsidiaries. Yet, rapid change is usually endemic in a highly inflationary environment. A premium is placed upon anticipation and flexible, rapid actions which implies that local management must be granted responsibility and wide latitude. Is this delegation compatible with tight, centralized control? Will the corporation that places severe restraint on its overseas personnel be able to attract and retain individuals with the attributes necessary to enable the affiliate to survive and prosper in an inflationary environment? I believe the answer is unequivocally, "No." An alternative approach of setting broad objectives jointly with operating management and giving them full discretion for achievement will be more effective. An implication of this principle is the determination of the few key variables necessary to understand the progress of an affiliate; corporate headquarters will receive information only on these important items and not burden the foreign operation with myriad forms and reports containing largely irrelevant data.

Two general rules for management can be stated. One, the greater the degree of uncertainty—for whatever reason—inherent in a plan, the greater the degree of freedom that must be accorded to local management if they are to be successful. Two, as inflation calls into question the usefulness and validity of long-term plans cast in monetary terms, there is a need to emphasize strategy and real measures of performance.

Sixth, some of my comments on the M-C paper were directed to the overall topic of the *risk element of debt*. Two additional aspects must be raised in discussing the firm's response to inflation.

Although the point is obvious, it is important enough to emphasize. The real rate of interest for a borrower is determined on a company-specific basis. Subtracting the CPI or GNP deflator from the nominal cost of debt gives a meaningless number for most individual firms. Rapidly growing medical costs may raise the price level for the United States as a whole, but the CPI implies nothing about Seagram's ability to charge more for a bottle of Seven Crown or Paul Masson wine.

In conversation, Dr. Modigliani took issue with my position, arguing that a general rise in prices erodes the value of a firm's debt. This diminution in the real value of liabilities occurs irrespective of the borrower's own capability to pass on cost increases. His point is valid but ignores the earning power of assets financed by this debt. If, because of technological obsolescence, foreign competition, general inefficiency, or any other factor, the firm's output cannot be sold at prices which compensate for inflation, then the holding gain from a net monetary liability position becomes somewhat illusory. The replacement cost of the steel industry's assets may be considerably greater than the book value, but few would assert that the former figure is a measure of true worth or an indication of the ability to service debt. As mentioned previously, perhaps too much of the academic investigation of the effects of inflation is directed to liabilities and too little to assets.

Looking beyond the risks of excessive debt for the total corporation, there are also dangers for individual foreign affiliates, particularly those in highly inflationary countries. The conventional wisdom is to borrow heavily in the local currency because rapidly increasing local prices will lead to devaluations, thereby reducing the U.S. dollar value of local debt. In addition, FAS 8-type foreign exchange losses will be reduced. There are a few problems with the proposition. First, for most of the decade of the 1970s, dollar debt was, in fact, less expensive than local borrowing in countries such as Brazil and Mexico. A policy of financing within the country would have caused an economic loss compared with the alternative of U.S. dollar funding. Second, credit crises occur periodically in these nations, which makes local financing virtually unavailable. The parent may then have to decide whether to allow its subsidiary to default, to curtail operations, or to inject financial support at a time dictated by events rather than of its own choosing.

Viewing both the entire corporation and individual affiliates, one cannot state categorically that debt is good. Its advantages must be compared with the true costs and risks. An attempt to optimize leverage may be extremely dangerous. Whether the debt is long or short term, it must be used judiciously. Then, the corporation's financial officers can repeat the comment of a Frenchman who, when asked what he had done during the Reign of Terror after the revolution replied, "I survived."

Seventh, *insurance coverage* must be scrutinized so that if an asset is lost the monetary recovery will be adequate. The secretary of our general manager in Argentina bought a little Fiat at the height of inflation there in the mid-1970s. She insured it fully at first but neglected to adjust the coverage. The automobile was stolen five years later, and she finally collected, after a one-year delay, from the state-owned insurance company. The amount of pesos was sufficient to purchase a new steering wheel.

Perhaps because the risk is so stark in hyperinflationary economies, most executives in them are fully cognizant of the danger of underinsurance. The problem is more likely to develop where the erosion in the value of a currency is gradual. In that environment, protection may become deficient as the policy year progresses, creating an economic loss as a result of insufficient insurance coverage if a claim is made.

Concluding comments on the corporate response to inflation

As Drs. Modigliani and Cohn state, tools which serve corporations well when prices are stable must be reinterpreted and adapted when inflation is virulent. However, there is at least one universal principle. An Argentine colleague says that the fastest way to go bankrupt in his country is to think in peso terms. His admonition applies equally even when inflation is less rampant. One must plan, monitor, control, finance, invest, and function with reference to a stable numeraire, not a standard that erodes.

Notes

1. Modigliani, F. and R. A. Cohn, "Inflation, Rational Valuation and the Market," *Financial Analysts Journal* (March-April, 1979).
2. All quotations from Modigliani and Cohn unless otherwise noted, are from the paper they presented at the Conference and printed above.

3. "Comments on Modigliani-Cohn," *Financial Analysts Journal* (May–June, 1981).

Fama, E. F., "Stock Returns, Real Activity, Inflation, and Money," *American Economic Review* (September, 1981).

Gordon, M. J., "The Impact of Real Factors and Inflation on the Performance of the U.S. Stock Market from 1960 to 1980," *Journal of Finance* (May, 1983).

Feldstein, M., "Inflation and the Stock Market," *American Economic Review* (December, 1980).

4. Modigliani and Cohn (this volume).

5. Kessel, R. A., "Inflation-Caused Wealth Redistribution: A Test of a Hypothesis," *American Economic Review* (March, 1956).

Shoven, J. B. and J. I. Bulow, "Inflation Accounting and Non-Financial Corporate Profits: Financial Assets and Liabilities," *Brookings Papers on Economic Activity*, 1:1976.

Von Furstenberg, G. M. and B. Malkiel, "Financial Analysis in an Inflation Environment," *Journal of Finance* (May, 1977).

6. Moore, B., "Equity Values and Inflation: The Importance of Dividends," *Lloyds Bank Review* (July, 1980). See also a criticism of Moore's position by Lawson and Stark in *Lloyds Bank Review* (January, 1981).

7. Hale, David, "Inflation Accounting and Public Policy Around the World," *Financial Analysts Journal* (September-October, 1978).

8. Abdel-Khalik, A. R. and T. Keller eds., *The Impact of Accounting Research on Practice and Disclosure* (Durham, N.C.: Duke University Press, 1978).

9. Sunder, S., "Relationship between Accounting Changes and Stock Prices," Empirical Research in Accounting: Selected Studies, 1973.

10. Ricks, W. E., "The Market's Response to the 1974 LIFO Adoptions," *Journal of Accounting Research* (Autumn, 1982).

11. For a summary of relevant studies see Griffin, P. A. "FASB Statement No. 8: A Review of Empirical Research on Its Economic Consequences," Financial Accounting Standards Board, Research Paper No. 482.

12. McCracken, P. et. al., *Towards Full Employment and Price Stability, OECD* (June, 1977).

13. Nordhaus, W. D., "The Worldwide Wage Explosion," *BPEA*, 2 (1972) and Perry, G. L., "Determinants of Wage Inflation Around the World," *BPEA* 2 (1975).

14. Computed from the *Economic Report of the President* (February 1983), pp. 170 and 186.

15. Regan, P. J., "Pension Fund Perspective," *Financial Analysts Journal* (September-October, 1983).

16. Much, M., "Pension Liabilities," *Industry Week* (November 16, 1981).

17. Modigliani and Cohn (this volume).

18. Corporate Accounting Reporter, 1983 and "FASB Preliminary Views

on Employers' Accounting for Pensions," a questionnaire prepared by the National Association of Accountants.

19. Feldstein, M. and S. Seligman, "Pension Funding, Share Prices, and National Savings," *Journal of Finance* (September, 1981). See also Shoven and Bulow, *ibid*.
20. Modigliani and Cohn (this volume).
21. 1983 Flow of Funds Accounts published by the Board of Governors of the Federal Reserve System.
22. Modigliani and Cohn (this volume).
23. Lintner, J., "Inflation and Security Returns,"*Journal of Finance* (May, 1975).
24. Leuthold, S. C., "Interest Rates, Inflation, and Deflation," *Financial Analysts Journal* (January-February, 1981).
25. Smith, G. R., "Inflation Accounting and the Financial Executive," *Financial Executive* (December, 1980).
26. 1983 Flow of Funds Account.
27. Fama, E., "Short-Term Interest Rates as Predictors of Inflation," *Journal of Finance* (June, 1975).
28. Modigliani and Cohn (this volume).
29. Altman, E., "A Further Empirical Investigation of the Bankruptcy Cost Question," *Journal of Finance* (September 1984).
30. See, for example, Moore, G. H., "Diagnosing the Problem of Inflation and Unemployment in the Western World," *After the Phillips Curve*: *Persistence of High Inflation and High Unemployment*, Conference Series No. 19, Federal Reserve Bank of Boston, June 1978.
31. Gordon, R. H., "Interest Rates, Inflation, and Corporate Financial Policy, *BPEA* 2 (1982).
32. Modigliani and Cohn (this volume).
33. Summers, L. H. "Inflation and the Valuation of Corporate Equities," Working Paper No. 824, National Bureau of Economic Research, Inc. (1980).
34. Brainard, W., J. Shoven, and L. Weiss, "The Financial Valuation of the Return to Capital," *BPEA* 2 (1980).
35. Kessel, R. A., "Inflation Caused Wealth Redistribution: A Test of a Hypothesis," *American Economic Review* (March 1956).

    DeAlessi, L., "The Redistribution of Wealth by Inflation: An Empirical Test with United Kingdom Data," *The Southern Economic Journal* (October, 1963).

    Lintner, J., "Inflation and Common Stock Prices in a Cyclical Context," National Bureau of Economic Research, 53rd Annual Report, 1973.
36. Modigliani and Cohn (this volume).
37. Ibid.
38. Fisher, L. and J. H. Lorie, "Rates of Return on Investments in Common Stocks," *Journal of Business* (July, 1968). 39.
39. Ibbotson, R. G. and R. A. Sinquefield, *Stocks, Bonds, and Inflation*, The Financial Analysts Research Foundation, 1977 and *Financial Analysts Journal* (July-August, 1979).

40. For example, Seed III, A. H., *The Impact of Inflation on Internal Planning and Control*, National Association of Accountants, 1981, and L. A. Bace, E. A. Schwallie, and G. W. Silverman, *Coping with Inflation*, Financial Executives Research Foundation, 1981.

41. Hicks, J. R., *Value and Capital* (London: Oxford University Press, 1939).

42. "A Grocery Mirrors the Pain in Brazil," *The New York Times*, November 3, 1983.

43. Rich, J. T. and E.E. Bergsma, "Pay Executives to Create Wealth," *Chief Executive* (Autumn, 1982). A. Rappaport, "New Measures of Executive Performance," *Business Week* (July 18, 1983), and "Executive Incentives vs. Corporate Growth," *Harvard Business Review* (July–August, 1978).

44. Loomis, C. J., "The Madness of Executive Compensation," *Fortune* (July 12, 1982). E. T. Redling, "Myth vs. Reality, the Relationship between Top Executive Pay and Corporate Performance," *Compensation Review* (Fourth Quarter 1981).

45. Rappaport, A., op. cit.

---

*This paper reflects my views and not necessarily those of Joseph E. Seagram & Sons, Inc.

15

Accounting Control versus Inflation—on the Brazilian Model for "Correcting" Financial Statements

Luiz Manoel Ribeiro Dias
Professor
Catholic University of Rio de Janeiro

Accounting Control versus Inflation—on the Brazilian Model for "Correcting" Financial Statements

Accounting records are kept in money. When money shrinks, the records are distorted. This paper intends to investigate the distortions caused by inflation in financial statements. It will ascertain that, under inflationary conditions, some accounts correct themselves but others don't; if they don't, correction must be applied to restore the reporting value of the statements. A seemingly logical path will lead to the Brazilian model of "correcting" for inflation. And a further step will discover that correction itself causes other distortions, which reach as far as corporate capital structure policy. Along the way some interesting complications will arise, but will be left aside for the sake of maintaining the discussions focused on the basic, elementary facts.

INTRODUCTION

As a starting point assume that, yesterday, Joe the grocer bought a bag of potatoes. He paid for it with 10 coins totalling $1; then he sold it, for $20 cash. Very pleased, he noticed that he had made a profit of $10 and that the $10 was in his pocket.

Today Joe buys another bag of potatoes. As he pays for it he notices that he now needs 11 coins to buy a bag exactly like the one he bought yesterday. A practical man, Joe sells it for $22 and reckons that he made a profit of $11. As he puts the $11 into his pocket, however, Joe notices that the new coins are smaller than the ones he earned yesterday. Surprisingly, though, the 11 new coins weigh the same as the 10 old ones. Always a practical man, Joe explains the anomaly as an effect of inflation,[1] and gets ready to pay more for the next bag of potatoes that he will buy.

The problem starts when Joe tries to buy a new crane for the shop. The one he has, bought a year ago, cost $1,000; a new one, exactly like the old, costs $2,000. Quite surprised, Joe notices that his accounting records are distorted. They show:

Fixed assets	
Crane	$1,000
Accumulated depreciation	(100)
Net value	$900

Obviously the old crane, even after a year of hard work, is worth more than $900. A new one costs $2,000!

The comparison, however, is not fair. The old crane was paid for with 1,000 big coins, the kind that circulated a year ago. Today the coins are much smaller. The crane manufacturer swears that 2,000 new coins weigh exactly the same as the 1,000 old coins. That is, the size of the coin has shrunk to one half; twice as many new coins are necessary to pay for anything. Since the phenomenon is general, there was an inflation of 100 percent in the period.

Such analysis lead to the conclusion that potatoes are different from cranes. The value of the potatoes, dynamically engaged in the operational cycle of the firm, corrects itself, compensating for the shrinkage of the coins. If Joe pays more for the potatoes, he sells for more to buy for more and so on. The inventory account will always reflect only one bag of potatoes, but its value will grow continuously, trying to reach the number of coins that will be necessary to buy the next bag.

But the fixed-assets account stopped in time. Unless something is done, it will always show the crane as worth $1,000,[2] regardless of the fact that the "1,000" means 1,000 old, big coins. The "obvious" solution to correct the anomaly is to translate 1,000 big coins into the equivalent number of small coins, the same ones used to evalute the potato inventory.

This discovery leads to a crucial dichotomy;

1. Some assets (the potatoes) correct themselves in the operating cycle; this is a characteristic of the *current assets*.
2. Some assets (the crane) do not participate in the operating cycle[3] and thus do not correct themselves spontaneously; this characteristic can be associated with the *fixed assets*.

The same dichotomy can be seen in the liabilities side:

1. Short-term loans correct themselves; the interest rates they bear take into consideration the shrinkage of the coins. The

same happens with accounts payable. When suppliers sell on account, prices include the time value of money.[4] Liabilities which correct themselves, because they are tied to the operating cycle, can be associated with the *current liabilities*.

2. On the other hand, other sources of funds generate liabilities of a permanent nature, not connected with the operational cycle of the firm. These form the *permanent capital*, that can be split into two groups:

   a. Liabilities, such as long-term loans in foreign currency, that explicitly incorporate a provision (the exchange rate) to correct for variations in the size of the coins.
   b. Sources, such as paid-in capital and retained earnings, that do not incorporate any correcting mechanism, neither spontaneous nor explicit.

The split between current and permanent can be orthogonally superposed to the assets and liabilities structure of a balance sheet. It follows that the balance sheet is built around a cross:

FIGURE 1

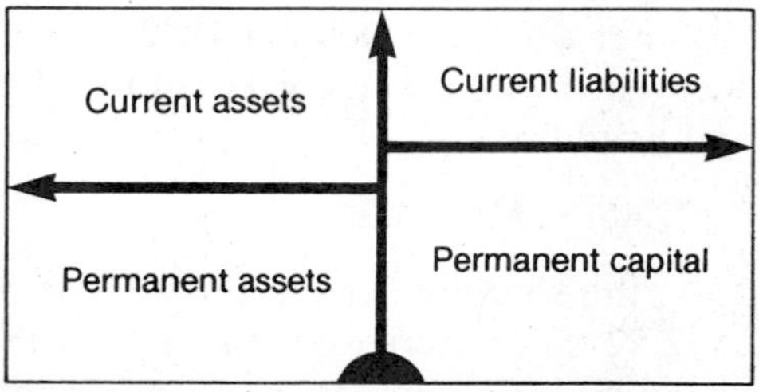

Current assets and current liabilities self-correct themselves, spontaneously, by circulating through the operating cycle of the firm during the statement year. Permanent assets and permanent capital do not. To convert them to the same monetary unit (i.e., to coins of the same size) used to evaluate the current, some form of correction must be made, either ex-ante, as in the case of foreign loans, or ex-post, by imposing an arbitrary rule.

The Brazilian practise for correcting the permanent accounts measures the size of the coins against a "stable" standard, a government bond called ORTN,[5] whose "price," in cruzeiros, should reflect the purchasing power (i.e., the size of the coin) of the cruzeiro.

The "price" of the ORTN is published monthly. Correction of financial statements is based on the price of one ORTN at the two dates involved. For example, a fixed asset with a book value of Cr$1 million in October 1982 will, in October 1983, have a book value (before depreciation) of

$$1 \times \frac{5{,}897.49}{2{,}398.55} = \text{Cr\$}2{,}458{,}777.00$$
$$\text{say MCr\$}2.46$$

Inflation, as measured by the ORTN standard, was 146 percent in the period.[6] And the book value of the said fixed asset would increase by Cr$1,458,777.00.

Then a complication arises. The increase in the book value of fixed assets reflects a kind of "profit" generated by inflation. The accounting entry to record the "correction" involves creating a new account; it will show:

Fixed assets	MCr$1.46	
Monetary correction of fixed assets		MCr$1.46

The same rule should be applied to net worth. Suppose, for example, that the firm's net worth, in October 1982, was Cr$2 million. In October 1983, net worth should be corrected to reflect the 146 percent inflation and would be

$$2 \times (1 + 1.46) = \text{MCr\$}4.92$$

Net worth, that is, the shareholders' claim against the firm, would increase by MCr$2.92. Such increase in the net worth reflects a kind of "loss" generated by inflation. The accounting entry in this case will show:

Monetary correction of net worth	MCr$2.92	
Net worth		MCr$2.92

It follows that the monetary correction of permanent assets and permanent capital generates profit and losses, because of inflation, as shown by posting a generalized form of the entries above.

Let: X = the permanent assets in the beginning of the period
Y = the permanent capital in the beginning of the period
k = the "correction factor" in the period

Then, the correction entries will be posted:

Permanent Assets		*Monetary Correction of Permanent Assets*		*Monetary Correction of Permanent Capital*		*Permanent Capital*	
X			*kX (1)*	*(2) kY*			*Y*
(1) kX		*(3) kX*			*kY (4)*		*kY (2)*

Inflationary Profit or Loss

(4) kY	*kX (3)*
	k(X − Y) (5)

The balance of the account "inflationary profit or loss" will show a "profit" if X is larger than Y and a "loss" in the opposite case. Since X and Y are the permanent assets and permanent capital and k is the same "monetary correction factor," it follows that a firm will have an "inflationary profit" if its permanent assets are larger than its permanent capital.[7]

There is, however, a fundamental difference between the *inflationary profit* described above and the *operating profit* illustrated by the bag of potatoes. The operating profit meant cash. The inflationary profit is confined to the books; it is reflected only in the accounting balances which measure the permanent assets and the permanent capital.

Regardless of such differences, the Brazilian model includes the inflationary profit in computing the *corrected profit*, which is the basis on which to calculate the corporate tax and, as a sequitur, the net profit.[8]

The several steps of the calculations can be organized by reshaping the income statement to separate:

1. A level-one operating profit (without depreciation), which depends solely upon the operation of the firm.
2. The depreciation, which depends only on the fixed assets.
3. The level-two operating profit, which takes depreciation into account.

4. The inflationary profit, which results from the monetary correction of permanent assets and permanent capital.
5. The corrected profit, defined as the sum of the operating profit plus the inflationary profit.
6. The net profit, which remains after deducting tax.

To emphasize the five levels of profit, the income statement will show:[9]

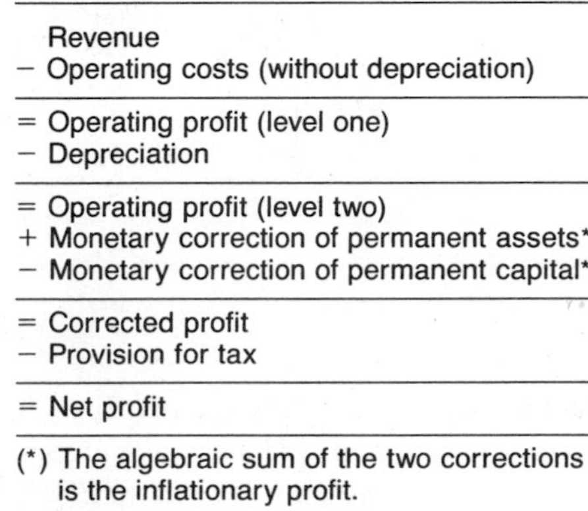

Revenue
− Operating costs (without depreciation)

= Operating profit (level one)
− Depreciation

= Operating profit (level two)
+ Monetary correction of permanent assets*
− Monetary correction of permanent capital*

= Corrected profit
− Provision for tax

= Net profit

(*) The algebraic sum of the two corrections is the inflationary profit.

With this algorithm, the effect that variations in the permanent assets or permanent capital will cause in the inflationary profit, therefore in the net profit, can be analyzed in a simple algebraic model.[10]

It can start by recalling that the essential structure of a balance sheet is a cross, this time with a pedestal:

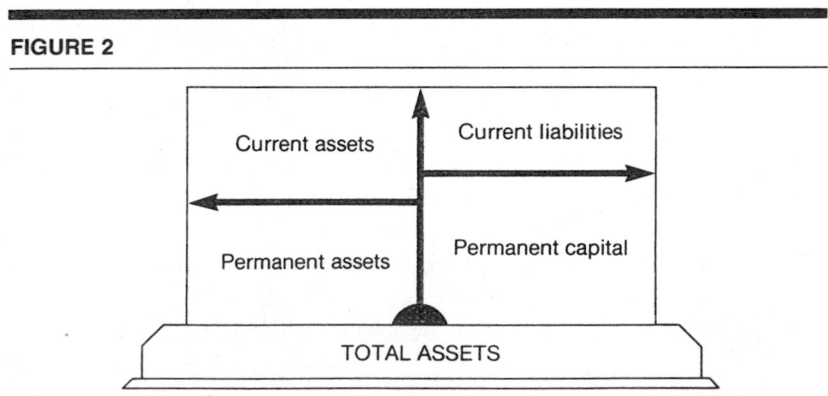

FIGURE 2

On this structure, two indices can be defined:

$$f = \frac{\text{Permanent assets}}{\text{Total assets}} \quad \text{thus permanent assets} = f \cdot A$$

$$k = \frac{\text{Permanent capital}}{\text{Total assets}} \quad \text{thus permanent capital} = k \cdot A$$

A third index, reflecting "pure" operating performance, can be defined ad hoc:

$$m = \frac{\text{Operating profit, without depreciation}}{\text{Permanent assets}}$$

thus operating profit (level one) $= m \cdot fA$

The rules of the game will define two final indices: (1) inflation, i, and (2) depreciation, d.

Then, the algorithm developed for the income statement can be applied to calculate the operating profit (level two):

Revenues	xxx
− Operating costs (without depreciation)	xxx
= Operating profit (level two)	$m \cdot fA$
− Depreciation	$-d \cdot fA$
= Operating profit (level two)	$(m - d) \cdot fA$

Along the same lines, the inflationary profit is:

Monetary correction of permanent assets
Monetary correction of permanent capital

And the corrected profit:

$$\begin{array}{r} i \cdot (1 - d) \cdot fA \\ -i \cdot kA \\ \hline i[(1 - d) \cdot f - k]A \\ (m - d) \cdot fA + i[(1 - d) \cdot f - k]A \end{array}$$

So compacted, the effects of monetary correction can be analyzed under two foci: (1) inflationary profit and (2) corrected profit.

Inflationary profit will be zero if

$$i[(1 - d) \cdot f - k]A = 0$$

A and i are, by definition, different from zero; then inflationary profit will be zero if

$$\frac{k}{f} = (1 - d)$$

It follows that a firm can aim at zero inflationary profit only by adjusting the equilibrium between permanent assets and permanent capital in order to include the depreciation rate. With leasing operations on one side and debentures (for instance) on the other, fulfilling the equilibrium condition is elementary. But the state of equilibrium, with zero inflationary profit, is only the tip of the iceberg. The immersed mass can be pushed to generate an inflationary LOSS, that does not involve cash flows, but reflects only the larger growth of the permanent capital, as compared to the permanent assets.

The sign of the inflationary profit is defined by the difference:

$$(1 - d) = k/f$$

If $k/f < (1 - d)$, i.e., if capital is dominated by permanent assets, the firm will make an inflationary profit.

If $k/f > (1 - d)$, i.e., if permanent capital dominates permanent assets, the firm will bear an inflationary loss, then can absorb operating profit and reduce corrected profit, therefore reducing income tax.

Corrected profit will be zero if

$$k/f = (1 - d) + [(m - d)/i]$$

The conclusion is compatible with the analysis of the inflationary profit. To reduce corrected profit, thereby reducing corporate tax, it is enough to push down the permanent assets and to increase the permanent capital until the index k/f reaches the desired level.

In the extreme case, tax can be completely "avoided" by a "proper" financial strategy, independent of the firm's operating strategy, that seeks to maximize the operating profit, reflected in index m.

It is relevant to realize that m is a "nominal" index. It compares the operating profit, without depreciation, with the permanent assets. The operating profit results from revenues and costs that self-correct themselves in the operating cycle. The permanent assets are frozen, until correction is imposed. If m is nominal, the Fischer effect applies.

Let n be the "real" return on the permanent assets. It follows that

$$(1 + m) = (1 + n)(1 + i)$$

The distortion caused by inflation is dramatic at higher rates.

If inflation is a moderate 5 percent per year, in order to obtain a "real" return of 20 percent (at operating profit level one) on the permanent assets, it is enough to aim at a "nominal" return of

$$(1 + m) = (1 + 0.2)(1 + 0.05) = 1.26 \qquad m = 26\%$$

On the other hand, with inflation soaring to 200 percent, the same 20 percent "real" return will require a nominal return of

$$(1 + m) = (1 + 0.2)(1 + 2) = 3.6 \qquad m = 260\% !!$$

At these high levels, accounting control has very serious problems in protecting the information content of its records and, a fortiori, the reporting value of the financial statements.

High levels of inflation exaggerate the distortions caused by a subreptitious, yet fundamental, flaw: Accounting procedures are blind to the time value of money. Up to a point, time effects are diluted and digested. The distortions they cause creep by unnoticed. Nevertheless, they exist.

New instruments, finer and faster, are called to face the challenge.

APPENDIX: THE MONETARY CORRECTION OF FINANCIAL STATEMENTS AND ITS EFFECTS ON CORPORATE TAX

In Inflation land there are six firms with almost identical performance. All of them: (1) close their fiscal year on March 31; (2) sell 5,000 coins per year; (3) have operating costs (without depreciation) of 2,000 coins; and (4) use their cash to maintain unchanged (at current prices) their current liabilities.

For accounting purposes, inflation is measured by the change in value of the National Adjustable Bond, NAB. In March 1982 one NAB was worth 1,600 coins; one year later one NAB was worth 3,200 coins. The monetary correction in March 1983, was (3,200/1,600 =)2. Inflation of 100 percent in the year!

For the sake of simplicity the balance sheets, given for March 31, 1982, were constructed to show only three levels of balance: 1,600, 3,200, and 4,800 coins, equivalent to one, two, and three NABs.

Also, all six firms had total assets of 6,400 coins, i.e., 4 NABs. To investigate the effect of the asset structure and of the financial structure upon the net profit, the six firms were grouped in three pairs:

---

* The original exercise was worded to present the problem gradually, using the numbers (kept simple on purpose) to illustrate the concepts and to investigate side issues such as the effect of depreciating first and then correcting, or vice-versa. It is worth noting that the monetary correction factor was made quite close to actual Brazilian conditions. One ORTN (see Note No. 5) was worth Cr$1.602,99 in March 1982 and Cr$3.292,32 in March 1983. Acutal inflation was 105.4 percent in the period.

1. The first pair compares the asset structure.
   a. In HIFIX the fixed assets dominate.
   b. In LOFIX the current assets are larger.
2. The second pair compares the financial structure.
   a. In HICAP the permanent capital dominates.
   b. In LOCAP the current liabilities are larger.
3. The third pair compares the net working capital.
   a. In HIWOR the net working capital dominates.
   b. In NEGWO the net working capital is negative.

The purpose of the exercise is to construct the income statement and the corrected balance sheet, on March 31, 1983, for all six firms and to compare the five levels of profit emphasized in the income statement:

1. The operating profit without depreciation.
2. The operating profit including depreciation.
3. The inflationary profit.
4. The corrected profit.
5. The net profit.

The exercise will show that the operating profit level one (which corresponds to the generated cash flow) that is, by construction, constant (3,000 coins), finds its way into the current assets.

The calculations, starting with the Income Statements and transferring the applicable figures to the Balance Sheets, are shown, for each pair of firms, in the following tables.

TABLE 1 Balance sheets

	NABS March 1982 (1,600) (coins)	*Coins* March 1982	*Coins* March 1983	*NABS March 1983 (3,200) (coins)*
HIFIX				
Current assets	1	1,600	4,600	1.44
Fixed assets	3	4,800	8,640	2.70
Total	4	6,400	13,240	4.14
Current liabilities	2	3,200	3,200	1.00
Capital	2	3,200	6,400	2.00
Provision for tax	0	0	1,820	0.57
Retained earnings	0	0	1.820	0.57
LOFIX				
Current assets	3	4,800	7,800	.44
Fixed assets	1	1,600	2,800	0.90
Total	4	6,400	10,680	3.34
Current liabilities	2	3,200	3,200	1.00
Capital	2	3,200	6,400	2.00
Provision for tax	0	0	540	0.17
Retained earnings	0	0	540	0.17

Income statements—coins Year ended March 31, 1983	HIFIX	LOFIX
Revenues	5,000	
− Operating costs	(2,000)	
= Operating profit (level one)	3,000	3,000
− Depreciation	(480)	(160)
= Operating profit (level two)	2,520	2,840
+ Correction of fixed assets	4,320	1,440
− Correction of capital	(3,200)	(3,200)
= Corrected profit	3,640	1,080
− Corporate tax (50%)	(1,820)	(540)
= Net profit	1,820	540

TABLE 2 Balance sheets

	NABS March 1982 (1,600) (coins)	*Coins* March 1982	*Coins* March 1983	*NABS March 1983 (3,200) (coins)*
HICAP				
Current assets	2	3,200	6,200	1.94
Fixed assets	2	3,200	5,760	1.80
Total	4	6,400	11,960	3.74
Current liabilities	1	1,600	1,600	0.50
Capital	3	4,800	9,600	3.00
Provision for tax	0	0	380	0.12
Retained earnings	0	0	380	0.12
LOCAP				
Current assets	2	3,200	6,200	1.94
Fixed assets	2	3,200	5,760	1.80
Total	4	6,400	11,960	3.74
Current liabilities	3	4,800	4,800	0.50
Capital	1	1,600	3,200	3.00
Provision for tax	0	0	1,980	0.12
Retained earnings	0	0	1,980	0.12

Income statements—coins Year ended March 31, 1983	HICAP	LOCAP
Revenues	5,000	
− Operating costs	(2,000)	
= Operating profit (level one)	3,000	3,000
− Depreciation	(320)	(320)
= Operating profit (level two)	2,680	2,680
+ Correction of fixed assets	2,880	2,880
− Correction of capital	(4,800)	(1,600)
= Corrected profit	760	3,960
− Corporate tax (50%)	(380)	(1,980)
= Net profit	380	1,980

TABLE 3 Balance sheets

	NABS March 1982 (1,600) (coins)	Coins		NABS March 1983 (1,600) (coins)
		March 1982	March 1983	
HIWOR				
Current assets	3	4,800	7,800	2.44
Fixed assets	1	1,600	2,880	0.90
Total	4	6,400	10,680	3.34
Current liabilities	1	1,600	1,600	0.50
Capital	3	4,800	9,600	3.00
Provision for tax	0	0	0	—
Retained earnings	0	0	(520)	(0.16)
NEGWO				
Current assets	1	1,600	4,600	1.44
Fixed assets	3	4,800	8,640	2.70
Total	4	6,400	13,240	4.14
Current liabilities	3	4,800	4,800	1.50
Capital	1	1,600	3,200	1.00
Provision for tax	0	0	2,620	0.82
Retained earnings	0	0	2,620	0.82

Income statements—coins Year ended March 31, 1983	HIWOR	NEGWO
Revenues	5,000	
− Operating costs	2,000	
= Operating profit (level one)	3,000	3,000
− Depreciation	(160)	(480)
= Operating profit (level two)	2,840	2,520
+ Correction of fixed assets	1,440	4,320
− Correction of capital	(4,800)	(1,600)
= Corrected profit	(520)	5,240
− Corporate tax (50%)	0	(2,620)
= Net profit	(520)	2,520

The contrast among the effects is emphasized by comparing the five levels of profit, as tabulated below:

TABLE 4

Coins	*HIFIX*	*LOFIX*	*HICAP*	*LOCAP*	*HIWOR*	*NEGWO*
Operating profit without depreciation	3,000	3,000	3,000	3,000	3,000	3,000
Operating profit including depreciation	2,520	2,840	2,680	2,680	2,840	2,520
Inflationary profit	1,120	(1,760)	(1,920)	1,280	(3,360)	2,720
Corrected profit	3,640	1,089	760	3,960	(520)	5,240
Net profit	1,820	540	380	1,980	(520)	2,620

It is interesting to notice that the corrected profit varies from a loss of 520 coins for HIWOR, to a profit of 5,240 for NEGWO, more than the sales revenue.

Also surprising are the balance sheets on March 31, 1983, after paying tax, as tabulated below:

TABLE 5

Coins	*HIFIX*	*LOFIX*	*HICAP*	*LOCAP*	*HIWOR*	*NEGWO*
Current assets	2,780	7,260	5,820	4,220	7,800	1,980
Fixed assets	8,640	2,880	5,760	5,760	2,880	8,640
Total	11,420	10,140	11,580	9,980	10,680	10,620
Current liabilities	3,200	3,200	1,600	4,800	1,600	4,800
Capital	6,400	6,400	9,600	3,200	9,600	3,200
Retained earnings	1.820	540	380	1,980	(520)	2,620

Now the champion of net profit, NEGWO, shows the smallest level (1,980) of current assets. And the loser, HIWOR, has the highest level of current assets. Tax-minded strategy has it price!

Notes

1. With due respect to economic rigor, inflation, detected by the increase in the price of potatoes, is actually a decrease in size of the coins.
2. Even worse! The crane's net value will fall, because every year Joe depreciates 10 percent of its original value.
3. Actually fixed assets and long-term loans do support the operating cycle, but their replacement cycle is much longer.
4. An interesting sideline emerges: Accounting procedures are blind to the time value of money! When Joe bought his first bag of potatoes, his

accountant charged inventory and credited cash for $10. Had he bought the same bag of potatoes on account, say at 30 days, for $12, his accountant would have charged inventory (and credited accounts payable) for $12. The $2 difference represents the price of credit, subreptitiously incorporated to the potatoes. Now, if Joe maintains his markup (100 percent on cost) and furthermore, follows his supplier's policy of adding 20 percent of the price for 30 days' credit, then he would sell the potatoes, at 30 days, for ($2 \times 1.2 \times 12 =$) $28.80. His accountant would debit accounts receivable and credit sales revenue for $28.80. When determining his gross income, Joe will subtract the cost of potatoes sold from the sales revenue and find that he had a profit of ($28.80 - 12 =$)$16.80, considerably more than the $10 he would have earned if he had bought and sold the potatoes for cash.

The "operational" profit, on the potatoes proper, is always $10. The difference, $6.80, reflects the time effect of the credit hidden in the commercial transaction. A first correction of this distortion would be made if accounting principles were persuaded to separate the time effect of the credit from the "pure" commercial transaction, as shown in the following condensed entries:

TABLE 6 Operation potatoes on account

Inventory	
(1) 10	
	10 (3)

Accounts Payable	
	12 (1)

Time Effect in Purchasing	
(1) 2	
	2 (5)

Accounts Receivable	
(2) 28.8	

Sales Revenue	
	20 (2)
(4) 20	

Time Effect in Selling	
	8.8 (2)
(5) 8.8	

Cost of Potatoes Sold	
(3) 10	
	10 (4)

Pure Commercial Profit	
(4) 10	20 (4)
	10

Profit from Time Effects	
(5) 2	8.8 (5)
	6.8

Entries:
(1) Buying on account.
(2) Selling on account, with 100 percent markup on cost and 20 percent charge for credit.
(3) Determining the cost of potatoes sold.
(4) Determining pure commercial profit.
(5) Determining profit from time effects.

The anomaly would be completely eliminated if selling price were calculated on the "pure" cost of potatoes (i.e., without the time effect on purchasing), always with a 100 percent markup and a 20 percent overcharge for selling on credit. Selling price would then be ($2 \times 1.2 \times 10 =$) $24 and the same accounting treatment would show a pure commercial profit of $10 and a profit from time effects of $2. Time-effect profit would be 20 percent (the price of credit) of the pure commercial profit, no more.

Under heavy inflationary pressure the "price of credit" can become preposterous. Nevertheless, the distortions denounced above creep unnoticed, under the generally accepted principles. But this is another problem.

5. The "Obrigações Reajustáveis do Tesouro Nacional", ORTN, were created in October 1964, with an original value of CR$10. Certificates are redeemable in two or five years. Their value, in cruzeiros, is based on the expurged general price index of the three last months. A second type of ORTN is readjusted by the variation of the U.S. dollar exchange rate. Besides having their value readjusted, ORTNs pay a moderate interest, in the order of 6 percent or 8 percent annum. Selected values of the ORTN are tabulated below:

TABLE 7

CR$ per ORTN in January of

1965–11,30	1970–42,35	1975–106,76	1980– 487,83
6–16,60	1–50,51	6–133,34	1– 738,50
7–23,23	2–61,52	7–183,65	2–1.453,96
8–28,48	3–70,87	8–238,32	3–2.910,93
9–35,62	4–80,62	9–326,82	

Cr$ per ORTN in 1983

Jan.–2.910,93	Apr. –3.588,63	Jul. –4.554,05	Oct.–5.897,49
Feb.–3.085,59	May –3.911,61	Aug. –4.963,91	Nov.–6.469,55
Mar.–3.292,32	June–4.224,54	Sept.–5.383,84	

6. It is worth pointing out that, if another standard is used, a different figure will arise. For instance, the variation of the U.S. dollar exchange rate will show:

$$\frac{\text{OCT–13–1983}}{\text{OCT–11–1982}} \quad \frac{\text{Cr\$780,00}}{\text{Cr\$214,68}} = 3.633$$

Increase, in the period, was 263 percent!

7. This is an oversimplification in that it assumes that all accounts which form the "permanent" groups are corrected by the ORTN. In actual practice, some accounts have individual correction criteria. For instance, the permanent assets can include shares of other firms, which may be corrected by ascertaining their "actual" worth. And long-term foreign debts must be corrected for the variation in the exchange rates.

8. Since net working capital is the difference of permanent capital less permanent assets, it follows that the condition to have a positive "inflationary profit" is to have negative net working captial.
9. Firms are allowed, however, to defer the tax on inflationary profit.
10. The same scalpel can be reapplied to further improve the analytical power of the income statement. The distinction between "pure" operating profits generated by the time effects in operational accounts (such as inventories and accounts payable), as discussed in footnote No. 4, can be introduced. Also, straight financial costs, i.e., interest due on loans (both long and short term), which do not depend on operation but only on the financial structure, can be separated. With the semantic limitations inherent to the capacity of words (English or Portuguese) to convey concepts, a more refined income statement model would break profit analysis into eight profit components:

TABLE 8

Pure operating revenues	
− Pure cost of goods sold	
= Pure operating gross profit	$X - 1$
Time effects on selling	
− Time effects on purchasing	
= Profit from time effects	$X - 2$
1. Operating costs (nonfinancial) (which can be treated as a negative component of the final profit)	$X - 3$
2. Depreciation costs (also a negative component, which depends on the structure of fixed assets)	$X - 4$
3. Financial costs (again a negative component which depends solely on the structure of the liabilities)	$X - 5$
Nonoperating revenues	
− Nonoperating expenses	
= Nonoperating profit	$X - 6$
Monetary correction of permanent assets	
− Monetary correction of permanent capital	
= Inflationary profit	$X - 7$
4. Corporate tax (another negative component of net profit, which depends on many things, most of which are severely distorted by the pressure that acted during the evolution of the present tax laws).	$X - 8$

It follows that net profit, a condition precedent for the firm to fulfill its duty as a transformer of resources, is dependent on eight components, each of them subject to independent decisions, policies and controls:

TABLE 9

Pure operating gross profit	X − 1
Profit from time effects	X − 2
Operating costs	X − 3
Depreciation costs	X − 4
Financial costs	X − 5
Nonoperating profit	X − 6
Inflationary profit	X − 7
Corporate tax	X − 8
Net profit	Total

Despite the semantic difficulties, the separation of the variables improves the capacity of analysis.

10. The model evolved from an exercise assigned to a managerial accounting class at PUC's MBA program. An adapted version of the exercise is presented in the appendix.
11. In actual practise, fixed assets are first corrected, then depreciated. It can be shown that, in either order, depreciation and correction lead to the same "corrected profit" and to the same "corrected value" of the asset.

Biographical Sketches

Edward I. Altman is Professor of Finance and Chairman of the MBA Program at NYU. He has been a visiting professor at the Hautes Etudes Commerciales and Universite de Paris-Dauphine in France, at the Pontificia Catolica Universidade in Rio de Janeiro, Brazil and the Australian Graduate School of Management. Dr. Altman has an international reputation as an expert on corporate bankruptcy and credit analysis. He is editor of the international publication, the *Journal of Banking and Finance* and two publisher series, *Contemporary Studies in Economics and Finance* (JAI Press) and *Wiley Professional Banking and Finance Series* (John Wiley & Sons). Professor Altman has published several books and over 60 articles in scholarly finance, accounting, and economic journals. He is the current editor of the *Financial Handbook* (John Wiley) and the author of the recently published book on *Corporate Financial Distress* (John Wiley, 1983). His work has appeared in several languages including Portugese, Japanese, German, and French. Dr. Altman's primary areas of research include bankruptcy analysis and prediction, credit and lending policies, corporate finance and capital markets. He has been a consultant to several government agencies, major financial and accounting institutions, and industrial companies, has lectured to executives in North America, South America, Europe and Asia, and has testified before the U.S. Congress on several occasions.

Saul Bronfeld is the director of the Foreign Department at the Bank of Israel. He received his M.A. in economics and business administration from the Hebrew University of Jerusalem. Previous positions with the Bank of Israel were: chief economist of the research department and director of state loan administration. Mr. Bronfeld contributed papers on the Israeli capital markets, monetary policy, and on taxation under inflation with special emphasis on the taxation of the yield on financial instruments. He has also lectured at the Hebrew University and Bar-ilan University.

Richard A. Cohn is Associate Professor of Finance at the University of Illinois at Chicago, where he teaches corporate finance. He was formerly on the faculties of Massachusetts Institute of Technology and the University of British Columbia. Professor Cohn is the author of many articles in academic journals.

Richard Karl Goeltz is vice president of finance and a member of the board of directors at Joseph E. Seagram & Sons, Inc., New York. Goeltz received an A.B. degree from Brown University, Providence, Rhode Island, and an M.B.A. degree from Columbia University, New York. He also studied at the London School of Economics and in the doctoral program at New York University. His papers on international finance have been published in magazines and newspapers, and he has given numerous speeches to professional societies, at university seminars, and to corporate and bank officers. Before joining Seagram in 1970, Goeltz was in the treasurer's department of Exxon Corp. He has appeared on panels at the Financial Executives Institute and the Financial Management Association.

John T. Hackett joined Cummins Engine Company, Inc., in 1964 and two years later was named vice president of finance. In 1971, he became Executive Vice President and Chief Financial Officer, a position he still holds.

He is a director of Cummins Engine Company, Cummins Engine Foundation, Irwin Union Corporation, the Ransburg Corporation, the Corporation for Innovation Development, the Heritage Venture Group, and the Ohio State Development Fund, and is president of the Indiana Secondary Market for Education Loans, Inc. He is a past director of the Federal Reserve Bank of Chicago.

Mr. Hackett graduated from Indiana University with a B.S. in economics in 1954 and an M.B.A. in business economics and public policy four years later. In 1961, he received his Ph.D. in finance and economics from Ohio State University, where he now serves on the Alumni Advisory Council. From 1954 through 1956, he served in the U.S. Army.

He served on the faculties of Ohio State, Case Western Reserve, and Kent State universities. Following completion of graduate work at Ohio State, he joined the staff of the Federal Reserve Bank of Cleveland and in 1963 was appointed Assistant Vice President and Economist.

Robert S. Hamada has been Professor of Finance since 1977 and Director of the Center for Research in Security Prices (CRSP) since 1980 at the Graduate School of Business, University of Chicago. His education includes B.E., Yale University, 1959; S.M., Massachusetts Institute of Technology, 1961; Ph.D. 1969.

He has been an instructor, Assistant Professor, Associate Professor and Professor of Finance since 1966 at the University of Chicago and finance faculty coordinator since 1975: visiting professor of finance at UCLA, University of Washington, University of British Columbia, and the London Graduate School of Business Studies. He had industrial experience with the Sun Oil Company in 1961 to 1963.

His research, teaching, and consulting interests are in: the effects of risk and taxes on the financing and capital budgeting decisions within the firm, on portfolio selection, and on the pricing of multiperiod capital assets. He received the McKinsey Award for Excellence in Teaching (1981) and was noted by *Fortune* Magazine (January 1982) as one of the eight outstanding U.S. business school professors. He is financial consultant to many financial institutions, corporations, law firms, and governments. He is on the Board of Directors, American Finance Association and NBER and is associate editor of *The Journal of Finance* and *The Journal of Financial and Quantitative Analysis.*

Thomas S. Y. Ho, Associate Professor of Finance, New York University. Graduated from University of Pennsylvania, Ph.D. (1978), MS (1975). Recipient of the Thouron Fellowship. Research interests include: fixed-income securities pricing, market-making and trading system designs, and hedging strategies. Articles have been published in journals including: *Journal of Business*, *Journal of Finance*, *Journal of Financial Economics*, and *Journal of Financial and Quantitative Analysis.*

Michael C. Jensen is Professor of Economics, Finance and Organization Theory at the Graduate School of Management, University of Rochester. He is also Director of the Managerial Economics Research Center which he founded in 1977. He was Assistant Professor at the University of Rochester from 1967–71, and Associate Professor from 1971–79.

Professor Jensen earned his Ph.D. in economics, finance, and accounting and his M.B.A. in finance from the University of Chicago. He received his A.B. from Macalester College.

Professor Jensen is the author of more than 30 published papers, comments, and articles on a wide range of economic, finance, and business-related topics. Dr. Jensen and his co-author, William Meckling, received the first Leo Melamed Prize for outstanding scholarship by business school teachers from the University of Chicago's Graduate School of Business for their paper, "Theory of the Firm: Managerial Behavior, Agency Costs, and Ownership Structure" in March 1979. Dr. Jensen was also awarded (with William Meckling) the Graham and Dodd Plaque given by the Financial Analysts Federation in May 1979 for their paper "Can the Corporation Survive?" He is the editor of *The Modern Theory of Corporate Finance* (with

Clifford W. Smith, Jr.) (McGraw-Hill, 1984) and *Studies in the Theory of Capital Markets* (Praeger Publishers, 1972). He founded the *Journal of Financial Economics* in 1974 and continues to serve as co-editor of that journal.

Dr. Jensen has served as a consultant to various corporations, foundations, and governmental agencies. He is currently a member of the American Finance Association Board of Directors, the Executive Committee of the Western Economic Association, and the Board of Advisors of the Pacific Institute.

Kose John is an Associate Professor of Finance at New York University, Graduate School of Business Administration. He holds a Ph.D. in business administration from the University of Florida. His doctoral dissertation, "Computing Equilibrium Paths of Continuous Families of Economies: A Homotopy Technique and Algorithms," was the winner of the 1979 AIDS National Doctoral Dissertation Award. Among his many awards and fellowships, he is the awardee of the Presidential Research Fellowship from New York University and the prestigious Batterymarch Fellowship. Professor John's research interests include corporate financial theory, capital markets theory, and information economics. His current research has focused on agency theory and signaling in corporate finance. He has published several articles in *American Economic Review*, *The Journal of Finance* and other leading journals.

Avner Kalay is an Associate Professor of Finance of New York University, Graduate School of Business Administration. He holds a Ph.D. in business administration from the University of Rochester. He is the awardee of the Presidential Research Fellowship from New York University and the Glucksman Fellowship for Research in Security Markets. His research focuses on the theoretical and empirical aspects of corporate finance and capital markets. Professor Kalay has published several articles in *The Journal of Financial Economics*, *The Journal of Business*, *The Journal of Finance*, *The Review of Economics and Statistics*, and other leading journals.

Andrew J. Kalotay is a vice president in the Bond Portfolio Analysis Group of Salomon Brothers Inc, where he is involved with a wide range of problems related to the management of fixed-income securities. He has particular expertise in areas relating to the retirement of debt, such as call features and sinking-fund provisions, and he has extensive experience with financial and regulatory issues related to the management of corporate debt.

Prior to joining Salomon Brothers, Dr. Kalotay was with the Corporate Finance Group of Dillon, Read. Previously to that, he had worked in the Bell System (Bell Laboratories, AT&T, New York Telephone) in various managerial and technical positions.

Dr. Kalotay received his B.S. and M.S. in mathematics from Queens University and his Ph.D. in statistics from the University of Toronto. His numerous papers have been published in the *Journal of Finance*, *Financial Management*, and *Management Science*, among others. Dr. Kalotay has taught at the University of Toronto, Bell Laboratories, Stevens Institute of Technology, and The Wharton School.

Robert S. Kay is National Director, Financial Service Programs, of Touche Ross & Co. in New York. He recently concluded a 12-year term as chairman of the firm's accounting and auditing professional standards committee. He received his B.S. degree (cum laude) in commerce from Loyola University of Chicago in 1955. Mr. Kay is a co-author of the *Handbook of Accounting and Auditing* (1981, updated annually) and is also the author of many published articles, has contributed to texts, periodicals, and has written numerous public position papers for his firm. He is currently a member of the American Accounting Association; the New York and Illinois Societies of CPAs; and the American Institute of Certified Public Accountants, where he has served on both the Accounting Standards and Auditing Standards Executive Committees. He has also served on the Financial Accounting Standards Advisory Council and several FASB task forces, including the task forces on business combinations, accounting for interest costs, and revenue recognition (conceptual framework).

Martin L. Leibowitz is a Managing Director of Salomon Brothers Inc, where he is in charge of the Bond Portfolio Analysis Group. He joined the firm in 1969 and was admitted as a general partner in 1977.

With Sidney Homer, former General Partner in charge of the firm's Bond Market Research Department, Dr. Leibowitz co-authored a book on bonds, entitled *Inside the Yield Book*, which was jointly published by Prentice-Hall and the New York Institute of Finance.

His recent work includes a series of studies relating to the subject of bond immunization and several studies developing a new approach to the analysis of financial futures. In another work, Dr. Leibowitz introduced the concept of a new structured approach to active bond portfolio management in a paper entitled "Contingent Immunization."

Dr. Leibowitz and his group have been particularly active in the development and application of techniques for the construction of dedicated bond portfolios to support specified liability schedules.

Michel Levasseur is Professor of Finance and Accounting at the Université de Paris-Dauphine in Paris, France. He received his Ph.D. in management science from the University of Paris in 1976. Prior to his present position, he was Professor of Finance at Université de Lille and the Hautes Etudes Commerciales. He has written several books in finance including

Options and New Futures (1980), *Introduction to Control and Financial Analysis* (1980), and *The Management of the Treasury Function* (1979). He has pioneered the application of option models to working capital management. He has taught courses in the theory of finance, portfolio analysis, options and futures markets, and financial accounting. Professor Levasseur has been an officer of the French Finance Association and is an associate editor of the *Revue Finance*. He is a member of the Scientific Council of the French National Center of Research for Economics and Management Sciences.

Scott P. Mason is Associate Professor of Business Administration at the Harvard University Graduate School of Business Administration. He received a B.S. in engineering physics from the University of Maine and an S.M. in finance from the Sloan School of Management at the Massachusetts Institute of Technology. After earning a Ph.D. in finance and economics at MIT, he joined the faculty of the Harvard Business School where he teaches finance in the MBA, executive, and doctoral programs. In teaching, research, and consulting he specializes in the theory and practice of capital markets.

Robert C. Merton has taught finance at the Alfred P. Sloan School of Management, Massachusetts Institute of Technology, since 1970. He is currently the J.C. Penney Professor of Management, having served as Professor of Finance from 1974–80; Associate Professor from 1973–74; and Assistant Professor from 1970–73. Professor Merton received his B.S. in engineering mathematics from Columbia University in 1966; his M.S. in applied mathematics from California Institute of Technology in 1967; and his Ph.D. in economics from Massachusetts Institute of Technology in 1970.

Professor Merton has served as an Associate Editor for the *Journal of Financial Economics*; *Journal of Banking and Finance*; *Journal of Money, Credit, and Banking*; *International Economic Review*; and *Journal of Finance*. He was the editor of *The Collected Scientific Papers of Paul A. Samuelson*, Volume III. He is a Fellow of the Econometric Society and a Research Associate of the National Bureau of Economic Research. He received the Leo Melamed Prize from the University of Chicago in 1983. Professor Merton is currently vice president and a director of the American Finance Association. He is also a director of the Nova Fund, Inc.; Tax-Managed Fund for Utility Shares; American Birthright Trust; and ABT Investment Services, Inc. He has served as a consultant to numerous financial institutions and corporations.

Professor Merton has published a number of articles in the areas of capital market asset pricing, portfolio selection, and the pricing of options and corporate liabilities.

Franco Modigliani, Institute Professor and Professor of Finance and Economics, is an internationally known authority on monetary theory, capital markets, corporate finance, macroeconomics, and econometrics. He received a doctorate in jurisprudence in 1939 from the University of Rome, and a doctorate in social science in 1944 from the New School of Social Research. Dr. Modigliani has served on the faculties of several colleges and universities, and was appointed to the MIT faculty in 1962. In 1970 Dr. Modigliani was appointed Institute Professor, an appointment that MIT reserves for scholars of special distinction to recognize accomplishments and leadership of high intellectual quality. He is the author of seven books, three volumes of his collected papers, and numerous articles for economic journals. He is a member of the National Academy of Sciences and a member of the American Academy of Arts and Sciences. He is a former president of the American Economic Association, the American Finance Association, and the Econometric Society, and an honorary president of the International Economic Association. He has served as a consultant to the Federal Reserve System, the U.S. Treasury Department, and a number of European banks.

James Poterba received his A.B., summa cum laude, in economics from Harvard College in 1980. He was a member of Phi Beta Kappa and received the John Williams Prize as the outstanding economics major. As a Marshall Scholar, he studied for three years at Nuffield College, Oxford University. His doctoral thesis, "Taxation and Corporate Dividend Policy," used financial data on both British and American firms to analyze the influences of personal taxes on corporate dividend payout ratios. The thesis, which was awarded the Webb-Medley Prize, showed that dividend policy responds to major changes in tax rates on dividend income.

Poterba has taught at MIT since 1982, first as an instructor in economics and later as an assistant professor. His current research focuses on several issues involving the interaction of taxes and financial decisions. One project extends his doctoral research in an attempt to discover how firms determine their dividend policies, and what factors influence the stock market valuation of firms with different payout rules. Poterba is also interested in the American housing market, and is mounting an empirical study of how tax policies toward homeowners and landlords have affected time-series movements in the level of home ownership. A final project examines the financial policies of municipal governments, and investigates the influence of expected tax changes on the yield spread between corporate and municipal bonds.

Luis Manoel Ribiero Dias is a chemical engineer who has had 30 years of technical and managerial responsibilities, mostly for American companies. He worked for Worthington, Liquid Carbonic, and Du Pont and served as priority analysis manager at Brasil's Economic Development Bank. He took his M.B.A. degree from Rio's Catholic University, where he teaches finance and managerial accounting, participated in the Training Trainers Programme at INSEAD in Fontainebleau, and is a business consultant.

Myron S. Scholes is Frank E. Buck Professor of Finance, Graduate School of Business, Professor of Law, Stanford University. Professor Scholes came to Stanford in 1983 after spending a year as the Distinguished Visiting Professor of Research in the Graduate School of Business in 1981–82. He is also a Research Associate of the National Bureau of Economic Research. Prior to coming to Stanford, he was the Edward Eagle Brown Professor of Banking and Finance at the Graduate School of Business of the University of Chicago. While at Chicago, he also served as the director of the Center for Research in Security Prices from 1974–80. From 1968 to 1973, he was an assistant and associate professor at the Sloan School of Management, Massachusetts Institute of Technology. He has published widely in noted academic journals. This is a sampling of his articles: "The Market For Securities: Substitution Versus Price Pressure and the Effects of Information on Share Prices," *Journal of Business*, 1972; "The Pricing of Options and Corporate Liabilities," *The Journal of Political Economy*, May 1973 (with Fischer Black); "The Effects of Dividend Yield and Dividend Policy on Common Stock Prices and Returns," *The Journal of Financial Economics*, 1974 (with Fischer Black); "Dividends and Taxes," *Journal of Financial Economics*, 1978 (with Merton Miller); "Dividends and Taxes: Some Empirical Results," *Journal of Political Economy*, 1982 (with Merton Miller). He is on the board of directors of the Capital Preservation Fund Group; Pacific Investment Management Co.; Dimensional Fund Advisors, and the advisory board of Wells Fargo Investment Advisors.

Clifford W. Smith, Jr. is Associate Professor of Finance and Economics at the Graduate School of Management, University of Rochester. He earned his Ph.D. in economics from the University of North Carolina, Chapel Hill, and his B.A. in economics from Emory University.

Professor Smith is the author of more than 20 published papers in the areas of corporate financial policy, financial institutions, and option pricing and is editor of *The Modern Theory of Corporate Finance* with Michael C. Jensen. His paper "Trading Costs for Listed Options: The Implications for Market Efficiency," co-authored with Susan M. Phillips, received the Pomerance Prize for Excellence in Options Research by the Chicago Board Options Exchange and his paper "Contractual Provisions, Organizational Structure, and Conflict Control in Insurance Markets," co-authored with David Mayers, was awarded the S. S. Huebner Foundation for Insurance Education Research Grant.

He is an editor of the *Journal of Financial Economics*; an associate editor of the *Journal of Accounting and Economics*; on the Editorial Review Board of the *American Real Estate and Urban Economics Association Journal*; and the Advisory Board of the *Midland Corporate Finance Journal.*

Martin G. Subrahmanyam is Professor of Finance at New York University, Graduate School of Business Administration. He holds a mechancial engineering degree from the Indian Institute of Technology, Madras, an M.B.A. from the Indian Institute of Management, Ahmedabad, and a Ph.D. in finance and economics from Massachusetts Institute of Technology. He has taught finance and economics at the Massachusetts Institute of Management for over eight years. He is chairman of the finance department at NYU. His articles had been published in several leading journals in finance and economics. His research interests are in the areas of capital market theory, corporation finance and international finance. He is the associate editor of *Management Science*, the *Journal of Banking and Finance* and the *Journal of Finance*. He has taught in graduate business programs and executive programs in England, France, India, Sweden, and the United States.

Lawrence H. Summers is Professor of Economics at Harvard University, where he specializes in macroeconomics and public finance. In 1983, he served as Domestic Policy Economist at the President's Council of Economic Advisers. Between 1979 and 1982, he was an assistant and associate professor at the Massachusetts Institute of Technology (MIT). Summers is a member of the Brookings Panel on Economic Activity and is a research associate of the National Bureau of Economic Research. He has published more than 30 articles in professional journals and books, concentrating primarily on the economics of employment and capital formation. Summers has served as a consultant to the Departments of Labor and the Treasury in the United States and to the governments of Jamaica and Indonesia.

Dr. Summers graduated from MIT in 1975 where he majored in economics and received his Ph.D. in economics from Harvard in 1982. His Ph.D. thesis on capital taxation and asset prices won the Wells Prize as the outstanding thesis at Harvard University and the National Tax Association's annual award for the outstanding dissertation in public finance.

Itzhak Swary is a faculty member of the Jerusalem School of Business Administration at Hebrew University, and a visiting associate professor at the Graduate School of Business Administration, New York University. He received his B.A. (1970) at Tel Aviv University, M.A. in economics (1973) at The Hebrew University of Jerusalem, Ph.D. (1979) at the University of Rochester. He also certified as a C.P.A. (Israel) in 1971. His current research interests include dividend policy, corporate bankruptcy, market-related empirical studies, taxation under inflation, and banking issues. Previous experience includes serving as assistant director, Open Market Operations

Department, Bank of Israel, and Income Tax Deputy Commissioner, Ministry of Finance, Israel.

Jean-Paul Valles received a bachelor's degree in mathematics in 1956 and graduated from the Ecole Superieure de Commerce de Paris in 1960. He obtained an MBA in 1961 and Ph.D. in 1967 from the Graduate School of Business Administration of New York University. Dr. Valles has been involved with multinational companies for many years. He was a business economist for five years at W. R. Grace prior to joining Pfizer Inc. in 1968 as an economist and long-range planning specialist. In 1970, he was named director of corporate planning and information services. He was elected controller of the company in 1972. Dr. Valles was elected to the Board of Directors of Pfizer Inc. at the shareholders meeting on April 24, 1980. Dr. Valles became vice president of finance on June 1, 1980.

Subject Index

P–Q

R

S

T

Name Index